Music, Race, and Nation

Map of Colombia

Music, Race, & Nation

Música Tropical in Colombia

Peter Wade

THE UNIVERSITY OF CHICAGO PRESS
Chicago and London

Peter Wade is senior lecturer in social anthropology at the University of Manchester and the author of *Blackness and Race Mixture* and *Race and Ethnicity in Latin America.*

The University of Chicago Press, Chicago 60637
The University of Chicago Press, Ltd., London
© 2000 by The University of Chicago
All rights reserved. Published 2000
Printed in the United States of America
09 08 07 06 05 04 03 02 01 00   1 2 3 4 5

ISBN: 0-226-86844-3 (cloth)
ISBN: 0-226-86845-1 (paper)

Library of Congress Cataloging-in-Publication Data

Wade, Peter 1957–
    Music, race, and nation : música tropical in Colombia / Peter Wade.
        p.   cm. — (Chicago studies in ethnomusicology)
    Includes bibliographical references and index.
    ISBN 0-226-86844-3 (cloth : alk. paper) — ISBN 0-226-86845-1 (pbk. : alk. paper)
        1. Música tropical—Colombia—History and criticism.   2. Music and race.
    3. Music—Social aspects—Colombia.   I. Title. II. Series.
    ML3487.C7 W33 2000
    781.64′09861—dc21
                                                                        99-088600

CONTENTS

PREFACE

Music has always been a central aspect of my relationship with Colombia, whether as an anthropologist or simply as a visitor to the country. It was in Colombia that I learned to love and to dance salsa, when I first went there in 1981 and lived in Cartagena for a year. Later, when I did a first spell of fieldwork in a small town near the Panamanian border, music and dance were important parts of my life and my research. I was looking at racial and ethnic identities in the town, focusing on the position of the black population, and I found that different musical tastes and dance practices were an integral part of racial and ethnic identifications. When I did another period of fieldwork with black migrants to the city of Medellín, the role of music and dance in the construction of identities was even more obvious—on occasion music even generated violent conflict as ideas about morality, territoriality, and identity became interwoven and expressed through ways of listening and dancing to music (Wade 1993a).

What I knew about Colombian music, however, was very much what filtered through the radio, television, and people's talk about music. My own tastes were also central to my interests: I liked salsa and had also grown to enjoy *vallenato* accordion music, mostly by dint of dancing and drinking for long hours with vallenato playing at high volume. My knowledge about the history of the music—as opposed to the way it functioned in particular processes of social identification—was very limited. As I learned more about the history of Colombian music, it struck me that it would make a very interesting way of understanding Colombian national identity and associated ideologies about race, class, region, sexuality, and gender in the country. The musical changes that had taken place over the twentieth century, which seemed to add up to a progressive "tropicalization" of the country, appeared vital to my interests in the place of "blackness" in Colombian society and culture.

At times during the research, I feared that I was wandering away from the economic, social, and political issues that had first engaged me in Colombia: racism and black resistance. Research on music and "popular culture" has often suffered from an image of triviality. However, in Colombia itself I found a much greater level of interest in my research on music than in my research on race. For the first time, I was interviewed on several occasions on the radio and in the press. This, of course, was in part precisely because popular music suited the image of leisure and entertainment that has made it seem trivial in "serious" circles. But it also seemed to indicate the importance of music to many people and the way one might use it to publicly address issues around the notion of race. During a later period of research, formally separate from this project, I was in Cali, which has the largest urban black population in Colombia. This population suffers from poverty to a greater extent than the nonblack population in the city, but this fact is quite difficult to establish and publicize and needs controlled research to demonstrate it. While I was there, the event of greatest public impact was the first festival of music from the Pacific coast, a region with a mainly black population that supplies many of the black migrants to Cali. A public space, financed by local government, had been created for "blackness," and that space was formed around music. Now, this is a double-edged sword. On the one hand, music can have great public impact; on the other, it is constantly subject to co-optation and trivialization. In this sense, we cannot be romantic about the contestatory possibilities of music. It is evident, however, that music is not by any means a realm of cultural practice that is disconnected from the issues that first drew my attention in Colombia. This is true whether one focuses on the blatant displays of racism that "black" music has sometimes attracted or on the more subtle and gradual ways in which Colombian popular music has interwoven with changes in the society and culture of the country as a whole.

The research was done in three cities: Bogotá, Medellín, and Barranquilla, with brief visits to Cali and Cartagena. I had originally intended to cover Cali in depth as well, but this proved to be impossible in the time I had available. As an anthropologist used to long-term participant observation, I found the type of research that this project involved rather different. First, there was a fair amount of library and archival research, covering secondary sources and especially the press. Second, listening to the radio and watching television became tasks rather than just pastimes. Third, I spent a good deal of my time on the telephone, arranging interviews which usually took place in people's houses or, especially if they involved people whose work was linked to music, in their work places. Interviews were generally quite temporally and spatially bounded affairs: they had a definite beginning and end and did not often give way to more informal interactions. Almost always I taped the interview, with the permission of my interlocutor.

The fact that the central focus of the research was historical obviously meant that participant observation was less vital, but aside from being important for the penultimate chapter, which looks at recent developments in the Colombian music scene, I found that it was useful in order to get something of a feel for people's sense of history—the things that were important to them; what, for example, the notion of tradition might mean to them. It was important to see what music was doing in people's lives in the 1990s in order to understand what was happening musically in the 1940s and 1950s. To some degree I of course relied on my past years of research in Colombia, which gave me a general sense of the country's musical culture and its geography. During this project, I also used more traditionally anthropological and informal avenues of inquiry where I could. This was fairly easy in Barranquilla, a relatively small city, where I found myself quite quickly integrated into some of the networks of the local intellectual and artistic circles. This meant I was able to socialize with music lovers— mostly of middle-class status—and accompany them to gigs and bars and visit their houses without having an interview in mind. This was also true for Medellín, a city where I had lived for a year in 1985–1986 and so had a wide range of contacts among both the middle and working classes. I found Bogotá was less easy to get to grips with in this way—a big, sprawling city with very marked patterns of class segregation—but I did get some sense of music in the city through my informal contacts with friends there, mostly middle-class people connected with university and intellectual circles.

To help with interviews and archival work, I contracted research assistants in each city (for more details of the interviews, see appendix A, the list of interviewees). In Bogotá, these were Rosana Portaccio, Javier Pinzón, and Lorena Aja; I also contracted Blanca Bustos and Natalia Otero to do specific pieces of research on Colombian national identity as revealed through school texts and other literary sources. In Medellín, I had the assistance of Manuel Bernardo Rojas. In Barranquilla, I hired Denirys Polo Calinda (who was assisted by Mónica Atequera). I am deeply indebted to them all for their thorough and careful work.

There were many other individuals who contributed to this research in one form or another, and I cannot name them all here. The original idea for the project emerged in a conversation with Egberto Bermúdez, and further conversations with him during the research were always stimulating. I must also extend my thanks particularly to the following people. In Bogotá, I stayed as usual with Clemencia and Jaime, whose flat was, as ever, a warm and hospitable abode and whose company was as intellectually stimulating as it has always been. Natalia, Blanca, Claudia, Germán, Margarita, and Carlos were great friends. In Medellín, I stayed with María Teresa and Fernando and exchanged ideas and music with them. Fernando's friends Moisés and Salvador were also unfailingly helpful and generous. I owe a special debt to Diana for all her assistance and support. The staff at a number of record companies in Medellín and Bogotá—Sonolux, Codiscos, Discos Victoria, and Sony—were also very accommodating, and I must thank the staff at Discos Fuentes in particular for all their help, especially Isaac Villanueva and Luis Felipe Jaramillo. In Barranquilla, I was welcomed with great hospitality by Gilberto and Mireya; Mariano Candela and Julio Oñate were also generous sources of information.

On an institutional level, I would like to thank the staff at the Biblioteca Luis Angel Arango in Bogotá and the Biblioteca Piloto in Barranquilla for their help. I am indebted to *El Tiempo, Cromos, El Espectador,* Sonolux, and Discos Fuentes for their help in finding photographic material and for permission to reproduce the photographs that appear in this book. The staff at the Photographic Unit in the University of Liverpool and at the Media Centre in the University of Manchester gave invaluable help with processing the photographs. Finally, the research was funded by a generous grant from the Leverhulme Trust, to which I am most grateful.

The editorial staff at the University of Chicago Press was also most efficient and helpful, and I must thank T. David Brent and Erik Carlson in particular.

A NOTE ON RECORDED MUSIC

Much of the music which I discuss in this book is difficult to obtain outside Colombia, especially that recorded between the 1940s and the 1960s. Some of the more recent material can be heard on *Tropical Sounds of Colombia* (Mango, CIDM 1058 846756-2, 1990) which, although it focuses mainly on music of the 1980s, does include a couple of older tracks. *Cumbia, cumbia* (World Circuit Records, WCD 016, 1989) is also mainly music of the 1970s and 1980s, but the follow-up album, *Cumbia, cumbia 2* (WCD 033, 1993), focuses on an earlier period, with tracks recorded between 1954 and 1972. Discos Fuentes is one of the best sources of the older music, since this record company has rereleased a great deal of this music on compact disc, but it is not easy to obtain many of their releases outside Colombia. Information on the company can be seen on their Web page (www.discosfuentes .com) which includes details on how individuals outside Colombia can order albums from their catalog. Information on modern vallenato is quite easy to obtain, since there are a number of relevant Web sites (e.g., http://209.143.145.169/vallenato/).

1 Introduction

This study is the result of a long-standing interest in racial and national identities, and in issues of cultural hybridity and multiculturalism in an increasingly globalized context (see Wade 1993a, 1995, 1998, 1999). Colombia is a prime site to address these themes for several reasons. To begin with, a master narrative for Colombian nationhood has been that of *mestizaje,* or "mixture," generally conceived in terms of race but also in terms of culture. Representations of hybridity have always been subject to intense manipulation, as they have in other Latin American countries with similar histories. In 1991, a new constitution was passed in Colombia which officially recognizes the country as a multicultural and pluriethnic nation and enshrines certain rights for indigenous peoples and black communities. New spaces have been opened for redefinitions of nationhood in which not only international concerns with democratization play a part, but also worldwide mobilizations for the promotion of ethnic and racial identities and rights. A multicultural nationhood emerges which seems to have as much connection to external identities as to internal ones. National identities have perhaps always been radically ruptured; in the Colombian case, this is officially recognized, even while the image of national unity is still projected.

Music, as a pervasive form of cultural expression and practice, has no simple connections with national identity, but one must be understood in relation to the other, just as both must be understood in relation to transnational circuits of commercial and cultural exchange. In Colombia, with communications technology well developed, commercial popular music has been ubiquitous for many years. Official representations of national identity have both conflicted with and been buttressed by different musical expressions, which occur within a musical environment constituted as much by non-Colombian as autochthonous styles.

The central concern of this book is how and why during the middle decades of the twentieth century certain musical styles, originally "folkloric" and confined to the Caribbean coastal region of the country, a region relatively marginal and rather "black" in the national frame, became the Colombian music which was most successful commercially in the country and the best known internationally—despite its apparent incompatibility with the dominant version of national identity and despite the initial resistance of some sectors of the population, which saw the music as vulgar, common, and sexually licentious. Alongside the more recent emphasis given to a multicultural nation, this music has become even more popular among ever-widening sectors of society, as have "modernized" versions of "yesterday's music."

This story is of interest in itself since the history of Colombian popular music is only partially written.[1] It is even more interesting if we are trying to understand how multiple and unequal representations of national identity relate to each other through contestation, appropriation, and transformation in a society stratified by class and race, how music reflects and constitutes identities, how musics and identities are racialized and sexualized, how races are musicalized, and how capitalism mediates and is mediated by popular culture. There is a changing politics of culture and representation involved here, in which "tradition" and "modernity" are crucial constituents of contest, each imbued with different potential meanings of nation, race, and music.

Much of this politics is also gendered and sexualized. Different perspectives on tradition, modernity, and national identity involve ideas about the proper places of men and women and of masculinity and femininity; ideas about "race mixture," since they imply sexual congress, are mediated by ideas about gender; the embodiment of music and especially dance has implications for the construction of sexual meanings about them. Finally, this cultural politics is, of necessity, spatialized. A nation has a territorial aspect, and—particularly in the Colombian case—cultural and racial diversity are often perceived and acted out through a spatialized politics of social relations. The way people think about identity and music is tied to the way they think about places.

This sketches out the terrain I will be exploring. In order to give some guiding coordinates for the journey, in the rest of this chapter I

look at theoretical approaches to the interconnections between national identity, race, gender, sexuality, and music.

National Identity

HOMOGENEITY AND HETEROGENEITY

In their influential work on nations and nationalism, Anderson (1983)
and Gellner (1983, 1994) both emphasize the importance of homogeneity in the emergence of the modern nation. A critical feature of the
nation is its "community of anonymity" (Anderson 1983: 40), the
identification of the citizen with other unknown compatriots in a common allegiance to the nation itself. This quality is created, according to
Anderson, primarily by spreading literacy and print capitalism, which
allow people to imagine a community of nationals. A precondition is
the emergence of a concept of "homogeneous, empty time" (Walter
Benjamin, cited in Anderson 1983: 28) in which people can imagine
their actions being simultaneous with those of others located elsewhere. For Gellner, "homogeneity, literacy and anonymity are the key
traits" (1983: 38). Modernizing production systems needed educated
people who could manage information (including instructions about
production). Thus, a literate "high culture," previously the prerogative
of rulers, began to pervade the entire society, creating an identification
with "an anonymous mass society" (Gellner 1994: 41). Gellner sees
the formation of actual nations in these general conditions as resulting
from the preexistence of specific languages and cultures through which
education (or print capitalism in Anderson's argument) could be articulated (cf. Smith 1986); also, since industrialization was geographically uneven, there were incentives for creating barriers to exclude
poorer neighbors or to protect weaker areas from the cold blasts of
market forces (cf. Nairn 1977). Segal and Handler criticize Gellner and
Anderson for implying that the nationalist idea of homogeneity within
a social unit preexisted nationalism itself, but they still propose that
the nations are "fundamentally constituted by a principle of equiva-
lence" (Segal and Handler 1992: 3).

These approaches give little room for conceptualizing heterogeneity
and the contestation and fracturing of national identity. As Taussig
(1992: 54) has noted, concerning writings on nationalism, "much of
anthropology . . . from Victor Turner to Michel Foucault, for example, claims something like an organic unity between the seal of the
symbol and the wax of the recipient, between the discourse and the

citizen. The Romantic aesthetics of symbol, from Hegel to Goethe on-
wards, and the structuralism of de Saussure converge on this point."
The analysis focuses on what nationalist discourse itself defines as
ideal—homogeneity—with little attention to the central paradox that
total homogeneity would entail the obliteration of internal differences
of hierarchy, whether of class, race, or region, which nationalist elites
themselves struggle to maintain. Gellner mentions the possibility of
an "ethnographic nationalism" which codifies and idealizes peasant
cultures as part of forging a new national culture (1994: 29), but this
potential difference simply becomes the homogeneous national culture. Bhabha has contended that the holism of which nationalism is
an example asserts "cultural or political supremacy and seeks to obliterate the relations of difference that constitute the languages of history and culture" (1989, cited in Asad 1993: 262), and Hall has argued that "national cultures help to 'stitch up' differences" into one
identity (1992: 299).

Heterogeneity is not ignored in these approaches, but tends to be
conceptualized as either the struggle of one potential nation within another nation—admittedly a vital issue—or a series of residual or resistant traditions or hybridizations set against the homogenizing im-
perative of the modern nation-state. The latter alternative is, in fact,
the common oppositional paradigm that pits a homogenizing national
elite (or, in recent literature, global capitalism) against a heterogeneous
popular, traditional, or hybridizing subaltern culture, seen as more or
less resistant. The problem with this, in my view, is the oversimplification of the basic opposition (not to mention the risk of imputing
strategic intentionality to the elite and/or the subaltern).

Bhabha's interest in ambivalence opens a perspective onto the
"space of liminality . . . of the national discourse" (Bhabha 1994: 149).
He identifies a "double narrative movement," a "contested conceptual
territory where the nation's people must be thought in double-time; the
people are the historical 'objects' of a nationalist pedagogy, giving the
discourse of authority that is based on the pre-given or constituted origin *in the past;* the people are also the 'subjects' of a process of signification that must erase any prior or originary presence of the nation-
people to demonstrate the prodigious, living principles of the people as
contemporaneity: as that sign of the *present* though which national life
is redeemed and iterated as a reproductive process" (Bhabha 1994:
145). Bhabha is not reiterating the well-known paradox noted by
Nairn, Anderson, and Gellner (and captured in Nairn's Janus-face met-
aphor [Nairn 1977]), according to which nationalism looks two ways

at once: forward to progressive modernity and backward to the legacy of tradition. In fact, both these gazes are located in the same teleological temporality that Bhabha detects in "nationalist pedagogy." Instead, he explores a different ambivalence between this "continuist accumulative temporality" and the "repetitious, recursive strategy of the performative" (Bhabha 1994: 145). This is a distinction between a historicist temporality—dependent on Anderson's empty homogeneous time—in which the nation is both timelessly ancient and moving forward, and a performative temporality in which the "cultural shreds and patches" (Gellner 1983: 56) of the nation are invoked. In the first mode, the nation and its people are a modernizing homogeneous whole, progressing through history toward their destiny. In the second mode, when deprived of this historicism, "the nation turns from being the symbol of modernity into becoming the symptom of an ethnography of the 'contemporary' within modern culture" (Bhabha 1994: 147). In this ethnography, the heterogeneity of "the people" necessarily comes to light. The point is that, rather than postulating a dominant state or ruling class bent on homogeneity and opposed against a varied populace who, to a greater or lesser extent, vindicate their heterogeneity, Bhabha shows that the nationalist narrative carries this split as a contradiction *within itself*, "sliding ambivalently from one enunciatory position to another" (Bhabha 1994: 147). In Colombia, for example, official or other public discourse on the nation includes claims both to the supposed homogeneity brought about by centuries of cultural and physical mixing and to the tremendous ethnographic diversity of a "country of regions." Indeed, this ambivalent sliding is no accident, but one of the central paradoxes of nationalism: the attempt to present the nation as a unified homogeneous whole conflicts directly with the maintenance of hierarchies of class and culture—and their frequent corollaries, region and race—that is wanted by those who are located in the higher echelons of those hierarchies. The ambivalent movement that Bhabha identifies is a result of this paradox, in which the dominant classes actually need the heterogeneity they also deny. To theorize this, it is necessary to go beyond simple oppositions between the homogenizing dominant class and the heterogeneous people.

The history of Colombian music, as the following chapters will show, supports such an approach. Yet a more oppositional perspective often underlies research on the relation between music and national identity. Pacini Hernández's work on Dominican merengue, for all the richness of its analysis, implicitly postulates an oppositional framework. The official urban merengue style imposed during Trujillo's dictatorship (1930–1961) is contested by other styles—salsa, *bachata, nueva canción*—that express the social identity of other social groups (Pacini Hernández 1991, 1995). Her forceful image is of a *lucha sonora* (a battle of sounds) as different musics compete for space in the market and the imagination. Here diversity is seen as originating "from below," from social locations opposed to the dominant nationalist discourse. Yet her work shows the boundaries are less than clear: the consumers of bachata, mainly poor urban migrants, also consume merengue and salsa; the musicians and producers of bachata mix merengue styles into their repertoires; one central bachata producer used to "clean up" bachata lyrics for commercial sale and encouraged urban migrants to become urbane consumers (Pacini Hernández 1995: 87–101).

The same type of oppositional approach can be seen in some of the contributions to *Music and Black Ethnicity,* edited by Béhague (1994). A common theme is the negation or minimization of blackness or Africanness by nationalist elites, whether in the Dominican Republic (Davis 1994) or even in officially *noiriste* Haiti (Averill 1994). Meanwhile, other people resist this marginalization and try to vindicate blackness and Africanness. Averill's analysis is interesting in that it shows how the different versions of Haitian identity are articulated by the middle and intellectual classes and thus avoids an opposition between elites and subalterns. Nevertheless, more African-oriented musics are seen as the "corollary to populist political movements" (Averill 1994: 178). This argument is refined in Averill's later book, where music is characterized as "a medium of the negotiation and communication of power" in which musics of resistance are not just "local" products but hybrids of "globally circulating practices, values and beliefs with those that are more properly 'local'" (Averill 1997: 210). Still, he states that "the movement of peasant and lower-class musics and expressive culture to center stage [in Haiti] has paralleled a stubborn bid for political centrality on the part of the oppressed" (1997: 211). This recreates a certain oppositionality which, it must be admitted, derives from the history of Haitian politics: as Averill shows, music was linked very directly to an explicitly racialized public politics in a way that has no close parallel in Colombia. The point I wish to make is that, while the negation and marginalization of blackness is also evident in Colombia, blackness is simultaneously and actively constructed by nationalist elites, even as it is assigned an inferior position (see chapter 2). That nationalist elites may intentionally seek to discipline diversity is clearly true,[2] but I think it is more productive to say that they resignify a diversity which they also partly construct: ethnographic variety is not just "out there" to be imported in disfigured form; its very existence in the nation is mediated by nationalist representations. In this sense, a nationalist project does not just try to deny, suppress, or even simply channel an unruly diversity; it actively reconstructs it.

This is evident in Reily's analysis of writings on music and Brazilian national identity by Mario de Andrade (1893–1945), author and musicologist. According to Reily (1994), Mario emphasized the synthesis between European, Amerindian, and African heritages, seeing this as a positive feature of national identity at a time when the idea of racial mixture was only just being vindicated against eugenicist notions of degeneration (see the section on race and nation below). Yet what also strikes me is the constant reiteration of diversity in Mario's writings, even as he focused on synthesis. Heterogeneity is constantly rediscovered, and thus recreated, by a nation-building discourse that seeks to mold unity from diversity.

As a theorization of the relation between the pedagogical and the performative, the notion that national discourse "slides ambivalently from one enunciatory position to another" (Bhabha 1994: 147) is a useful advance, but it is not very clear what this involves. How do individuals intent on interpellating "the people" as a homogeneous object and the nation as a modern progressive entity with a continuous cultural tradition deal in practice with heterogeneous popular cultures? Here we need some theory of transformation and appropriation.

TRANSFORMATION AND APPROPRIATION

Processes of transformation and appropriation were very common in Latin America (and other areas) from the late nineteenth and into the twentieth century. Societies in the region urbanized, with extensive rural-urban migration and the differentiation of urban space into class-stratified zones. They became increasingly capitalized: internal frontiers were pushed back in aggressive colonizations, national industries grew, and economies were linked more and more to global circuits of exchange. Cultural nationalism was widespread and expressed itself in musical nationalism. Part of this was the appropriation of "traditional" elements in art music circles (Béhague 1996), but more important was the emergence of national popular music styles: tango in Argentina, samba and maxixe in Brazil, *danza* in Puerto Rico, *ranchera* in Mexico, *son* and rumba in Cuba, and so on. In many ways, these were musical styles that developed in the working-class barrios of

Latin American cities, often by adapting European styles and combining them with African-derived (and to a much lesser extent Amerindian) aesthetics and rhythms, and that were then fastened upon by the middle classes, "cleaned up," modernized, and made into acceptable national symbols.[3] "In the typical pattern," writes Manuel (1995: 15), "lower class syncretic forms gradually percolate upwards, acquiring more musical sophistication and eventually coming to be enjoyed by the upper classes," and perhaps gaining the status of national music.

Moore notes that, "Given the centrality of this mainstreaming phenomenon to musical production in Brazil, the United States, and other countries, surprisingly little attention has been devoted to it by music historians" (1997: 6), and, although the idea of "percolation" gives a general sense of a common trajectory, it is important not to oversimplify the processes involved. It is necessary, first, to appreciate the syncretic nature of the lower-class forms, which fed off a host of different musical currents. This helps us to avoid falling into an oppositional model in which the musical style in question is formed entirely by subaltern classes, located "in the barrios" and then taken and modernized. There is no simple opposition between the local and the national (or between these and the global), or between the traditional and the modern. Instead, the music "in the barrio" was actually created in complex processes of interchange, class mediation, and appropriation that worked in ambiguous spaces between country and city, between social classes, and, not infrequently, between the national and the international.[4] In Colombia, important exponents of new urban popular music styles were often moving across the boundaries between small town and big city, between working classes and middle classes, and between home and abroad. Second, it is necessary to appreciate that the music that is modernized and nationalized has to be defined against something else that remains putatively traditional and nonnational (i.e., local): if everything is appropriated and made national, then the danger of erasing hierarchies of class and culture rears its head. Like any meanings, national meanings are defined relationally, both with respect to other nations and to forms within the nation that are defined as inferior. So appropriation implies a parallel process of differentiation. In sum, we need quite a complex notion of appropriation to deal with this material.

In her study of Guyana, Brackette Williams develops ideas about processes of transformation and appropriation (Williams 1991). National processes of homogenization may work on heterogeneity "by assimilating elements of that heterogeneity through appropriations that devalue them or that deny the source of their contribution"; this is a "transformist hegemony," a concept she derives from Gramsci (although it is similar to Raymond Williams's idea of "selective tradition").[5] If marginal persons and groups insist on their ownership of certain cultural elements in the national mix, these are devalued and their owners defined as "not 'true' members of the ideologically defined nation." If they try to appropriate higher-value elements claimed by other groups, they may "stand accused of riding to the pinnacle of civilization on the coattails" of these other groups, which are defined as "the real producers." Those claiming status as the real producers of the core elements of national culture have the ideological power to redefine the meaning of the elements appropriated from marginal groups. Heterogeneity is never erased altogether, but continues to emerge from variations in the objective conditions under which groups live and from the differing interpretations people make of the same cultural elements (Williams 1991: 30–31). As I mentioned above, this is not accidental, but necessary to the maintenance of hierarchy.

Gramsci actually hardly developed the idea of transformism, but it is worth pursuing some aspects of the notion of hegemony here, since the construction and representation of national identity is generally something organized by dominant groups in a class society but which resonates well beyond those groups. Hegemony can be understood as a specific historical constellation of multiple social forces, in which there is a deep and wide-ranging degree of social and moral authority, agreed on by a broad collective of allied classes or class segments. It is not static, but always in a process of change, including its own growth and demise. There is also a shifting boundary between explicitness and tacitness, between the degree to which particular notions are open to debate and the degree to which they are taken for granted. Hegemony is not orchestrated in a simple sense by a single class or state which simply imposes its will: civil society is penetrated by the moral leadership of dominant forces, and this evokes a measure of consent. But particular segments of society do have more power than others, not only to impose force when necessary, but to penetrate civil society in this way and project such leadership (Hall [1986] 1996a). Hegemonic discourses will always be complex ensembles including elements (ideas, symbols, values, practices) from varying sources. These elements can be "read" in various ways, their meaning and organization are not fixed and are always partial, and they may submerge into and reemerge from tacitness in unpredictable ways. But some readings are made dominant and tacit and commonsensical through the work done in particular projects by particular sets of people (e.g., in the field of education or music or economic production) which give these readings moral authority. Thus, the ideological field is not a free-for-all of readings, but is given some unity—and its class character—by the articulation of particular sets of ideas with the more powerful social forces. The dominance of these ideas depends not just on their connection with dominant social forces, but also on their resonance with real, but partial, aspects of different people's experiences. Any ideological element can be transformed by working on it and "rereading" it, placing it in a different relation to other elements. Ideological struggle is thus a struggle over the appropriation of elements (Mouffe 1979: 193; Hall [1986] 1996b).[6]

Whether one uses Gramsci's notion of hegemony or Williams's development of the concept of transformist hegemony, the point is, first, that "the function and significance of the heterogeneous elements are determined by their place in the system and not by the meaning they had formerly in their source culture" (Barber and Waterman 1995: 240), and, second, that the struggle that Mouffe refers to is rarely a simple fight between the dominant class and the underdogs; a host of different processes of appropriation and resignification occur in which, however, certain dominant values tend to pervade. A nationalist project can articulate a variety of elements that have different locations, in terms of, say, putative class or racial origin, and give them some coherence as part of a hegemony, without fixing their meaning completely. Thus, music from the Caribbean coastal region of Colombia could be resignified as a national music by relocating it in relation to other elements rather than by simply obliterating its former meanings. Its blackness did not disappear, but was diluted stylistically; meanwhile, other, "blacker" musics which were not as popular commercially remained to signify "true" blackness. But its blackness was still available to be read by some as a stigma, thus reaffirming the hegemonic value of whiteness. Or its blackness might be read by others as a positive feature, whether for marketing the music as exciting and "hot" or for vindicating the position of the Caribbean coastal region in the nation. The same music might be modernized in its instrumentation and presentation, but its image as rooted in regional tradition could be read both as a negative thing, connecting it to rural black culture, and as a positive thing, lending the music an authentic Colombian identity. Meanwhile, its modernity could be good, implying progressiveness and international prestige, but also bad, related to the erosion of "traditional" values, to loose, immoral behavior, and to shallow commercialism. In short, these multiple meanings existed and were involved in ideological struggles but were structured by hegemonic values of whiteness and modernity (themselves articulated to racial hierarchies and processes of economic change), which meant that certain readings had more power than others.

Processes of ideological appropriation are, of course, carried out by human agents, despite the temptations of seeing hegemony as a self-reproducing totality. As Hall ([1986] 1996a) argues, people pursue specific social and political projects and it is out of these that hegemonic ideologies arise. Hall's argument does not entail an overly instrumentalist focus only on the self-conscious power strategies of nationalist or class elites. Hegemony may be perpetuated in a general sense by elite interests in the nation, but everybody works within it. Thus, for example, much of the appropriation practiced on musical styles from Colombia's Caribbean coastal region, which transformed them into commercial forms popular across a range of classes and ultimately into authentic "Colombian" music, was actually done by musicians from provincial and rural middle-class or even working-class backgrounds; much of the promotion of this music on radio and record was done by middle-ranking businessmen who were more interested in making money than in constructing representations of national identity;[7] and, of course, it was a very wide range of people who consumed the music produced. Colombian popular music and Colombian national identity were thus transformed over a number of decades, moving in stereotypical terms from "Europhile" to "tropical," yet tropicality was appropriated and rearticulated in particular ways that maintained certain aspects of Colombian identity as not very "black" and as rooted in authentic tradition yet progressive and modern.

NATIONALISM AND TRANSNATIONALISM

In her account of transformation and appropriation in an ideological hegemony, Williams touches on another important aspect for understanding Latin American and other postcolonial nationalisms. The dominant groups in 1980s Guyana who attempted to orchestrate a national hegemony were, she argues, themselves under the sway of a "foreign" hegemony of Anglo-European (and presumably U.S.) values. In Colombia, too, ruling elites have been and still are strongly influenced by these values. This adds another dimension to ideas about homogeneity and heterogeneity and modernity and tradition. The notion of the modern homogeneous nation in Latin America owes a great deal to European models, not just for the structures of the nation-state, but for the basic cultural values of "civilization" espoused by elites. This has led to debates within Latin American political and intellectual elites about "imitation" and "authenticity": some nationalist currents have felt that a "proper" nation cannot simply be a copy of some other (notionally original) societies and cultures; there must be some authentic cultural traditions to create originality, difference, and hence identity.[8]

This concern with a distinctive yet modern identity may be resolved by Gellner's "ethnographic nationalism" or the glorification (perhaps even "invention") of objectified autochthonous culture under the traditionalist eye of nationalism's Janus face. Yet, as I have argued, if we focus on Bhabha's ambivalent movement between the nation as a homogeneous modern whole and the nation as the symptom of an ethnography of the contemporary in modern culture, then ethnographic nationalism is always called into question. In Colombia this century, much of contemporary culture at various class levels was (and still is) seen as highly modern and also of "foreign" origins. Much popular music, for example, came from Europe, the United States, Cuba, Argentina, and Mexico, to name only the most prominent. The search for modernity could lead to imitation and to heterogeneity of a radical kind. Looking to "the people" as a repository for traditional roots would again bring nationalists—or anyone else, for that matter—face to face with foreign modernity, since the working classes were as avid consumers of foreign music as anyone else. Thus, any attempt to consider a nationalist project must look beyond national boundaries.

The transnational dimension is an important corrective to some conventional wisdom about nationalism. In a minimal sense, a supranational level is admitted by any analysis, since a nation must be defined in relation to others. In more recent discussions, it is argued that globalization, rather than undermining nationalisms, can activate and underwrite them (Hall 1992). Nations are still important actors in world capitalism (Arnason 1990), and localities remain of great significance in a global world (Keith and Pile 1993; Miller 1995b). Homogenization goes hand in hand with fragmentation as "two constitutive trends of global reality" (Friedman 1990: 311). This is fine at the global level, but what happens within the nation? Anderson's image of an imagined community created by the spread of print capitalism (or education, or—less often mentioned[9]—music capitalism) suggests internal coherence within a nation; the boundaries of the nation and thus of the imaginations of its citizens are said to derive from preexisting language differences, administrative divisions, and so forth (Anderson 1983; Gellner 1994). But the very same media allow people to imagine themselves far beyond these boundaries and think themselves in a world of different places. In Colombia, and in most of Latin America, music from the 1920s onward could transport people to the United States, Cuba, Mexico, and Argentina; film had a similarly transnational realm of the imaginary. In this sense, it is again necessary to see a nationalist project not as simply the obliteration of difference by sameness, but as mediating a tension between these two. Indeed it may make sense to say that the nation, as the symptom of the ethnography of the contemporary in modern culture, is radically fragmented; it is an unstable conjuncture of parts of interlocking transnational cultural diasporas.

Gilroy uses the concept of diaspora as part of his attempt to explode an ideological opposition between tradition and modernity (1993: 199). In this case, "tradition" is that invoked by Afrocentric black nationalists (often North Americans) as a pure, continuous current of authenticity stretching back to and recoverable via Africa; in this view, "modernity" is the erasure of that tradition in hybridity and creolization. The black Atlantic diaspora with its crisscrossing connections in space and time—music being a crucial medium—introduces an "explicitly transnational and intercultural perspective" on identity formation (Gilroy 1993: 15). The absoluteness of "tradition" is undermined, and blacks' relation to modernity is reconceived as a form of "double consciousness," located within modernity (and indeed prefiguring some of the crises of identity that have affected it) but also highly critical of its attempted exclusion of them and its separation of knowledge, morality, and aesthetics, which helped the ideology of progress to coexist with racial oppression. Gilroy's approach helps to see national identity within its transnational context, to understand what makes up the heterogeneity within the nation that stands in such an ambivalent relation to constructions of homogeneity. It is also suggestive in its use of musics to explore this precisely because "they exceed the frameworks of national or ethnocentric analysis with which we have always been too easily satisfied" (Gilroy 1993: 35).[10]

So far, I have been moving toward a view of nationalism and national identity in which homogeneity and heterogeneity are seen as two sides of the nationalist coin, rather than facing each other across a nationalist divide; in which cultural elements from a wide variety of sources, "traditional" and "modern," "foreign" and "national"—all ambivalent terms—can be recombined and resignified, without their meaning being exhausted or fixed by simplistic oppositions between elite and masses, but without this implying that they are totally autonomous from basic power inequalities and hegemonic value hierarchies or from nationalist projects guided by elites; and in which the heterogeneity of national cultures is located in a transnational frame with all that implies for the fragmentation of imagined communities. I will now look at how meanings of race become entwined in all this.

Race and Nation

Let me be clear about what I mean by "race."[11] I am referring to the changing categories and concepts created primarily by Europeans as a result of their contact with, and subordination of, non-European peoples through colonialism and imperialism. These categories focused on aspects of physical difference deemed salient (primarily skin color, but also hair texture and certain facial features) and worked them into "racial" signifiers which came to bear a vast load of social and cultural meanings organized primarily by hierarchies of labor exploitation, power, and value. Meanings have varied over space and time, influenced by many factors, such as economic and demographic structures, the development of scientific understanding of human difference, and political and cultural struggle over the categories and meanings themselves (Wade 1993b, 1997). Partly because of their construction of heritable phenotypical variance, racial categories have, to a greater or lesser extent, been naturalized: the cultural differences that physical difference is taken to indicate are held to be rooted in a natural essence which is heritable through sexual reproduction; this naturalization has varied according to historically changing conceptions of human nature as well as changing structures of social relations, particularly those involving inequality.

This approach to race emphasizes the *process* of racializing, naturalizing identifications and derives from my experience of Latin America, where racial identities are often more ambiguous, changeable, and context dependent than in other regions, but I think the approach is widely applicable and helps avoid reifying racial categories. In this sense, rather than studying "races" or "blacks" or "whites"—even as socially constructed groups—one studies processes of racialized identifications and the racialized social relations that go with them.[12]

Racial identifications are very important in understanding constructions of national identity in Latin America and elsewhere.[13] If nationalisms work between homogeneity and heterogeneity, then the presence of people who identify themselves and others as belonging to different racial categories is a vital aspect of diversity, a possible threat to putative national purity, or perhaps a crucial resource for future versions of homogeneity; this is all the more so since racial categories may be thought to involve deeply ingrained characteristics that are transmissible across generations. As far as Colombian music is concerned, racial identifications are also important because the musical styles which are the subject of this book were often labeled black or even African. Even when the styles were not explicitly labeled in this way, discourses about Colombian popular music very often included, and still include today, a concern with origins, attributed to African, native American, and European cultures or "races."

In theories of nationalism, in keeping with the common emphasis on myths of homogeneity, nationalist discourse on race is often seen as mainly excluding or marginalizing "races" seen as "impure" or "foreign" (see Anthias and Yuval-Davis 1992: 39; Gilroy 1987; Segal 1991; and Williams 1989). The more nuanced view of nationalism advanced above raises the possibility that to focus only on an ideology of exclusion may be too simple. In fact, at least for much of Latin America, there is a subtle balance between inclusion and exclusion (Stutzman 1981, Wade 1993a).

Mestizaje, or mixture, both physical and cultural, is a master narrative of national identity for much of Latin America (see especially Graham 1990; Skidmore 1974; Stepan 1991; Stutzman 1981; Wade 1993a, 1997; Whitten 1981, 1986; Whitten and Torres 1998; and Wright 1990). It involves inclusion and exclusion, affirmations of homogeneity and heterogeneity. To portray, say, Colombia as a mestizo nation implies that everyone is the same, but for the idea of mixture to have any meaning it must invoke the idea of difference: mestizos and mulattoes are "made from" blacks, whites, and indigenous people. When mixture is understood as progressive whitening, black and indigenous peoples may be classed as so different that they are marginalized or even denied, but they may also be included as potential recruits to mixedness.[14] Every mention of mixture, of hybrid, or of creole inevitably reaffirms the difference which is apparently being dissolved in the speech act. This is a general phenomenon, but it can be seen specifically in what Béhague (1991) identifies as the overriding concern of many Latin American musicologists with studying the origins of what is admitted to be music of triethnic derivation: the theme of African, native American, and European origins is constantly harped upon.

An illustration of the persistence of a symbolics of origin alongside a symbolics of mixture which might seem, logically, to erase origins can be drawn from Venezuela, where there is a similar ideology of nationhood founded on everyone being mixed and the color of *café con leche* (Wright 1990). Despite that ideology, as Taussig (1997) and Placido (1999) show, there is widespread religious activity centered on a host of spirits and saintlike figures in which three are central: María Lionza (usually a white, but occasionally an indigenous, woman), El Indio Guaicaipuro (an indigenous man), and El Negro Felipe (a black man). That is, the original racial ingredients are still vital symbols for many Venezuelans. The state has also appropriated aspects of the María Lionza cult, often constructing her as indigenous in relation to the "white" independence hero, Simón Bolívar.

Processes of racial identification in Colombia (and elsewhere in Latin America) are thus intimately bound up with nationalism and national identity: homogeneity and heterogeneity are imagined as the community and diversity of "natural" essences; transformation and appropriation are imagined through the hybridizations of mestizaje in which notional fragments of racialized essences may be resignified by rearticulation in a different representation, often overshadowed by a hegemonic principle based on an ideological link between whiteness and modernity; and, of course, globalized categories such as black, white, and indigenous cannot be thought of only in the national frame—racial identifications are a transnational process. The following chapters will show how important racial identifications were to the interplay between music and national identity in Colombia: the putative blackness of Colombian tropical music was a central concern, whether it was to denigrate it or exoticize it.[15]

Nation, Gender, Race, and Sexuality

NATION, GENDER, SEXUALITY, AND RACIAL IDENTITY

Nationalism is "constituted from the very beginning as a gendered discourse, and cannot be understood without a theory of gender power" (McClintock 1993). Women are interpellated in nationalist discourses and practices in various ways: as reproducers of biological offspring ("to govern is to populate"), as producers of cultural offspring who will "know who they are," as symbols of national boundaries and national identities, and as participants in national struggles (Yuval-Davis and Anthias 1989: 7). They are often seen as guardians and civilizers, but, as in the case of Argentinean prostitutes, they may also be seen as threatening the national body politic (Guy 1991; see also Stepan 1991;

and Parker et al. 1992). Many of these ideas owe much to Foucault's argument that the concern of the European bourgeoisie with individual sexuality—and the discursive construction of "sexuality" as an object—was tied to a concern with the reproductive vigor of the nation (Foucault 1979).

Doris Sommer takes an intriguing line on the relation between gender and nationalism. She argues that the romantic novels that became required reading in Latin America in the late nineteenth and early twentieth centuries reveal a marriage between Eros and Polis in a project of national consolidation. The novels' "erotic passion was . . . the opportunity (rhetorical and otherwise) to bind together heterodox constituencies: competing regions, economic interests, races, religions" (Sommer 1991: 14). The romantic liaisons of the novels' heroes and heroines suggested the possibility of reconciling different social origins. They also intimated the seductive quality of the nation within which such a reconciliation was possible, especially when the private family affairs of the political elite were often also public affairs of state. At the same time, successful love affairs, ending in marriage (and in the Latin American romances of the time, they generally did, unlike their more tragic European counterparts), held out the prospect of social fruitfulness based on sound family life.

In the realm of music, Monsiváis makes similar observations about bolero in Mexico in the early decades of the twentieth century. The rise of romantic songs, with their "language of rapture," effectively united "social classes and regions, moods and prejudices, real and imagined loves." Although bolero initially put the "guardians of public chastity" on guard, romantic songs eventually "consolidate[d] the home, becoming the means by which the new frankness and audacity proper to the growing capital city [were] made 'decent'" (Monsiváis 1997: 171, 173, 168, 174). This ambiguous appeal to profane sexuality and moral decency is one that will recur in subsequent chapters.

Savigliano links the gendered embrace of late-nineteenth-century tango to emerging nationalism, but she detects the profound contradictions underlying the link. On the one hand, "Tango started as a dance, a tense dance, in which the male/female embrace tried to heal the racial and class displacement provoked by urbanization and war"; then, "After the unification of the country, which forced Argentina into a new national identity that focused on Buenos Aires . . . tango's embrace became a must" (Savigliano 1995: 30, 31). Criollo nativism fought to establish a whitened national identity and chose the exotic tango as a symbol. On the other hand, such a project "was born to fail in the hands of the tango" (165), which, because it "emerged out of mutual admiration and scornful disdain among the different races, classes and ethnicities lumped together in the city [of Buenos Aires]" (32), reenacted division as much as unity. The contradictions and ambiguities that Monsiváis and Savigliano reveal are, as I will show, also present in the case of Colombian popular music.

The important connection between gender and images of nationhood becomes all the more significant when, as with the tango, ideas about race mixture are involved. Since mestizaje involves notions of "blood" and essences or fragments of essences passed on down generations, it is mediated by gender relations and sexuality. Often, as with ideas about the nation, women are seen as a locus of possible purity, the guardians of family honor under patriarchal control, and thus also as a potential threat to that purity (see, e.g., Martinez-Alier 1974; see also Stepan 1991; and McCaa 1984). Such ideas about honor and shame are not, of course, at play only in contexts in which racial identifications are being made (see, e.g., Peristiany 1965), but they take on further meanings when ideas about race are involved. Stoler (1995) has described in detail how the maintenance of racial hierarchy in European colonies involved the policing of the boundaries of the sexual and moral behavior of both men and women. In a rather different way, Gilroy has suggested that "gender is the modality in which race is lived." In the black Atlantic diaspora, an "amplified and exaggerated masculinity . . . and its relational feminine counterpart become special symbols of the difference that race makes," meaning that "racial sameness [is experienced] through particular definitions of gender and sexuality" (Gilroy 1993: 85). This draws our attention to the general proposition that racial identification is always a deeply gendered process.

Of particular relevance to this book is the relation between racial identity and sexuality, which turns fundamentally on the imputation by "whites" of a lascivious, powerful, unrestrained sexuality to "blacks," a notion deeply embedded in the history of Christianity and Western colonial domination. Bastide (1961) argues that the imputation derives from the relation of domination itself, since it gives dominant men the opportunity to "use" subordinate women without shouldering the responsibility of social paternity. According to bell hooks, "Sexuality has always provided gendered metaphors for colonization" (hooks 1991: 57). Nederveen Pieterse (1992: 172–174) notes the ambivalent repression and eroticization of "Others" which is also an ambivalence about the sexuality of self; he also suggests that psychoanalysis has reinforced the common connection made from an early date in Western cultures between Africans and sexuality. At the risk of dehistoricizing, it seems that from an early date blacks' sexuality has been made a seedbed in which nonblacks—particularly men—have cultivated ideas about themselves: ideals of civilization, purity, and control over (human) nature were opposed to black sexuality seen as bestial, primitive, and contaminating; and, by the same token, the fear of alienation from qualities defined as base but also powerful, vital, rooted in nature, potently masculine, and seductively feminine was imagined in relation to "white civilization" seen as constrained, over-refined, and impotent (see also Fanon 1986; Gilman 1986; Hernton 1970; hooks 1991, esp. chap. 7; Jordan 1977: 32–40; McClintock 1995; Wade 1993a: 246–250; and Young 1995). Of course, those identifying themselves as blacks have been able to appropriate this ambivalence in order to exploit such fears, assert a "natural" superiority in certain spheres, and, perhaps, form part of what Gilroy (1993) sees as a questioning of Western values of modernity. Interestingly, this "primitivism"—that is, Western constructions of "savage," usually racially differentiated others—although it "by then had a long prehistory of its own" (Barkan and Bush 1995: 2), became a growing ideological force in the late nineteenth and early twentieth centuries, due partly to the expansion of European imperialism during that period (see Barkan 1995; Franco 1967; Honour 1989; Kuper 1988; Rhodes 1994; and Torgovnick 1990). As before, images of lasciviousness were a constant presence, but blackness could be very ambivalent. In an essay on Josephine Baker, the African-American dancer especially popular in interwar France, Martin notes that in the United States at that time, "the black body represented unrestrained, illicit desire and black sexuality was associated with satanic chaos and bestiality. At the same time, black culture represented freedom from routine, predictability, rigidity" (1995: 318).

This picture of primitivism and its ambivalences is complicated by the existence in specific contexts of comparable sets of images mediating relations between classes and between men and women themselves—showing what might be called a certain interchangeability and compatibility between discourses of class, racial, and gender inequality with respect to a fundamental ambivalence of fear and desire. Donna Guy's (1991) study of prostitution in Argentina, for example, shows how prostitutes and lower-class women in general could be seen as both potentially polluting and highly attractive (see also Gilman 1986).[16] Washabaugh (1998b: 7–8) argues that the nineteenth-century

Romantic fascination with introspection and passionate emotionality was realized partly through emerging popular musics which took off "on womanly wings, propelled by the promise of wholeness that could only be realized by contacting the femininity of the cosmos." Yet the woman's voice was "elided and usurped by the man's." Monsiváis remarks that if women—even prostitutes in some cases—were exalted in boleros, these songs also had a "clearly masculinist orientation . . . , mediated by the myth of the Housewife" (1997: 191).

In Colombia, the sexualization of national and racial identifications can be seen in what I have called the cultural topography of the nation (Wade 1993a).[17] I will describe this in more detail in the next chapter, but the aspect I wish to stress here is that the ambivalent space between homogeneity and heterogeneity in discourse on the nation is necessarily spatialized in the tension between, on one hand, a national project of territorial and cultural integration through "development" and, on the other, the continuing variety of regional cultures, which also have different racial identities. This tension is expressed partly in the intertwined sexual and racial imagery attached to given regions and is mediated through the sexual interactions between men and women of different regional origins, who define each other partly in terms of these images, not just as regional or racial types, but as regionalized and racialized men and women. Thus, the Caribbean region of the country is often seen as "hot" and the Andean zone as "cold," climatically and sexually speaking. The Andean zones have been and still are more piously Catholic, while in the Caribbean region the moral control of the church has been less powerful; patterns of marriage are less "orthodox" there. Over time, however, the rest of the country has "heated up," and in this process the Caribbean region has played a vital role, in great part by means of its music.

The music and dance from the Caribbean region of the country was initially identified by many people in the interior as linked to blackness and also (and as a result) morally suspect and sexually explicit when danced, but it was also seen as exciting, liberating, and vital. Such images obviously had different impacts for women and men, given prevailing gender relations and the perceived value of a controlled sexuality for women. The music was implicated in a whole process of change in sexual morality that was occurring in Colombia, as it was elsewhere in Latin America,[18] partly due to changes in sexual divisions of labor and gender relations. That some of the tensions between homogeneity and heterogeneity should be worked through in terms of music must be due in part to the power of music capitalism to generate imagined communities, but it is also because the connections between music, dance, the body, and sexuality made of music an evocative and powerful mediator of the differences located in the sexualized cultural topography of the nation.

MUSIC, DANCE, THE BODY, AND SEXUALITY

Connections between music, dance, the body, and sexuality are a complex area.[19] In people's talk about music in Colombia, the use of the body in dance was most often mentioned in connection with sexuality or perceived impropriety. But how have these meanings emerged and what significance does the embodiment of meaning have?

What Middleton (1990: 258) calls the "instinctualist view" of the relation between music and the pleasures of the body is tempting, but too crude. This position simply holds that music—or, rather, some forms of music, especially rock and Afro-American styles—is directly linked to the physical body, and thus to the libido, because of an "immediate material relation to the music" (Grossberg, cited in Middleton 1990: 259); for Frith, "black music expresses the body, hence sexuality" because "sound and beat are *felt* rather than interpreted" (Frith, cited in Middleton 1990: 259).[20] This naturalistic approach tends to dehistoricize the body, neglecting "its specific representations [and] culturally available shapes" (Middleton 1990: 259). Just as problematic, in my view, is the automatic link made between physicality, sexuality—"the body, hence sexuality"—and bodily pleasure: the mere fact that music, and even more obviously dance, engage the body does not make them *necessarily* sexual or even pleasurable. This approach overprivileges and even naturalizes the relationship between music (or dance) and the body. All human practice is embodied—embodiment is "the existential ground of culture and self" (Csordas 1994)—and the practice of music or dance is not inherently closer to the body than, say, the practice of sport or work.

A social constructionist view of the body, in contrast, sees "the body not merely as a natural object but as one socially and historically constituted" (Cowan 1990: 21). In this view, any links between music, dance, the body, and sexuality are constituted entirely by social relations and categories, or in Foucault's terms, by discourse (Shilling 1993: 70–99; see also Cowan 1990: 21–27). This approach is undeniably powerful. The connections often made in Colombia between people from the country's Caribbean region, their music and dance, and their "hot" sexuality, have been constructed, and not just imposed, in a particular history which includes slavery in the region, African cultural influences, and domination by a colonial power for which dancing was often defined as sinful—connections and history which could be traced in varied forms in many regions in the Americas. From an early date, Africans were seen by Europeans as both highly sexual and fond of music and dance, and in the colonial Americas this connection persisted, with music and dance seen by the authorities both as an escape valve for slave emotions and as a possible threat to the established political and moral order. In the nineteenth and twentieth centuries, the same link has been made (see, e.g., Aretz 1977; Barkan and Bush 1995: 3; Cooper 1993; Levine 1977: 242–244; McClary and Walser 1994; Nederveen Pieterse 1992: 132–151; Ortiz [1950] 1965; Savigliano 1995: 30–35; and Wade 1993a: 278–281). The equation between potent sexuality and musical and dance skills has been elaborated by black people as well, although for different reasons and with different moral judgments involved.

Shilling objects, however, that a pure social constructionist approach tends to make the body as a physical entity disappear (Shilling 1993: 100), a concern shared by others (see Butler 1993; Csordas 1994; and Turner 1994). After all, the entire historical process by which blackness has become sexualized and, so to speak, musicalized could be recounted without reference to the body as anything more than the simple vehicle for complex meanings. Embodiment itself becomes a residual fact. Washabaugh (1998a: 43) observes that, while once it was assumed that dance simply revealed meaning in a denotative or metaphorical way, it is now argued dancers "exemplify and embody the world that has marked their bodies." Yet this formulation still sees the body as a relatively passive vehicle on which meanings are "inscribed." This neglects two important aspects. First, dance, in particular—and this book largely concerns dance music—involves bodily effort, even if there is no privileged connection between the body and dance, as opposed to other physical activities. Daniel argues that "The aesthetic force of rumba in combination with the physical release of tension govern its potency" (1995: 140). This implies an enactment of meanings which adds to their emotional intensity. Second, dancing ability is not just a meaning constructed on the body, but a material product of working through the body understood, in Shilling's terms, as an unfinished project (Shilling 1993: 114). The motor skills of the body are altered, changing a person's embodied physical capital during his or her lifetime, particularly a young person. This transformation then feeds back into processes of social constitution as apparently "natural" evidence of the connection between, say, the Colombian Caribbean region and dancing skills. This helps account for the frequent naturalization of dance skills, often seen as a "natural attribute." The constructed connection with sex—which although it is a socially constituted activity is also generally seen as a "natural function"—is clearly eased by this process.

Any connections between the body, musical and dance forms, and sexuality are cultural constructions, but it is important that these constructions take place not just *on,* but *through,* the body—seen as constructed, but not infinitely malleable. If music in Colombia is a powerful mediator of the differences located in the sexualized cultural topography of the nation, this is mainly because of the historically constituted links between music—and particularly dance—sexuality, and (racialized) region; but it is also important to pay attention to the embodiment of dance and sexuality and also, indeed, to the embodied experience of region—the literal heat of the Caribbean region, the cold of Bogotá, or the actual rise in climatic temperature of the Andean cities in the last decades. These are, after all, some of the most commonly mentioned features of people's experience of regional difference.

Music, Identity, and Music Capitalism

MUSIC AND IDENTITY

In her book on zouk, Guilbault notes that "Musical genres have often played a crucial role in the expression and negotiation of identity" (Guilbault 1993: 203).[21] Much of the literature on this theme, while it may admit that musical styles have a complex relation to identities and social positions, nevertheless does not always theorize this difficult area in much depth. A notable exception is Middleton, who makes a comprehensive attempt to assess the study of "popular music in culture" (Middleton 1990: 127–171). A central characteristic of many studies within this perspective, according to Middleton, is the idea of a relation of homology between musical form and social structure (which can be said to include the social positioning from which identity is held to arise). He presents a detailed argument which, in brief, concludes that many of these studies tend to overstate the tightness of fit between the two levels, may understate conflict over musical meaning within the social group whose identity is supposedly being reflected, and, in the case of those studies which posit a countercultural music reflecting a subcultural group, may overstate the element of subversion. In general, there is a tendency to see social identity as a preformed thing which music simply expresses.[22] Finally, in some cases, this tendency can lead to an emphasis on the value of the "honest" representation of this social identity through "authentic" music. This neglects the ideological nature of the notion of authenticity, which, Middleton argues, is rooted in a Romantic critique of industrial society (or more generally modernity), in the nationalist idealization of tradition, and also in bourgeois attempts to devalue urban industrial working-class culture (Middleton 1990: 130, 168–169).[23] Also, of course, any tendency to link music and identity mechanically will, when applied to the nation, run into the problems discussed previously of opposing elites and subaltern masses in an overly simple fashion.

Middleton himself adopts a Gramscian approach which is not far removed from that espoused by Hall and Jefferson (1976) and is in line with that outlined earlier in this chapter (Middleton 1990: 7–11). This allows much greater flexibility of fit between music and social structure or social identity (whether based on class, ethnicity, or gender, although Middleton refers specifically to class structure), without abandoning the possibility of explaining that fit in terms of social structures and identities—for example, in terms of appropriation—as opposed to simply describing the historical connections between these and musical forms. It is often very difficult to link particular musical styles to particular class locations—Finnegan, for example, found no clear correlations within the varied music scene of Milton Keynes, U.K. (Finnegan 1989: 312). Slobin also recognizes the difficulties of using class as an analytic principle in the study of music. But when he says that music is "a wild card in a game for which there are no known rules" (Slobin 1993: 16), he resigns himself to mere description.

It is also necessary to see music as constitutive of social identity rather than merely reflective. Middleton points out that poststructuralist accounts criticize a culturalist position for seeing culture as a preconstituted totality which can be simply expressed (Middleton 1990: 166). Instead, cultural meanings are generated in the process of signification. From the poststructuralist perspective, "There are no essences to be captured by appropriate linguistic formulations" (Giddens 1987: 85). This can lead to problems in accounting for the reference of meanings to anything other than themselves: a "retreat into code" (Giddens 1987: 84) which raises the question of "the possible need for some conception of the *real,* if any practices of valuation and politics are to survive" (Middleton 1990: 166). A pragmatic way out of this impasse is perhaps in Stokes's point that "musical images do not just reflect knowledge of 'other places' [or other identities] but preform them in significant ways" (Stokes 1994b: 5). He gives the example of stereotyped images of "Eastern music" preforming people's knowledge of, say, Turks or Iraquis. Of course, these images do not arise from nowhere; they derive from a specific history, implying a more dialectical process. Drawing on Waterman's idea in his study of Nigerian *jùjú* music that "good juju *is* good social order" (Waterman 1990: 220), Stokes also argues some social events are thought to need an atmosphere—in effect, a constitutive context—which can be created only by music and dance (Stokes 1994b: 5). This gives us a way of seeing how meanings are generated in the process of signification without divorcing them from reference to a concrete social context.

Another way of looking at this is through Anderson's argument, applied to language but also relevant to music, that, "It is always a mistake to treat languages . . . as *emblems* of nation-ness. . . . Much the most important thing about language is its capacity for generating imagined communities" (Anderson 1983: 122). Music can also be seen as constitutive of social realities in this way, as I suggested earlier in relation to national identities (see also Frith 1996).

The foregoing argument is necessary in order to conceptualize the Colombian material. In a society where hybridity is the rule rather than the exception and where a transformist hegemony operates, it is impossible to think in terms of simple equations between music and social position. Musical styles from the Caribbean coastal region, especially as they became increasingly commercialized, are very difficult to relate in any simple way to class positions or ethnic or racial identities. Without being divorced from these, the music crossed boundaries quite fluidly and changed its associations over time, as I shall show in the ensuing chapters. A focus on the constitutive nature of music helps to grasp changing relations between musical style and identity since, instead of seeing a given style as essentially linked to a given identity, one can see how the same or similar musical styles can help constitute various identities in different contexts. Finally, since in Colombia there is constant debate about the authenticity of different styles, it is important to understand the ideological nature of notions of authenticity and their roots in Romantic critiques of modernity. Claims about authenticity—playing precisely on an assumed essential link between music and identity—are involved in a power struggle over the ownership of value in which tradition and modernity are key terms.[24]

MUSIC CAPITALISM

A crucial feature of the story behind music from the Caribbean coastal region is its commercialization, which, far from being unique to those styles, was part of the technification, massification, and commoditization of the communications media in Colombia and across the globe. Films, records, and radio all became increasingly commercial products from about 1930 in Colombia, with television following in the early 1950s. It is therefore necessary to address the question of how changing technologies of communication, specifically those in the music industry, have mediated the tension between cultural homogeneity and heterogeneity in the national frame.

Discussions of the massification of the media have often centered on the extent to which this has resulted in the homogeneity, standardization, and increased social control through strictly channeled consumerism that Adorno views so negatively or, on the other hand and especially in the last few decades, the extent to which it has opened up possibilities for increased democratization, increased diversity of production, and more social participation through greater access by more people to the means of production and consumption of information (see García Canclini 1989; Manuel 1993; Martín-Barbero 1987a, 1987b; Middleton 1990: 34–100; Miller 1995a; Rowe and Schelling 1991; and Wallis and Malm 1984). As with the parallel discussions about the impacts of globalization in destroying and recreating localities, the answer seems to be that both processes can occur. Massification under Fordist regimes of accumulation may involve standardization, but this depends on the product. The economies of scale involved in production-line car manufacturing create pressures to standardize, since change involves great cost; musical production tends to be more flexible, since instruments and recording equipment can be turned to many uses. Middleton discusses other reasons why Adorno's vision of musical standardization is exaggerated and concludes that the circuit of production and consumption of popular music is like "a constantly mutating organism made up of elements which are symbiotic and mutually contradictory *at the same time*" (Middleton 1990: 38).

Many people in Colombia—journalists, disc jockeys, television announcers, musicians, and other listeners—expressed to me the fear that commercialization leads to a loss of "authentic," local traditions, a fear commonly heard elsewhere.[25] But, as Wallis and Malm (1984: 269–311) point out, commercialization brings international cross-fertilization, which may also open new opportunities. Describing Dominican bachata music, Pacini Hernández says that cross-fertilization, rather than resulting in a "homogeneous and insipid muzak for the global village," can lead to musicians "strengthening and revitalising their local and/or national musical traditions" (Pacini Hernández

1992a: 361). Manuel comments: "mass media can and often do enrich as well as alienate" (1993: 8). He notes that homogenization can be good or bad depending on what is being purveyed (e.g., values of tolerance or acquiescence to social inequality), and diversification can mean democratic grass-roots cultural autonomy or fragmentation into divisive bigotry (12).

The commercialization of the media in Colombia meant that standardization occurred in specific ways. Some Colombian styles became successful—and thus pervasive—at the expense of others which, in the new commercial climate, remained purely local or faded into the background; those genres that did become popular also often became more standardized, losing aspects of their internal diversity. The tendency of capitalist production toward economies of scale clearly worked here. But commercialization also introduced a whole new range of styles of music onto the national market—Argentinian tangos, Mexican corridos, Cuban rumbas and guarachas, U.S. fox-trots, and so on, as well as Colombian styles previously limited to particular regions. It also permitted greatly increased possibilities of transnational cross-fertilization. This is often discussed as a recent phenomenon dependent on newly globalized markets, but although electronic communications have certainly sped up the interchange and arguably opened it up to more people, it has a long history, especially in music (see Roberts 1979).[26]

If both standardization and diversification can occur with the same technologies, then the question is, What influences the development of these alternatives? One answer is given by Martín-Barbero in his account of the massification of the media in twentieth-century Latin America, according to which the state and/or a capitalist ruling class and their relations with the working class are the main influences (Martín-Barbero 1987a: 178-179; 1987b). In his view, from the 1930s to the 1950s, there was a strong emphasis on the construction of national cultures by elites, using new technologies such as the radio to address the growing urban masses with a discourse of populist compromise and modernization. From the 1960s to the 1970s, communication was seen more as a means to economic development. Television helped to construct the image of a single public with a homogeneous set of consumer demands which were increasingly transnational. From the 1970s, electronic media have held out possibilities of increased state control and capitalist investment in production for an ever more fragmented market. This, however, has also increased the diversity available, breaking with the previous projects of homogenization. Still, nowadays each person—given the economic wherewithal—is also able to plug in more individually to the products she or he wants to consume, ignoring the rest.

This is quite a persuasive account in many ways: it is clear that the spread of radio and television allowed new pervasive, immediate, constant, and potentially centralized ways in which people could be interpellated as national subjects and shown what the state and the elites who controlled the media considered to be in good taste and representative of nationhood. But Martín-Barbero overestimates the solidity of a state or ruling class armed with a specific cultural project. In Colombia, the state did not regulate the record industry except in so far as it was a business like any other; legislation for radio was fairly unobtrusive, at least as regarded the content of programming. There was no defined cultural policy as such until the 1970s. What existed was something like Middleton's "constantly mutating organism," run by musicians from a variety of backgrounds and by businessmen with overridingly commercial ends in view, catering to an increasingly diverse market with rapidly changing tastes. There are clear contrasts here with more authoritarian regimes: for example, the Dominican Republic under Trujillo (Austerlitz 1995; Pacini Hernández 1995) or Haiti under Duvalier (Averill 1997).

This does not mean that music in Colombia was some kind of free-for-all. Consumers' tastes and musicians' and record producers' ideas of what to create or what might sell are always in a complex and dynamic process of mutual influence in which, although the music industry arguably has a powerful hand, it is hard to generalize. The point is that, in Colombia, these tastes and ideas were all being formed within the whole changing ideological fields of nation, race, gender, sexuality, modernity, and tradition that I have already discussed. There were overarching hierarchies of morality and of taste and distinction (Bourdieu 1984). In this field, we cannot think in terms of the state or the ruling elite imposing homogeneity in some simple way. Commercialization seems to have increased musical heterogeneity in some ways, but diversity continued to be judged, appropriated, and transformed within an ideological field structured by hegemonic values. The capitalization of music and the technological developments in its dissemination mediated the tension between homogeneity and heterogeneity by expanding and diversifying the market for music but at the same time opening up that cultural space to more pervasive forms of ideological evaluation.

* * *

I have been trying to map out a theoretical perspective for understanding nationhood and cultural and musical diversity in which the
ambivalent, tensioned space between homogeneity and a transnation-
ally constituted heterogeneity is seen as worked through in an ideological field of hierarchical class, racial, gender, and sexual identifications, mediated by the capitalist circulation of commodities and
information. All this can be seen anew in the Colombian state's recent
experiments with official, constitutionally recognized multiculturality,
occurring alongside a number of related but diverse phenomena: projects of *el rescate de lo nuestro* (the rescue of what is ours) in the Caribbean coastal region, based on reaffirming regional culture and identity, resting heavily on music, and imbued with notions of authenticity
and regional pride; the recent proliferation in the mountain city of
Medellín, industrial center of the recording industry, of dance schools
based on *porro*, one of the Caribbean regional styles that began its
commercial career in the 1930s; the resounding success in 1993 of Carlos Vives, a soap opera actor and ballad singer, with "modern" cover
versions of old *vallenato* songs, originally from the Caribbean coastal
region—success that has broken all record sales in Colombia and
crossed previously quite resistant class and national boundaries to this
music. These all partake in the "tropicalization" of Colombia that began decades ago, but they also fit easily into images of postmodern
multiculturality, seen as a reaffirmation of nationhood rather than its
dissolution. The evident historical continuity indicates that, in fact, the
same sort of tensions are operating in an ideological field which has
changed in its balance of elements and is now mediated by new technologies of capitalist circulation, but which still retains much of its old
structure. I will take up this theme again in the conclusion, when the
details of the history of the "tropicalization" of Colombia through its
music are clearer.

2 La Costa and Música Costeña in the Colombian Nation

This book is concerned with how and why music from the Caribbean coastal region—popularly known as *la costa*[1]—came to be central to Colombia's popular music repertoire. The identity of both Colombia as a nation and La Costa as a region within it are clearly central to this concern. These identities will emerge in detail in the ensuing chapters, but here I want to give a sketch of the overall contours of the ideological field in which these identities are constituted by first looking at the nation and then the place of La Costa within it. I will conclude with a brief account of how music from the region fitted into the national music scene in the early twentieth century, before this music became a national success.

The Colombian Nation

Like elites in other countries in Latin America in the late nineteenth and early twentieth centuries, Colombian political and intellectual circles were striving to define their nationhood. They were faced with a heterogeneous country, broken into regions which could communicate only with difficulty due to poor infrastructure and a broken terrain, all of which had large populations seen as mixed and several of which had large numbers of people identified by elites as *negros* (blacks) or *indios* (indigenous peoples).

A major element of perceived difference within the nation stemmed from its strong regionalization and the uneven distribution of the mixed descendants of the Europeans, Africans, and native Americans, which had led to a specific spatial pattern of racial identifications, still operating today. From the perspective of the highland interior, the

Pacific littoral was black, the Caribbean coastal region (i.e., the coastal belt and its hinterland) was highly mixed, with significant numbers of black and indigenous people, the jungles of the Orinoco and Amazon basins beyond the eastern cordillera were largely populated by native Americans and missionaries (although *los llanos,* the plains between the cordillera and the jungles, had long since been colonized by a wide variety of people), while the interior of the country was mainly white and mestizo with some indigenous populations in isolated rural areas and some black and mulatto people in particular areas of the inter-Andean valleys. The interior of the country, especially in its urban centers, was the focus of power, wealth, "civilization," and whiteness.[2]

Bushnell (1993: viii) notes that "it is a commonplace to say (with Colombians often saying the first and the loudest) that the country lacks a true national identity or a proper spirit of nationalism." It was not until 1886 that, after numerous constitutional experiments swinging between federalism and centralism, Rafael Núñez imposed a strongly centralist constitution—and also incidentally composed the words for Colombia's first national anthem. This centralization occurred on the basis of economic and political changes, in progress since the 1850s, that were breaking with colonial structures and giving rise to a "national social formation" characterized by intensive peasant colonization of virgin lands and increased integration of the peasantry into national and international markets via a commercial bourgeoisie (Fals Borda 1981: 82B). It was at this time that the first Academia Nacional de Música was founded (1882), and, from about 1887, a national anthem began to be standardized, based on the words by Rafael Núñez and set to music by Oreste Sindici (1837–1904), an Italian immigrant.[3]

Another important era for nationalist sentiment was the 1930s—"the nationalist years" (Uribe Celis 1992: 57; my translation)—when a series of liberal and modernizing reforms under Alfonso López Pumarejo endeavored to open up the education system and incorporate the rural and urban working classes more fully into state structures. It was at this time that "the *national* frame became a point of political reference for the 'oligarchies' as well as the popular strata" (Palacios 1986: 138–139). Intellectuals also pondered over the possibility of a national art: for example, the first congress of music was held in 1936 and aimed to "promote musical culture in Colombia, recognizing its great importance for nationalism," in the words of Daniel Zamudio, a composer and musicologist who participated in the congress (Zamudio 1978: 398); there were also discussions about national values in art, with painters and writers tackling indigenist themes and regional cultures (see also Medina 1978: 185; Universidad Nacional 1984; and Uribe Celis 1992).

These moments did not give rise to a "hyperbolic nationalism" (Bushnell 1993: viii), but it would be wrong to suppose that the question of what Colombia was or is as a nation has not preoccupied intellectuals and the state, or that national identity has not been subject to powerful representations. These form a vital context for understanding the place of the Caribbean coastal region and its music. There are many starting points from which to cut into the field of representations of national identity and especially the ambivalent space between sameness and difference. Here, I will look briefly at three of these: the writings of intellectuals, textbooks used in the education system, and state cultural policies.

THE LITERATE ELITE

Representations of national identity produced by a literate elite in the late nineteenth and early twentieth centuries generally disparaged blackness and indigenousness, privileging whiteness at their expense. *Negros* and *indios* were not simply ignored in these representations, as if denied by an image of homogeneous, whitened mixedness; in fact, they formed a constant point of reference for imaginings of the nation, symbolizing the backwardness and primitivism against which the future of the citizenry was defined and against which elite superiority was perceived.[4] Elsewhere I have documented in more detail the varied discourse of intellectuals on Colombian nationhood (Wade 1993a, 1994b), but it is worth looking at two crucial figures of the twentieth century to give a flavor of the thinking involved.

Luis López de Mesa was an important figure in intellectual and government circles; his posts included minister of education, 1934–1935. His writings, especially his book *De cómo se ha formado la nación colombiana* (1934), have been subjected to various analyses. Bagley and Silva (1989), Restrepo (1988), and Helg (1989) emphasize his racism, conditioned by ideas of contemporary science about race and eugenics. He is generally pessimistic about mestizaje and derogatory about black and indigenous people. In a piece called "El Factor Etnico" (1927), written for a special committee of experts on the problems of Colombia and circulated only to the clergy and the national authorities, López de Mesa said: "The mixture of the indigenous with the African element and even with the mulattoes that derive from it would be a fatal error for the spirit and wealth of the country; the defects of the two races would be added, rather than eliminated, and we would have a *zambo* [indigenous-black mixture] who was astute and indolent, ambitious and sensual, hypocritical and vain at the same time, not to mention ignorant and sickly. This mixture of impoverished bloods and inferior cultures brings about unadaptable products . . . which fill the asylums and the prisons when they come into contact with civilization" (cited in Restrepo 1988: 379–380).

It is certainly true that López looked at the world through the racist spectacles of his era (albeit a slightly anachronistic era), but there is also evidence of a characteristically Latin American view of mestizaje in his writings. He is in favor of European immigration, since this would "enrich the qualities of [Colombia's] racial fusion," but immigrants would bring new skills and customs as well as contributing to "the enrichment of [Colombia's] good stock." In a stance typical of Latin American adaptations of Anglo-American eugenic thought (Stepan 1991), he remarks that, although racial heritage and mestizaje are bad influences, he does not "want to assign them excessive importance in the formation of the creole character"; the social environment is also crucial and "From this it is clear that if creole laziness is conditioned by elements which can be dominated, such as poor health and lack of discipline, then it [laziness] should not be considered a fundamental obstacle to the constitution of a historic race." Mestizaje is also democratic force: "We are Africa, America, Asia, and Europe all at once, without grave spiritual perturbation" (López de Mesa [1934] 1970: 122–123, 20–21, 14).[5]

Laureano Gómez, Conservative leader and president of Colombia (1950–1953), was more uncompromising in his views. In his essay *Interrogantes sobre el progreso de Colombia* (1928), he states that "Our race comes from a mixture of Spaniards, *indios* and *negros*. The latter two flows of heritage are marks of complete inferiority." Although the Spanish heritage includes elements of fanaticism and ignorance, "It is in whatever we have been able to inherit from the Spanish spirit that we must look for the guiding lines of the contemporary Colombian character." These views were the blueprint for a political system in which the few, better racially endowed, ruled the many with a rod of iron (Gómez [1928] 1970: 44–47; see also Helg 1989; cf. Wright [1990: 79] on racial ideologies and dictatorship).

Both these writers were thinking in the tense, ambivalent space between homogeneity and heterogeneity. Large portions of their works are taken up with documenting and pondering on diversity in their country; homogeneity is asserted at the same time as heterogeneity is constantly mentioned. Often present difference is seen as a resource to be plundered for future sameness, but difference is also irreducible, otherwise they themselves, or their intellectual descendants, would be the same as the *negros, indios,* and mestizos they berate. Blackness and indigenousness (and in some accounts mixedness itself) are there as a temporal other for a future of national civilization, but also as a present other for the personal civilization claimed by those on the upper rungs of a class, regional, and racial hierarchy. As such, *negros* and *indios* were an integral part of representations of the nation.

A similar tension between affirmations of sameness and recognition of difference can be seen in more recent writings. The well-known writer, journalist, and politician Eduardo Caballero Calderón stresses the heterogeneity of the Colombian nation, which is "a sample of the Hispanic-American racial mosaic" in which "racial integration still does not exist" due to "geographic and racial incoherence," on top of which the state exists as a European-derived "artificial construction," giving the mere "appearance of national unity." He refers often to blacks, generally in derogatory terms, noting that blacks are "the most primitive and uncouth [*basto*]" element in the racial mix but that black culture has become predominant in areas such as the Caribbean coastal region of Colombia "because not only in the economic sphere is good money dislodged by bad" (Caballero Calderón 1960: 21, 85–86, 49). More recently, the sociologist Uribe Celis (1992: 205–206) writes of the "perfecting of mestizaje" which took place in Colombia but also mentions the "regional diversity" of the country. Perhaps the writer who most emphasizes homogeneity is the politician and essayist Otto Morales Benítez: he is concerned with establishing that Latin America as a whole has a sui generis mestizo identity which is different from European identities (Morales Benítez 1984).

School Texts

This same tension between sameness and difference can be seen by looking briefly at school textbooks from about the 1930s onward.[6] These texts are an excellent source because, as Gellner (1983) has argued, education is a critical tool for the creation of a national culture. The attempt to create a common education system in Colombia dates roughly from the centralizing 1886 constitution; the Catholic Church had a central role in organizing pedagogy.[7] In the 1930s, liberal reforms sought to diminish elitism, extend education to the masses, and reduce the role of the church (Helg 1987).

The idea of the nation as a single unity is evoked in various ways in these textbooks. History books portray a common trajectory of the birth of the nation from conquest, through colony, to the republic; the civilizing role of the church and the deeds of certain hero figures, particularly Simón Bolívar, "the Liberator," are stressed. The idea that Colombia is a country of mestizos, the product of mixtures between Europeans, Africans, and native Americans, receives continuing and constant emphasis in both history and geography books: "from the fusion of the European and the Indian races [blacks are ignored here] came a new race with excellent qualities and virtues" (Granados 1949: 10); "There has been extensive mixture in the country, Spanish, Indian, and African blood being combined in very diverse measures" (Ramón 1967: 141); "The contemporary population of Colombia is the result of the mixture of three historical groups" (Valencia 1977: 80). Alongside this, there is the reiteration of what constitutes Colombia as a nation: its political boundaries, its cities and landscapes, its flag, and so forth. The history books often have a chapter teaching the basics of *civismo* (public-spiritedness, but also patriotism) which emphasize the national symbols and the unity of the "Colombian race" and describe the country's political institutions.

Diversity is, however, also a long-term and constant theme. Colombia is "a country of regions" or a "sea of landscapes" (Valencia 1977: 38) which can offer the visitor "a great number of beauties" (Martínez 1924: 58). Some regions, however are seen as more important than others, and it is the Andean region which is given pride of place: "The Andean region is the most populated and the most important from every point of view" (Valencia 1977: 100); "The Andean region is . . . the most important" (Ramón 1967: 82). In terms of racial identifications, the same picture emerges. At the same time as an overall mestizaje is evoked, writers unfailingly refer to the great variety of human types in the country, producing thumbnail character sketches of the "mestizo" and the "mulatto," and of regional types such as the *costeños* (from the Caribbean costal region) or the *antioqueños* (from Antioquia Province; see Ramón 1967; Sánchez 1966; Vergara y Vergara [1901] 1974; and Valencia 1977).

Prior to the 1970s, this diversity was often explicitly harnessed to hierarchy. The *criollos,* as the "white" American-born sons of Spanish fathers were generally known,[8] were portrayed as the illustrious rebels who led the fight for independence: according to Brother Justo Ramón, a member of a religious order whose texts span a long period (1948– 1967), they were helped by "the Indian, obedient soldier . . . the black, submissive soldier, [the] valiant mulatto, and the mestizo . . . a daring horseman" (Ramón 1948: 246). A 1941 history primer, alongside text describing "the race" as a mixture of "Europeans, Indians, and blacks," has an illustration of a white, book in hand, standing beside, or rather above, a native American and a black, each holding a hoe (Bernal Pinzón 1941: 119). Simple statements that blacks, indigenous people, and a majority of the mixed population were concentrated in the lower strata during colonial times are mixed in with value judgments: Henao and Arrubla, for example, who wrote school texts from 1925 to 1967, say that "the mass of colored men and the indigenous race, unthinking and hard working, were in a deplorable state everywhere" (Henao and Arrubla 1967: 276). Ramón describes the "African contribution" as generosity, festivity, physical resilience, and laziness, while the Europeans brought "a sense of measure, moderation of reason and emotion, haughtiness of spirit, and a great stock of knowledge" (Ramón 1967: 141). The characteristics of control (measure, moderation) spelled out here are important in view of the emphasis given in education to "good manners." An important text by Manuel Antonio Carreño, *Manual de urbanidad y de buenas maneras,* was widely used in schools over an astonishingly long period from the mid–nineteenth century to the 1960s.[9] The manual stresses the need to maintain the moral standards of the church, the strict rules governing good behavior in society, and the necessity of hierarchy: "urbanity esteems highly the categories established by nature, society, and God himself" (Carreño n.d.: 26).

Blacks and indigenous people were—and are—a constant presence in these representations of Colombianness but were relegated to an inferior position. Homogeneity was invoked in terms of citizenship and a shared heritage; heterogeneity was never denied and could be praised in terms of the abundance of variety which Colombia had to offer, but it was subjected to hierarchy, especially in racial terms. In more recent decades, hierarchy has become less explicit and tends to be established, for example, by the identification of blacks with the rural and poverty-stricken Pacific coastal region.[10]

CULTURAL POLICY

A different angle on representations of, and attempts to shape, national identity comes from a brief examination of state cultural policy (Mena Lozano and Herrera Campillo 1994). Prior to the 1960s, the promotion of culture had always meant the promotion of "cultured values," that is, the cultural activities associated with intellectual European circles and closely connected with formal education and the arts. In the

1930s, for example, the Ministry of Education also looked after fine arts, libraries, public monuments, and archaeological relics.

Other areas were controlled by the appropriate ministry. Radio broadcasting, for example, was covered by the Ministry of Communications, which dealt with basic legislation organizing use of the airwaves, and the Ministry of Education, which made programs for the state radio station, the Radiodifusora Nacional. The state was concerned from the start with making sure radio stations were registered and approved, but in the first legislation controlling commercial radio, decreed in 1936, there was little mention of national identity. By 1954, during the dictatorship of General Gustavo Rojas Pinilla, radio transmissions were required to "disseminate and increase culture," and they could not endanger "Christian morals or good manners." A 1966 law stated that radio should "affirm the essential values of Colombian nationality," but said nothing more specific. In 1974, this requirement was reiterated and given some substance by articles stipulating that musical programming must contain at least 25 percent of works by Colombian authors and 35 percent by Colombian artists. By 1992, perhaps in line with the internationalization of the economy, a new decree dropped this requirement, contenting itself with vague phrases about "exalting national traditions." [11] The Radiodifusora Nacional, started in 1941, took a more substantive line by transmitting mainly classical music, news, plays, and educational programs. However, there was some airtime for short programs such as *Regional Music of Colombia* and *Popular Latin American Music*.[12]

From about the late 1950s, cultural policy advanced in two parallel channels. The first channel was in the national development plans, which began at this time and featured the promotion of "culture" as a small element supposed to help in the social and economic modernization of the country. One plan mentioned the mobilization of "human resources which are needed in the economic, cultural, social and political development of the country." Another plan talked in general terms about disseminating "national culture," without specifying what this comprised, and added that "national folklore" should be cultivated. Presenting the 1983 plan, Change with Equity, President Belisario Betancur similarly spoke of the need for "the affirmation of our cultural identity and the strengthening of our culture." The plan spoke of the stimulation of the "diverse cultural expressions" of the population, which would "strengthen our cultural identity, protecting and disseminating the constitutive values of our historical personality." [13] These plans saw culture—understood as artistic and intellectual production, whether elite or popular—as a socially cohesive force, even in its diversity.

The second main channel was in the formulation of cultural policies by institutions especially charged with this task. This really took shape in 1968 with the creation of Colcultura (the Colombian Institute of Culture), attached to the Ministry of Education.[14] This entity lasted until 1997–1998, when it was replaced by the Ministry of Culture. The institute, via its various cultural policies, tended to privilege "cultured" culture: the conservation of the national patrimony (e.g., monuments, buildings), museums, libraries, archives, fine arts, theaters, and so on. However, cultural diversity was recognized from the start in measures designed to promote the study of "the sociocultural manifestations of the different regions of the country" and, later, to decentralize the institutionalization of culture and achieve the "effective participation of the community" in designing "cultural programs adapted to the different sociocultural zones of the country."[15] This emphasis was increased in the mid-1980s to 1990s with strategies to promote regional cultures as elements in a national culture—with ethnic minority cultures being increasingly included in the 1990s. The most recent plans have been created in the context of the internationalization of the economy and thus seek to reinforce national identity while participating in a global culture (Mena Lozano and Herrera Campillo 1994: 164). The 1990 cultural policy plan nevertheless uses a discourse by now familiar when it says that "To enrich Colombian cultural identity" it is necessary to recognize that "Colombia is Indo-America, Afro-America, and Hispano-America at the same time. Parallel with this, mestizaje has been an important factor of national integration. . . . In the diversity of cultural expressions, Colombia is and must be one. Its unity depends on the meeting of varied cultures and on a critical recognition of their diverse values" (DNP and Colcultura 1990: 14).

In both these channels of state activity, diversity is harnessed to national integration based on a cultural identity which, though varied, is a common heritage. Although a definite shift is visible over time from an almost undiluted emphasis on bourgeois European culture to the gradual inclusion of popular, regional cultures—the latter still, however, outweighed by the former—integration has been a continuing aim. Hierarchies of value are, of course, reiterated in the enduring institutional oppositions established between "popular culture" and "culture" *tout court*—that is, the unmarked category—but in mediating the tension between sameness and difference, it has rarely been a question of simply imposing homogeneity. From its inception, cultural policy sought out diversity and actively constructed it, first through investigation and more recently by, for example, organizing Regional Days of Popular Culture aimed at the "retrieval" (*recuperación*) of regional history and the display of local traditions (see Bonilla 1990: 26–27; and Triana 1990).[16]

A recent example of this process of construction is the exhibition *Millenia of Cultural Diversity*, housed in the National Museum in Bogotá and designed with advice from the Colombian Institute of Anthropology, a section of Colcultura. The Gold Museum—part of the state's Banco de la República—has long given a public space to the notion of Colombia's Amerindian heritage, but this exhibition was the first in the National Museum to explicitly embrace cultural diversity. Much of the display was dedicated to pre-Colombian Amerindian cultures, with one room dedicated to contemporary ethnic minority cultures, including "Afro-Colombians." The overwhelming impression was that *indígenas* (indigenous peoples) were nowadays located in the Amazon region, remnants of pre-Colombian cultures that were shown as having once been widely distributed. Likewise, although one or two of the Afro-Colombian exhibits came from the Atlantic coastal region, most of them came from the Pacific region, creating the same type of congruence between region, race, and culture. Within the exhibition itself there was no reference to the history of enslavement, although on a different floor there were exhibits which explored this theme from Africa to the Americas—among the standard displays of items from an elite colonial and especially Republican history. Notable also was the representation of "cultural diversity" as comprising (Pacific coast) blacks and (Amazon) indígenas: the rest of the country was not on display: nonblack and nonindigenous people were the unmarked category against which "diversity" was defined. Still, an important exhibition in a museum which is a typical venue for school visits, *Millenia of Cultural Diversity* sought out and celebrated difference, taming it into certain molds and actively constructing it as a national patrimony.

La Costa in the Nation

The Caribbean, or Atlantic, coastal region has a particular place in the country's racialized cultural topography. It is a place characterized by a certain ambiguity: it is black, but also indigenous and white; it is poor and "backward" (although not as poor as the Pacific region or the Amazon region), but has also been a principal point of entry for "modernity" into the country; it has been politically vocal, but economically weak. It is also the source of much of the country's commercially and internationally successful cultural products: musical styles such as *cumbia,* authors such as Gabriel García Márquez, and painters such as Alejandro Obregón and Enrique Grau.

The Caribbean ports of Cartagena and Santa Marta were early colonial settlements, and the former was also the main entry point for slaves destined for the territories of New Granada and other Spanish possessions. While maintaining a presence in these and a couple of other provincial cities, the bulk of the Spanish colonial enterprise soon shifted to the Andean interior around Bogotá and Tunja, in search of gold, more easily exploited indigenous populations, a more equable climate, and security from pirate attacks. La Costa was characterized by land-intensive cattle farming and agriculture, while the gold mining so crucial to elite accumulation elsewhere in the colony was more or less absent.

By the late eighteenth century, a census classified the majority of the population as mixed, with smaller proportions of whites, slaves, and indigenous people.[17] Physical mixture between these groups had been extensive, but the population was unevenly spread: those classed as whites tended to concentrate in the cities and generally formed an exclusive aristocratic elite; many of the slaves were found in or near Cartagena; those still classed as *indios* were generally in more isolated rural areas; the "mixed" people were widely distributed, but tended to have more African heritage along the coastal belt and the banks of the main rivers.

In the nineteenth century, economic activity in La Costa was dominated by the ports of Cartagena, Santa Marta, and after about 1870, Barranquilla (which prior to the 1850s had been a small town). These ports connected the interior of the country to external markets and were subject to the boom-bust cycles of exports from the interior such as tobacco (1850–1870) and coffee (which became important after about 1890). La Costa did experience agricultural growth—tobacco was grown there too, and bananas were a major export from United Fruit Company plantations in the Magdalena area during the first forty years of this century—but in general this was limited and slow growing; rural areas were dominated by cattle farming that required large areas of land but little input of labor. Industrial activity grew in the ports, which were rather disconnected from these hinterlands.

Barranquilla, especially after the construction of a rail connection to a suitable harbor bay in 1871, rapidly outstripped Cartagena and Santa Marta as the commercial and industrial center of La Costa, with important brewing, milling, and textile industries.[18] In 1891, a United States–born resident wrote: "We believe . . . that no other city of South America has had such a signal progress as ours" (cited in Nichols 1954: 173). By 1920, it was the third most important Colombian city after Medellín and Bogotá. Because of its position as a port facing across the Caribbean and the Atlantic, because of the extensive immigration from countries such as the United States, Italy, and Germany, and because of its early wealth, Barranquilla competed at least on an equal basis with Bogotá in the trappings of urban modernity—indeed, it boasted several "firsts." Soccer entered the country through Barranquilla in about 1903—as an elite sport—and the first Colombian Football Association was founded there in 1918. Baseball and basketball also made their first appearance in Colombia via Barranquilla. The country's first airline, the Sociedad Colombo-Alemán de Transportes Aéreos, was founded there in 1919 by German immigrants and Colombian partners. In 1918, a U.S. immigrant, Karl Parrish, Sr., founded an urban development firm to create Colombia's first planned elite residential neighborhood, El Prado. In 1925, amid the national borrowing spree of the so-called Dance of the Millions, the city negotiated a loan from the Chicago Illinois Trust Company to improve piped water supplies and sewage disposal, and to tarmacadam roads and pave sidewalks; the country's first municipal public utility company was created, run by the North American Samuel Hollopeter.[19] Barranquilla had the first radio station, La Voz de Barranquilla, founded in 1929 by Elías Pellet Buitrago, the grandson of a North American immigrant who had been the U.S. consul in Barranquilla and had owned a publishing company. In the 1930s, the city was home to the first Olympic stadium, the first Exhibition of National Products, and the first automatic telephone exchange. Along the coast, in Cartagena, the country's first record company, Discos Fuentes, was founded by Antonio Fuentes in 1934, and Barranquilla was second in line with Discos Tropical, founded about 1945 by Emilio Fortou, son of a French immigrant.[20] Apart from these firsts, in the 1940s, the city hosted its own philharmonic orchestra and opera company, both founded by Pedro Biava, an Italian immigrant, and the University of Atlántico was also established (see Bell Lemus 1984; Espriella and Quintero 1985; Posada Carbó 1986, 1987b; and Solano and Conde Calderón 1993).

Underlying this spectacular growth were the seeds of decline. The opening of the Panama Canal in 1914 made the Pacific port of Buenaventura, located conveniently near the coffee-growing regions, an increasingly serious competitor to Barranquilla. From 1934, Buenaventura took the upper hand in tonnage of exports and, from 1941, in tonnage of imports. After the Depression of the 1930s, the adoption by the government of policies to protect domestic industry initially stimulated industrial growth in Barranquilla, but eventually weakened Barranquilla's position. Industries grew faster in the interior, feeding markets protected for them by the high cost of transport from the coast. In the late 1930s, the main textile manufacturer in the city, Tejidos Obregón, closed down. Government tariff policy did not favor local regional agricultural products such as cotton, helping instead wheat production centered on the Andean zone. The weak hinterland economy of La Costa weighed against its cities, and the so-called golden triangle of Medellín, Cali, and Bogotá increasingly monopolized industrial and commercial wealth. Despite this, Barranquilla retained its importance until after the Second World War, and between 1948 and 1958 it experienced a relative respite based on favorable trade. Thereafter, it entered into crisis. Taking the region as a whole in 1985, the seven provinces of La Costa—except for the tiny Atlántico Province, the capital of which is Barranquilla—had levels of poverty 20–40 percent higher than the national average, with illiteracy at 19 percent compared to a national average of 14 percent (Bell Lemus and Villalón Donoso 1992; López de Rodríguez n.d.; Meisel Roca 1992; Meisel Roca and Posada Carbó 1993; Piñeres Royero 1991; Rodado Noriega n.d.).

The Identity of La Costa

I do not want to present here a comprehensive analysis of Costeño identity, since this would preempt the ensuing chapters. Instead I want to present some of the principal ways in which Costeño identity has been constituted. Rather than giving a sketch of the identity of the region as if it were a synthetic totality, I will outline the most salient fields of ideology and practice within which that identity exists.

The field of racial identifications is central. Since a discourse of mestizaje involves evoking the original constituents of the "racial mix," there has always been the possibility of stressing the blackness of La Costa. An important element in helping to make that identification are the beaches of La Costa, which have been a tourist destination for better-off people from the interior of the country from early this century. Tourism, a central element of modernity, has been shown to be important in constructing images of place, and La Costa is no exception (Graburn 1995; Shields 1991; Urry 1990, 1995). Many people easily identified as blacks and mulattoes—especially for a visitor from the highlands—live along La Costa's beaches and also in Cartagena, a major tourist destination, where they form a servant class for the tourists. The image of La Costa from this point of view is "Caribbean": tropical sun, sea, sand—and blacks.

On the other hand, it is possible to stress the mixedness of La Costa, drawing attention to the mixed appearance of the majority of the people and the whiteness of the elite, which stems in equal proportions from aristocratic lineage and—particularly in Barranquilla—from more recent European and Middle Eastern immigration. This ambiguity makes Costeño culture, including Costeño music, a very potent operator in mediating the cultural transactions taking place in the ambivalent space between sameness and difference that opens up when talking and thinking about the nation. Things Costeño can be black or not black—or more or less black—at different times or in different contexts, or even at the same time and in the same place, depending on what one wants to see. Things Costeño are highly subject to appropriation and resignification in terms of their racial identity.

A second vital ideological field is that of tradition and modernity. During its heyday, Barranquilla was, or claimed to be, the most modern city in Colombia. Despite its location in a region subject to identification—often via blackness—with backwardness, the city had the symbols of modernity and had strong connections with the United States and Europe via its large immigrant population. In intellectual circles, this was evident with the publication of one of the country's only avant-garde magazines of the early twentieth century, *Voces* (1917–1920; Bacca 1990, 1991; Gilard 1991; Williams 1991: 56, 102). Musically, Barranquilla and Cartagena have always led the country in hosting the latest sounds, whether the Costeño music itself that became so popular in the interior, or the fox-trots and rumbas of the 30s, or the salsa of the 70s, or the more recent Dominican merengue, Jamaican reggae, Afro-Caribbean, and African styles.[21] (It should be noted that the Pacific coastal port of Buenaventura has also been important as a point of entry for new styles of music; see Hurtado 1996; Ulloa Sanmiguel 1992: 445; and Waxer 1997, 1998.) Again, then, there are contradictory possibilities for connoting La Costa as a region: on one hand, rooted in tradition with large, isolated rural areas, apparently based on archaic haciendas,[22] and with many dark- skinned people living in rudimentary conditions; on the other, with modern cities, ports of entry of outside influences, and tourist locations with the last word in entertainment. Since the decline of Barranquilla, the former image has tended to dominate, and nowadays it is helped, ironically, by music, since La Costa is seen by people inside and outside the region as being a rich repository of traditional "folklore."

Both of the preceding ideological fields are linked to a third, in which the competing values can be termed reason and emotion or perhaps realism and magical realism. This is the view, propagated just as much by Costeños as by people from the interior—and usually with a more positive evaluation—that, compared to the highland interior, Costeño cultural practice is less inhibited, more open, more emotional, more sincere, more fun, more "sexy" (in the various modern connotations of that term), and also more superstitious, more magical, less Europeanized, less bound by the constraints of scientific and bureaucratic rationality, and thus more liable to the eruption of the bizarre.

The Barranquilla carnival and the location of the annual national beauty contest in Cartagena have helped sustain this image of the coast since before the Second World War.[23] Such a view can also be traced back in the field of arts and literature to at least the 1940s—black Costeño poet Jorge Artel's *Tambores en la noche* (Drums in the Night) was published in 1940, evoking a sensuous rhythmicality for the region (see Prescott 1985b)[24]—and has found its major exponent in the magical realism of the novels of García Márquez (Gilard 1986). The paintings of Barranquilla artist Alejandro Obregón, with their bold, bright colours and their interest in the vernacular and in the sensuality of women, including black women, also underwrote this view (see Medina 1978: 367).[25] It goes without saying that music has been a crucial realm in which these images are purveyed. Again, all these areas and ideas relate to a view of La Costa as linked to a general Caribbean culture.

Ideas about family and male-female relations are also involved here: Costeño men are said, by themselves and others, to be womanizers; Costeño women may be thought of by non-Costeños as sexually loose; there are stories about how poor families sometimes sell their daughters to rich men. These all create a picture of male-female relations and sexuality which are less restricted by Catholic piety than in the interior.[26] Sexual liberation may, however, be seen as both traditional (unrestrained primitivism) and modern (breaking the bonds of traditional morality).

The image of sincerity and openness has a further important con-notation—peacefulness. Colombians—like many other Latin Ameri-cans—are intensely aware of the violence in their country. This has been manifested in many bloody civil wars and more recently in guer-rilla activity, state repression, and drug violence. La Violencia, un-leashed in 1948 by the assassination of Liberal leader Jorge Eliécer Gaitán and lasting into the late 1950s, was a period of particularly in-tense and often barbaric civil strife which happened to coincide with the rising popularity of Costeño music, although after its initial urban manifestation, La Violencia was mainly rural, while Costeño music was consumed primarily by urbanites. Interestingly, La Costa is gener-ally spoken of as having been less violent during this period than the interior of the country. Sánchez observes that "on the Atlantic Coast . . . the Violence was minimal or non-existent" (1992: 100). Partridge (1974) found that the Costeños he worked with in the 1970s still saw people from the interior as more prone to violence than themselves, and I also found this in my fieldwork in La Costa (1993a: 166, 254). In the late 1980s and the 1990s, the region has been losing that repu-tation in some respects, with both guerrilla and more recently para-military violence affecting some areas of the region, but during the pe-riod with which this book deals, La Costa was reputed to be relatively peaceful.[27]

The final field in which Costeño identity is constituted is that of po-litical power and powerlessness. The rise of a regional consciousness among the Costeño political elite (as opposed to complaints to the cen-tral government from Cartagena elites about local and personal issues) is generally said to have emerged in the 1830s with Juan José Nieto, a Cartagena-born Liberal leader (1804–1866; see Bell Lemus 1993; and Fals Borda 1981; see also Delpar 1981; and Park 1985). The stance taken then set the agenda thereafter. It was said that (1) La Costa as a region had certain economic interests which were unfairly disfavored by central government in Bogotá, (2) the region's politicians needed more autonomy and more representation in central government to de-velop these interests (which would also be in the nation's favor—full separatism has rarely been an issue),[28] and (3) the Costeños' customs, capabilities, and mode of speech were looked down upon by people from the interior.

Since then, collective action by the region's political and economic elites has been uneven but visible. Beginning in 1919 with the Costeño League formed to lobby the central government for regional interests, various assemblies and associations have come and gone which have expressed a regional viewpoint.[29] Regional consciousness was also reinforced as, from the 1960s, central government planners, often pushed by Costeño initiatives, began to look at the region as a unit for planning purposes.[30] An important recent stimulus has been the creation of regional television channels, the second of which was Telecaribe, established in 1986 (Abello Banfi 1994).[31] Finally, over the last decade, a small group of Costeños has emerged which combines a regional political project with an intellectual one: people such as Gustavo Bell Lemus (historian, ex-governor of Atlántico Province, and current vice-president), Eduardo Posada Carbó (historian and ex-director of a Barranquilla newspaper), and Adolfo Meisel Roca (historian and ex-director of ICETEX, the government body that deals with international educational links) have worked extensively on the history of the region, being concerned to raise its political and cultural profile at the same time.[32]

Costeño political elites—a category that overlaps with economic and to a lesser extent intellectual elites—have thus for a long time had some conception of the region as a single entity, politically and culturally, even if actual economic structures, centered on Barranquilla and Cartagena, do not reflect that conception. For these elites, the fields in which racial and cultural identifications compete have presented opportunities and problems: blackness can be a drawback but can be avoided by stressing mixedness, which can also be presented as a particularly Colombian quality; backwardness can be offset by claims to (foreign) modernity or revalued by claims to the solid authenticity of (local) tradition; a "warm" and "emotional" culture can be made to seem authentic but also irresponsible and lacking seriousness; rich creativity in art and literature is a useful support in asserting the value of regional culture but can backfire if others stress the presence of commercial dance music classed as "frivolous"; a "Caribbean" leaning may be useful in depicting the region as warm and creative, but this may also make it seem too foreign from the point of view of the interior. As the inaugural speaker of the first Forum of the Atlantic Coast in 1981 said: "Our happy temperament has been confused with irresponsibility; our generosity and bonhomie with a lack of culture [i.e., culturedness] and when the executive cadres of the country were under consideration, this region was not taken into account" (Paulina de Castro Monsalvo, cited in Primer Foro de la Costa Atlántica 1981: 1). In my view, it is all these ambiguities, opening opportunities for mul-

tiple readings and resignifications, that are a root cause of the popularization of Costeño music.

Colombian Popular Music and Costeño Music

As in other Latin American countries, popular music began to develop
as an urban form, more or less distinct from rural music in its performance context, from the early nineteenth century, with art music
traditions already well established in the cities.[33] In rural areas of
Colombia, there was a wealth of musical and dance styles, with certain
broad regional differences and a host of more local variations. Lack of
documentation makes it very hard to know what these were. Colombian writers on music tend to refer to twentieth-century regional patterns, dividing "folklore" into subgroups characteristic of the Andean,
Caribbean, Pacific, and Los Llanos regions. Attention is then paid to
questions of origin, usually focusing in a rather timeless way on the relative admixture of African, European, and Amerindian traits. The history of a style during, say, the nineteenth century receives less attention, except in an anecdotal fashion.[34]

In urban areas during the nineteenth century, dances originating in
Europe, such as the long-standing quadrilles, minuets, waltzes, and
contradanzas, or the newer polkas and mazurkas, were popular among
"respectable" people, played in their salons on piano and string instruments, although they would have been heard by a range of classes
when played by military bands during public festivals. Light operatic
pieces and other songs popular in Europe were increasingly common
all over the Caribbean and Latin America, often circulating among the
Colombian middle and upper classes in sheet music form with arrangements for voice and piano, although the six-string guitar was also used.
These European forms were sometimes "creolized" to produce new
forms, such as the *pasillo*, a form of waltz popular in Venezuela,
Colombia, and Ecuador (Riedel 1986), or the *danza,* which developed
in Cuba and Puerto Rico and spread all over Latin America. Such music was typically played both in salons and in more working-class contexts, although with different instrumentation (see Manuel 1994: 253;
1995: 32).

For the upper classes, regional variation in European-based music
was not very marked: the same music would be listened and danced to
in Bogotá and Cartagena. However, there were also urbanized versions
of more varied regional rural styles—which included, for example,

bambuco, popular in Bogotá and other cities of the interior from at least the mid–nineteenth century (Ochoa 1997; Restrepo Duque 1991: 126; 1988: 529).[35] The upper classes looked down on certain of these musical styles, but even if they did, it was often the case that the men consorted with the women, and thus also the music, from classes lower than their own.

Also important in urban areas were brass bands, of military origin. These became increasingly popular from the early 1800s and, with instruments imported from Europe, played marches, waltzes, polkas, and the newer creole styles such as the pasillo and danza. Bands played in the salons, but also in festivals in provincial towns, often sponsored by local elites who paid the musicians and in some cases imported instruments and sheet music. These bands spread popular European styles into rural areas, especially those linked to international trade networks, such as the Caribbean coastal region (Bermúdez et al. 1987: 84–87).[36]

Toward the end of the nineteenth century, music in Colombia began to be integrated into discourses about national identity, and it was bambuco of the interior region's string ensembles that took pride of place.[37] The pasillo, which was if anything more widespread, did not acquire the same nationalist overtones. The author, journalist, and politician José María Samper (1828–1888) said of the bambuco that "[there is] nothing more national, nothing more patriotic than this melody which counts all Colombians among its authors. It is the soul of our *pueblo* [people, nation] made into melody." According to Baldomero Sanín Cano (1851–1957), an educator, critic, journalist, and politician, "Bambuco resounds with the heartbeats [*palpitaciones*] of the fatherland." In the words of the historian Luis Angel Cuervo (1893–1954), "The history of bambuco is the history of the whole Republic, of its societies and its individuals." Writing in 1960, Eduardo Caballero Calderón (b. 1910), writer, journalist, and politician, affirmed that "Without bambuco, the fatherland would not be conceived" (all cited in Perdomo Escobar 1963: 308; see also Añez [1951] 1970: 19–24).[38] Other modern writers concur: folklorist Abadía Morales, for example, says that bambuco "is the most important and representative musical and choreographic expression of our folklore" (1983: 152).

Bambuco had already become an urban form by the time of Pedro Morales Pino (1863–1926), the so-called "father of Colombian popular music," with whom the folk music of the Andean region "gained entry to society" (Restrepo Duque 1991: 121, 112). Born in Cartago of humble origins, he began as a painter in the bohemia of Bogotá. There he also studied in the National Academy of Music and made an impact in the city with a waltz, "Los Lunares." He played with various trios and quartets of guitarists and mandolin players before forming his famous Lira Colombiana in about 1897, a lineup of some ten musicians playing bambucos, pasillos, and danzas.[39] The Lira Colombiana toured nationally before setting off for Central America and the United States. The original Lira Colombiana broke up around 1908, but Morales refounded it in Bogotá and toured other countries in South America. Despite his popularity, Morales died in penury in Bogotá, leaving the bambuco "Cuatro Preguntas" as perhaps his best-known song (Restrepo Duque 1991: 121–125).

Morales Pino's groups produced other important figures in the popularization of bambuco. These people were also some of the first to participate in the emerging international record industry, based in New York. Emilio Murillo (1880–1942), a disciple of Morales Pino and a figure in Bogotá's bohemian world, formed his own Estudiantina Murillo in about 1908 (an *estudiantina* is a string ensemble). In 1910 and in 1917, he made some recordings with the Columbia Gramophone Company and the Victor Talking Machine Company in the United States. These included some pasillos, a two-step, a one-step, *gavotas,* polkas, waltzes, and the Colombian republican hymn, and they were played either with solo piano, a piano and flute, or tiples and piano; Murillo also directed the Banda Española for a couple of numbers (Spottswood 1990: 2145–2146). No bambucos were included in these sessions, which is surprising, since these and pasillos were principal components of his repertoire: "Canoíta," a bambuco, is one of his best-known pieces (Restrepo Duque 1991: 110–114). Apparently, at this early stage bambucos did not interest record companies, which were catering to an international Latin American market.

Alejandro Wills (1884–1943), born in Bogotá to a well-off family, played in an early lineup with Morales Pino and went on to form duets, briefly, with Arturo Patiño and, more famously and lastingly, with Alberto Escobar. With their bambucos, pasillos, and waltzes, both duets were very popular in Bogotá, playing alongside the many other duets and trios in bohemian cafés, in cinemas between film showings, and on serenades. In about 1914, the Victor company recorded Wills and Escobar on a portable recording machine in Bogotá, and in the following years they toured the country, the Caribbean, and finally the United

States, where in 1919 they recorded some Colombian songs, before visiting Mexico (Restrepo Duque 1991: 125–130). Among others, Murillo and Wills and Escobar were chosen to represent Colombia at the 1929 Exhibition of Seville.

Jorge Añez (1892–1952) was born in Bogotá to a family in comfortable circumstances. He studied music in the conservatory in Bogotá but also played in Morales Pino's reformed Lira Colombiana before moving to the United States, where he lived between 1917 and 1933. With Víctor Justiniano Rosales, a Colombian tenor who had already made some recordings in 1910, Añez recorded a series of bambucos and pasillos with Victor in New York in 1920, using guitars and tiples. In 1923, he teamed up with a Panamanian singer, Alcides Briceño, who made scores of recordings in New York between 1919 and 1936, and the duet recorded with Victor, Columbia, and Brunswick for a decade, although bambucos and pasillos were only a part of their repertoire, alongside Mexican and Argentinean songs. Between 1929 and 1931, he also directed the Estudiantina Añez in a series of recordings for Victor, Columbia, and Brunswick which were mostly pasillos and bambucos (Añez [1951] 1970; Restrepo Duque 1991: 1–3; Spottswood 1990: 1637, 1696–1707, 2275–2276). For Añez, bambuco was "the lyricism of our blood, the artistic echo of our race transformed into song" (Añez [1951] 1970: 21).

In Medellín too, the 1910s witnessed the boom of bambucos and pasillos, plus other similar styles from the Andean interior such as *torbellinos* and *guabinas*. As in other cities, this music started in bohemian quarters and moved into cinemas, serenading, and finally upper-class clubs (Londoño and Londoño 1989: 362). Important Medellín figures included Pelón Santamarta (real name Pedro León Franco, 1867–1952), a tailor whose musical talents led him to Bogotá when bambuco was booming under the influence of Morales Pino. With his companion, Adolfo Marín, another tailor, he voyaged to Cuba in 1905 and thence to Mexico, where they recorded for Columbia and reportedly gave rise to the *bambuco yucateco* (Restrepo Duque 1988: 29; Betancur Alvarez 1993: 184–201). From a more elite background came the Uribe brothers, Daniel, Luis, and Samuel, who accompanied Emilio Murillo to New York in 1910 and recorded some pasillos and bambucos as a trio. Also from the province of Antioquia, of which Medellín is the capital, came the important Lira Antioqueña, founded in about 1908 after the model of Morales Pino's group. Unlike the latter, however, in 1910 the Lira Antioqueña managed to make recordings in New York, with Emilio Murillo as director, playing mainly pasillos, plus the odd danza, *schottis,* waltz, and *marcha*—not to mention the national anthem (Restrepo Duque 1988: 532, Spottswood 1990: 2009).

All these artists played styles other than bambuco—they might play pasillos, waltzes, danzas, torbellinos, and guabinas—and one-steps. They were recording in an international music industry catering to a Latin American audience: Jorge Añez's 1920 recordings included a Cuban bolero, an *aire colombiano,* and a Mexican ranchera; Alcides Briceño recorded fox-trots, marches, tangos, and Cuban *habaneras;* Alejandro Wills played a carpenter's saw in New York! (See Restrepo Duque 1991: 2, 128; see entries for Briceño in Spottswood 1990, vol. 4.) Nevertheless, bambuco came to be seen at that time as the most authentic national music of the country. Its origins have, not surprisingly, excited some discussions, which have essentially focused on the relative weight of African, native American, and Spanish influences; some of the debate has centered on the origin of the name, rather than the music as such. An African origin has been ruled out by some, although possibilities of indigenous influences have remained (see, e.g., Abadía Morales 1983: 154–156; Añez [1951] 1970; Davidson 1970, vol. 1; Ocampo López 1988: 103; and Perdomo Escobar 1963: 311–313).[40] Ochoa (1997: 42) may be right when she says that "Behind the negation of the African element in bambuco, of its rhythmic complexity which resists being confined to a single meter, there is a creolization of the genre, a process of making it acceptable as a symbol of the nation." Yet the debates on bambuco are typical of discourse about Colombian national identity in the constant repetition of the classic mantra of triethnic mixture, counterpointing difference against sameness in the same breath.

Whatever else observers thought, there was agreement on the basically *criollo* (native-born) nature of bambuco and on its origins in the Andean interior, making it a good symbol in a nationalist discourse managed by elites based in that region. In the process of urbanization, it acquired erudite overtones, suiting it further to use as a national symbol: Abadía Morales (1983: 156) notes how bambuco, like other "acculturated airs" such as pasillo and danza, had as lyrics "select poetry, taken from a universal repertoire or sometimes from eminent poets." He also writes of the dance as having a "delicate sentimentality" and a "decent *cortesía* [politeness, graciousness]" (1983: 295–296).[41] In the current of musical nationalism that swept Latin America at the time, bambucos were also set to classical arrangements by, for example, Guillermo Uribe Holguín, a prominent composer and director of the Conservatorio Nacional de Música from 1910 to 1935 (Perdomo Escobar 1963: 231, Béhague 1996: 317). It is thus not surprising that the term *música colombiana* was frequently used to refer to musical styles from the interior of the country, as if music from other regions was not Colombian.

This type of bias has proved long lasting. The sleeve notes on an early long-playing record (LP) by Dario Garzón and Eduardo Collazos, a famous duet which sang bambucos and other styles from the interior of the country over four decades from 1938, say: "Here sings this nation and these are some of its most precious native [*telúricas*] songs" (*Pueblito viejo,* Sonolux 0003, early 1950s). More recently, in a songbook entitled *The Most Beautiful Songs of Colombia,* over half the three hundred or so songs are classed as bambucos, with another sixty-one pasillos (Rico Salazar 1984). Another recent songbook, *The One Hundred Best Colombian Songs,* lists thirty-six bambucos and fourteen pasillos (Restrepo Duque 1991).[42]

This, then, was the situation when Costeño music began to make an impact outside its own region—and, indeed, within it. Bambuco and other styles from the interior dominated the scene from the late nineteenth century until the 1920s and remained important into the 1930s, just at a time when vast changes were beginning to take place which would alter beyond recognition the possibilities for music. Record companies emerged in the United States—Victor was established in 1901 and Columbia in 1903—and they recorded Latin American music from early on, both in the United States and in Latin America.[43] Gramophones in private houses and public establishments were increasing in popularity and were quite widespread by the late 1920s. Radio sets followed behind record players, with Colombian radio stations starting in the 1930s, although some listeners could pick up foreign stations prior to that. Meanwhile, between 1912 and 1928, the population of six major cities increased by 130 percent, even though the country's urban population was still only 31 percent of the total in 1938 (Bushnell 1993: 208, 287). In the longer term, however, it was Costeño music that really reaped the benefits of these changes, leaving bambuco and other related styles behind as increasingly "folkloric" music.

3 Origin Myths
THE HISTORIOGRAPHY OF
COSTEÑO MUSIC

In this chapter, I want to look at the way the origins of twentieth-century Costeño popular music have been written about. My argument will be that this music is presented as having very long roots into the past, although certain transformations are, of course, admitted. This representation is possible partly because it may be true, although the scarcity of sources available makes truth more of a moot point than it might otherwise be. Such a picture also has great resonance because it fits into paradigms of thought in which local regions—especially ones with significant black and indigenous roots—are associated with authentic traditions that, with the increasing impact of modernity in the twentieth century, are perceived to come under attack from commercialization and lose their authenticity. In the commanding ideological opposition between tradition and modernity, then, La Costa comes out, in the writings of folklorists, amateur historians, and academics, as on the side of tradition.

Cultural Dynamics in the Nineteenth Century

As we have seen from the previous chapter, the scant sources on music in La Costa before the impact of radio and the record industry permit only a rough sketch of the situation. The music scene was evidently quite complex: art music, popular music, and military music from Europe entered through urban channels, but *bandas de viento* (wind bands), for example, spread well beyond the cities and most musicians in the bands, military or otherwise, were working people.[1] Small towns had their bands too, not infrequently directed by a foreigner.[2] Many

black slaves and their descendants lived in urban areas, since there was
not a mining or plantation economy in the region, so that they were ex-
posed to elite musics as well as reelaborating African-derived styles in
their own circles and *cabildos*.[3] Indigenous people also lived in urban
as well as rural areas.

In towns and cities, elites listened to European music—quadrilles,
polkas, waltzes, mazurkas, contradanzas, minuets—but also some local styles or *bailes de la tierra* (dances of the land, i.e., "local-born"
dances) which probably included danzas.[4] These urban elites also pa-
tronized and organized some of the musical festivities of the lower
classes. Posada Gutiérrez's widely cited account of the music and dance
of Cartagena's lower strata in the 1830s mentions the indigenous *gaita*
flutes and the blacks' cabildos, in which they danced currulao and
which participated in masked processions that were organized by the
authorities (Posada Gutiérrez 1920: 338, 347).

A later source, less often used, is the history of Cartagena by Urueta
and Gutiérrez de Piñeres, which describes fandangos in the late nineteenth century. Urueta and Gutiérrez de Piñeres describe "nocturnal
civic processions" with carnival-style floats accompanied by a "music
band" but also by an "African drum," with women singing improvised
verses and clapping. There were three fandango associations which
made up the floats, and they were financed by the political parties and
distinguished families (Urueta and Gutiérrez de Piñeres 1912: 474–
475; cited in González Henríquez 1987: 80). For Barranquilla, the late
nineteenth century saw the beginnings of attempts by the elite to organize lower-class street celebrations at carnival time into an increasingly controlled event in which the elite also participated (Friedemann
1985; Jiménez 1986; Orozco and Soto 1993; Rey Sinning 1992).

In short, complex cultural dynamics were at work, which historical
research has barely begun to explore.[5] Ideology operates strongly in
current writings on the topic of La Costa's musical history. I do not
mean to imply that more data would evict ideology in some simple
way, but the scarcity of the former certainly gives the latter much lee-
way. Thus, the current literature deals as much with a mythology of
musical origins as with their historiography.

One tendency in the literature is to simply adduce the old, mixed
origin of styles of Costeño music—saying that a mixture of African, indigenous, and European elements is involved—and then move straight
to contemporary "folk" styles, with the tacit or explicit implication
that, being "traditional," these can be taken as a proxy for older forms

(see, e.g., Abadía Morales 1983; Escalante 1964; List 1980, 1983; Ocampo López 1988; Perdomo Escobar 1963; and Zapata Olivella 1962). It may be true that the lineups and styles found today, or documented and recorded thirty or forty years ago, are some indication of musics that existed a hundred or even more years ago:[6] the point is that the idea of changes and transformations in these forms is rarely addressed, except perhaps to bemoan a loss of "authenticity." As Bermúdez (1996: 116) points out, however, the heterogeneity of the rural styles, which were probably consolidated in the late colonial period, makes it difficult to argue for straight continuities with rural styles found in the early twentieth century, let alone more urban styles.

Another tendency in the literature is to give accounts of the "birth" of particular styles, locating their origin in specific places and, while arguing that they were new forms, also implying that there were strong continuities with existing autochthonous forms. This is evident in accounts of the emergence of porro, one of the main commercial genres of Costeño popular music of this century, which will appear extensively in later chapters.

Porro

The literature on porro's history recognizes porro as a recent development rather than something that extends back into the mists of time, but there is nevertheless an air of origin myth about these narratives. As Bermúdez (1996: 114–115) shows, wind bands began to be popular in the 1840s and existed in cities and provincial towns all over Colombia. One account of the emergence of porro focuses on the town of El Carmen de Bolívar, south of Cartagena, which between about 1850 and 1875 was the center of a tobacco boom that brought in many migrants—merchants and small cultivators—to this traditionally cattle-farming savannah area. The local elite was entertained by wind bands, composed of local musicians but usually directed by a formally educated musician, and these bands were also used for festivals, often on religious occasions, sponsored by elite families (González Henríquez 1987, 1989b).

This account then uses a widely cited piece of oral history published by Fals Borda. He reconstructed the experiences of Adolfo and Agustín Mier, two brothers of humble origins from Mompox, on the banks of the Magdalena, who had learned trumpet and *bombardino* (a type of tuba) from a Mason who ran a band there. In the 1850s, the brothers ended up in El Carmen, having heard of the tobacco boom and that "bands and orchestras were forming to play at the fiestas and *berro-ches* [dances] which the new rich people and foreign merchants were having." They joined the Banda Arribana, which had a tuba, two trumpets, a bass guitar, a bugle, a snare drum, a bass drum, and some cymbals, playing waltzes, pasillos, danzas, contradanzas, and marches. Then a crucial transition occurred: Agustín also began to play local styles on the clarinet, and this was the beginning of porro; the title reputedly came from a drum of the same name (see Fals Borda 1981: 103A–111A; see also González Henríquez 1987).[7] The mythical quality here derives especially from the fact that the fragments in the recounting of this story are presented as if Adolfo Mier were telling his life story, when in fact the text is a reconstruction by Fals Borda from stories apparently told to him by Adolfo's grandson, although this is nowhere explicitly stated (Fals Borda 1981: 29A).

In this way, porro is read as the continuation of an existing traditional folkloric form. The new wind instruments are traditionalized, so to speak, and the integrity of authenticity is maintained: the hardware of globalizing modernity is subordinated by the power of local tradition. It is just as possible, however, to read the transformation as the "localization" of musical styles which were pan-Caribbean dance forms such as the *danzón* and the danza. The end musical result—the porro—is the same, but the implications for understanding the music as a local product which underwrites local identity are rather different. In metaphorical terms, instead of a tale in which a local son borrows from the global scene and still remains a local hero, we have a global father figure spawning a child in the provinces.[8]

A different myth of origin for porro centers on the town of San Pelayo, near Montería, outside the tobacco-growing area, and the host since 1977 of the Festival del Porro, an event created by local intellectuals to rescue the music from what they perceived as degeneration and oblivion. Not surprisingly, investigations by local historians and folklorists have focused on the town as the birthplace of porro (Fortich Díaz 1994). The basic story is similar: the emergence of wind bands in the late nineteenth century to entertain the local elite, this time owners of cattle haciendas. The crucible for transformation is the *fiestas de corraleja*, festivals involving the fighting and running of bulls, arranged by landowners on their haciendas or in the local towns: the use of wind bands made the music in the fiestas more audible. Alzate states that the different barrios of the towns engaged in musical rivalry which reflected class and party political differences (Alzate 1980: 32, 33). In this story, Alejandro Ramírez Ayazo is the central founding figure (Alzate 1980; Fortich Díaz 1994). Born in 1883 in Montería to a prosperous merchant, he was educated in Montería and Cartagena and moved to San Pelayo when he was eighteen. There he learned the clarinet from Manuel Zamora, a musician from near Barranquilla who directed a local band, and he started playing traditional music. He is credited with the composition of a famous porro, "María Varilla," reputedly based on a local washerwoman of that name who was a marvelous dancer. Also important is the merchant Diógenes Galván Paternina, who, setting off to the United States in 1913, was charged with buying a new set of instruments for the band of San Pelayo, a commission he eventually discharged in 1915 after many adventures (see also Lotero Botero 1989).

As before, porro emerges from old traditional music being played by new instruments in new contexts. Fortich Díaz (1994) is very explicit about this. Porro is said to derive essentially from the traditional *conjuntos de gaitas*, groups (based on flutes of Amerindian origins, together with drums)[9] which are documented as existing at least as early as the 1830s (e.g., in Posada Gutiérrez's description [1920]) but which are simply said by Fortich to have origins "so remote that they become confused with legend" (1994: 2). This thesis is based on a structural similarity (a particular drumming technique) which Fortich detects between the "most traditional porros" of the region as played by existing wind bands and the porros played by existing conjuntos de gaitas (1994: 11–12). "Traditional" folklore of the late twentieth century is used to legitimate arguments about origin events that occurred in the mid–nineteenth century. In addition, since the gaita is an Amerindian instrument, Fortich is giving weight to indigenous elements in the tripartite racial calculus which forms such an important part of these debates about origins.[10] On the other hand, as is usual in these discussions, the drums are attributed to African influence and Fortich then makes tangential reference to voodoo and Santería—without actually linking them to Colombia or porro—before mentioning an African secret society called *poro*, found in Liberia, Sierra Leone, and Nigeria—again without making an explicit connection (1994: 12–15).[11]

Fortich then proceeds with a more specific historical argument, focusing on the founding father figure Alejandro Ramírez Ayazo. According to oral testimony from his son (who must have been unborn when the events he is narrating unfolded circa 1900), Ramírez, who had learned the clarinet from a trained musician, liked to invite conjuntos de gaitas to his house, where he would then play clarinet with them (Fortich Díaz 1994: 67–68). This was the key transition—apparently occurring some fifty years after the same transition in El Carmen—in which "the old porro of the *gaiteros* served as a nucleus which musicians with some academic training could develop" (1994: 6).

Yet the word *porro* does not appear prior to the late nineteenth century to indicate an existing style which could be taken over in this way; terms such as *fandango, currulao, mapalé,* and *bunde* were used.[12] Also, Fortich himself shows very clearly how one influential formally trained band director in the region, José de la Paz Montes, was a stickler for musical correctness, inspiring terror in one of his pupils, José Dolores Zarante, who in the 1880s and 1890s was an important band leader in the area and composed numerous waltzes, danzas, polkas, pasillos, marches, and mazurkas—but no porros (1994: 49–61). Fortich is also insistent on Ramírez's high level of education and literacy. All this casts some doubt on the straightforward continuity that Fortich claims between traditional tunes and the new porro.

A different line of argument centers on the fandango, a style that forms part of the repertoire of wind bands alongside porro. Fandango itself is a very old form, deriving from Spain and documented in Colombia from the early eighteenth century, generally as almost any kind of collective dance. It is often described for the Caribbean coastal region as a circle of people dancing around drums and hand-clapping singers (Bensusan 1984; Davidson 1970: 2:197; Fortich Díaz 1994: 18–38). It is reasonable enough to suggest that, during the late nineteenth century, the bands simply took on a role as the musical core around which dancers circled (Fortich Díaz 1994: 33), but it is by no means clear what the musical continuities might have been in this case. Certainly, today, during celebrations known as fandangos wind bands play porros and other such styles (Fortich Díaz 1994: 22), and as a musical style fandango is virtually the same as porro.

The kind of ancient rootedness that Fortich constructs by linking porro to "remote" and legendary conjuntos de gaitas and to an African secret society is reproduced by others. Portaccio, for example, a Costeño and retired radio announcer and amateur historian, sketches the history of the wind bands at the turn of the century, before referring to the obligatory "triethnic" origins of porro: from "the white" came the dance, specifically the "minuet"-style opening of the music; from "the black" came the drum; from "the Indian" came the cane flute, precursor of the clarinet (Portaccio 1995, 1:44–45). The sleeve notes that accompany a compact disc (CD) of Totó la Momposina, a black Costeño singer who specializes in "traditional" Costeño music and has collaborated with Peter Gabriel to export it to Europe, also suggest that the music her band plays originates in the distant past. The notes mention how African rhythms and Spanish romantic narratives have combined; "our music," says Totó, "can be described as the result of a musical project that perhaps began its process over five hundred years ago." Her gaita player, Roberto Guzmán, wrote a short piece on the gaita flute for the sleeve notes and also described the early integration of African, European, and indigenous cultures giving rise to gaita musical styles; porro was mentioned as a variant that "is conserved today" (sleeve notes of Totó la Momposina, *Carmelina* [MTM, 7262-008026, 1996]).

It is not my purpose here to argue that porro or fandango are basically European forms with little or no African or indigenous input; this would be manifestly untrue as well as little short of racist. My aim is to avoid constructing yet another formula in the tripartite racial calculus that always accompanies debates about the origins of Costeño music. Whatever the "truth" of the matter—and processes of musical syncretism, apart from being incredibly complex, are always subject to post hoc reinterpretation[13]—the point is that the line of connections chosen by Fortich and others always privileges continuity and traditional roots. These roots certainly exist (as do other multiple influences, less often foregrounded): a selective emphasis on them creates a certain image for Costeño music.

In any event, by the first decades of the twentieth century, porro (and fandango) was established as a form played by *banda de viento* lineups with trumpets, tubas, clarinets, drums (mainly the *bombo* bass drum and the *redoblante* or snare drum), and cymbals. The players were local people, usually men, generally of humble origins, part-time musicians contracted by landowners, politicians, and other members of the elite for specific fiestas and political events.

There are several varieties of porro played by wind bands, but a typical porro has an eight-bar introduction which is said to sound like a Cuban danzón.[14] This is followed by a section of more regular rhythm carried by the bombo and the cymbals in which the trumpets form a sort of call-response dialogue with the clarinets and bombardinos. There may be a section (called the *bozá* by Fortich) in which the trumpets cease, the bombo player keeps the beat with a stick on the frame of his drum, and the clarinets and bombardinos interweave their melodies (Bermúdez et al. 1987: 86).

Cumbia

The mythology surrounding cumbia, the other main style which became commercial this century, is rather vaguer, but also simpler. It is generally presented as a very old and traditional form. Specifics, however, are never presented, antiquity instead being evoked by adducing mixed indigenous and African origins, with frequent claims to an African origin for the name and some mention of European influences (Abadía Morales 1983: 201; Escalante 1964: 149; Ocampo López 1988: 190; Zapata Olivella 1962: 190).[15] The sleeve notes of *La candela viva,* a CD by Totó la Momposina, say of cumbia that it is "a fine example of the combined sentiments of Indian, Spanish, and African culture" and goes on to say that it originated as "a courting dance . . . between Black men and Indian women when the two communities began to intermarry" (Totó la Momposina y sus Tambores, *La candela viva* [MTM/Realworld 7260-008019, 1993]; the sleeve notes are in English). Yet neither I nor Egberto Bermúdez (personal communication) has found the word *cumbia* used by contemporary observers from before the late nineteenth century, although dances are often described that sound very like what is now called cumbia. There was clearly a long-standing tradition of men and women dancing around a group of seated musicians, which received various denominations in the nineteenth century—fandango, currulao, mapalé, and so on—and various others nowadays (including bullerengue, *chandé,* etc.). Because this is how folkloric forms of cumbia may be danced in the twentieth century, the continuity is assumed. This topic would need more archival research, but it is probably the case that, while the actual musical and dance forms that have been called cumbia have colonial roots, the term itself is not as old as commonly thought.[16]

In any event, cumbia, also known as *cumbiamba,* a term usually used to refer to the festivity during which the music and dance occur, is often labeled as the principal folk style of the region (List 1980). It is played with either the transverse caña de millo (cane flute) or two gaitas (long vertical flutes), which repeat a simple melodic phrase. They accompany a 4/4 rhythm played by one or two single-headed conical drums and often a double-headed bass drum, a rattle, and the maracas. It is usually instrumental, but may have verses (octosyllabic quatrains) sung in a call-response fashion with a refrain. It is danced by couples of men and women who do not touch each other but circle around seated musicians; the women may hold aloft bundles of candles (List 1980).

Alissa Simon's study of the way sexuality is perceived in cumbia adds an interesting dimension to this mythology (Simon 1994). The dance is commonly seen as a courtship dance, since the man circles the woman, who maintains a certain aloofness. In several sources, the man is referred to as black and the woman as indigenous; occasionally, a Spanish influence may be mentioned. For example: "The characteristics of their [the man and woman's] dance are the result of a social process, in which the man takes the place of the black and the woman that of the Indian; to the Spanish can be attributed the clothing and of course their influence on social behaviour" (Londoño 1989: 123; cited in Simon 1994: 195).[17] The indigenous people are seen as reserved and aloof; the blacks as energetic, extravert, and communicative. Cumbia is taken to represent the sexual union between indigenous woman and black man—or the sexual conquest of the first by the second—giving rise to the process of mixture which is seen as characteristic of the Colombian nation. In these accounts, the mixture is not Eurocentric: black-indigenous mixture was discouraged by colonial authorities and frowned upon by republican elites. Instead, the mixture has a specifically non-European, popular, Costeño style. Regional identity—like the national identity of which it is a special case—is held to spring from an act of sexual congress which is both represented by and encouraged by music and dance. Music, sex, and nationhood come together in a powerful triad. The historiography of cumbia, debating the relative weight of Amerindian, African, and European heritage, sees its own reflection in the dance itself, as a dramatic replaying of an original—and in this case subversive—act of mixture.

Vallenato

Another mythology surrounds the emergence of *vallenato,* accordion music which has become highly commercially successful: since the 1970s it has become the best-selling Colombian style in the country. I will be dealing in more detail with vallenato in a later chapter, since its popularity came later and the mythological constructions around it are complex, but I will present the basic narrative here. There existed in La Costa, as in all Latin America, a tradition of versification that included *romances* (ballads), *coplas* and *trovas* (rhyming verses), *décimas* (ten-line stanzas), *cantos* (songs), and different forms of oral poetry; these included work songs and ritual songs as well as secular and romantic ones (Bermúdez 1996: 116; cf. Pacini Hernández 1995: 5). They were sung unaccompanied or perhaps with a guitar; many of them seem to have been of European origin, although African origins are often adduced for the remaining fragments of work songs and some funerary songs found in La Costa and for oral poetry in general.[18] In about the 1880s, the accordion began to appear in the region, imported from Germany via the coastal ports, and began to be used in this corpus of songs, probably as something of a rarity; it was also used to play the styles usually played by traditional lineups and wind bands (Bermúdez 1996: 116; Londoño 1985: 128; Posada 1986: 20).[19] The accordion has usually been described as in the hands of the *juglar* or wandering minstrel, perhaps accompanied by a small hand drum (now known as a *caja*) and a scraper (*guacharaca*).[20]

Costeño accordion music now generally receives the name of *vallenato*, a term which means born in the valley and which is usually taken to refer to Valledupar, a town in the eastern part of La Costa, and its surrounding areas—often simply called *la provincia*. At least as early as 1903 the term was used in that locality to refer not to music, but to local people, particularly lower-class people (Quiroz Otero 1982: 16).[21] Much of the literature which has been written on vallenato, the most studied and debated Costeño musical style by a long shot, argues that it derives in a fairly straight genealogical line from the songs and verses that began to be accompanied by an accordion in the late nineteenth century. It is often also argued that, although accordion music of roughly the same type can be found all over La Costa, the music originates specifically in the region around Valledupar.[22] No particular reason is given for this; instead, the names of many local heroes are adduced to support this proposition (Araújo de Molina 1973: 102–107; Gutiérrez Hinojosa 1992: 439–488). Early exponents include the semimythical figure Francisco "El Hombre" Moscote (b. 1880), who was reputed to have had a musical duel with the devil (Restrepo Duque 1991: 70–73). There are many others who were never more than locally known, but names which are now more widely recognized in Colombia include Chico Bolaños (b. 1903), Pacho Rada (b. 1907), Emiliano Zuleta (b. 1912), Alejandro Durán (b. 1919), and Leandro Díaz (b. 1928).

A later but particularly important figure is Rafael Escalona, born in 1927 in the village of Patillal, near Valledupar, to the well-to-do family of a colonel. After primary education in Valledupar and during secondary education in Santa Marta, Escalona began to compose songs which became widely known in the local region. Despite his origins and despite local elite disdain for accordion music, he, like some other upper-class men, used to spend time partying with accordion players and *hombres parranderos* (partying, fun-loving men) of a lower social status.[23] His songs fitted into their mold. Although he never played any instrument or made any recordings, his songs were interpreted by many famous vallenato artists and became fundamental to what was consolidated as the vallenato corpus from the 1950s onward (Araujonoguera 1988).

This version of origins displays a tendency similar to that seen in accounts of porro. There is an old local tradition, originally formed mainly from black and indigenous inputs and generally seen as being in the hands of wandering players who carry songs, gossip, and news from place to place. Into this, the new accordion is assimilated, itself becoming a traditional element, as with the new brass and wind instruments in the case of porro. Gradually, this local tradition becomes better known, partly as a result of the efforts of brilliant local composers, and it is later commercialized in the new radio and recording industries. Along the way, at some indeterminate point between 1900 and 1950, it takes on the name *vallenato*. All this takes place principally in one small area, which is the birthplace of the music. In short, this story has the same combination of elements of modernization and localization as narratives about porro.

Gilard (1987a, 1987b) criticizes this origin myth of vallenato. He argues first that vallenato is not "traditional," but emerged only with the mediation of modernization; "vallenato" was created in the 1940s when early recordings were made and a few journalists and folklorists began writing about it (to be followed by Gabriel García Márquez— Gilard's own specialist topic—from the late 1940s onward). This is not just a question of a new label for the same basic tradition; the musical style itself emerged at this time.[24] As Bermúdez notes (1996: 116), the type of accordion associated with the "vallenato" style appeared only in the late 1930s. This was also a time when the area of *la provincia* around Valledupar had been opened up and linked more to other regions with modernizing projects backed by President Alfonso López Pumarejo, whose mother came from Valledupar (Araujonoguera 1988: 59–61).

Gilard then argues that the region around Valledupar was constructed as the source of this music when local elites (which included Escalona and other songwriters of a similar social status, such as Tobías Enrique Pumarejo, Freddy Molina, and Gustavo Gutiérrez—all well-known names in the vallenato genealogical tree) began to claim the local manifestations of this music as a tradition special to their area, partly by writing songs themselves (or perhaps registering local songs as their own). Gilard sees this emerging regional chauvinism as the modernization of local forms of elite domination. Quiroz Otero (1982: 19) suggests that these provincials were reacting against the disdainful opinion of the snobbish Santa Marta elite. Claims to local particularism were reinforced in the 1960s with campaigns for a new *departamento* (administrative province), El Cesar, separating the Valledupar area (and regions south) from the vast Magdalena Province. This petition was granted—after much pressure by people such as Escalona who, of course, used vallenato music extensively in their campaigns. This argument implies the corollary—which Posada (1986: 20) and Londoño (1985: 127) support—that, from the turn of the century, *música de acordeón* existed unevenly in many areas of La Costa, not just around Valledupar, although it is probably true that the instruments themselves followed riverine and maritime trading routes.[25]

In sum, then, Gilard contests the continuity and the local specificity of the origins of vallenato as presented in standard histories of this style. I would also argue that there is little evidence of a real *tradition* of accordion music as a specific style going back to the late nineteenth century or even the early decades of this century: the instruments were probably rather few and far between and used to play a range of styles from sung verses, through cumbias, to polkas.[26]

Conclusion

This brief look at the origins of some styles of Costeño music reveals certain important features in the writings about those origins. There is a tendency to project styles such as porro and vallenato and, even more, cumbia back into the past, assuming continuity rather than examining it. A similar tendency is evident in accounts of the carnival of Barranquilla, which all commentators date from the late nineteenth century in its organized form. Nevertheless, very long-standing continuities are sometimes emphasized. Friedemann (1985: 36), for example, writes that "the carnival of Barranquilla still conserves a varied core, fresh and marvellous, which is the traditional music, the *danzas* (masked dance groups) and the masks and disguises of rural origin. And those that recall colonial situations in cities such as Cartagena, Mompox, and Santa Marta." Orozco and Soto (1993) are more indirect: they simply tie elements of the carnival to old European, African, and native American myths and oral traditions, implying continuity.

Of course, the arguments for real continuities in musical styles are sometimes well made: after all, forms such as porro and vallenato must have received influences from many different angles. The point is that these continuist arguments always get pride of place. When change is recognized, it is seen as the reestablishment of the dominance of tradition, with new instruments or influences being subordinated to existing styles. Later on, as we will see, change, in the form of commercialization, is also seen by some as a process of degeneration, a loss of authenticity.

A second, related tendency is to root particular styles in specific places, as if porro or vallenato were "born" in one locale, child of a fruitful union.[27] This gives these locales special status as the authentic "cradle" of a certain music—and writers do use precisely the reproductive terminology which meshes neatly with the notion of mestizaje as a process of sexual reproduction. Something similar happens in some accounts of the Barranquilla carnival: it is recognized that a process of institutionalization dates from the late nineteenth century, but the fact that carnival celebrations existed in Cartagena, Santa Marta, and Mompox loses significance in the face of the Barranquilla celebrations and is given only a passing mention, while the classic moments in the mythology of the Barranquilla carnival are reproduced.[28] The current association of the event with the city is projected back into the past.

Both these tendencies obey, in different ways, a desire for authenticity. In one sense, that desire stems from the nostalgia that Turner (1990: 7) calls "a crucial product of modernization" since it derives from the doubts and uncertainties that Weber and many others have seen as being the dark side of modernity. It is no accident that the origins of these musical styles are generally seen as being rural, "folk," and rooted in gemeinschaft and as such more distant from the deformations that modern gesellschaft is thought to entail (see Middleton 1990: 127–146). In another related sense, the desire has its basis in a sense of local or regional identity: the location of originality and authenticity in one's own area, however that is defined. This nostalgic attitude toward "tradition" has, of course, long been connected with the creation of unique identities, particularly national ones (see Robertson 1990; see also Hobsbawm and Ranger 1983; and Nairn 1988).

In these accounts of the origins of Costeño music, there is also endless play on the classic indigenous-black-white triad underlying the mestizaje which is always adduced when Costeño music—and Colombian national identity—are discussed. This, of course, is inevitable in the sense that the music is a product of complex cultural fusions: the interesting aspect is how writers deal with the theme (see, e.g., the works already cited by Abadía Morales, Gutiérrez Hinojosa, List, Ocampo López, Perdomo Escobar, Triana, Delia Zapata Olivella, and Manuel Zapata Olivella). It is common to tie individual instruments, styles, or elements of styles to particular racialized origins: the maracas are indigenous, the drums are African, the lyrics are Spanish, the *pito atravesado* (transverse flute) could be either African or indigenous; the carnival itself is European, but some of the masked dance groups (*danzas de congo*) show African origins, while others are native American; the woman in the cumbia dance is indigenous, the man is black; and so on. Whatever the oversimplification of the complexities of cultural hybridization (Tagg 1989), the end result is the constant reiteration of the founding myth of Colombian nationality, spoken through the medium of La Costa, where the indigenous and African elements are said to have had a strong impact. As is always the case in talking about mestizaje, the music is seen as a symbol of fusion, of the overcoming of difference, but the representation of that symbol involves the continual reiteration of difference. Hierarchy is also involved, although it is ambivalent: black and indigenous people are seen as the eventual repositories of true tradition (European popular traditions are rarely mentioned), but as a result they can be seen as both backward and authentic.

4

Music, Class, and Race in La Costa, 1930–1950

Class in Barranquilla, 1920s–1940s

Music associated with the lower classes in La Costa gradually made its way into the middle and upper classes of the region over a period of some two to three decades. In examining this process, I will focus on Barranquilla, where change has to be seen in the context of the racialized class structure of the city. This structure was more fluid for Barranquilla than for other major cities in the region. During its rise to regional dominance, merchants and others had immigrated from cities with a traditional colonial elite, such as Cartagena, Santa Marta, and Mompox, but they had not instilled their old aristocratic values into the city. The many immigrants from Europe, the Middle East, and North America were, almost by definition, not of elite status in their home countries. The city, with a population of 65,000 in 1918 (but growing faster than any other Colombian city, to reach 152,000 in 1938), was based on a commercial sector which had only begun to grow in the 1870s and on industries which took shape from about 1900 (Posada Carbó 1987b; Solano and Conde Calderón 1993). Archila Neira (1991: 65) argues that the city breathed "values of tolerance and cosmopolitanism" and that the elite "did not have the aristocratic pretensions of other cities with their time-honoured lineages."

Nevertheless, class differences were marked and the elite strove to define some boundaries. To begin with, and helped by widespread European and North American origins, the elite identified themselves as white in relation to the lower classes, generally seen as black, indigenous, zambo, mulatto, and so on. This created an important element of solidarity despite the divergent national origins and religious affiliations of the upper class. Residential class segregation also grew from the 1920s. The original elite residences were, as in other Latin American cities, in the town center, with the lower classes living in surrounding barrios. In the 1920s, the elite began to move to the north of the city with the creation of an American-style elite residential neighborhood, El Prado, initiated by Karl Parrish (1874–1933), an influential North American immigrant. Over the ensuing decades, the city center increasingly became a central business district, the south expanded with *barrios populares,* while the middle classes occupied zones between the center and the rich north and the poor south.

Class identity was also expressed powerfully through the creation of elite social clubs. The first Club Barranquilla was founded in 1888 and refounded in 1907, just after the Club del Comercio in 1902. The Club ABC (Arte, Belleza y Cultura: art, beauty, and culture), founded in 1915, was subsumed within the Club Barranquilla in 1926, and this remained one of the most select clubs in the city. Immigrants formed their own clubs as well—for example, the Club Italiano, the Club Alemán, the Centro Español, the Club Alhambra—and later came the Club Unión and the Country Club, the latter founded by Karl Parrish. Clubs still exist today, some old, some newer: they too moved gradually into the northern sector of the city. The most prestigious today include the Country Club, the Club Barranquilla, and the more recent Club Campestre (Londoño and Londoño 1989: 353; Posada Carbó 1986; Sojo 1942: 82).

The emergence of clubs should be seen in the context of changing forms of diversion in general. As Archila Neira (1991: 167–188) shows for various Colombian cities, new industrial forms of work discipline were accompanied by elite—and indeed organized working-class— campaigns against the consumption of alcohol that took place in the taverns, bars, and brothels which catered to the growing urban working population. These places were seen as insalubrious and a threat to moral decency, to the stability of the family and, in some accounts, to the vigor of "the race." The brewing industries fed their workers beer during breaks and the working class was an important market for commercially produced alcohol of all kinds, but work discipline had to be maintained. The domestic production of alcoholic beverages was also frowned upon. Elite social clubs emerged in opposition to the proliferating bars and taverns of the urban working class, and, not surprisingly, there was a great emphasis on propriety and good behavior in their precincts.

Carnival is an interesting location to examine class difference, especially since I found during fieldwork that carnival was used by some

Barranquilla intellectuals to sustain an argument about the democratic nature of their city. As mentioned in previous chapters, the city's elite took more and more interest in organizing carnival celebrations from about the 1880s. Prior to this, celebrations had been held on the streets by the general populace and in private houses by the rich. In the 1870s, there was already an official announcement of carnival with the reading of the *bando* (proclamation) in late January. Also during this period, two of today's important *danzas* (costumed dance groups) were established—El Congo Grande (with the characteristic very high top hats, elaborately decorated with multicolored flowers) and El Torito (with a bull-face mask)—organized, it seems, by people of nonelite origins. It is probable that local barrios used to elect their kings and queens to preside over celebrations, but by the 1880s there was a president for the whole city, and by the end of the decade, after the founding of the first Club Barranquilla, this figure and his court were members of the elite. In 1899, a Junta Directiva (organizing committee) was created by the elite to run things; in 1930 this task was taken over by the Club Barranquilla and then in 1940 by the Sociedad de Mejoras Públicas (Society of Public Improvements). From 1918, a queen of carnival began to be elected by popular vote, and she has always been a woman from the elite. In 1903, the Batalla de Flores (Battle of Flowers) was established as an event for carnival Saturday by General Heriberto Vengoechea: this created an opportunity for the elite to come out onto the streets in their carriages and participate in an ostentatious procession.

Carnival in the 1920s was still a fairly segregated event, whatever opportunities the ritual atmosphere created for crossing and defying boundaries. At the turn of the century, the elite clubs organized dances in the Salón Fraternidad and the Escuela Pública, and after 1903 in the Teatro Emiliano, which were only for club members. From the early 1920s, these dances moved to the club precincts themselves, and the announcements for these events that appeared in the local press from the 1930s reminded readers that entry was only for members and their guests with tickets. Workers and artisans held their festivities in the street, in local taverns, and in the *salones burreros* (donkey taverns, so called because people tied up their donkeys outside). Such celebrations were temporary affairs sponsored by local merchants (who doubtless also sold the beverages consumed there). A contemporary observer commented: "while the high class had fun in the clubs . . . in the lower barrios the animated dances of the Africans and aborigines carries on, to the sound of the drum, caña de mijo [cane pipe], and guacharacas [scrapers], instruments of primitive music" (Jorge Abello, *Diario del Comercio,* 14 February 1926, cited in Friedemann 1985: 51; for other details on carnival, see Jiménez 1986; Orozco and Soto 1993; and Rey Sinning 1992). The middle strata, apparently, held parties in their own houses.

Class differences were thus evident enough, but they were not as rigid as in some other cities and depended less on family tradition than on economic wherewithal. The boundary between the middle classes and the elite does not seem to have been a strong one: anyone who had the money to sustain the kind of lifestyle expected of the elite and who behaved appropriately could gain entry to the clubs. There were also mechanisms for crossing class boundaries. One such, which extended beyond the carnival and indeed was an institution in La Costa, was for men from the upper or middle strata to have fun with the men and particularly the women of the lower strata during festive events. This is commented on by Posada Gutiérrez (1920: 342) for Cartagena in the 1830s when he notes that the men in the high-class dances "furtively deserted" their own women in search of women at less prestigious celebrations. President Juan José Nieto (1804–1866) himself had children by a lower-class *cuarterona* (quadroon) whom he met during a fiesta, according to Fals Borda (1981: 47A). Although the Protestant morality of some of the North American and North European elements of Barranquilla's upper classes doubtless braked this somewhat, the same thing happened during carnival, where the use of masks and *capuchones* (hooded cloaks) could disguise the identity of the man. Many interviewees, recalling the social life and particularly the carnivals of their youth, commented on upper-class men leaving their clubs to dance and drink in less exclusive surroundings. Rafael Campo Miranda, a composer from Barranquilla, observed: "So when the dances in the Country Club or the Club Riomar had finished, the men went to *echar colita* and they would go to the [Salón] Carioca, but in disguise, and they used to say that was the real fun; and they'd stay there until dawn, but in their masks—during carnival. They couldn't go without a mask; that would be criticized" (interview; see appendix A for details of interviews).[1]

Outside the confines of festivals, it was and is quite common practice in La Costa for men of means to have relationships, often of quite long standing, with women of more humble origins, crossing both class and racial boundaries (Gutiérrez de Pineda 1975). This is a classic process of mestizaje, highly sexualized and loaded with images of desire and embodied emotion—of the supposed passionate intensity and physical sensuality of blacks in general and the sexual ardor of black women in particular. Class and culture, both racialized, were mediated through these embodied practices of sex, celebration, and dance. Hierarchy did not, of course, disappear: on the contrary, hierarchies of gender, race, and class were reiterated. But certain possibilities were also opened for cultural hybridization.

Over the period 1920–1950, the city elite was in a fairly consolidated position in what was still an important commercial and industrial city, despite the threats to its economic base during the 1930s and 1940s. The middle classes were becoming a more important element in this picture, as in other Colombian cities (Uribe Celis 1992: 52). It would be false to portray an entrenched elite fighting off an ascendant middle class because, in Barranquilla at least, such boundaries were not well defined. But some saw it that way. Rafael Campo Miranda, composer of well-known Costeño music hits such as "Playa," was one such member of the middle class. Born in 1917, just outside Barranquilla, he has been a commercial employee all his life and composed as a hobby, without formal musical training:

> The middle class in ascent was in the first place a university-educated class. There were many graduates whose parents had no position from the social point of view, but who in contrast [had been to] the universities, mainly those in Medellín and Bogotá—because at that time we didn't have a university [in Barranquilla]—I'm talking about from 1940 to 1945. And commerce: there was a multitude of employees because Barranquilla was flourishing commercially at the time. So the commercial establishments were packed with employees who had a more or less average culture. (Interview)

Educational opportunities were becoming more available than before, partly as a result of the 1936 educational reforms increasing access to public education, and students were going in small but ever greater numbers to the universities of the interior. Often these were the children of the elite, who could afford the costs involved, but they also included the sons (and less often the daughters) of the middle classes. The important point is that nonelite people (who perhaps wanted to be part of the elite) were becoming more educated and eager to participate in the cultural life of the city. Campo Miranda goes on: "This collection [of employees], seconded by the university graduates and professionals, made up this large group, this great movement of leadership of our Costeño music. Because the gentlemen of the clubs were insistent that not this music, but only European currents [of music] would enter the clubs." As I shall show, the clubs were not quite as exclusive as Campo Miranda makes out—nor were the employees as committed to local music—but he indicates an important element in the overall picture.

Changes in Music, 1920s–1940s

In the 1920s, the music listened to by the elite and the middle classes in Barranquilla and La Costa underwent a process of change that would end up admitting more vernacular forms, albeit slowly and with some ups and downs. As I showed in chapter 1, this was a process that had occurred in many regions of Latin America and the Caribbean. In Barranquilla, it started in the 1920s with the impact of North American music, which was, in fact, felt all over Colombia. By the 1930s, in line with a nationalist tendency in the country to avoid European and North American models, Latin American styles became the rage, with Cuban music especially popular.[2] In the 1940s, Costeño music began to make an impact in elite circles, always in a highly orchestrated and stylized form. Instrumental in this process were the numerous local bands and orchestras which emerged during this period and which included locally born musicians, often from humble backgrounds. The middle classes to which Campo Miranda referred were also important. Of vital significance, too, was the emergence of a local recording and radio industry run by the elite and middle-class elements. I will examine these different aspects in turn.

PATTERNS OF CONSUMPTION

Prior to the 1920s, the music listened and danced to included waltzes, pasillos, bambucos, contradanzas, polkas, and so on. In the 1920s, with the arrival of records, Mexican, Cuban, Argentinean, and North American musics began to make an impact. The program of the Club ABC for a carnival dance in 1923 gives a good idea of what the elite danced to at that time. The president of the club, Señor Dugand, had contracted the Panama Jazz Band, quite possibly the first "jazz band" to play in Barranquilla (González Henríquez 1989c: 88); this band alternated with an orchestra of fourteen musicians. After the obligatory hymn of the club, the first piece was a waltz, followed by a danza, a fox-trot, a one-step, and a pasillo, after which fox-trots alternated with one-steps ending with a request session which might include paso dobles and the "tune of the moment, The Charleston" (Rey Sinning 1992: 17).

The themes chosen for the carnival dances in the Club Barranquilla also show an interesting variety. In 1936, these were "A Night on the Argentine Pampas" and "Charro Disguises" (a *charro* is a Mexican cowboy). In 1937, they included "On the Banks of the Volga," "A Night in Honolulu," "Kongo Country," and "El Tambor de Alegría" (The Drum of Happiness, the title of a hit by the famous Cuban musician Ernesto Lecuona). Carnival of 1938 saw "In the Palace of the Mummy" and "The Panamanian Tamborito" (*tamborito* is a Panamanian dance, usually associated with blacks). A photograph of a *comparsa* (dance group) of the club in 1937 shows the participants dressed in the Congo Grande uniform, indicating that a dance of plebeian origins had been accepted into the club, at least for carnival purposes (Sojo 1942: 102–113).

Press announcements are a further indication of certain aspects of the music scene of the period, showing the varied influence of foreign musics.[3] Papers from 1925 to 1930 featured advertisements for records (see below), gramophones, and presentations by artists. The latter included the Compañía Centro Americana de Operetas y Zarzuelas, playing in the Teatro Cisneros;[4] the Spanish singer Emilia Benito; the Jazz Band of the Club Barranquilla, made up of a group of *profesores* (i.e., trained musicians); a recital by a pianist; a concert in the Conservatorio del Atlántico by three Italian musicians, Alfredo Squarcetta and the *profesores* Brunetti and Bacilieri;[5] a debut by the American tap dancers and singers Miss Ellen and Texas Bill in the Teatro Colombia; a debut by the Compañía de Revistas Lupe Rivas Cacho (a revue or variety show company), presenting the works "México Típico" (Traditional Mexico), "Cielo de México" (Mexican Sky), and "Si Yo Fuera Presidente" (If I Were President). There was also an advertisement for the Jazz Band Barranquilla which detailed the repertoire it would play in the clubs during the 1927 carnival season; these numbers (i.e., the originals), it said, could be obtained on record in the shop of the Victor agent, and they included a fox-trot, a paso doble, a tango, a danza, a waltz, and a pasillo.

In contrast to the above, between 1930 and 1940 the great majority of press notices were for orchestras or jazz bands, and, from 1936, these were frequently for dances in elite clubs or hotels. The remainder of the advertisements included ones for a piano recital, operetta, child singers, a couple of comedians, the Viennese Ballet, a duo of tango singers, and dance exhibitions, usually of Cuban rumbas. An advertisement for the latter, to be performed by Las Cubanacán in the Hotel Esperia, a smart, out-of-town venue, was quick to point out that "They will present a series of stylized dances of absolute morality, modern and attractive" (*La Prensa,* 21 December 1935).[6] Cuban music was clearly important, and there were many visits by Cuban artists, including the Trío Matamoros in 1934 and Los Piratas de F. Maya in the same year.[7]

There were agents for the Victor, Columbia, and Brunswick record companies in the city, and they all sold records and gramophones. One notice placed by the Brunswick agent advertised the Panatrope gramophone and listed some of the buyers of these machines in Barranquilla during the last four months of 1927. The list comprised about 450 customers, including some businesses (mostly the Magdalena River steamboat companies, which always provided music, live and recorded, to entertain the passengers). Since record players had first entered the country in the 1910s, it would seem that they were quite widely distributed among Barranquilla's middle and upper classes.[8]

The record lists advertised by these agents in the press from the late twenties to early thirties give some idea of musical taste among buyers. The lists used over sixty terms to label styles of music, but if these are condensed very roughly into broad categories, then "European" music (e.g., waltzes, mazurkas, polkas, paso dobles, and including for these purposes creole styles such as bambuco and pasillo) ranked alongside "Cuban" music (danzón, bolero, son, plus other Caribbean styles such as plena and merengue) and also "North American" music (fox-trot, blues, one-step), with "Argentinean" tangos slightly behind.[9] Equally important were *canciones* (songs), which do not fit into even these heuristic regional categories. There was a strong Mexican influence here, since the *canción mexicana*—for example, in the guise of the ranchera—was a powerful force in Latin America, but the term could cover music from other regions too (see Béhague 1985: 6; Londoño and Londoño 1989: 363).[10] It has to be remembered that, for example, Mexican and Cuban music had been cross-fertilizing for decades already (Roberts 1979), that artists might travel and record in New York, Mexico, Havana, and Buenos Aires, and that much of this music was recorded by resident orchestras in New York from sheet music sent in from Latin American countries. An artist such as Juan Pulido, who was born in the Canary Islands, lived in New York, Cuba, and several other Latin American countries, and recorded many canciones for Victor in this period, is typical of the transnational nature of this style. Colombian music was poorly represented among these recordings, with only three bambucos and a score of pasillos, all performed by international artists. However important bambuco was as a symbol of national identity, it did not compete equally on the international

Latin American record market with Cuban, Mexican, North American, and Argentinean musics.[11]

No record lists appeared in *La Prensa* between 1934 and 1940, for reasons that are unclear, but a few did appear in 1941 and 1946. Given the small sample, not too much can be read into these, but they show that Cuban styles are very dominant (bolero, guaracha, conga, rumba, plus some danzón and son), while North American fox-trots are a minor presence, along with tangos and Mexican songs. Waltzes and other styles of "European" music have almost vanished, but there are a couple of porros listed, recorded by Colombian artists with Victor.[12]

The new music styles of the 1920s and 1930s made most initial impact in elite circles, partly because of their recorded format and because the orchestras that played them (even the local ones) were large and fairly expensive to hire. Middle-class tastes are harder to judge, but the middle classes were not necessarily the champions of Costeño music that Campo Miranda implied they were, at least not at this time. For example, the radio programs of La Voz de Barranquilla sponsored by the Association of Commercial Employees in 1934 comprised classical music, canciones, bambucos, and pasillos, interspersed with talks entitled "Instruction and Culture" (*La Prensa*, 15 December 1934; 12 January 1935).

For the lower classes in Cartagena, according to the Costeño writer Manuel Zapata Olivella, who was about fifteen years old at this time, there were conjuntos playing gaitas, cañas de millo, drums, and scrapers on the streets—for example, around the old marketplace—in the afternoons; there were also many small groups of amateur or semiprofessional musicians in guitar trios or in Cuban-style sextets and septets which played local and Cuban styles, pasillos, and so on; there were Saturday-night dances in the barrios in people's houses (often belonging to families which were known for regular parties; interview with Manuel Zapata Olivella). Other venues for entertainment which could include music were bars, taverns, brothels, and billiard halls (Archila Neira 1991: 169).

Recorded music had an increasing impact outside elite circles, especially in the 1930s. Gramophones and pianolas (automatic pianos) existed in cafés, bars, and other places to which the general public had access, and in the 1930s *traganiqueles* ("nickel-swallowers," i.e., jukeboxes) were increasingly common (Londoño and Londoño 1989: 363; Restrepo Duque 1988: 533).[13] Radio sets were very expensive in 1930, but by 1936 their price had dropped a good deal, and in any case radio broadcasts filtered into public spaces via the loudspeakers directed into the street by commercial establishments with radio sets and by the radio stations themselves, which were located in the city center.[14]

Cinema was also a crucial influence, and the *teatros* (theaters) were places where both rich and poor would go. Bogotá had regular showings from the 1910s, in the Di Domenico Brothers' Salón Olympia, and all the major cities soon followed suit. The teatros of the period were huge halls, seating thousands, which served as venues for all kinds of public events. In Barranquilla in the 1920s, the two main teatros were the Teatro Colombia (owned by the Di Domenico Brothers) and the Teatro Cisneros. In early times, the screen was placed in the middle of the hall, and the cheapest seats were behind it. A special reader was employed to decipher the mirror image of the silent films' subtitles (Londoño and Londoño 1989: 365; Rasch Isla 1928). The early films were from Hollywood and also from Europe, and accompanying music was played by local orchestras from sheet music that came with the film. With the advent of sound in the early 1930s, Mexican and Argentinean films also became popular, especially among the illiterate, who could not read subtitles. (Dubbing of Hollywood films was not common.) In these films, music was a vital ingredient, and indeed many films were basically musicals. The Mexican film industry also incorporated Cuban themes and several famous Cuban artists, among them the singer Rita Montaner, who had recorded many of Ernesto Lecuona's songs, and the dancers María Antonieta Pons and Ninón Sevilla. Hollywood films frequently used Latin American musical styles that had become popular in the United States, such as tango, bolero, Mexican ranchera, and Brazilian samba and maxixe. The popular film *Rio Rita* (1926), for example, which featured a U.S.-Mexican romance set to Mexican-style music, reached Barranquilla in 1929. Other well-known films included *The South American Way* and *Down Argentine Way,* both with the Brazilian star Carmen Miranda. The Spanish-born Cuban musician Xavier Cugat also made an early impact on Hollywood films. Cinema thus made many kinds of music, both North American and (often highly stylized) Latin American, accessible across a wide class spectrum (Díaz Ayala 1981; King 1990; Roberts 1979; Sevcenko 1995).

Also in the 1930s, various venues emerged in Barranquilla which were cheap enough to allow middle-class access. From about 1936, newspaper advertisements indicate that places such as the Salón Arlequín, Salón Carioca, Jardín Aguila, Bar Americano, Salón Noel, and Salón de las Quintas all emerged, many of them lasting into the 1950s. These varied from tearooms to dance halls and varied in status as well;

the Jardín Aguila, for example, was quite a respectable place where the Orquesta Sosa frequently played and where members of the elite would also go to dance. Visiting orchestras which played the elite clubs also played these venues, and they sometimes played teatros which were cheap enough to allow working-class access. Thus, in 1936 the all-women Orquesta Cubana Topacio played the Club Unión, various *salones*, and the Teatro Rex (alternating with a Hollywood film), allowing access to their music across a broad class range.[15] Most famously, the Cuban Orquesta Casino de la Playa, with lead singer Miguelito Valdés, came to Barranquilla in 1939, where they were mobbed by fervent crowds. They played the Club Barranquilla, the Country Club, and various teatros (*La Prensa*, 18–25 August 1939; interview with Marco T. Barros, who witnessed their visit).

The Costeño elite was thus on the crest of the wave of modernization and artistic modernism that was slowly breaking over Colombia. Its place as a Caribbean port and the elite's varied origins helped to place it at the forefront of cultural innovations. The same kinds of changes were taking place in Bogotá, and also Medellín and Cali, but Barranquilla competed on at least equal terms with the capital.[16]

The elite had an ambivalent relation to some of these new styles, however. On the one hand, they were modern and desirable; on the other, some of them were seen as vulgar. It is difficult at this distance to pin down exactly in what this vulgarity was thought to consist—after all, this music was not straightforwardly associated with Barranquilla's black and mulatto working classes; it was stylized international music coming out of New York, Hollywood, and various Latin American capitals. But immorality was perceived to threaten, whether in the lyrics, the hot rhythms of some styles and the dance movements that went with them, or a vague reputation of popularity and plebeian (and even black) origins. As Cooper (1993: 7–9) shows for Jamaica, vulgarity, "low" culture, and indecent sexuality were linked together in elite eyes. In some cases, the lyrics were clearly part of the problem. Alfredo de la Espriella, local historian and curator of the Museo Romántico in Barranquilla, commented that some of the records raised eyebrows in respectable circles. The song "Tóqueme el Trigémino, Doctor" (Touch My Trigeminal Nerve, Doctor) by the Orquesta Típica Panameña (Columbia 3708), which was a hit in 1930, struck some people as risqué, since the location of the trigeminal nerve (the face) was hardly well known. The same went for the hit "Paran Pan Pin": "The other one was [he sings] 'Con tu cara de paran pan pin, yo te he visto con María en la puerta del solar.' But that was very vulgar.

And then: [sings] 'Ya tú no soplas como mujer.' That was very dis-
agreeable. And the other was worse: [sings] 'Te lo ví, te lo ví, no lo es-
condas que te lo ví'—that was nothing less than a vulgarity" (interview).[17] The threat of immorality went further, however, and The
Hotel Esperia was clearly alive to these problems when it assured pro-
spective clients that the rumba dances programmed would be "stylized" and of "absolute morality," but still "modern and attractive."
Cuban dance styles had a reputation for "vulgarity" that needed to be
preempted. The image of blackness, associated with Cuba, threatened
elite notions of morality, and this danger had to be held at bay. The
Cuban orchestras were, indeed, made up of whites and light-skinned
mestizos. (Miguelito Valdés, the lead singer of Orquesta Casino de la
Playa, was a mulatto, but this was an exception, both in Cuba and in
Colombia.)[18] A further problem for the elite (especially for its older,
more conservative elements) was that the new styles of music—especially Cuban and Mexican varieties—were already the taste of the
masses: the working classes flocked to the cinemas to hear Mexican
songs, and they mobbed the Orquesta Casino de la Playa when it arrived in the city. Many of the elite therefore wanted to accept new
styles as modern and new, while trying to avoid the plebeian tones of
their massification (which could only be compounded by any overt
connotations of blackness or vulgarity). The elites thus enjoyed these
new styles of music, as long as immorality and plebeian overtones were
kept at arm's length and admitted only in particular conditions. The
members of the Club Barranquilla might dress up in the uniform of the
Congo Grande, but this was strictly for carnival purposes.

LOCAL BANDS AND ORCHESTRAS

In the midst of all these influences, many "jazz bands" and orchestras
began to form in Barranquilla and elsewhere that played these types of
music.[19] For example, during its visit to Barranquilla in 1923, the Panama Jazz Band left behind a trumpeter, Simón Urbino, who influenced
various local musicians including the pianist Carlos Zagarra, who later
directed the Jazz Band Colombia, and Simón Gómez, who later directed
the Jazz Band Atlántico, both functioning from about 1931–1932
(Candela n.d.).[20] Other such bands included the Jazz Band Barranquilla (1927), the Orquesta Nuevo Horizonte (1929, based originally
in Cartagena), Orquesta Sosa (c. 1934), and the in-house orchestra of
the newly formed radio station La Voz de Barranquilla (1929).

Most of the musicians involved were local people. Some of them
were from reasonably well-off families, and most of them were unlikely

to be identified as blacks or even mulattoes by an elite audience. But others were of humble, occasionally rural or small-town, origins—and a few were blacks or mulattoes. This opened up the possibility of elements of Costeño wind band styles such as porro and fandango—and even perhaps of traditional rural styles—being included in the repertoire of these bands and thus entering into elite social circles. I will examine a few of these orchestras in order to show the social backgrounds of their members and also to introduce some central figures in the commercialization of Costeño music.

In Cartagena, the Orquesta de los Hermanos Lorduy, formed in about 1920, played a typical mixture of Cuban and North American music, plus some Costeño music (González Henríquez 1989c: 87).[21] The trombonist in this band was José Pianeta Pitalúa, who, in the late 1930s, formed the well-known Orquesta A Número Uno which played an important role in commercializing Costeño music, making recordings in Colombia. The pianist of the Lorduy lineup was Angel María Camacho y Cano, who later became the first Colombian musician to record Costeño music in New York and whose career shows interesting features. Born in about 1903, he came from a relatively well-to-do background, studying law in the University of Cartagena; he must have played with the Lorduy brothers at this time. Later, he practiced law briefly and then traveled around La Costa, founding the Instituto Musical in Montería in 1927 and then directing an orchestra in the Café Paris in Medellín. In 1929, he met Ezequiel Rosado, a merchant and the Brunswick agent in Barranquilla, and went to New York to record with Brunswick, the next year recording with Columbia under the name Rafael Obligado. In New York, the Puerto Rican Rafael Hernández—a central figure in Caribbean popular music of this era, who, with his Grupo Victoria, made many recordings of Cuban and later Dominican music in New York between 1917 and 1939—put together musicians (trombonist, trumpeter, bassist, and drummer) to accompany Camacho.[22] Strangely, in 1931 Camacho ceased composing and playing and threw himself into a bohemian lifestyle—which included being a disc jockey in Barranquilla—until 1945, when he composed "Colombiafonia No. 1," which was played by a philharmonic orchestra. Although Camacho came from what must have been at least a middle-class background, he was clearly connected to other social circles in La Costa, and this is presumably what led him to record songs labeled "cumbia," "porro," and "mapalé" alongside rumbas and fox-trots. (I discuss these recordings in more detail below.)

Also in Cartagena was the Orquesta Nuevo Horizonte, originally formed in 1929 by Francisco Tomás Rodríguez in the town of Arjona, not far from the city. Rodríguez had studied music with a teacher who used to visit Arjona from Cartagena. In an interview, Pompilio Rodríguez, his son, said that this band played mostly Cuban music, but also local porros, performing in the city's social clubs and more popular bars. With the start of the Second World War in 1939, the orchestra moved to Barranquilla, where it played in the Salones Carioca, Arlequín, and Paraíso. In the Carioca, it alternated with the Orquesta Casino de la Playa. A photograph of the band in Cartagena (presumably in the early 1930s) showed that the lineup included clarinet, trumpet, trombone, one soprano, one tenor and two alto saxophones, violin, bass, drum kit, *tumbadora* (conga drum), and maracas.[23] Pompilio mentioned that there was also a banjo. The musicians included Francisco's four sons: Lucho Rodríguez on clarinet and sax, Tomasito on vocals, Efraín on drums, and, from when he was about twelve years old, Pompilio, who took over on drums. In about 1946, the band went to Bogotá, where they played in a *cabaret* (a bar where men picked up women), before returning to Barranquilla in 1948. The importance of this band is that it appears to have included porros in its repertoire as early as the 1930s—although this is impossible to confirm—and, at any rate, by the 1940s. Also in about 1956, after a more extended visit to Bogotá, it became the basis of the Orquesta de Pacho Galán, a famous Costeño group based in Barranquilla (see below).

An important orchestra in Barranquilla was the Orquesta Sosa, directed by Luis Sosa, a *cachaco* (i.e., born in the interior of the country, in this case Boyacá Province)[24] who also directed the Atlántico Province Police Band. Sosa started off with the Jazz Band Barranquilla in 1927, and the Orquesta Sosa seems to have formed in the early 1930s, lasting until about 1939. Sosa died in 1938, but his son-in-law, Pedro Biava, had already taken over the direction of the orchestra. Biava, born in Rome in 1902, took over the Police Band after Sosa's death, founded a philharmonic orchestra and an opera company in Barranquilla in the 1940s, and taught music in the Escuela de Bellas Artes (School of Fine Arts; Candela 1992). The Sosa orchestra played the Club Barranquilla and the fancy Hotel El Prado (fig. 4.1), a major elite and middle-class venue, from the mid-1930s; advertisements for their presentations usually pointed out that the musicians were all *profesores,* and photographs show them to be mostly white or very light-skinned men, resplendent in white tuxedos. However, they played less exclusive venues as well. This orchestra had strong connections with art music and other styles accepted by the elite, and it is significant in

4.1 Hotel El Prado, Barranquilla. (By permission of Casa Editorial El Tiempo Bogotá.)

this story because it also served as a training ground for some important musicians of more humble origins; it also included El Negrito Jackie, a black Peruvian singer and percussionist, on drum kit and Antonio María Peñaloza (fig. 4.2), a mulatto, on trumpet.

Antonio María Peñaloza, later to become a well-known composer and arranger of Costeño music, was born in 1916 in Plato, a small town on the Magdalena River. He grew up with his mother on a large cattle hacienda belonging to a Santa Marta landowner. There he had contact with a number of *juglares,* wandering minstrels who played the accordion, and with local conjuntos which played cumbias, fandangos, and such on the traditional instrumentation. He then moved with his mother to Fundación, a town which acted as a commercial center for the Magdalena banana plantations run by the United Fruit Company and thus attracted many immigrants from all over Colombia and abroad. There he began to learn the trumpet with a music teacher from El Carmen de Bolívar (one of the mythical origin sites of porro), and, with great sacrifice, his mother, who made and sold bread, bought him an Italian trumpet. With this he would tour the town, playing paso dobles in a group which advertised the local cinema's forthcoming attractions. After twelve years in Fundación, he went to the nearby town of Aracataca, where he improved his skills with a local player of the

4.2 Antonio María Peñaloza. (By permission of Casa Editorial El Tiempo Bogotá.)

bombardino, before moving on to Ciénaga, the largest town in the region after Santa Marta. There he found work in the *academias* (dance "schools" where men would pay women to dance with them), playing waltzes but also styles such as porro and fandango; a few Cuban pieces were also included. Peñaloza was already composing at this time and would serenade a girl he met in Ciénaga, playing the trumpet and accompanied by her uncle on guitar.

In 1935, Peñaloza arrived in Barranquilla. The son of the family where he found lodgings turned out to be a trumpet player in the Banda de la Policía, directed by Luis Sosa, and through him and his own skills as a trumpeter, Peñaloza entered the band. He began to study in the conservatory, under Pedro Biava, and to play in the Orquesta Sosa; it was here that he felt the influence of North American music. After Sosa's death, Guido Perla, a trombonist with the orchestra, went on to form the Emisora Atlántico Jazz Band (a resident orchestra for the Atlántico radio station) which dominated the Barranquilla scene for a decade: the orchestra took on many of Sosa's players, and Peñaloza played with them for a time. Peñaloza went on to com-

pose many well-known songs and to play and arrange for many orchestras and bands, both in La Costa and in the interior, and his name
will crop up again later. Peñaloza is significant for the way he mediated
between rural and urban areas, between classes, and between musical
traditions (interview with Antonio María Peñaloza; see also Peñaloza
1989; Giraldo 1989; and González Henríquez 1989c).

The Orquesta Sosa had a second trumpeter, Francisco "Pacho"
Galán (fig. 4.3), who went on to form one of the most successful orchestras of La Costa. Galán was born in 1906 in Soledad, just outside
Barranquilla. He was white by Colombian standards and came from a
family with enough means to buy him music lessons when it was evident that he had some aptitude in that direction. He was taught violin
and saxophone by Julio Lastra (who had his own orchestra from the
late 1930s and directed the house orchestra of radio station La Voz de
la Patria) and also received lessons from Pedro Rolong, a trumpeter. At
an early age, he formed the Orquesta Pájaro Azul, which played danzas, polkas, and waltzes, but also porros, according to his son, Ar-

4.3 Pacho Galán (*left*). (By permission of El Espectador.)

mando (interview). Galán then studied under Biava at Bellas Artes in Barranquilla and played in the Banda de la Policía and the Orquesta Sosa. He went on to play with Guido Perla's Emisora Atlántico Jazz Band in 1940 and became one of the orchestra's main arrangers and composers, going on to direct it for a time, according to some accounts. The connections between the old Sosa orchestra, Pedro Biava, and the Emisora Atlántico Jazz Band were strong, and the latter might, on occasion, play classical music, although the main repertoire was the usual combination of North American (including now Glenn Miller), Cuban, and European music. However, by the 1940s, orchestrated porros, fandangos, and cumbias were making an appearance, even in the sets played at the Hotel El Prado, where the Emisora Atlántico Jazz Band had a contract. Like Peñaloza, Pacho Galán, who by 1950 had his own orchestra, proved to be very influential, and his name will also reoccur.

The final person who must be introduced here is Lucho Bermúdez (fig. 4.4), as the most influential exponent of Costeño music, not only within La Costa, but even more in the cities of the interior.[25] He was born in 1912 in El Carmen de Bolívar to a teacher and his wife. His father authored a number of novels and rose to be rector of the University of Cartagena, but died early, leaving Lucho to be brought up by his grandmother, a seamstress. His maternal uncle was director of the local brass band, and Bermúdez began to play flute with the band from a very early age. In 1926, he moved to Santa Marta (where his father's family came from) and managed to get a place in the military band there, ending up after some seven years as its director. Due to lack of resources, he did no formal education beyond a couple of years of secondary school, but he had musical training and could write music. During this time, he also composed—mainly bambucos, pasillos, waltzes, and so on, recalling this later as "a real obsession with music from the interior" (Arango Z. 1985: 24). He took up the clarinet, the instrument for which he was to become known. Military bands were dissolved in the early 1930s, and Bermúdez had to leave Santa Marta, taking up the unpaid directorship of a small village band for two years before being appointed the director of the Bolívar Provincial Band in Cartagena in about 1935.

At this time, he joined the Orquesta de José Pianeta Pitalúa (the trombonist in the Lorduy brothers' band—see above) and became the leader of Pianeta's Orquesta A Número Uno, directing it in early recordings. He was also linked to the radio stations, Radio Cartagena

4.4 Lucho Bermúdez. (By permission of El Espectador.)

and Emisora Fuentes, as an artistic director. After some three years in Cartagena, he formed his own Orquesta del Caribe with backing from Daniel Lemaitre, a poet, songwriter, industrialist, and member of the city's elite, and from José Vicente Mogollón, a member of an important commercial family in Cartagena and in Barranquilla (where J. V. Mogollón was the RCA Victor agent). The idea was to compete with the best Barranquilla orchestras. It was apparently during this period in Cartagena, that he began to compose and orchestrate Costeño music. In 1938 he composed and had a hit with a porro, "Marbella," and a mapalé, "Prende la Vela"; both were hits in Cartagena's Eleventh of November independence celebrations. In 1938 too, Daniel Lemaitre's porro "Sebastían, Rómpete El Cuero" was a success in the Barranquilla carnival.[26] Bermúdez's numbers were likewise hits in the 1939 Barranquilla carnival, and the Orquesta del Caribe played them in the Country Club. In the same year, he played these pieces in Cartagena's Club La Popa, alternating with Orquesta Casino de la Playa.

Bermúdez cites as his influences the formally trained musicians

Pedro Biava, Ernesto Lecuona,[27] and Rafael Hernández, the Puerto Rican musician who played with Camacho y Cano in New York (Arango Z. 1985: 34); the Orquesta del Caribe also played Cuban music, Mexican songs, tangos, and so forth, but Bermúdez's compositions were among the first porros to be played in elite social clubs in La Costa. Interestingly, an early photograph of the orchestra shows several men who might easily be classified as black by an elite audience—these did not include Bermúdez himself, who was very light skinned with straight hair. Slightly later photographs of the band in Bogotá, where Bermúdez first went in about 1942, show a lesser "black" presence (Arteaga 1991).

A firsthand account of the move from village band to radio orchestra is that of José del Carmen "Cheíto" Guerra, born in 1925 in Arjona near Cartagena, whose account also gives a flavor of local fiestas in the 1930s.

> I've been a musician all my life and I arrived at that profession by accident. As a child, I liked music and in my village they still celebrate the patron saint festival for the Virgin of La Candelaria. Bands used to go along, from Sincelejo, Soplavientos, Corozal. They'd put four bands in the *corralejas* [bull-fighting corrals] and they'd alternate, and the bull runs were with forty or more bulls in one afternoon. The rich man, the one who had [money or bulls] and could contribute most . . . There was a famous rich man there called Gregorio Zarate, and [people would say]: Today is Gregorio Zarate's afternoon—and you knew that there would be at least forty bulls, and good bulls, and at least five deaths. As well as the bands, there would be *conjuntos folklóricos* [folkloric groups] of cumbia from San Pablo, and, as a child, I was curious and they'd let me play the guacharaca. So I began to play the maracas, and I found that I had rhythm. I learned music from when I was about fourteen or fifteen years old and I started with swing; I played solos. I inherited a saxophone from my father and he gave me the first lessons in music. Later he sent me to a teacher—I didn't know what kind of a musician he was. In my village, I joined the band, a small orchestra, and this orchestra would go to a small village called Sincerín, where there was a sugar mill called El Batey, and that was every Saturday and Sunday. We used to go to the famous carnival in Barranquilla, and I got better known. The bands only went to play in the patron saint festivals: in Cartagena the Virgin of La Candelaria, on February 2, the processions in Arjona were well known as very pretty, the ones in San Roque as well.

Then I went to Cartagena and they asked me to start an orchestra for a radio station called Radio Cartagena—which doesn't exist any more—and the musicians who they got together elected me as the director of the orchestra. I already wrote music and did little arrangements of pieces of music. I was in Cartagena from '45 to '51. I worked in the Orquesta Fuentes in Cartagena, and we worked in the Hotel Caribe [Cartagena's premier hotel at the time]. (Interview)

These short histories show that the emergence of the local orchestras is a varied phenomenon. Musicians are often very difficult to tie to a class background, and therein lies a source of creativity. People such as Bermúdez and Galán came from backgrounds that had strong elements of the provincial middle class but had some links with rural lower-class experience as well; they had formal musical training, not always in a conservatory, but they were also familiar with Costeño instruments and styles from traditional peasant repertoire and from the bandas de viento. They knew, played, and often composed a wide range of styles, including bambucos and pasillos, but they wanted to bring Costeño music, albeit in highly adapted form, into the same arena—this was their way of making a mark. Elites accepted this music into their clubs because it came on the coattails of North American, Cuban, Mexican, and Argentinean music, also recorded and played by these orchestras, and because it had been heavily stylized by mainly nonblack composers and musicians.

The vernacular music that the elite and middle classes knew from observation and perhaps at closer range during carnival celebrations—and that many men knew more intimately from their open or semi-clandestine contacts with the lower classes and especially women of the lower classes—became more acceptable in this stylized form. Even so, some resistance remained. Alfredo de la Espriella recounts that in 1947, as a young man and a member of an elite Barranquilla social club, he wanted to organize a carnival dance group based on the porros and cumbias of Lucho Bermúdez. The president of the club refused to allow the dance group into the club itself, saying that they would have to stay out in the street (interview). This appears, however, to have been an unusual case, since Bermúdez's porros had been in the clubs for a decade.

In addition, there was a growing number of educated middle-class people, and, while some tended to imitate the elite, others—such as Rafael Campo Miranda—wanted to undermine what they saw as antiquated and Europeanized tastes. Some of the latter category also became involved in the radio and record business, as I will explain below.

Duos, Trios, and Small Groups

The music business was also important for other types of musical lineup which existed alongside the orchestras but which are less visible in retrospect because they do not seem to have played in the clubs at this time, or if they did their presence was not advertised and has been forgotten. These were the duos, trios, and small conjuntos based on guitars or accordions. There is very little information about these groups, but they must have been a varied set. I have already referred to the accordion players who go back to the 1880s, when the accordion was first imported. These could be solitary wandering figures or accordion players who entertained in their own villages and towns. At any rate, they were probably rather few and far between. There were also guitar players who might play singly and in duos and trios. Antonio María Peñaloza, for example, mentioned that his grandfather was an accordionist who played mazurkas, waltzes, and polkas, while his father played the guitar.

One trio which bridged the time and space between purely aural and recorded music was the Trío Nacional, formed in 1927 by three black men in Cartagena, with two guitars and maracas. They dressed in Cuban peasant garb and played Cuban music—mostly boleros—but they also played regional styles such as paseos, porros, and cumbias. They made recordings in Cartagena in the early to midforties and their sound was often strengthened by the addition of a bass, a sax, and a clarinet (Muñoz Vélez 1995). Another such group was Trío Los Romanceros. Their founder, Alberto González, recounted that his group played boleros (their strong suit), but also "porros and whatever else came along" in radio stations in Barranquilla in the early 1940s; they also recorded in Cartagena, before moving to Medellín (interview).

If the guitar trios do not seem to have played the clubs, it is fairly certain that the accordion players did not. This music was seen as very plebeian by the elite, and the social club in Valledupar itself did not allow accordion music (although the statutes also forbade guitars and "parrandas parecidas" [suchlike parties]; Araújo de Molina 1973: 52). Accordionists such as Pacho Rada, Alejo Durán, Abel Antonio Villa, and Luis E. Martínez—the latter two best known for being the first to record local-style accordion music—had very local followings, although in the midforties they began to reached a wider audience through radio performances and recordings.

4.5 Guillermo Buitrago (*center*) and his group. (By permission of Discos Fuentes.)

A critical figure who bridged the gap between the guitar trios play-ing boleros and the accordion groups playing paseos and sones was Guillermo Buitrago (fig. 4.5).[28] Born in the town of Ciénaga in 1920— he must have overlapped there with Peñaloza—he studied little but played guitar from an early age and began to play on radio programs in Ciénaga and Santa Marta in the late 1930s. At this time, he com-posed and played waltzes, pasillos, and Mexican-style rancheras. In 1938 in Ciénaga, he met the singer Socrates Medina, nicknamed El Negrito Figurín, and accompanied him on a radio show. Buitrago was impressed by the singer's repertoire of Costeño music and began to tour Magdalena Province looking for songs, basing himself in Fun-dación, in the banana plantation zone. He took up and later recorded songs by composers from the Valledupar region such as Tobías En-rique Pumarejo, Emiliano Zuleta, and Rafael Escalona, at a time when they were figures more or less unknown outside their own region; he also recorded his own compositions in the same style. In 1942, he arrived in Barranquilla with a group which included guitarist Julio Bovea, a figure not unlike him, also born in Ciénaga, who went on to popularize a similar sort of music, especially Escalona's songs, with his own group, Bovea y Sus Vallenatos. Buitrago made some record-ings with the European firm Odeon which were pressed in Buenos Aires and also recorded with a Colombian company, but he died very young in 1949, a victim of alcoholism and tuberculosis. Despite this,

4.6 José María Peñaranda (*with accordion*) and his group. (By permission of Casa Editorial El Tiempo Bogotá.)

his records became very popular in the interior and were an important channel for the popularization of Costeño music there. He is still quite a well-known figure whose songs are played especially at Christmas. Bovea was still performing in the 1990s.

Another similar artist was José María Peñaranda (fig. 4.6), born in Barranquilla in 1907. From a nonmusical family, he did manual work and wrote songs on an informal basis, performing them on the guitar. He also performed on local radio stations, and some of his songs were recorded by the early local record industry. In about 1940, while working as a technician in Emisoras Unidas, he wrote "Se Va el Caimán," based on a mythical beast, half man, half caiman, which he had read about in the newspapers. The song made little impact initially but reemerged in 1945 after the Venezuelan Rosita Perón had a hit with it in her country. Peñaranda had the music written up by Pacho Galán, so the story goes, and the local RCA Victor agent suggested sending it to be recorded in Buenos Aires. It became a major national and international hit, still covered regularly in Colombia today. Peñaranda went on to record many songs, taking up the accordion in 1950, and toured in the United States and Puerto Rico in the 1960s (interview with

Peñaranda; see also Restrepo Duque 1991: 27–28; Ruiz Hernández 1983: 227–231; and *Semana,* 3 May 1994, pp. 74–75).

The particularity of these artists was that they performed most of their songs with a lineup of guitars, bass, guacharaca, and, in Buitrago's case, a small hand drum; some of Buitrago's records made with Los Trovadores de Barú also had the accompaniment of wind instruments. They generally avoided the accordion, thus providing a distancing from the very plebeian connotations of this instrument (although Buitrago made some early records with Abel Antonio Villa on accordion, as did Peñaranda with Luis E. Martínez). They proved immensely popular both in La Costa and in the interior of the country. All three were also white or at least very light skinned, in contrast to accordionists such as Pacho Rada, Alejo Durán, Abel Antonio Villa, and Luis E. Martínez, who were black or mulatto. The latter set all came from clearly peasant origins, while Buitrago and Bovea, at least, came from the slightly higher social classes of a major provincial town.

RADIO BROADCASTING

The emergence and rapid growth of radio broadcasting was fundamental to the growing popularity of Costeño music. Radio began in La Costa, and stations were generally founded by middle-class men with a commercial mentality who found sponsorship from the private sector. Although radio programming was quite varied, music was a staple item and Costeño artists found a new medium for their music.

The first radio station in Colombia was founded in Barranquilla in 1929 by Elías Pellet Buitrago, the grandson of a U.S. immigrant, who had studied electrical engineering in the United States.[29] It was called La Voz de Barranquilla, and its inaugural program of 8 December included a Bach aria (played on the cello by Guido Perla—the trombonist of the Orquesta Sosa—with Emirto de Lima on piano), other classical pieces played by the resident orchestra, directed by Emirto de Lima, a pasillo played by Carlos Zagarra (director of the Jazz Band Colombia), a talk on sport, and so on. It is said that the first record played was the notorious "Tóqueme el Trigémino, Doctor," although it seems this was by mistake.

This innovation took place in the context of an already fervent interest in radio transmission in the whole country, with local amateur enthusiasts' clubs in the major cities and primitive antennae sprouting up from private houses, receiving shortwave broadcasts from places such as Cuba, Mexico, and the United States. Other radio stations quickly followed in Barranquilla. In 1934, a Barranquilla technician and a Venezuelan poet founded the Emisora Atlántico with the financial backing of Miguel Angel Blanco Solís, the Costa Rican consul who owned a chemical and drug laboratory in the city. It was this station that maintained the famous Emisora Atlántico Jazz Band from 1940, although prior to that the Orquesta Sosa played there frequently. In 1936, the Venezuelan consul, who was also the RCA Victor and Kodak agent, Emigdeo Velasco, started up La Voz de la Víctor, and, after Pellet died as a young man in 1939, Velasco bought up La Voz de Barranquilla, the two stations together becoming known as Emisoras Unidas. Also in 1936, La Voz de la Patria was founded by Clemente Vassallo Manfroni, an Italian merchant, and his son, who had the technical expertise. (Other early Barranquilla stations included Radio Barranquilla and Emisora Variedades.) The role of commercially minded immigrants in broadcasting and technological innovation in Barranquilla was clear.

In Cartagena, the first radio station was La Voz de Laboratorios Fuentes (later simply Emisora Fuentes), founded in 1934 by Antonio Fuentes (1907–1985), whose family owned Laboratorios Fuentes and who had been educated in the United States, in Philadelphia. In other cities—Santa Marta and Ciénaga, among others—radio stations also began to spring up. Naturally, in Bogotá and Medellín stations were being founded at the same time. An official government station was inaugurated in Bogotá in 1929, and commercial stations soon followed, notably La Voz de la Víctor (1930), Radio Santa Fe (1933), and Emisora Nueva Granada (1933) in Bogotá and La Voz de Antioquia (1931) and Ecos de la Montaña (1931) in Medellín.

Sports, news, humor, talks, plays, and religious instruction were important parts of 1930s and 1940s radio programming—and politicians used the new medium from the midthirties to promote their platforms—but music was also fundamental from the very start, and records and live music, classical and popular, formed a major part of radio broadcasts. The music played generally reflected the elite and middle-class tastes that I have described.[30] Radio stations generally had a *radioteatro* (a theater) on the premises, and national and international artists would be contracted to play there. Tickets were distributed, often free of charge, and people watched the artists during live broadcasts. Commercial interests quickly saw the potential of advertising and of owning radio stations. In Medellín, for example, a collection of major industrial interests (including Coltabaco, the textile firm Fabricato, the brewers Cervecería Unión, Nacional de Chocolates,

4.7 Carmencita Pernett. (By permission of Cromos.)

and Café La Bastilla) formed the Compañía Colombiana de Radio-difusión, which owned La Voz de Antioquia. All over the country, individual firms or brand names sponsored their own musical programs: Coltabaco, Fabricato, Kresto (a chocolate drink manufacturer), Sal de Uvas Picot (a digestive salts product), and Café Almendra Tropical, to name but a few.

Radio opened a means for local Costeño musicians to get more widely known. Carmencita Pernett (fig. 4.7) began singing with the Orquesta Emisora Fuentes in Cartagena, appearing later on Emisoras Unidas in Barranquilla in 1941 (billed as the "romancera de la radio," the balladeer of radio) and in the Jardín Aguila in 1942 (see Restrepo Duque 1991: 10; *La Prensa*, 30 January 1941; 6 February 1941). Perhaps helped by her European looks—enhanced by dyed blond hair—she went on to fame in Mexico (she married a Mexican and emigrated to Mexico). In 1950 she triumphed in New York on NBC with Afro-Cuban music and "stylizations of Colombian porro" (*El Tiempo*, 21 August 1950, p. 20). The same might be said of Estercita Forero, another Barranquilla-born singer, who became well known in Puerto Rico and Mexico, with the backing of Rafael Hernández (the man who originally helped Camacho y Cano in New York). But more locally known artists also got airtime: Buitrago and Bovea, of course, but also artists such as the accordionist Pacho Rada, a wandering minstrel born in 1907, who played La Voz de la Patria in 1936 in a show run by Camacho y Cano; Abel Antonio Villa joined him there at about the same time (Hinestroza Llano n.d.: 45–47).

THE RECORDING INDUSTRY

The recording industry, then as now, was closely linked to radio and again facilitated the entry of Costeño music. As I have shown, the records available in the 1930s came from abroad, mainly the United States, and among these were a few Colombian hits. As I mentioned in chapter 2, some Colombians went to record bambucos and other such styles as early as 1910, but the first Costeño music recorded in the United States seems to have been the song "La Pringamoza," a "danzón colombiano," sung by the Spaniard Pilar Arcos and the Cuban Miguel de Grandy and written by Cipriano Guerrero, a Barranquilla saxophone player (Columbia 2749-X, 1928). Camacho y Cano's recordings of 1929 soon followed. These entered the Colombian market, and, although he also recorded fox-trots and rumbas and even his Costeño music was sometimes given vague labels such as *parranda* or *aire colombiano*, one advertisement for his records invites readers to "dance in this carnival to music that is genuinely ours": the terms *cumbia, mapalé,* and *porro* also appeared on his records (*La Prensa*, 7 February 1931).[31] It is clear that it was important to establish the music as Colombian and, indeed, Costeño.

The national recording industry started in Cartagena when Antonio Fuentes, a keen musician himself, began tinkering with rudimentary recording technology in his radio station, giving rise to Discos Fuentes.[32] He sent recordings to be pressed in the United States and Buenos Aires, although not many of these have survived.[33] About 1943, he purchased his own record presses and began to produce records in a more businesslike fashion. He was followed soon after by Emilio Fortou, son of a French immigrant and a technician who did work for radio stations and the Avianca airline and who ran his own electrical goods shop in Barranquilla. He set up Discos Tropical in his own house, probably in the midforties (interview with Tony Fortou, his son; Emilio Fortou himself resolutely refused to talk to anyone about his experiences). Then, in about 1949, a well-off local merchant called Gabriel Buitrago, together with Emigdeo Velasco (owner of La Voz de la Víctor) and various associates from the interior of the country, founded the Atlantic record company, which kept going until the midfifties, when Velasco bought out his partners and formed the Eva label. Antonio Fuentes's much younger brother, José María "Curro" Fuentes (b. 1925), helped out in Discos Fuentes and had a chain of shops called La Múcura, where he sold records he imported personally from New York, plus the Discos Fuentes products. Curro Fuentes also started his own label, Discos Curro, in the early 1950s.

These early companies recorded a range of material, but the over-whelming emphasis was on Costeño music. Records of Cuban styles were also very popular, some recorded locally and the majority im-ported or pressed under license from other companies. Atlantic re-corded the big local orchestras, but kept accordion music on a separate label, Popular. Fuentes was less fussy, and in the Fuentes 1954 catalog, which has recordings going back to the early to mid-1940s, there are numerous porros, gaitas, and fandangos, plus a few cumbias, as well as merengues, paseos, and the odd number labeled "son vallenato," al-though the latter three categories would have been played mostly by groups based on guitars rather than accordions. There are also pa-sillos, some tangos, and even the odd bambuco. The Orquesta Emisora Fuentes predictably figures large, and there are other orchestras, such as Orquesta Melodía. Abel Antonio Villa and Luis E. Martínez—two of the first to record accordion music—also appear, as does an artist and composer from El Banco, near Mompox, who was to become more famous than either Villa or Martínez, not only for his composi-tions of Costeño music, but for tangos and boleros—José Barros. The Trío Nacional, the Trío Los Romanceros, and Julio Bovea are all there, and the biggest earner at the time was Guillermo Buitrago: the Fuentes Building in Calle del Sargento Mayor in the colonial sector of Carta-gena is reputed to have had a plaque saying "This building is owed to Guillermo Buitrago." Fuentes also recorded conjuntos based on gaitas and other traditional instruments: for example, several records by Manuel Silvestre Julio y su Conjunto de Gaitas are listed under a sep-arate label, Caribe. For Discos Tropical, one of the main early artists was Julio Bovea, and Pacho Galán also made some early recordings with them.

Procedures were by all accounts fairly flexible. Antonio Fuentes ran the business personally and, being a musician himself, took a major hand in the arrangements. The same musicians would play in different bands, and the same bands had varied lineups: Fuentes would simply swap people around for a given recording session, trying out different sounds and arrangements. Bands such as the Trovadores de Barú and the Piratas de Bocachica appear with different artists—Buitrago, Barros, and others—and were simply resident backing bands. Some people claim that an equally flexible attitude was taken with the authorship of songs and that some pieces were not registered under their authors' names. "La Múcura," for example, was registered under Fuentes's name and recorded by two singers from Trío Nacional, backed by the Trovadores de Barú (Fuentes 0082). It was recorded again in 1949 by a Panamanian singer, Bobby Capó, who got into trouble with Fuentes when he claimed it as his. Pérez Prado, the king of mambo, also recorded a version in the 1950s. But it appears that the real author was Crescencio Salcedo, a poor wandering flute player, who also claimed such classics as "Mi Cafetal" and "Se Va El Caimán" (see Arteaga 1991: 112; and Villegas and Grisales 1976).[34]

The national record industry was confined to La Costa until about 1949, when competition started almost simultaneously with Sonolux in Medellín and Discos Vergara in Bogotá (see chapter 5). Costeño artists also continued to work for foreign companies in the hope of reaching a wider market. In the early 1940s, for example, Buitrago and Abel Antonio Villa made some recordings that were pressed by the European firm Odeón, which had branches in Chile and Argentina. Lucho Bermúdez went to Buenos Aires in 1946 and recorded some sixty songs for RCA Victor. This visit was particularly important for the impact it had on local band leaders such as the violinist Eugenio Nóbile, leader of the Orquesta Panamericana, and Eduardo Armani, leader of his own orchestra, both of whom had already been playing Cuban music in Buenos Aires. Bermúdez's recordings were made with local orchestras—he and two singers, Matilde Díaz and Bob Toledo, were the only Colombians present—and this was an early chance for Argentinean musicians to hear Bermúdez's versions of porros, gaitas, and cumbias (Arteaga 1991: 56–59). Eduardo Armani went on to record a great deal of Costeño music in Argentina, and his orchestra sold many records in Colombia.

THE RECORDINGS

A brief look at the lyrics of the Colombian songs recorded in New York in the late 1920s underlines why the Costeño elite might have had reservations about them. "La Pringamoza" (The Stinging Nettle) for example, a lively danzón sung by a male-female duet accompanied by violins, piano, and guitars, includes the following lines in its chorus:

> Ya me la encontré, ya me tropezó
> Es un rasca-rasca que lo sentimos los dos
>
> .   .   .   .
>
> Si me lo quito, también se lo quito yo
>
> I've found it now, I've stumbled on it
> It's an itchiness which we both feel
>
> .   .   .   .
>
> If I get rid of mine, I'll get rid of yours too

The double meanings possible in ideas about itchiness and scratching, especially when sung by a male-female duet, must have been evident to listeners then. More open is Camacho y Cano's "Por lo Bajo" (Brunswick 40873), a "parranda" with two male vocals accompanied by a violin, a trumpet, a trombone, a bass guitar, and maracas, which has a single refrain:

> Yo quiero, negra, que tú me quieras
> Sólo por lo bajo
> Ay quiéreme, negra
> Por lo bajo
>
> I want you, *negra*, to love me
> Only under cover
> Oh, love me, *negra*
> Only under cover[35]

The theme of covert sexual relations with a woman, possibly a black (and thus by implication lower-class) woman, was a well-known one in La Costa, and it is interesting that Camacho y Cano, as a white Costeño male, chose to refer to this particular intersection of race, gender, and class. Common it might have been, but it was not necessarily something the elite wanted in their clubs. Suddenly, however, rather than being referred to by local lower-class songsters, it was sung by a white man, recorded in New York and sold alongside all the other international Latin American hits. Most of the songs recorded by Camacho y Cano did not have sexually suggestive lyrics—although titles such as "Grab It/Him from Behind" and "Getting Hot" ("Agárralo por Detrás" [Brunswick 41011] and "Calentándose Va" [Brunswick 41150]; both listed in Spottswood 1990: 1722–1723) perhaps did— but the presence of the occasional risqué number is indicative of some of the changes that were taking place as Costeño music made its way into elite circles.

The recordings made in Colombia, however, are less easy to characterize given their large quantity and varied nature, and especially when rather few are available to be heard. Listening to a selection of numbers recorded by the Orquesta Emisora Fuentes and the Orquesta A Número Uno in the early 1940s indicates that risqué lyrics were uncommon—in any case, many of the porros and cumbias were instrumental. Instead, pieces frequently referred to local Costeño themes, often rural ones. Thus "La Vaca Vieja" (The Old Cow, Fuentes 2001) laments the loss of an old cow. "No Como Conejo" (I Don't Eat Rabbit, Fuentes 0037), with Carmencita Pernett on vocals, talks about how vixens eat rabbits even though they are fleet of foot. However, it also goes on to say that there is a good hunter in Sincelejo (a Costeño town) who "killed doña Leonor's rabbit." This is certainly a sexual pun, since *conejo* can mean a woman's sexual organs. "La Fiesta de San Roque" (Fuentes 0038) mentions incidents from a local fiesta with cumbia dancing and recounts that women were being scared by "la vaca loca" (literally, a mad cow, but here a person carrying a set of flaming cow's horns with which he chases people in a carnivalesque open-air fiesta). In "Muchacha Cartagenera" (Cartagena Girl, Fuentes 0035), Carmencita Pernett sings about dancing porro until daybreak in the barrios of Cartagena. Early Lucho Bermúdez numbers such as "Borrachera" (Drunkenness), "Marbella" (a place near Cartagena), and "Prende la Vela" (Light the Candle) refer to romantic themes, local beauty spots, and dancing to cumbia and mapalé.

Buitrago's songs tend to focus on male-female relations, but with little sexual innuendo, and on partying. In "Las Mujeres a Mí No Me Quieren" (Fuentes 0078), he laments that women do not like him because he is poor, while on the B side, "Compai Diodoro" (usually known as "Compae Heliodoro"), he invites his compadre to go drinking and partying with him. In "Dame Tu Mujer, José" (Fuentes 0114), José is told that he should hand over his woman to Buitrago as a recompense for unpaid debts. "Grito Vagabundo" (Fuentes 0095) is a general lament about the difficulties of life: "¿Cómo me compongo yo, si vivo triste?" (How am I to sort myself out, if I live in sadness?). "La Araña Picua" (Fuentes 0096) describes an odd-looking and tricky spider, and "La Piña Madura" (Fuentes 0122) talks about the tasty juice of the ripe pineapple which is valued by the women of Ciénaga. "La Hija de Mi Comadre" (Fuentes 0079) relates that the daughter of his comadre has left town, apparently because she has stained the family's honor (presumably by becoming pregnant outside marriage).[36]

Rafael Escalona's songs, popularized particularly by Bovea y Sus

Vallenatos, explore similar themes, with an emphasis on local personalities and events. "Hambre del Liceo" recounts his problems getting
enough to eat at college in Santa Marta. "Mi Honda Herida" is a lament about the deep wound caused him by a woman whom he loves
but who has forgotten him. Many of his songs are addressed to people,
male and female, whom he knows and who are known in his region of
origin.[37]

In short, then, this corpus of recordings presented its audience with
thematic variation, but regional and rural references were common.
The lyrics did not hide plebeian origins, and instead often used a
slightly picaresque tone to make these amusing and unusual. Partying,
dancing, music, and drinking formed a major theme, and the songs
were self-reflexive in this sense: cumbias and porros might have lyrics
saying how much fun it was to dance cumbia and porro. Love was an
important topic, but frequently male-female relations were dealt with
in a down-to-earth and even light-hearted way which contrasted with
the tragic tone of many tangos or Mexican rancheras, for example.
There were different possibilities in these lyrics, in terms of the appeal
of these styles of music to elite social circles and urban audiences in
other regions. On the one hand, with its insider references to people,
places, and rural themes, some of the music seemed very tied to La
Costa; on the other hand, general themes such as partying and love
also had an appeal which could prove more general and, indeed, the
evocation of La Costa—by referring to a few well- known elements
such as sea and sand, rather than little-known villages or individuals—
could help to sustain that appeal in other regions.

A difficult question is that of the musical continuity between the
orchestrated and recorded styles that emerged in the late 1930s and
1940s and the music played by the provincial wind bands or other
peasant or small-town musicians. As I argued in chapter 3, when
narrating origins, the historiography of porro or vallenato tends to
imply that the traditional body of the musical style remained the same,
simply overlaid by a new arrangement or orchestration. The same
pattern is evident for this later period. In an oft-repeated phrase, Lucho Bermúdez, for example, took porro and *lo vistió de frac* (dressed
it up in tails).[38] That is, the body of the music remained intact but was
glamorized with an outer covering. Portaccio, for example, states that
porro was considered rather plebeian at the time; Bermúdez "took up
elements of the big bands of the era, above all [those] of white origin,
softening porro and thus giving it a greater circulation" (Portaccio
1995: 46).

The musical repertoire of the bandas de viento—porro and fandango—was to a large extent formed within a pan-Caribbean musical matrix that owed much to European forms, so continuities were quite feasible. Yet it is undeniable that the music of Lucho Bermúdez—who, as I said, cited as his influences Pedro Biava, Ernesto Lecuona, and Rafael Hernández—was very different in its overall presentation from that of the provincial wind bands. One can certainly hear similarities between records such as "El Pollo Pelongo," labeled a fandango,[39] and fandangos played by wind bands in the 1980s (if indeed the latter are a real guide to wind band fandangos of the 1920s): there is a similar call-and-response dialogue of trumpet with clarinets and other brass instruments; there is a similar part where a clarinet solos against a refrain played by the rest of the brass section. But there are also big differences: there are a piano, bass, and drum kit playing, for example, and the overall sound is much more polished. Of course, there is a even greater distance between this orchestrated sound and the music of the rural peasant conjuntos playing cane pipes and drums.

Thus, in 1950, when Gilbert Chase updated Gustavo Durán's guide to recorded Latin American popular music, he added a section on porro, noting its recent popularity but saying, "From a folkloric or nationally characteristic point of view, however, the porro offers no special interest, for it is a cross between a danzón and a rumba, and in general follows standardized patterns of modern commercialized dance music. In duple time, usually 2/4, and moderately fast tempo . . . the porro presents typical Caribbean rhythmic patterns" (Durán 1950: 37). So, although it would be wrong to deny real musical continuities, I think it is vitally important that composers of orchestrated porros— and the record companies and many of the later commentators on the music—were seeking a distinctive label, something that would give their music a particular identity that made La Costa shine within Colombia and the nation stand out in the international Latin music scene.

Music, Class, and Race in La Costa

Between 1920 and 1950, important changes in the production and consumption of music took place in the cities of La Costa. At the beginning of this period, rural populations listened mainly to their own local musics played on homemade instruments, with brass bands also present in towns and during local rural fiestas; city populations listened to both the former styles, but among the elite the preference was

for European music and styles from the interior of the country, particularly pasillos and bambucos. With the advent of imported records,
North American, Mexican, Argentinean, and Cuban music all began
to penetrate, first into elite circles, but very soon into the social strata
below them. Cuban music was especially influential, and, indeed, there
were already long-standing links with Cuba which existed outside
the elite. Then, with radio and the emergence of the local recording industry, new styles began to make an impact which were partly based
on local rural or small-town music, using certain distinctive features
which evoked this music and evincing a good deal of local flavor in
their lyrics. Some of this music began to be accepted in the elite's clubs:
it tended to be light-skinned musicians using orchestral lineups or, to
a lesser extent, guitar-based conjuntos who effected this move. Members of the elite might class some of this music as vulgar and offensive,
but it was not seen as sufficiently vulgar by enough people to keep
it out.

If we look at these changes in terms of broader issues, a number of
themes come to light. First is the question of local elites and processes
of appropriation and transformation in an ideological field dominated
by certain values. Costeño elites were in an ambivalent position with
respect to the changing musical scene and especially the gradual expansion of vernacular local styles beyond lower-class circles. At stake
was their self-image at a regional level and above all at a national
level—where the Costeños felt politically and culturally discriminated
against. For the elite, music could help construct images of modernity,
but if all the modern music came from abroad, then modernity ran the
risk of being too imitative and not autochthonous enough and, to the
extent that Barranquilla outdid even Bogotá in being cosmopolitan, of
perhaps distancing La Costa from the core of nationality, from the
bambucos and pasillos. On the other hand, local music could be woven into ideas about and possible claims to regional cultural particularity, but if the music was too evidently black, rural, and traditional—
let alone "vulgar"—this could cause problems; in addition, if it was
too different, this could appear to be creating space between La Costa
and the interior. A balance between modernity and tradition could be
struck, and music could represent this, but it was an insecure balance
because the music could be "read" in different ways, according to the
point of view.

Music and its representation were therefore of importance to the
elite, but it would be overly instrumentalist to imagine that the dominant classes of Barranquilla, let alone La Costa as a whole, had a co-

herent project of control in relation to music. There is little evidence, for example, that the Costeño elite or even the middle classes used music in an explicit way to represent Costeño culture and identity—for example, by writing about it extensively in the public media—until about the 1950s. Nevertheless, music formed a crucial part of elite social life, in which much time, effort, and money was spent on musical entertainment in the clubs and, in the case of Barranquilla, carnival celebrations. With the emergence of radio and record production, music became an increasingly important part of economic activities, through direct involvement with radio and records and through advertising by means of music.

The main project pursued by elites and in fact the middle classes was the development of communications media in the region— through which local music expanded its audience, whether or not this was their explicit intention. They organized club dances and carnival celebrations, and they set up radio stations and record companies. More important than class conflict between the elite and a rising middle class—as remembered by composer Rafael Campo Miranda— was the fact that an educated middle class was expanding and taking part in the cultural life of the cities, giving added life and diversity to the production and consumption of culture as a commodity. There is an alliance, rather than a conflict, of classes evident in the similarity between Antonio Fuentes, from a rich Cartagena family, and Emilio Fortou, a middle-class technician, with their common interest in developing (and making money from) recording, and doing this with local musicians. There is no denying that some people in the elite, and doubtless in the middle classes too, objected to what they saw as vulgar music of plebeian origins, but this was not a uniform response. The eagerness of some members of the upper and middle classes to develop modern technologies of communication opened up opportunities for local music.

Radio was developed as a commercial venture, advertising everyday products. Programming had to appeal to a wide audience, and this meant playing popular music. Much of this was Cuban, Mexican, or Argentinean, but the presence of local musicians meant that local styles began to be played with similar orchestration and arrangements. Figures such as Fuentes were very important here in bringing musicians together and arranging musical productions; musicians such as Bermúdez, Galán, Peñaloza, and Buitrago were crucial in their ability to mediate between class levels.

But local music, as we have seen, was not admitted to middle-class and elite circles in an unaltered fashion. The commercialization of vernacular styles, putting them into the fast lane of modern life, went hand in hand with the establishment of new hierarchies of value. Previous hierarchical distinctions between Europeanized elite music and local lower-class music became more complex, as North American, then Cuban, and finally some local music gained elite status. The fact that the music listened to by elites was less exclusively upper class than before meant that other signs of high status acquired increasing importance, such as the performance of music by an orchestra in a club, the exclusion of "vulgarity," the maintenance of a certain etiquette in dances, and so forth.

New hierarchies shared much continuity with previous ones. The musicians were mostly white or at any rate not evidently black, they might be advertised as profesores, and they wore tuxedos; the music was stylized and played with an orchestra lineup associated with modern tastes. In short, elements of traditional Costeño music were rearticulated with other musical and nonmusical elements to resignify Costeño music as an authentically regional but also modern product, as a style with some roots in blackness but now made respectable—*vestido de frac* (dressed in tails)—and hence whiter. The process of rearticulation was thus structured by some basic hegemonic values of racial and class hierarchy. The process of rearticulation was carried out by many different people, pursuing different motives, but in the context of hegemonic values: some older elite people rejected the music entirely; others of the elite enjoyed its exotic appeal; musicians mediated between different class contexts in search of new music that would be successful in the clubs and in the new media; the owners of radio stations and record companies wanted successful products for an audience that, though broadening, was still more middle class and above than solid working class.

The second theme arising from this story relates to the perspective on national identity outlined in the first chapter. It is important to recognize that this recombination of elements did not mean blackness was simply written out of the script; it was always there to be evoked, and Costeño music in its new guise was open to different readings. I will give examples of this in the next chapter, but here it is worth mentioning a 1945 piece on national music in *La Prensa*. This noted that pasillo was the music for which Colombia was best known and that the diversity of autochthonous musics meant that artists preferred "the languor of an Argentinean tango, the heat of an Afro-Cuban rumba, the ancestral protest of the Aztec Indians, or the hybridity and heterogeneity of Brazilian music." But in the Barranquilla carnival, the dominant music was porro, an essentially African music found in La Costa because the region was like a colony of distant Africa (Ortega 1945). Even at a date by which porros had been in the social clubs for over half a decade and Lucho Bermúdez was a hit in Bogotá, the writer of the article chose—in the context of carnival—to emphasize the blackness which was available to be evoked but which was played down in other settings.

This is not just accidental. The Costeño elite prided itself on its whiteness, which was contrasted to the blackness (and indigenousness) of the lower classes. Eliminating reference to blackness would undermine the contrast. It was one thing to purvey an image of a regional identity represented by music rooted in local rural traditions; it was another to obscure the differences between the rural (black and mulatto) populace and urban (white) elites. The tension between a unified identity and class hierarchy could not be entirely overcome.

In addition, blackness (or indigenousness), although carrying a powerful stigma, could also be constructed as a source of strength, especially if it could be presented as "tamed." The sexuality attributed to blacks was guarded against by the elites in their clubs but pursued by middle- and upper-class white men in more covert ways. This was one reason why blackness was not simply eradicated from Costeño music, since musical and sexual enjoyment were linked for the very sort of men who were the prime movers in the commercialization of Costeño music. To completely excise blackness from the music would mean constricting the possibility of channeling sexual desire through this music, and this option, even if necessarily subliminal, was an important frisson.

Upper- and middle-class women were far from excluded from these frissons or from desiring black men, but in social terms their sexuality was more controlled and they participated much less in the commercialization of the music, so that their own experiences of, or imaginings about, black sexuality would have had less influence on the music and its representation. Nevertheless, female singers such as Carmen Pernett and Ester Forero did capture the sexual imagination of audiences, and, indeed, female singers were often popularly supposed to be morally loose, perhaps especially if singing Costeño music. Mercedes de Coronel, for example, who sang for a while in the early 1950s with the Orquesta Emisora Fuentes and the Orquesta de Roberto Lambraño in Cartagena, said that her mother was always careful to accompany her to gigs to avoid any possible misunderstandings. She also gave up singing and became more "respectable" with a view to getting married (interview). Matilde Díaz, the acclaimed singer in Lucho Bermúdez's orchestra, said of her early career: "I was the first woman to sing in an orchestra and I said I was Mexican because if I'd have said I was Colombian, well, they would have humiliated me; who knows what they would have said." She admitted to being Colombian when the recording career of the orchestra was well established (interview).

In sum, then, this new ideological complex of Costeño music was not adopted by the political elite as an explicit self-representation in political struggles against the interior of the country, not even when the music of Lucho Bermúdez and others became a huge success in the cities of the interior. Popular music was not serious enough for formal politics; it was too open to trivialization. But the process of the creation of new types of Costeño music was certainly mediated very heavily by the elite and by the middle classes, and, although the emergence of these styles was not the result of a purposive strategy, they fitted well with an upper- and middle-class self-image of being progressive and modern while at the same time being the owners of a region with something particular to it. Costeño music in its new "tail coat" had qualities which expressed richly and with productive ambiguity the tensions between modernity and tradition, between blackness and whiteness, between the region as distinctive and as part of the nation in progress, and between sexual desire and moral propriety. As the music spread into the interior, it did begin to appear as a more definite symbol of Costeño identity both in the micropolitics of migrants' everyday lives and in the public arena of the press and other media. There is no doubt that it strongly influenced the image of La Costa in the rest of the country and indeed recast the image of the nation itself.

5 ¡Alegría! Costeño Music Hits the Heartland, 1940–1950

Bogotá and Medellín before Costeño Music

Bogotá and Medellín in the 1930s were cities which, like Barranquilla, were undergoing rapid change. Before this time, observers commented on the isolation of Bogotá, its provinciality, and the weight of church influence there. Iriarte notes that in 1910 the capital "was still submerged in the stagnation and the state of marginality which . . . kept it notably behind the most important Ibero-American capitals"; it was still a capital "quasi-isolated from the world in the redoubt of its lofty Andean meseta" (Iriarte 1988: 187). In 1901, the geographer Vergara y Velasco wrote that the residences of Bogotá were "individual family houses, with patios, melancholy and still, somber gardens, surrounded by rooms, and with orchards at the back" (cited in Puyo Vasco 1992: 182). A student from Barranquilla, resident in Bogotá at the turn of the century, commented on the city's "fogs, its melancholy and rainy days, [and] its dark and tedious winter nights," although he also admired the local flora (Palacio, cited in Peralta 1995: 30). The French traveler Jorge Brisson noted that there were thirty-two churches in the city, practically one for every block (Brisson 1899, cited in Archila Neira 1991: 77, n. 40).[1] Peralta, after reviewing Bogotá's pleasures and diversions in the nineteenth century, concludes that "in relation to pleasures, the personality of the Bogotanos became secretive, inauthentic, imitative, repressive, and nostalgic. With all these limitations, Bogotanos became lazy, bored, sedentary, and grey" (1995: 156).

Medellín was also a very provincial city, isolated in terms of communications infrastructure, but some visitors found it livelier. Pierre d'Espagnat, another French traveler of the same period, found that it lacked the "sad mysticism" of Bogotá, but he still noted that people led a limited social life and were rather strict and abrupt in manner. Brisson wrote that "life is very serious in Medellín," revolving around work, commerce, and the family. He also observed that "priests [are] very abundant here" although less so than in Bogotá.[2] An earlier local commentator, writing in the 1850s, noted that there were dances in Medellín: despite the overriding atmosphere of the "most Christian, the ascetic, the orthodox city," people realized that life had "not been created solely to do penance" (Kastos 1972: 205).

Barranquilla, with its easier external links, although still seen by turn-of-the century travelers as very provincial, was a more open city, where the clergy was a lesser presence and the carnival gave the city an aspect of animation.[3] Both Medellín and Bogotá were, however, undergoing the same sorts of changes as Barranquilla: telephones, electricity, piped water, urban transport, industry, and air, road, and rail connections to the rest of the country were all expanding, not to mention cinema and radio.

The two Andean cities also differed from each other. Bogotá was the capital and sported the self-appointed title of the Athens of South America; its elite was very European in aesthetic and intellectual values and quite conservative in attitude and in politics, adding to the city's reputation for being rather somber. The Barranquilla-based avant-garde cultural magazine *Voces* (1917–1920) developed a trenchant critique of what its Catalan editor, Ramón Vinyes, saw as Bogotá's intellectual and artistic stuffiness (Gilard 1991). Medellín had emerged as a major competitor with the advent of coffee cultivation in the 1860s; its subsequent precocious industrialization made it the country's industrial leader by the 1940s. The Antioqueño elite, rather like its Costeño counterpart, felt somewhat discriminated against by the central government in Bogotá, and a strong—and by the early twentieth century, quite vociferous—regional identity existed, based on the idea of *la raza antioqueña* and glorifying the image of a unique Antioqueño breed which was hard working, commercially shrewd, adventurous, self-reliant, democratic, and white—or at least nonblack and nonindigenous. The image of democratic egalitarianism is questionable, but the elite was certainly less European in orientation than was the elite in Bogotá; Antioqueño writers—for example, novelist Tomás Carrasquilla—were often strongly regionalist and also critical of Bogotá's cultural conservatism.

Blackness was denied in literate representations of Antioquia, despite the attested presence of many slaves in the colonial period and many blacks and mulattoes in the region and in Medellín itself.[4] The

Antioqueño elite, being of rather recent origins, like the Barranquilla elite, wanted to prove itself; the difference was that Antioquia as a region and the Medellín elite as a social group were more powerful and more internally coherent than were the La Costa and Barranquilla elites. The Bogotá elite, by comparison, had less to prove, having the advantages of long-standing political and cultural centrality. Also, although indigenous heritage was apparent in the city's population, the elite did not really have to deny blackness, since it had never had much of a presence there.

The class context of diversion and music in the Andean cities was similar to that in Barranquilla. A fundamental division between the elite and the lower classes was being complicated during the first decades of the twentieth century by an expanding middle class and by immigration and a growing urban industrial working class, although in Bogotá artisans remained numerous in this period. Class differences were expressed in residential segregation, with elites living either in the center or, from the 1920s, beginning to locate in smart neighborhoods north of the center—for example, El Prado in Medellín, and Teusaquillo and Chapinero in Bogotá. The lower classes crowded into multioccupancy housing in the city center (often old elite residences) and a few newer planned urbanizations and unplanned peripheral settlements. Elite clubs also emerged or were consolidated in both cities: for example, the Gun Club, the Jockey Club, and the Country Club in Bogotá (note the English names), and the Club Unión and the Club Campestre in Medellín. Archila Neira's account of elite and middle-class moral campaigns against working-class drinking establishments, which I mentioned in the context of Barranquilla, applied just as much to Medellín and Bogotá—indeed, more so, to judge from his examples (Archila Neira 1991). Antioqueño novelist Tomás Carrasquilla's characterization of Medellín high society in his novel *Grandeza* (1910) was equally valid for Bogotá: "More important than family, more even than money, was good bearing, good taste, elegance, and good manners" (Carrasquilla 1964, 1:261).

A difference between these two cities and Barranquilla was that sexual relations between men of the upper and middle classes and women of the lower classes seem to have been more covert. The strong Catholic ethic of both cities meant that such behavior, where it occurred, had to be more clandestine. On the other hand, these sexual relations were channeled through prostitution, which was widespread and legal. In Medellín, the *zonas de tolerancia* (red-light districts) were in Guayaquil, a working-class sector of the city center, teeming with cheap residences, bars, and taverns—and music—and there were also brothels in Lovaina, just north of the city center. It was normal for middle-class men (and boys, although those under sixteen were not allowed by law) to patronize these places, where they also listened and danced to popular music. For Bogotá, I have less detail, but prostitution seems to have been more geographically dispersed, although still located in the more working-class areas near the city center.[5]

For the elite and middle classes in Bogotá and Medellín, music and dance in the 1920s and 1930s were rather similar to the scene in Barranquilla: bambucos and pasillos were still very popular, and recorded music from North America, Mexico, Argentina, and Cuba was increasingly important. In the interior, Mexican and Argentinean music were rather stronger relative to Cuban styles than in La Costa, but Cuban music was still important in opening the way for Costeño music in the interior. Cuban music came in not only via records and radio (shortwave radios in Medellín and Bogotá could pick up Cuban stations), but also by means of visits by Cuban artists. When the Trío Matamoros toured Colombia in 1934, they included Medellín and Bogotá in their itinerary; the tenor René Cabell debuted his Colombian tour in Bogotá in 1940; Rafael Hernández—who was actually Puerto Rican but played mostly Cuban music—also toured Colombia in that year, starting in Bogotá (see Betancur Alvarez 1993: 253–256).

Social clubs were live music venues for the elites, while, from the 1910s, the cafés which sprouted in the city center, often dedicated to particular types of clientele—students, businessmen, bohemians, and so on—often had small guitar groups, pianolas, and, later on, jukeboxes. There were also night clubs, such as Covadonga in Medellín or El Metropolitan in Bogotá: these catered to elites and the middle classes. Open parks, such as the Bosque de la Independencia in Medellín, also had live music on Sunday afternoons and attracted people of all social classes. As most houses did not have running water, many people went to the public bathhouses, where recorded and live music was also played; these were mainly for better-off families, but some catered to the middle classes and workers. For the working classes and artisans, the principal places for entertainment were bars, taverns, billiard halls, and, especially in Bogotá, *chicherías,* where home-brewed *chicha* (a fermented drink usually made from maize) was served— seven million liters of it in Bogotá over the first four months of 1929, according to contemporary figures.

Foreign recorded music was available, and the numerous bars of Guayaquil in Medellín hummed to a great variety of styles. Guayaquil was a vibrant sector, the location of the railway station, the bus stations, and the marketplace, the first destination for myriad rural migrants, and a place packed with small-scale commerce, cheap rented accommodation, and entertainment of all kinds. It was for the lower classes, but the music played there—for example, boleros, bambucos, and pasillos—was often the same as that played in the social clubs (see Archila Neira 1991: 168–173; Iriarte 1988; Londoño 1988; Londoño and Londoño 1989; Mora Patiño 1989: 27–45; Puyo Vasco 1992; and Restrepo Duque 1988; on Guayaquil, see also Viviescas 1983). Clearly, the local musical styles which became popular in Bogotá and Medellín were different from those favored in La Costa: they were bambucos, pasillos, torbellinos, guabinas, and other guitar-based styles. It was these that had been elevated to the status of a national music such that, while bambucos were listened to in La Costa—and indeed composed by Costeños such as Peñaloza and Bermúdez— Costeño music was simply absent in Medellín and Bogotá.

The newspapers of the early 1940s give the impression that popular music and dancing were less prevalent in Bogotá than in La Costa. Whereas the Barranquilla press carried many advertisements for dances, whether in elite social clubs, more middle-range dance salons, or cheap theaters, these are rather rare in *El Tiempo,* the major Bogotá daily.[6] For the whole of 1940, there are only five advertisements: one reporting the arrival of Rafael Hernández for his tour, sponsored by a digestive salts company; one for a "folkloric Argentine group," one for a "folkloric group" from the Antilles called Estrellas del Caribe, one for a Red Cross charity dance with Orquesta Ritmo and Orquesta Cristancho, and another by the Kresto soft drink company, which was sponsoring a radio program with the singers René Cabell and Josefina Meca (*El Tiempo,* 16 May 1940; 16 June 1940; 29 June 1940; 5 September 1940; 17 November 1940). In comparison, *La Prensa* of Barranquilla carried twelve such notices just in the weekend editions published in December through February.

Memories of Urban Life in the Interior

Oral histories which go back to this era are, of course, not easy to come by, but the few my assistants and I were able to collect help give a feel for the place of music and dance in people's lives. My point in what follows is not to present memories and images as true or false—they are clearly selective stereotypes which are nevertheless widely agreed on— but to show how people thought about the cities where they lived, in their musical aspect, before the arrival of Costeño music. All the data presented are edited versions of taped and transcribed interviews (see appendix A for more details of interviewees).

Adalberto Pinzón was born in Bogotá in 1911 and worked with the railway company all his life. In the following extract, he talked about the 1930s in Bogotá.

> As a rule, people used to have *pachanguitas* [little parties] in their houses.[7] In my house, that's what we'd do. [People] danced and drank beer and *aguardiente* and played a lot of *tejo*.[8] [We'd dance to] pasillo, danza, bolero. . . . [We'd have parties] usually on weekends. You would come out of work at midday and, about three in the afternoon, you'd start playing tejo, until about seven, eight, or nine at night. Then you'd go home with a few beers in your head. [At Christmas or New Year] we'd drink beer and *trago* [spirits] and we'd dance in the house until dawn. Sometimes we'd hire an orchestra, or if not, just with the radio.[9] [The orchestras were] tiple, mandolin, and guitar. [The radio] was a Telefunken, [which we bought] in 1930. There were two or three stations which broadcast news. Music, very little: pasillos. Modern stuff started from the seventies. I liked to go to the *retretas* [open-air band concerts]; they'd give them in the Plaza de Bolívar and we'd go there. Orchestras—the Symphonic was very good.

From a more middle-class background, Ema Valderrama, daughter of an accomplished player of the *requinto* (a small tiple) and a teacher by profession, remembered the early 1940s, when she had begun secondary school education in Bogotá:

> We used to have lovely parties, almost every Saturday. We'd have gatherings, to play cards, to listen to music. It was very common for the girls to play the guitar, the tiple, the mandolin, and the violin. In the wealthier houses, the more prestigious ones: the piano. The piano was an instrument of great social rank . . . in those days, the piano gave a touch of distinction. . . . In my house, almost all of us learned to play an instrument; I played the tiple very well and played it until I graduated. [We played] mainly music that was called national music then, which was a way of saying Andean music, the music from the center: Boyacá, Santander, Tolima, Cundinamarca. It was pasillos, bambucos, torbellinos—joropos, because many influences came from the Llanos and from Venezuela.[10] Danzas and contradanzas were very common, and the groups of musicians would be made up with guitars, mandolins, tiples—maracas sometimes.
>
> We would dance, because then there weren't as many record players

as now. . . . With the radio, if there wasn't a record player in the house, which was usual since only rich people had those [although her family did in fact have one]. But in the houses, there was a simple little radio, and with that people danced all night and with the music played by the young people of the house and their parents and friends. . . . [On the radio there was] classical music, there were special radio stations, the National Radio all the time [the state radio station], . . . and music which, as I said, was called national music, because in those days we made a distinction between national music which was from the center and Costeño music which we didn't like much then. It seemed less elegant to us, because it seemed scandalous, it seemed less refined, and we always looked on it as unimportant.

When we arrived in Bogotá [in the early 1940s] we acquired a *radiola* [combination radio and record player]. For the dances, we'd put on pasillos and paso dobles . . . a few rumbas and some dances from the [Atlantic] littoral like mambo, porro, cumbia—that was just beginning. . . . Ah! and the boleros, I haven't mentioned them . . . Bolero was for love, for despair, for sadness, for happiness, for longing: bolero was all that and it was listened to a lot and people had many bolero records. We loved Mexican music immensely. . . . Who didn't dream, who didn't cry, who did not become romantic to the highest degree with all those songs, and who didn't dance a *zapateado mexicano*, a *jarabe*, a *corrido* and things like that? . . . We also assimilated Cuban music a lot: conga, danzones, all that. It was really beautiful, it was a very beautiful time of life.

Ligia de Márquez, born in Bogotá in 1925, received a university degree and also became a teacher. In the 1940s, as a secondary school student, she lived with her parents in a well-to-do barrio of the city and remembered a much more restricted life:

In my barrio, [we had] very little fun, because my father didn't let us have dealings with anyone and, well, we'd say hello to the girls of the same age as ourselves, but intimate friendships, no chance, my father was very serious. I started going to parties practically when I went to the university. We went to mass with my mother, we'd go into town to go window shopping, to watch the people. We did have [a radio] and we listened to music all day long. We'd listen to Colombian music, beautiful waltzes, very nice classical music as well. [Question: What do you mean by "Colombian music"?] Bambucos, pasillos, those lovely pasillos; by then, there were boleros as well. [We had] a gramophone and records; the records were pasillos, waltzes; there were some from my mother's time which were danzas, and we listened to the Charleston too. We hardly ever had parties in our house; we'd celebrate birthdays, Christmas, New Year, and so on, but we never danced.

Later, when she was at the university, there would be *empanadas bailables* (a sort of tea dance, with empanadas, a fried snack) in her house or at friends' houses with "the parents keeping watch the whole time." Ligia does not make a direct contrast with La Costa, but she remembers that there was a lot of prejudice against the Costeños, who were said to be "libertines and *atarbanes* [rude, loud, vulgar]."

Oral testimony that describes Medellín in the 1930s or even the 1940s is rather scarce in my data.[11] However, one interview with Oliva Zapata, born in about 1924 in Anorí, Antioquia, from a rural, peasant background, gives a few indications. "At that time, people didn't dance much. They danced the twist [sic] . . . I'm talking about Anorí, in about, maybe, the 1920s? The twist, marchas, pasillos, and the marimba. The musicians played tiple, guitar, they played what's called *música guasca*, that old music. . . .[12] I first came across a radio sometime about 1930 in Anorí. They just played those pasillos and, like I said, that guasca music." Anorí is in the northern part of Antioquia, quite close to La Costa, and Oliva also lived for some years in Barranquilla, where, she said, "there was *mucho ambiente*" (a lot of atmosphere), that is, animation and festivity. She recalled, of course, dancing cumbia in the carnival: "there was more *parranda* [partying] in Barranquilla than in Medellín," although in the factory where she worked in Medellín there were parties with dancing.

Teresa de Betancur was born in 1937 in Medellín and worked in domestic service before she married a textile factory worker in 1955. In the early 1950s, she used to go out with groups of friends to Guayaquil and to Barrio Trinidad (which in a 1952 decree was defined—not very realistically—as the only official red-light district of the city and was thus a place with plenty of nightlife). There were dances to live groups and to jukeboxes. Despite the moral ethos of the time—"everything was a sin, more or less. I was with my husband three years [before we got married] and I can tell sincerely that I never even kissed him, because everything was shocking"—she did a lot of dancing both before and after marriage. They would also go to an *estadero* (a large, out-of-town establishment for eating, drinking, and dancing) known as La Primavera, on the outskirts of the city, which was a well-known venue for working-class and some middle-class people: "you'd go on foot to redeem a promise to God[13] and you'd stay there dancing; then in the evening, you'd catch a bus and come home." The music they danced to was varied, with boleros, paso dobles, bambucos, and pasillos, but also rock and roll, mambo, and porros from La Costa. According to her, Costeño music was appreciated by her friends and family, but she recalled that middle-class people often had different ideas: "They'd say that music was very boring." This is an odd comment, because, as we shall see, Costeño music was most frequently seen as *alegre* [happy, joyful]. It may be that Teresa de Betancur was trying to capture the idea that middle-class people sometimes saw Costeño styles as musically simple and therefore monotonous.

Tomás Botero went to Medellín to study as a live-in student. He was born in about 1920 in Aranzazu, Caldas Province, where he was later mayor three times and founded the Club Aranzazu. He recalled that as a youth he used to go dancing with his friends "to the clubs and to the places where there were parties—there were many parties at that time." In the Club Medellín, "they had famous orchestras which played a more stylized music, not so *popular* [working class]." [14] He mentioned La Primavera estadero, where Teresa de Betancur used to go, although he thought that "*la gente popular* [the common people] couldn't afford to get out there." In contrast, Guayaquil was "very *popular;* high-class people rarely went there, although the men would go; it was a men's place." There, "people listened to all kinds of music," although Costeño music had not made an impact by then; "it was more rumba, waltz, tango." He remembered the impression the Costeños made when they did arrive: "When a Costeño arrived [at a party], people would say 'Ah, the Costeños have arrived. What fun! They can light a match under water.'"

The music scene in Medellín and Bogotá was evidently varied, even before the advent of Costeño music, but the major styles were the bambucos, pasillos, and canciones of the interior, and international Latin American styles such as bolero, tango, and romantic Mexican songs. Tango was especially popular in and around Medellín: Carlos Gardel, the world-famous tango singer, died in an airplane crash in Medellín in 1935, and this fueled the popularity of tango, with a local cult emerging around the dead singer. Clear class divisions do not seem to have existed in musical taste: interviewees of different social positions, recalling the 1930s and 1940s, talked of listening and dancing to a similar range of styles. There was a slight tendency among the middle- and upper-class interviewees to talk more about bambucos, pasillos, and paso dobles and, almost without fail, boleros, but working-class people also remembered these styles.

However, it was usually only working-class people who referred to música guasca or *música de carrilera*. Although the latter is usually associated with Medellín and surrounding rural areas, people in Bogotá used the term as well. Restrepo Duque (1988: 538) defines música de carrilera (literally, railroad music) as "the recorded music which went out [from Medellín to the villages], in the arms of delivery men and via the railways, and which has as a common denominator a strong [sense of] the sadness of the common people, with *despechos* [spite, rancor, despair], dead and absent mothers, depressions and suicides"; he dates the term from the mid-1940s. The music itself could be Mexican rancheras and corridos,[15] tangos, Colombian songs recorded by Argentinean artists in Buenos Aires, and a bit later, similar styles recorded locally. Although the music is associated strongly with small towns and rurality, it was, and still is, also popular in the city. People often used the terms *música de carrilera* and *música guasca* interchangeably, probably because of the context in which they are heard—typically, the cantina.

One of the main emotions that people connect with música de carrilera and tangos is despecho, which can mean simply "spite" but which also conveys a much deeper and more tragic sense of anger and despair at the cruel blows delivered by destiny and especially by unrequited or ill-starred love. It is seen as a violent emotion, associated with hardship, poverty, and tragedy. As Julio Estrada, the Colombian salsa artist more commonly known as Fruko, put it when describing his native Medellín barrio in the 1950s, tangos were "songs of thugs, fighters." Mexican music such as corrido "also had this message, music of despecho, of fights" (interview). In an interview, Fabio Betancur, a sociologist and writer on Cuban and Colombian music (Betancur Alvarez 1993), put it another, more philosophical way: "Medellín is a very existentialist, thoughtful city, very preoccupied with the being, with the human condition. So the Antioqueño, apart from being entrepreneurial, commercial, and so on—within that there is a permanent preoccupation with what he is. . . . I think that has a lot to do with the fact that tango settled in Medellín, because tango is existentialist too: it poses the problem of life, the human condition, women, sexuality."

In summary, people remembered Bogotá and Medellín as being quiet and peaceful compared to the images of urban chaos and violence that they generally evoked for the same cities today: one could go out without fear, one could leave the front door open, and so on. The demise of this idyllic scene is often held to have begun with La Violencia, which erupted in 1948 when populist Liberal leader Jorge Eliécer Gaitán was assassinated in Bogotá, sparking the so-called *Bogotazo,* a short period of mass rioting and civil unrest which soon spread to much of the country. The subsequent decade of virtual civil war, as the Conservatives unleashed a regime of repression and terror, actually took place outside the major cities, even if city dwellers could not ignore its existence.

People also made—were invited to make—comparisons with La Costa, whether they knew the region or its people personally or not, and, as I have shown, Bogotá was felt to be relatively restrained, even somber; people saw Medellín as perhaps livelier—Guayaquil was always portrayed as an animated area—but still introspective, concerned with the tragedies of life represented in the lyrics of tangos and rancheras. In contrast, as we shall see in more detail below, Costeño music was associated by many with happiness, fun, good times, dancing, and a sexuality seen not in terms of cruelty and tragedy, but in terms of seduction and comedy.

The Beginnings of Costeño Music in the Colombian Interior

La Rumba Criolla

The first taste of Costeño music for the audiences of Bogotá, Medellín, and other places of the interior of the country came in the form of the records made by people such as Camacho y Cano that I mentioned in chapter 4. Knowledgeable people with whom I discussed the impact of Costeño music in Bogotá and Medellín almost never mentioned his name—whereas those in Barranquilla mentioned him frequently—so, even given the effect of their remote date, it seems likely that these records made little impact there.

More often mentioned by the collectors and older music lovers of the interior are figures such as Emilio Sierra, Milciades Garavito, and Efraín Orozco, names associated with the so-called *rumba criolla* and *bambuco fiestero,* which were a sort of "heated up" bambuco, played with a jazz band lineup.[16] These men were musicians born and raised in the interior of the country, who learned their trade in local bands or church orchestras. They all went into popular music, composing and playing bambucos, pasillos, waltzes, and such. In the rapidly changing musical scene of Bogotá and Cali, however, they experimented with new sounds, mixing orchestrated bambucos with boleros and, later on, a few porros—albeit "touched with *cachaquismo* [the feel of *cachacos,* people of the interior]" (Restrepo Duque 1991: 66).

In 1940, Sierra recorded some numbers which included the hit "Vivan Los Novios" (Long Live the Fiancés).[17] This was baptized a rumba criolla, and Zapata Cuencar (1962: 170) describes the style as "just between hot music and the music of the altiplano." Rumbas criollas by Emilio Sierra y Su Orquesta and by the Orquesta Garavito had a varied instrumentation which included violins, trumpets, trombones, saxophones, maracas, piano, double bass, and sometimes bongos. Generally they retained the mixed 3/4 and 6/8 rhythms characteristic of bambuco. One track, "Es Algo Que Tiene Gracia," by the Orquesta Garavito, starts with a Cuban rumba rhythm, with the claves clearly audible (on the album *Así se bailaba en el Medellín de los años 40* [LP002 of the privately produced collectors' series Lo Que Piden Mis Amigos, published in Medellín, 1989]). Although the term "rumba" was used to associate the music with fashionable Cuban styles, Sierra himself defined the rumba criolla as a "fandango, the younger brother of bambuco, but happier than the latter and just as Colombian" (Ruiz Hernández 1983: 111). The concern with defining a national style amid the burgeoning musical scene is evident.

Efraín Orozco was a more international character, touring Latin America with a band he founded in Cali in 1923 and later living in Buenos Aires, where he made recordings from the late 1930s. His repertoire included many styles of popular music, with bambucos and pasillos prominent among his recordings. He also recorded some Costeño music, although Restrepo Duque (1991: 25) notes that "what he presented under the names porro and cumbia had nothing to do with these airs from the Colombian coast and were really bambucos fiesteros."[18] The label and reputation of Costeño music was clearly an attractive trapping.

I have already shown that the music scene of the 1930s in Bogotá was quite varied, but it is interesting that commentators tend to see Garavito and Sierra as introducing an important change into the music of the city. A 1941 article in a local magazine said: "Bogotá lacked its own music. Bambuco, pasillo, and guabina are typically national, they are born in any Boyacá chichería, in the fights of Santander or in some corner of Antioquia. But Bogotá [itself] had no music." The author credited Sierra with having supplied the city with its own style, and indeed Sierra mentioned that his music was also called *rumba bogotana* (Restrepo Duque 1991: 66, 67; Restrepo Duque quotes an article by Próspero Morales Pradilla in *Estampa,* 13 December 1941). In the same vein, Ruiz Hernández (1983: 113) writes that the music that came before Sierra—that is, the bambucos of Emilio Murillo or Alejandro Wills—"had more of a *campesino* [rural, peasant] than a city accent" and that Sierra broke this mold. As in previous instances, there is an evident concern here with locating a musical style, both in time and space. Bogotá gains a musical identity and the rumba criolla is given a birth certificate.

The rumba criolla also penetrated Medellín, where something different but related occurred with the duo Fortich and Valencia. Roberto Antonio Valencia, a black guitarist from Quibdó, Chocó—a province of the mainly black Pacific coastal region—teamed up with Cartagena-born guitarist Gustavo Fortich during Christmas 1942 in Honda, a river port near Bogotá, where both were playing separate gigs. Eschewing Bogotá, they went to Medellín. They played many boleros, which, of course, had been popular for some time, and—despite their own origins—they also played many bambucos. These were in a new upbeat style, however, which Ruiz Hernández calls a *bambuco costeñizado* and Restrepo Duque labels "bambucos with a modern style." Their main impact was via recordings, since they were contracted by RCA Victor to record in Buenos Aires and stayed there until the end of the decade (Restrepo Duque 1991: 42; Ruiz Hernández 1983: 87–91). Again, then, there was an attempt to "heat up" bambuco by mixing it with elements of Cuban and Costeño music.

COSTEÑO MUSICIANS

The real impact of Costeño music came with the arrival of Lucho Bermúdez and his Orquesta del Caribe, playing porros. According to Bermúdez's biographers, he was invited to inaugurate a new night club, El Metropolitan, in the basement of a building in the city center. As usual in the accounts based on oral histories, dates vary, but this seems to have been in 1944. This was the first time live porros, gaitas, and cumbias had been played in Bogotá by a Costeño orchestra. The band members soon tired of the cold of Bogotá: they returned to Cartagena, accompanied by Lucho's wife and child, who had come along, leaving Bermúdez on his own and announcing the effective end of the Orquesta del Caribe.

This marked an important transition for Bermúdez. His old Costeño musicians—a number of them more or less "black"—were gone. From now on, Bermúdez began to collect around him musicians from the interior—much "whiter" in appearance, from higher-status social backgrounds, and schooled in classical music and styles of the interior. Bermúdez also began to look to more international horizons.

Meanwhile, his marriage to Leda Montes, a woman from his hometown, dissolved.

On his own in Bogotá, Bermúdez found work with the city's radio stations and in 1944 in the studios of Radio Nacional, he met Matilde Díaz, the woman who was to become his second wife and the orchestra's star singer (fig. 5.1). Born in 1924 in a small town in the southern province of Tolima, Díaz learned to sing and play bambucos and pasillos there with her family; she also grew up listening to Mexican rancheras and tangos. She recalled that she first heard something "happy, sort of similar to Costeño music, in Emilio Sierra's rumbas criollas." However, when the family moved to Bogotá to give her and her sister an opportunity as Las Hermanas Díaz, she was taken under the wing of Emilio Murillo, the famous exponent of bambuco. With him, she sang only pasillos and bambucos on the radio programs which he arranged for the sisters. "He never let me learn [anything else]. He said, 'You're never going to sing foreign music—nothing, not boleros, nothing but Colombian music.' And we listened to him. But he died in '42 and that was when Lucho Bermúdez arrived." For Murillo, then, Costeño music was "foreign." After her sister married, Díaz met Lucho while working at the Radio Nacional. She sang with his orchestra a few times in El Metropolitan nightclub, before joining fulltime in 1945. Soon after, they married (interview with Matilde Díaz; see also the sources cited for the biography of Lucho Bermúdez in chapter 4, especially Arteaga [1991] and Portaccio [1997: 67]).

In 1946 Lucho and Matilde made an important trip to Buenos Aires to record with RCA Victor. Again, Lucho was playing his music outside the context of his Costeño orchestra—this time with Argentinean musicians such as Eduardo Armani and Eugenio Nóbile, who adopted Costeño music with enthusiasm. On their return from Buenos Aires, Lucho and Matilde joined Orquesta Ritmo, directed by the saxophone player Alex Tovar and the house band of the Hotel Granada, the smartest night spot in Bogotá. In 1947, the band began to appear as the Orquesta de Lucho Bermúdez. Its principal players were all from the interior of the country.

Alex Tovar himself had been a soloist with the Berlin Symphony Orchestra and was a member of Efraín Orozco's band when he met Bermúdez in 1946. As an illustration of his background and of the changing musical tastes of the time, it is interesting to examine his celebrated 1948 song "Pachito Eché," dedicated to Hotel Granada manager Francisco Echeverri, which was an international hit and one of the

5.1 Lucho Bermúdez (*far right at the back*) and his orchestra, with Matilde Díaz on vocals. (By permission of El Espectador.)

first big successes for Barranquilla's Discos Tropical. (It was later covered by the king of mambo, Pérez Prado, with the Cuban Beny Moré on vocals.) Tovar arranged it first as a bambuco, but in view of a tepid reception by the hotel's clientele, he rearranged it as a more danceable *son paisa* (paisa is the colloquial term for Antioqueño). The reign of bambuco was already virtually over as jazz bands all over Colombia either heated it up or abandoned it for rumbas, guarachas, and porros.[19]

Another saxophone player who joined Bermúdez and Tovar was Gabriel Uribe, son of one of the Uribe brothers who had recorded bambucos with Emilio Murillo in New York in 1910. Finally, Bermúdez contracted bassist Luis Uribe Bueno.[20] Uribe's own speciality was bambucos and pasillos—with which he later won the national music competition four times between 1948 and 1952—but he was also playing with local jazz bands in Bogotá at the time. He was an important figure in Lucho's new orchestra, directing the band on some occasions, until he left in 1952.

With these players in his orchestra, Lucho went to Medellín in 1948 with contracts to appear on La Voz de Antioquia and at the Hotel Nutibara, premier radio and nightlife venues. Bermúdez now had a band staffed mainly by musicians from the interior, formally trained and weaned on bambucos and pasillos. He was also a raging success.

Other important Costeño musicians in Bogotá at this time included the trumpeter Antonio María Peñaloza and composer and singer José Barros, both of whom I mentioned the previous chapter. Peñaloza, who would go on to be an influential arranger in the 1950s, had arrived in Bogotá in about 1940 and landed a job with the resident orchestra of the Emisora Nueva Granada, which also included Alex Tovar and Gabriel Uribe. Although he was not directing his own orchestra in Bogotá, as was Bermúdez, he was also integrated into musical contexts that were defined by people such as Tovar, Uribe, and Francisco Cristancho, the director of the Nueva Granada Orquesta, who had been a member of Morales Pino's classic estudiantina and composer of the famous bambuco "Bochica."

José Barros (fig. 5.2), a singer and composer born in 1915 in El Banco, in the Mompox area of La Costa, was another who headed for the interior of the country in search of his fortune. After taking a prominent role in the early Fuentes recordings, he arrived in Bogotá in the mid-1940s and sang with various orchestras there, learning music from Luis Uribe Bueno, Bermúdez's bass player. He also obtained a recording contract with Jaime Glottman, the RCA Victor agent. His

5.2 José Barros (*front center*) in 1942, when he directed Los Trovadores de Barú. (By permission of El Espectador.)

classic song "El Gallo Tuerto" (The One-Eyed Cock) was recorded
first by the Orquesta Garavito with Barros on vocals and covered later
by many others. Barros also worked in Medellín, recording other
perennials such as "Mompoxina" (Mompox Woman) and, most famous, "La Piragua" (The Canoe).[21] Like Bermúdez, then, Costeño musicians such as Peñaloza and Barros interacted with a wide range of
musicians from the interior, often the same individuals, both learning
from them and opening opportunities for them.

Costeño music did not infiltrate only in the medium of orchestras.
The Trío Los Romanceros, for example, left Barranquilla in 1945,
looking for better work opportunities. They boarded a Magdalena
riverboat and, playing *en route* for food and tips—all the steamers had
live and recorded music for their passengers—they arrived in Medellín, where they found work in La Voz de Antioquia radio station.
Recalling that time, Alberto González, one of the trio, remembered
that were no manifestations of Costeño music at the time: "It was as
pure as this photo shows [he showed a photograph of him singing
with an estudiantina]. They even put ponchos on us and gave us bambucos and pasillos so we could sing them too." The trio's main strength
was boleros, but they also played porros and other Costeño styles;
González also sang with an orchestra from time to time. As well as radio stations, they played in social clubs and at private parties for
middle-class families and the elite (including those given by the president, Mariano Ospina Pérez); serenading was also a source of work.
This gives a feeling for the tremendous eclecticism of the musical scene:
although boleros were their forte, these working guitarists played anything and everything to a very wide range of people.

Radio was, of course, a vital medium for the diffusion of Costeño
music. As I showed in the last chapter, radio stations in the interior
were just behind the pioneers in Barranquilla. The programming of
these stations was similar to their counterparts in La Costa in the
1930s: records and live bands playing fox-trots, pasillos, bambucos,
boleros, and other Cuban styles, with a good measure of Mexican
songs and Argentinean tangos; the recorded material was still filtered
through the international Latin American music recording industry
based chiefly in New York. In the 1940s, as the oral testimonies above
show, this picture retained a good deal of its shape. However, Costeño musicians were also playing in stations in Bogotá and Medellín.
Records from Discos Fuentes and Discos Tropical were also getting
through, although this seems to have happened toward the end of the

decade, when advertisements for their products first appear in the Bogotá press.[22]

An important venue for Costeño music was special programs dedicated to these styles. In 1942, La Hora Costeña (The Costeño Hour) was started on La Voz de la Víctor by Costeño migrants to Bogotá Enrique Ariza, a law student, and Pascual del Vecchio.[23] It began as a half hour on Sundays and soon expanded to a longer slot, playing records and presenting live artists such as Lucho Bermúdez, Matilde Díaz, and Carmencita Pernett. The program lasted well into the 1950s.[24] Meanwhile, in 1949 Medellín's Emisora Claridad started its own Sunday morning Hora Costeña, presented by Eduardo Villa Alba, a Costeño disc jockey, who received records direct from Discos Fuentes. (His show was still running in 1995 on La Voz de las Américas.)

In these shows, airtime was also given to Costeño artists who did not travel to the interior of the country to play live. Pacho Galán, for example, seldom ventured out of Barranquilla, but his records were available for radio stations to play.[25] Another important figure here was Guillermo Buitrago, who died in 1949 after a recording career of only a few years. His guitar-based vallenato music became popular in Medellín in the late 1940s and 1950s, as did that of Julio Bovea, his contemporary, although the latter also played live in Bogotá and Medellín, including the elite clubs.[26]

Accordion music was relatively rare in the 1940s in the interior, although records by artists such as Abel Antonio Villa and José María Peñaranda were available late in the decade.[27] Tellingly, one of the first accordion groups to become known in the interior was made up of Bogotano musicians: Julio Torres y Sus Alegres Vallenatos. This band, playing with a mixed lineup of accordion and guitars, had a big hit in 1950 with a merengue called "Los Camarones" (The Prawns), recorded by a new Bogotá record label, Discos Vergara. Torres himself had never been to La Costa, although his song referred to themes of sea and sand; when he visited Cartagena not long after his success, he drowned in the sea! (See *Semana,* 30 December 1950, p. 26; see also Ponce Vega 1994.) Vallenato music from La Costa thus made its first impact via the guitars of Buitrago and Bovea or the guitar and accordion lineup of a Bogotá band: in any case, all these musicians were light skinned.

One of the first Costeño accordion players to perform live in Bogotá was Fermín Pitre (b. 1910), taken there in May 1952 by the black Costeño writer Manuel Zapata Olivella, who had studied medicine in the capital and was involved in local intellectual and artistic circles. Pitre played alongside conjuntos of traditional Costeño flute and drum players and a group from the old maroon community Palenque de San Basilio, so the context was explicitly a "folkloric" presentation of traditional Costeño music and, with the San Basilio group present, clearly "black" (García Márquez 1981: 599; Quiroz Otero 1982: 114). On the one hand, accordion music might occasionally succeed in the hands of musicians from the interior mixing it with guitars; on the other, it was eminently folkloric.

The general picture, then, was of a growing number of key Costeño musicians in Bogotá and Medellín, working closely with musicians whose experience was generally in musical styles of the interior and perhaps in classical music. These musicians and radio stations and night spots were all beginning to experiment with presenting Costeño styles to audiences of the interior. The principal Costeño style—at least in terms of the labels that were used at the time—was porro, with related styles such as gaita, fandango, and mapalé also present; cumbias were not very common at this time. There were also the paseos, merengues, and sones vallenatos usually played on guitars and occasionally accordions; the orchestras might also play the odd merengue. In any case, Costeño music would be mixed with other styles: a Lucho Bermúdez gig would include boleros, paso dobles, and North American jazz alongside porros. The big Costeño-led orchestras played mainly in elite venues, but Costeño music itself was widely accessible through radio and records. Nevertheless, the big band sound had something of an upper-class image, while the songs of Buitrago were more "popular," in the Latin American sense of the word.

The racial identity of the Costeños was varied. Lucho Bermúdez was identifiable as light mestizo; Barros was rather darker and might be identified as mestizo or, by some, as *moreno* (literally, brown, a common euphemism for a "black" person in Colombia); Peñaloza could be easily identified as moreno or perhaps even black to a Bogotá resident. There were occasional more definitely black figures: the singer Luis Carlos "El Negro" Meyer, born in Barranquilla in 1920 to a poor domestic servant, and El Negrito Jack, singer and percussionist, who played Costeño and Cuban music with various orchestras and bands in Barranquilla, Bogotá, and Medellín.[28] The orchestras the Costeños played in were generally white or light-skinned mestizo: people such as Matilde Díaz, Luis Uribe Bueno, Alex Tovar, and Gabriel Uribe were all white in Colombian terms. Lucho Bermúdez's orchestra had a black drummer, Manuel Gómez, at this early stage, but would not have a black or dark-skinned singer until the mid-1950s (Bobby Ruiz) and 1960s (Henry Castro). The variety of possible racial identifications that was typical of Costeños and Costeño music was thus set in an overall context of whiteness which still maintained a certain racial ambiguity: blackness was usually not very evident, but its shadow or possibility was always there, especially in the rhythm section.

Costeño Music: Reaction and Counterreaction

EARLY REACTIONS TO COSTEÑO MUSIC

Despite the success of Costeño music in penetrating the consciousness of the audiences of the interior of the country and the success of artists such as Lucho Bermúdez in winning entry into elite entertainment circles, not all reaction was favorable—some was actively hostile—and there was some controversy about porro, seen as the main style of Costeño music.

The Radio Nacional, founded in 1940 as the state radio station, concentrated on providing what was seen as "cultured" material with the aim of improving the minds of the masses. There were plenty of classical music, news, drama, and educational programs. The station was not averse to some popular music, but still maintained its own standards. In 1940, *El Tiempo* carried an article about the new radio station, in which the author said:

> Do you want to listen to all kinds of music? Orchestras, artists, estudiantinas are all there [on the Radio Nacional]. Do you want to dance? There are several hours of jazz. Are you an idiot? Look for vulgar and stupid records on another station. Our people, our lovely people who adore "Tú Ya No Soplas" [Mexican corrido] and who do not get beyond "Vereda Tropical" [Mexican bolero] and "Perfidia" [Mexican bolero] and "El Vacilón," do not realize that on this station there are hours of great chamber music conducted by the master Espinosa, *música brillante* [light music], a marvelous string quartet, several hours of jazz-band, traditional music by [Alejandro] Wills. . . . Because the mission of an educational radio station is to purify the tastes of the public, ennobling the artistic senses, [and] improving judgment, by means of high-level programs about music, art, literature, history, religion, sport, and science. (*El Tiempo*, 18 March 1940, p. 13)[29]

There is no mention here of Costeño music, but the condescending attitude toward popular Mexican hits contrasts with the explicit acceptance of North American "jazz" and, of course, bambucos and pasillos.

The class references are very selective, because boleros were listened to by the elite as well as other classes, just as U.S. music crossed class boundaries, but the complex musical scene is being ideologically read from a particular class perspective here, linking North American films and music with the middle classes and elite, while Mexican films and music were associated with "the people." The Radio Nacional did not program Costeño music at this time: the program of "popular Colombian music" scheduled for Tuesday afternoon on 2 March 1940 included only pasillos, bambucos, and a guabina (*El Tiempo*, 2 March 1940, p. 2).

Of course, 1940 was rather early for Costeño music to have made an impact, but as late as 1961 the Radio Nacional's program bulletin saw fit to publish the text of a talk entitled "The Musical Folklore of Colombia," given by Daniel Zamudio on the occasion of the first Congress of Music in Ibagué in January 1936. Zamudio, a composer and musicologist, thought that the Africans "came with their music which, mixed with Spanish music, has given us a hybrid and harmful product." The rumba belongs, in his view, "to black music and is a faithful translation of the sentimental primitivism of African blacks." In fact, he said, "this music, which does not deserve the title, is simian." He lamented that "the rumba and its derivatives, porros, sons, boleros, are displacing our traditional autochthonous airs, taking a favored place in social dances and salons" and added that "although this is not of great importance from the artistic and aesthetic point of view, it is none the less certain that a process of purification is taking place which, if it is too late, will give rise to a *new confusion,* since 'fashion' may ruin the little truly genuine that we have." Black Colombians he sees as potentially useful since "culturally speaking, there is the possibility of *desrumbarlos* [de-rumba-izing them] despite their atavism" since, as negro spirituals demonstrated "the black race has valuable musical representatives at the level of higher sentiments" (Zamudio 1961: pt. 1, p. 1; pt. 4, p. 77). In this racist diatribe, Costeño music is lumped together with Cuban music as foreign, black, and threatening to national identity.

Some writers in the press took a similar line. One piece titled "Christmas and Nationalism" bemoaned the "foreign" influences evident at Christmastime and defended older customs: "The manger, the Christmas carols, the music, the Christmas gifts, and all the traditional motifs have been forgotten. An explosive African-sounding orchestra now threatens festivities from which the feeling and simplicity typical of previous celebrations are absent" (*El Tiempo*, 12 December 1940,

p. 5). Here the author is likely to be referring to a variety of musical styles — Cuban, Mexican, rumba criolla, perhaps North American jazz too — but foreignness is equated with Africanness, and hence blackness, and is set up as an inclusive emblem in opposition to an unidentified traditional purity which is implicitly located with the writer in the interior of the country.

Under the pen name Trivio, another writer addressed the theme of "the sweet music of porro" in satirical style:

> From a purely personal point of view, a concert given by a cow being dragged by the nose, three canaries, a broken can being beaten with a broomstick, and an idiot selling alcohol would be more harmonious than the sublime harmonies thrown out or extracted from a musical group in the midst of proclaiming to the world that Santa Marta has a train [the title of a porro], that Cartagena has no mountains, and that "eeeeepa" and that "eeeeeepa" and that "daaaaale compareeee" [shouts typical in Costeño music] and so forth.[30]
>
> In a porro orchestra there are usually only three types of instrument: the clarinet, the drums, and a black man howling.

The dancers were no better in his view, since they move with the grace of "a sausage suspended on a string, supposing that the string in question were attached to the tail of a dog chasing a cat." When the dance has finished "the couples exhausted by the contortions, the shoves, the death-defying leaps, and the crazy races they have executed, immediately ask for it to be repeated" (*El Tiempo,* 23 October 1943, p. 5). Notable here is the identification of the music with blackness and the constant animal imagery. The overall impression is one of lack of measure, lack of control, excessiveness of bodily movement, noise, and emotion.[31] Something similar can be seen in a characterization of the Pacific coastal currulao penned by the anonymous "H.M.G.": "it is the most genuine manifestation of Pacific *negrería* [typical black behavior]. Euphoria, madness, human overflowings, sobs, and howls are its constitutive elements" (*El Tiempo,* 4 November 1946, p. 5). One is reminded of Carreño's manual on urbanity and good manners (see chapter 2), which stated: "In order to please God . . . and to be good citizens . . . we must dedicate our whole existence . . . to establishing in our hearts the gentle empire of *continence*" (cited in Quintero Rivera 1996: 162). As Quintero Rivera argues, manners were fundamental to establishing class hierarchy and were somatized so that they inhered in the body itself. When class had racial connotations, manners, or the lack of them, could be seen as natural characteristics.

All this is clearer still in a 1944 article entitled "Civilization of Color." José Gers commented that "modernism requires this: that we should dance like blacks in order to be in fashion and in line with the tastes of the latest people"; the culture best received "is that which has the acrid smell of jungle and sex." According to him,

> the blacks have decided to avenge themselves of the bitter fate they bear on their shoulders [i.e., slavery] . . . and the attack is advancing against what the previous masters held most dear—against their art. . . . Pairs of blonds must dance with effusive movements of the belly, jerks, contortions, leaps, and savage shouts. The Versailles waltz is dead. The dancer and his partner must jump, swivel their eyes while raising one leg, move their hips in lewd gyrations, cross their eyes, and spread their legs like frogs. . . . Meanwhile, the drums beat, the gentlemen of the orchestra screech with a tragic fury, as if they were seasoning a joyful picnic of some "mister" [i.e., a white boss] in a jungle in Oceania. (The Bogotá weekly *Sábado*, 3 June 1944, p. 13) [32]

Again, Costeño music is identified as foreign, black, immoderate, and vulgar; it is also explicitly linked to sexual license. But it is also very modern, or more precisely, part of the artistic currents of modernism which had become popular in North America and Europe and which often included an element of primitivism (see chapter 1). This modernism was making itself felt in Colombia partly through Costeño music, although other literary and artistic trends coming out of La Costa were also important (see below). The seemingly odd reference to Oceania by Gers is explicable in this context. In European primitivist art circles, Oceania was an important source of imagery, and, for Gers, it makes as much sense to mention a jungle in Oceania as one in Africa.

Making what was, for this type of commentary, an unusual connection between culture and politics, Gers went on to say that "the blacks have also intervened in politics, to which they have brought the red [i.e., Liberal] belligerence of their intrepid aggression. They occupy parliament and they confront and impose themselves on the ancient masters." Gers was writing in 1944 during a period of Liberal hegemony (1930–1946) which had superseded three decades of Conservative rule and had seen President Alfonso López Pumarejo's "Revolution on the Move" program of reform (1934–1938). Both the Atlantic and Pacific coastal regions were traditional Liberal strongholds—and López's mother came from Valledupar—so it is possible that this sparked Gers's observation. [33] Gers—clearly a conservative—wove together the overthrow of traditional political hierarchies, cultural upheaval, and moral decline, all symbolized by Costeño music and blackness.

In 1947, the controversy continued with a spate of letters in *Semana*, the Bogotá-based national weekly, sparked by a letter from one Fabio Londoño Cárdenas of Medellín in which he accused Costeño music of being "noisy and strident rhythms, manifestations of the savagery and brutishness of the Costeños and Caribbeans, savage and backward peoples." In subsequent weeks Costeños wrote defending their music (see below), but Londoño was unrepentant and replied "porros, bundes, paseos (what paseos!), etc., are not music, nor do they have any rhythm, they are savage and deafening noises, and they express neither feelings, nor sadness, nor longings, nor happiness (although they may express an orgiastic and bacchanalian happiness), rather on the contrary these airs imitate very well the racket made in the jungle or the forest by a pack of monkeys, parrots, or other wild animals." The following week, the editors closed the debate with a final letter from another Antioqueño who wrote: "Porros are indeed a manifestation of culture. Of the culture that Costeños have (I do not refer to Rafael Núñez). And I will not be more explicit for fear of offending against morality. With regard to my compatriot [Fabio Londoño], I am Antioqueño, I do not know why he insists on saying that Africans are black [i.e., on stating the obvious]." Rafael Núñez, a Costeño, was also a national political hero, and the writer wanted to avoid tarring him with the same brush as he did the Costeños with the implication that their culture was immoral. The spurious use of the African image to make his final point—that porro was evidently "savage"—was hardly accidental (*Semana*, letters section, 15 November 1947; 6 December 1947; 13 December 1947).[34]

In 1947, an unsigned piece in *El Tiempo* (7 December 1947, p. 5) commented on these debates over porro and noted excesses on each side, with one critic having been "unequivocally unjust" to porro while its defenders gave the impression that Lucho Bermúdez should have been baptized Ludwig van Bermúdez! The writer admired the Costeños' stalwart defense of their music and noted its success in other countries, but asked: "would it not be advisable to civilize it a little, to lighten all that—and it is a lot—which evidently makes it painful to the ears of those who are not accustomed to it?" He advised composers to limit their inspirations to the music and leave lyrics aside, since there had been "truly inadmissible excesses" in that area: he cited a couple of songs that referred to pigs and the tastiness of pork and added: "Anyone can recognize that these are things that cannot be said, much less sung, in an elegant place." Again, porro is seen as crude and vulgar and is associated with animals.

Agustín Nieto Caballero penned a long piece on modern dancing, which, for him, lacked decorum and propriety. He gave a long description of people "gesticulating" and going through "odd contortions" which seemed to him more like "an attack of epilepsy" than anything else, noting that "it is not necessary, and indeed may be an inconvenience, to be of sound mind" when dancing in this way. In one sense, this could be seen as simply a stuffy old conservative patronizing new styles which appear to him ridiculous—a familiar enough story. Interestingly, however, he made constant connections between these "modern" dances and blacks. Thus, mambo (which had been popularized by the Cuban Dámaso Pérez Prado at about this time) was, according to an "erudite ethnologist" of his acquaintance, derived from a war dance in Mozambique. Nieto referred to "the craziness of African dances" and linked merengue and fandango to the rhythm which arrived from Africa "with that strange and soporific cadence which only the blacks possess." The dances, he guessed, "must be like the parties in the Congo." Finally he recounted how, when a female companion had said to him that these dances were "real folklore" and that everything else was "foreign," "a black man [*un negrito*]" who overheard the sentiment "showed his teeth in a broad smile of satisfaction on noticing, doubtless, how distant Africa had made itself so intimately our own" (*El Tiempo,* 16 November 1952). It was about this time that Miguel Angel Builes, an Antioqueño archbishop, condemned the mambo as a mortal sin and said that "porro, rumba, *la americana* [?], and other dances are evil due to the very grave danger of sin that they contain" (cited in Betancur Alvarez 1993: 289).[35]

COUNTERREACTIONS

These derogatory, satirical, and often racist commentaries did not go unchecked by Costeño intellectuals and were not subscribed to by all the Bogotá intelligentsia. Gilard (1986, 1994) looks briefly at some of this process, focusing on the Costeño intellectuals Antonio Brugés Carmona, Manuel Zapata Olivella, and Gabriel García Márquez. Gilard argues that improving communications and greater internal and external migrations brought a crisis in ideas about Colombian identity, based until then on creole elites' insistence that Colombia "would be indistinguishable from Europe if it were not for a supplementary dose of identity added in their struggle for independence." I showed in chap-

ter 2 that elites were not, in fact, as "allergic to the concept of mestizaje" as Gilard makes out, but I think he is right to observe that
changes in identity were taking place, spurred by the "discovery" that
the "Atlantic coast was an integral part of the Caribbean world" (Gilard 1986: 41).

Gilard argues that this uncomfortable fact was initially admitted
through a sort of literary *negrismo* (*négritude*) which presented romantic images of blacks' suffering and pain, often linked to slavery—
an institution by then, of course, apparently well in the past.[36] This can
be seen in the context of the *afrocubanismo* which developed in Cuba
between 1920 and 1940, itself partly a response to the aesthetic primitivism popular in Europe and the United States (Moore 1997: 3).

Gilard cites what he sees as the "very conventional *negrismo*" of the
Costeño poet Jorge Artel (1909–1994), whose major work, *Tambores
en la noche* (Drums in the Night), was published in 1940 (on Artel, see
Prescott 1985b). Eduardo Carranza, a well-known poet of the 1930s
and 1940s who was interested in adopting the vernacular into his poetry, wrote of Artel: "Artel carries the singing voice of the dark race
which, on the shores of our seas, in the dramatic loneliness of the jungles, and along the banks of our immense and mysterious rivers,
dreams and suffers, loves and labors, contributing with its dark blood
to the complete integration of our nationality" (Carranza 1944). Artel's poems make frequent reference to music and dancing, and Carranza comments that in Artel's "torrid world" mulatto women dance
"while in the shadows the drums and accordions play and the tame, re-
signed pain of the shadowy race slips by." Another commentator was
less optimistic about "integration." José Camacho Carreño thought
that the African and Spanish elements in Artel's work, and indeed in
the poet himself, were not fused, but simply juxtaposed and clearly
separable. Camacho Carreño talked of the African in terms of eroticism, lasciviousness, and the melancholy heritage of slavery; in contrast, Spanish elements were seen as clean and harmonious (*El Tiempo*, 4 March 1940, p. 4). While today's commentators may see
Artel's poetry as "an early exception to the flight towards whiteness
which was adopted [by many blacks] in Colombia" (Friedemann
1984: 533), contemporary intellectuals in Bogotá clearly took a more
paternalist stance—which nevertheless sometimes admitted elements
of a romanticized blackness more positively into ideas about Colombian national identity.

In Gilard's view, when it came to music, the Bogotá intellectuals
were less enthusiastic, and he cites the contribution by José Gers,

quoted above. But there were also more measured responses. Gilard (1986: 44) mentions two Bogotano intellectuals who took a more open-minded view of Costeño music, and it is worth delving into their writings in more detail than Gilard has space to present. One was Enrique Pérez Arbelaez, geographer, botanist, and priest, who, in *El Tiempo*'s monthly magazine, described the people and culture of Magdalena Province, where he owned a house and had spent a good deal of time. It was, in his view, an isolated area with "a musical, happy, and easy-going people who have their own literature [i.e., oral traditions, stories, poetry, music] . . . which deserves wider recognition because it reveals a particular mentality and because its forms are rooted in the distant depths of our nationality." He admired the sincerity of the Costeño, who "knows no fiction [i.e., lies] and does not adopt postures of solemnity, of reserve, or false circumspection." This made the Costeños "the only Colombian group on which *naturalidad* [naturalness, spontaneity] blows, from childhood, from all sides" (Pérez Arbelaez 1945: 378; see also Pérez Arbelaez 1952). This idea of natural, easygoing, unhypocritical sincerity is still a powerful element in perceptions of La Costa, whether by Costeños or others, especially when contrasted with the highland interior, where nature (seen as "truth") is often said to be covered up by layers of artifice and mannerisms, just as people's bodies are spoken of as covered by layers of clothing against the cold.

Gilard's second "cachaco" defender of Costeño culture is Octavio Quiñones Pardo, who, writing in the same magazine, noted that "porro has had more challengers than promoters in these romantic lands of the altiplano," due to a difference in temperament. Costeños had "the sensual happiness of rumba" which they injected into everything: "Costeño cumbia takes hold of the blood of its musicians—like porro—and, making it bubble, brightens life with offers of pleasure." In contrast, "the bambucos and torbellinos of the altiplano take hold of the heart and, by possessing it, embellish the melancholic landscape of our existence." Costeño music had a definite "Afro-Antillean" influence and was full of sensuality: "cumbia bites the flesh with the passion of a woman fired by desire; cumbia is desire made into flames." One should not, in his view, write diatribes against porro, but instead seek to understand it. However, this involved a reflective, not an emotive, sympathy: the idea was to "contemplate, from on high, the joyful manifestations of another's emotion" (Quiñones Pardo 1948: 83, 85). Interestingly, these commentators barely mention blackness, and instead there is a greater emphasis on naturalness, happiness, sensuality, and sexual pleasure. These qualities are seen as positive and part of a varied Colombian identity, although only, perhaps, to be viewed "from on high." Quiñones Pardo, for all his lascivious delight in the cumbia, could not publicly recommend that all Colombia's good citizens indulge in it.

There were other such voices. For example, *Semana* published an issue in 1949 with Lucho Bermúdez taking pride of place on the front cover. A long article dedicated mainly to Bermúdez also explained aspects of Costeño music to its readers, noting that porro is "currently the most popular of the festive airs of Colombia," but that "many people in the interior maintain that it is the noisiest, and some that it is the most vulgar": none however denied its *alegría* (happiness, gaiety). The reasons for its victory over bambuco and other styles of interior were, according to the article, its sensual undercurrent, the public's snobbish desire for new rhythms, the orchestral arrangements (which bambucos did not have), the presence of a Costeño colony in the interior, and the lack of active composers of bambucos. It ended with the hope that "the characteristic airs of the different regions of Colombia may achieve in the not too distant future something like a musical synthesis . . . a certain artistic unity." Certain musical styles needed to be "nationalized" in order to be widely accepted (*Semana*, 1 January 1949: 24–27; also reproduced in *Semana*, 3 May 1994: 72–76).

Semana also published an article on Julio Torres, the leader of the vallenato group from the interior which had had a hit with "Los Camarones." According to this, music was "one of the means by which national sentiment is expressed." Moreover: "to despise the importance of popular music . . . is a critical absurdity. To exalt so-called classical music as suitable for the people and cultured minorities, is another sociological error. Art music does not have to forcibly exclude popular music, nor vice versa" (*Semana*, 30 December 1950; cited in Ponce Vega 1994). Absent from both these pieces is any mention of blackness, while the only mention of eroticism is the idea that Costeño music has an "underlying sensuality"; instead, the "happiness" of the music is emphasized. Nevertheless, the suggestion that music needed to be "nationalized" implies a process of refinement.

Costeños themselves often defended the music of their region. The reactions in the letters pages of *Semana* to the contribution by Fabio Londoño Cárdenas, cited above, bristled with indignation at the Antioqueño's slights, which, in the eyes of one correspondent, betrayed a belief that "Medellín is the only Colombian city which deserves the epithet of civilized." Other writers invited Londoño to visit La Costa, where, one noted, the minister of labor, also an Antioqueño, had himself recently danced porro in the Club Cartagena. One letter defended porro as the "authentic expression of the euphoria of a healthy and optimistic people" (*Semana,* letters section, 15 November 1947; 6 December 1947; 13 December 1947).

Costeño intellectuals also took up the challenge, without necessarily escaping from characterizations of Costeño culture that fitted with some of the negative depictions. To some extent, their statements reflected the modernist primitivism that had become successful in preceding decades in North America, Europe, and some countries of Latin America (see Barkan 1995; Franco 1967; Honour 1989; Kuper 1988; Rhodes 1994; and Torgovnick 1990; on Cuba see Moore 1997). They defended Costeño culture—without necessarily being explicit about blackness—but they also saw it as natural, spontaneous, sensual, and earthy.

Antonio Brugés Carmona (1911–1956), a lawyer, journalist, and politician from Santa Ana, Magdalena Province, wrote a series of articles in *El Tiempo* and *Sábado* which were somewhat whimsical descriptions of characters, musical styles, and events from La Costa. In 1943, he described how porro was born from the traditional music of La Costa: "since it [porro] was of the same family as cumbia, under the hot and brilliant nights in which cumbia was danced, the younger son appeared in the circle [of dancers] lit by madness, bringing new rhythms to the monotonous rejoicings of cumbia. . . . The cumbia circle became less random and more regular, with more ordered happiness . . . [porro] took over the festivities and finally went beyond the borders of its predecessors, becoming not Costeño but Colombian." Porro had been so successful because it captured a variety of influences, while being at the same time definitively Colombian. Sexually speaking, it was "the song of the liberated Costeño man who shows to anyone who observes him a boastful demonstration of Dionysian joy in the face of life." Porro "exalts happiness [and] laughs at those who do not know how to enjoy themselves" (Brugés Carmona 1943). Another description of porro talked of "the drummer [and] his mulatto and lascivious music" which "expresses the vital happiness of the people who produce it" (Brugés Carmona 1945).

In a later article describing the fates of Frenchmen who had ventured into the Costeño hinterland, Brugés Carmona focused on one who had settled there: "The jungle, with its invisible tentacles, drew him in, bit by bit. . . . He learned the simple musical airs of the Sinú [a zone toward the west of La Costa] and enjoyed the tenderness of a

pretty mulatto woman, to the sound of the native drums. . . . He became drunk with the tasty fermented liquor of the tropical environment" (Brugés Carmona 1949).

These depictions, while generally positive about Costeño music, are
also filled with images of La Costa and Costeño culture as enticingly
sensuous, sexual, and *alegre*. Brugés Carmona was not aggressive, or
even really defensive, in his accounts of Costeño culture, which, as Gilard points out (1986, 1994), tended to be harnessed to the folkloric
and picturesque. Only once did he take a more forthright stand, when
in 1946 he protested that Costeño music was being excluded from the
National Music Competition by the judging panel which "admits as
national music only bambuco, guabina, and other airs of the interior
of the republic, excluding all those from the Atlantic littoral which are
thought to have Antillean and negroid influences" (Brugés Carmona
1946).

Manuel Zapata Olivella, being black himself, has tended to defend
blacks in general as well as La Costa as a region. He was more active
than Brugés Carmona, taking Costeño musicians to Bogotá, doing
many investigations of traditional Costeño culture, and writing many
novels, his first being published in 1947. This is not the place to review
Zapata Olivella's extensive oeuvre of fiction and nonfiction, but some
basic tendencies in his position are worth outlining. On the one hand,
Zapata Olivella has been very influential in drawing attention to black
people and culture in Colombia and to problems of racism. On the
other hand, there is in his work an attachment to mestizaje—a mestizaje ideally undifferentiated by hierarchies of color, ancestry, or cultural tradition—as the basis for a uniting identity for Colombia. Another feature has been his treatment of black, and Costeño, culture
within the framework of "folklore" (or sometimes in his novels in
terms of what was later known as magical realism). Thus, his early presentations of Costeño music in Bogotá circles explicitly identified this
music as pure and folkloric, juxtaposing and interweaving images of
Costeño culture, blackness, music, and traditionality for the intelligentsia of the interior. Later, he founded the Colombian Foundation
for Folkloric Investigations as a vehicle for studying black culture. His
ideal of a democratic form of mestizaje was thus somewhat at odds
with the inclusion of blackness in a way which tended to reinforce for
people of the interior the image of alterity which surrounded it.[37]

Gabriel García Márquez is possibly the most crucial figure in the resignification of La Costa in the Colombian landscape, if only because
of his international success. Again, this is not the place to discuss his

work as a whole, which has been the object of extensive critical treatment. His importance in the context of my argument is that he defended images of Costeño culture and he publicized and valorized the early vallenato music that was being recorded—the more "authentic" the better, as far as he was concerned. Gilard (1986) argues that García Márquez broke the narrow bounds within which Zapata Olivella confined himself and embraced the effervescence of modern popular culture, especially in its Costeño and Caribbean forms, being altogether less concerned with defending tradition and cultural purity. This was undoubtedly evident in his early journalism when in 1951 he endorsed the new fashion for mambo and laughed at the absurd calls for the excommunication of Dámaso Pérez Prado (García Márquez 1981: 449, 508, 539). But these pieces were alongside others in which he praised Zapata Olivella for organizing the presentations of Costeño music in Bogotá and wrote approvingly of what he saw as the most authentic accordion music. Thus, as early as 1948, in a piece on the accordion, he argued that "The true, legitimate accordion is that which has become a national citizen among us, in the valley of the Magdalena [River]" (García Márquez 1981: 66). In the same year, he depicted the poet Jorge Artel in cold Bogotá, but with the "musical secret of the gaita sounding in his hand . . . [and] the dawn of Cartagena in a bottle." Artel was a "black patriarch measuring the pulse of the fever in the belly of a drum," and present with him was "a fruitlike mulatta, made from the same wood as the gaitas, watching him age toward the abyss of the first nightmare" (García Márquez 1981: 94). These are images—directed in this case at a local audience, since they were published in the Cartagena daily *El Universal*—which are not far removed from those of Brugés Carmona, although this vision of La Costa has been vastly more influential in the hands of García Márquez.

García Márquez also praised Zapata Olivella's "embassy" of "folkloric music from the Atlantic littoral" in his column in Barranquilla's *El Heraldo*, to which he had moved by the early 1950s. He said that Fermín Pitre would be able to show the Bogotanos "how vallenato music is pure and our own [i.e., the Costeños'] and that the Afro-Cuban ingredients that have supposedly been found in it are the individual and deceptive product of poor artists" (García Márquez 1981: 600, 622). Other comments by García in his column suggested that, in his view, these artists included Buitrago and Bovea, or at least some of their records. Discussing whether bambuco or vallenato was superior, he noted that one would have to look at "authentic vallenato and bambuco, of course, because Guillermo Buitrago—who had a beautiful singing voice—left behind some merengues composed by him which are truly lamentable," and he added that "there is always a Bovea who sings well, but without that poetic sense . . . of Pacho Rada, Abelito Villa, and Rafael Escalona" (García Márquez 1981: 167). García Márquez also indulged in that favorite pastime of "authenticators"— the search for the real author of such-and-such a song—in this case with reference to some songs by Escalona (García Márquez 1981: 506–507; see also 178–179). At least in his early writings, then, García Márquez subscribed to a discourse of authenticity and degeneration with respect to vallenato. In this case, the degeneration was associated not only with commercialization, but with the popularization of the music in the interior, whither La Costa sent "embassies"—as if to a foreign country—to show people there what the "real thing" was like.

These writings would have had little impact in Bogotá or Medellín, since they were published at the time in local Costeño papers. When, in 1954, García Márquez moved to Bogotá to work on *El Espectador,* he also wrote about La Costa, although not extensively. Apart from one brief piece on the Barranquilla carnival—which highlights the intensity of the festivities—the pieces are early examples of magical realism, depicting an isolated area of La Costa and focusing on witchcraft, superstitions, legends, and traditional curers (García Márquez 1982, 2:108, 117, 137, 145, 161).[38] The overwhelming impression is of a strange tropical region where rationality is suspended.

García Márquez was part of the so-called Group of Barranquilla, which emerged in the late 1940s. This group of writers and journalists to some extent owes its recognition as a group to García Márquez's later preeminence, but it was also important in its own right as a channel for literary modernism in Colombia. Formed under the wing of Barranquilla-born novelist José Felix Fuenmayor, author of *Cosme* (1927), and the Catalan Ramón Vinyes, editor of the short-lived avant-garde cultural magazine *Voces* (1917–1920), the group included people such as Alfonso Fuenmayor, Alvaro Cepeda Samudio, and Germán Vargas. Zapata Olivella socialized with these writers on occasion, and García Márquez used to meet with Rafael Escalona, who became his compadre in the early 1950s (see Bacca 1990, 1991; Bell Lemus 1981; Gilard 1991; and Williams 1991). Music was not a concern of the group as a whole, but Costeño society and culture were, and this was important for how intellectuals in the interior saw La Costa. Taking García Márquez's *Cien años de soledad* (1967)—famously defined by García Márquez himself as a 450-page vallenato—as the culmination of the work of this group, Raymond L. Williams (1991: 121) highlights the "coexistence of a conservative primary oral culture based on the rural Costa's tri-ethnic oral culture and a progressive modernity of a group of readers of modern literature." In this sense, the tension between tradition and modernity that I have described as a critical dimension for the constitution of Costeño identity was also strongly present in regional literature.

Conclusion

The irruption of Costeño music into the interior posed certain problems and opened certain possibilities for thinking about Colombian national and regional identities. For elites in Bogotá and Medellín the points of cultural orientation were located in Europe and in their own regions; these magnetic points also shaped the ideological force fields of national identity as a whole. Costeño culture, with its underlying potential of blackness, was present in these force fields and, although marginalized in some respects by elites of the interior, was also a crucial point of orientation: Costeño culture could be made to signify the backwardness, irrationality, indiscipline, and immorality against which the opposites of these qualities were defined. On the other hand, during the 1930s and 1940s, Colombia was going through a period of organized modernization and national consolidation, with industrialization and social and political reform. The 1940s and early 1950s were a period of economic growth based on high coffee prices. The elite of Barranquilla was outward looking and rather avant-garde in some respects; Costeño culture could also signify the modern, the cosmopolitan, and the new—an image many Costeños were keen to purvey. The avant-garde could also involve a certain primitivism, popular in some North American and European avant-garde circles, and again, some Costeño intellectuals were able to exploit the contradictory ways that primitivism might lend an image of modernity to their region.

Then, in 1948, the intense strife of La Violencia broke out all over the country, but with particular ferocity in the interior. La Costa seemed fairly peaceful by comparison, and this reinforced yet another possible reading of the region as one in which positive traditional community values reigned. The role of ideas of peace and violence is hard to judge, since the sources I have used barely mention La Violencia, which terrorized rural areas more than big cities. But it may be that city folk were particularly open to "happy" music at a time when their country was being ripped apart by partisan strife. While La Violencia

had a certain literary expression, it is hard to detect its impact on popular music.[39] Costeño music with its celebratory style certainly ignored
it. Perhaps the música de carrilera—deeply indebted to Mexican rancheras and Argentinean tangos, stereotypically associated with provincial cantinas of the interior regions of the country, and betraying an
obsession with ill-starred love, depression, and tragedy—is a partial
reflection of the terror and strife that tore apart Colombia's countryside in the 1950s, even though the emergence of that music predates
the worst of La Violencia. There may thus be a connection between
this provincial music of the interior regions and a more direct experience of violence, while Costeño music perhaps reflected an urban es-
capism that reveled in the economic growth of the period, turned its
back on civil strife, and looked forward to a bright new tomorrow
which was nevertheless still rooted in a peaceful, communitarian
morality.

In assessing the way Costeño music could be read as modern and/or
traditional, there was not a simple opposition between the elites of the
interior defining Costeño culture as backward and Costeño elites defining it as modern. First, the elites did not divide up simply in this way:
a few people in the interior praised Costeño culture. More importantly,
aspects of tradition in Costeño culture were harnessed to a project of
cultural modernity, and this happened both in music and literature.
Thus, Costeño "folkloric music" could be presented as "pure" and
"authentic" to Bogotá audiences, reinforcing an image of traditional
Costeño particularity and regional identity. At the same time, fragments of a mythologized Costeño history and culture could be woven
into a discourse about liberation, freedom from the restrictions of a
grey, bureaucratic rationality or a prohibitive religious morality, and
release from the reputed sombreness of Bogotá or the seriousness of life
in Medellín, centered on work and business. To borrow Daniel Bell's
terms, Costeño culture could be made to represent the experimental
critical cultural modernism which has long existed in tension with the
rationality and utilitarianism of social modernity (Bell 1976). In this
case, however, that cultural modernism was partly constructed around
elements of *traditional* openness and sexual freedom.

The image of Costeño culture as *alegre*—happy, joyful, carefree,
lighthearted, unaggressive—may conjure up ideas of triviality, and this
has certainly been one connotation, as shown by the newspaper ex-
tracts quoted above. On the other hand, I would argue that ideas about
happiness are also deeply embedded in Western concepts of modernity
and tradition. Both these concepts have been imbued with happiness

and sadness, pessimism and optimism. Tradition can be seen as the bad old days, a straitjacket of custom, ignorance, and intolerance, to be superseded by a bright, new, modern tomorrow, a liberation from hidebound views, oppressive authorities, and arbitrary violence. At the same time, tradition can be seen from a romantic perspective as a repository of solid, genuine, humane, community values, rich with sentiment, sincerity, and peacefulness, which is being corrupted by modernity, thought of as some combination of the prison of bureaucracy, the inhumanity of commercial imperatives, the glossy sham of rapidly changing appearance, and increasing violence to humankind and nature. Happiness—more broadly understood as contentment, being at one with the world and oneself—may lie in either, or both, directions, depending on one's point of view.[40]

In this sense, comments about Costeño happiness have a deeper meaning. They conjure up the possibility of the brighter tomorrow of modernity, figuratively loosening the collar and tie of a traditional, oppressive society—such as Bogotá, according to some. At the same time, they play on the possibility of the happiness brought by the frankness, sincerity, community, and peacefulness attributed to tradition, when this is seen from a more romantic standpoint.

Costeño music fitted in well here: its defining quality was its *alegría,* its happiness. In the form introduced by Lucho Bermúdez and others, it could be seen as modern not only in its jazz band or big band orchestration, but also in being a liberation, a blast of warm, sensual air in the cold climate of Bogotá or the work-obsessed atmosphere of Medellín. On the other hand, Zapata Olivella took to Bogotá accordion players from around Valledupar and black singers from Palenque de San Basilio who were representatives of an old "tradition." Not accidentally, the "modern" jazz band artists were young people, while Zapata Olivella's bearers of "tradition" were older. Also, with the eruption of La Violencia, the image of La Costa as a peaceful region could be linked to traditional community values. But music, especially happy popular music, could also be seen as simply trivial, and its happiness as the gaudy and ephemeral wrappings of modern fashion: this is why the Costeño political and even intellectual elite did not, in the majority, appropriate Costeño music as a public representation. García Márquez and Zapata Olivella may have talked and written about music, but the political elite was not very interested—at least not at this stage.

In sum, then, Costeño music could be read in very different ways. Its power lay in its ambivalence, in the multiple possibilities it presented for ideological rearticulation. It mediated ambivalently between notions of tradition and modernity. This is perhaps obvious enough, and, for example, Pacini Hernández (1995) for bachata and Austerlitz (1995) for merengue attribute much of the popularity of these styles to their bridging the divide between traditional and modern worlds. But it is important to see the ideological construction of notions of tradition and modernity, the ambivalence inherent in each term, and the dynamic way they define each other. Tradition is not just "there," it is constantly recreated in opposition to modernity: "this is the 'progress' we live by, a progress that must constantly inflate, exaggerate and create 'the old' as part of introducing 'the new'" (Wagner 1981: 67). This makes the mediating role of music more complex.

The ambivalence of Costeño music proved especially potent in a different but related realm, that of the tension between homogeneity and heterogeneity in national identity. If progress toward modernity also meant national homogenization, then tradition signified heterogeneity, but, as I have argued, homogeneity had always to be held in check, lest hierarchies of class, race, and region (not to mention gender) collapse into indistinction. In Colombia, national identity was constantly thought of in terms of mestizaje and hybridity, so the tension between difference and sameness was always acute and Costeño music clearly operated on that tension.

This was mainly through the role blackness played in Costeño music and regional identity. It was an evident part of the music, whether in the actual—but only occasional—presence of black singers, drummers, and guitarists or in the attributions of Africanness to the music and its associated dances. But it was also an ambivalent and negotiable presence. Africa was not always mentioned in relation to the music. Many of the musicians were not black, and their musical careers were linked to the musical styles of the interior and, in some cases, to classical music as well. As I have shown, many important Costeño musicians became closely connected with white musicians from the interior. In this sense, and by means of the orchestration of the styles, commercial urban Costeño music was whitened, compared to the rural or even the urban styles of La Costa.

The possible presence of blackness was, however, very important, such that whitening did not consist of simply erasing all traces of it from the music as a social practice and a cultural form. Blackness could be held to represent primitiveness, moral indiscipline, and lack of "civilized" values—but also, and by the same token, happiness and freedom from care (Wade 1993a: 245–250). Crucially, blackness also had possible connotations of potent sexuality, of freedom from the strict bonds of a pious sexual morality. I want to explore this in greater detail in a later chapter, in the context of oral testimonies and a brief look at changing gender relations, but already I have shown the clear sexual associations made with this music by observers from the interior and La Costa. A more "liberated" sexuality, while threatening to a pious morality, was also seen as more modern, especially from the point of view of the younger generation, and the supposed primitiveness of black sexuality was thus also paradoxically open to being read as modern.[41]

A third area in which Costeño music formed an ambivalent term was the tension between the national and the transnational. This period was an important one for Colombia in terms of the development of communications, including radio, the roads, and airlines. In Anderson's formulations on nationalism, improved communications facilitate the construction of national identity by allowing a common culture to be conceived, practiced, and transmitted nationally. But communications are not nationally bounded and also ease transnational identifications, thus threatening national unity. In Colombia, "foreign" influences of many kinds in the economy and popular music became geographically and socially pervasive, and, while they were valued as modern and progressive, they also they stimulated the assertion of nationalist sentiment. The same communications technologies opened the way for regional music to become more national, and, as I have shown, Costeño music was sometimes marked as "foreign," usually African or perhaps Antillean, or in need of "embassies" to promote it. In their derogatory observations, some commentators clearly thought exclusion was the right response. The articles cited from *Semana,* on the other hand, took a more inclusive stance, favoring the "nationalization" of regional musics or simply supporting popular music as a valid expression of national sentiment—both referred to Costeño music. Costeño intellectuals adopted an ambiguous position: they defended Costeño music and culture as legitimate expressions of national identity, but they also marked their difference as a specific (and even a superior) regional culture. In short, Costeño music could be read as alien, nationalizable, national, or regional, depending on the ideological project one had in mind.

There was thus a constant tension between homogeneity and heterogeneity, between sameness and difference, constituted both nationally and internationally (although these two frames were not clearly distinguishable, since, for some, elements of national culture looked "foreign"). Different people took different stances on how this tension should be resolved, but in my view, part of the success of Costeño music was the ambivalent potential it had for being read in different and contradictory ways: for being black, white, and mixed; for being traditional and modern; for being regional and national.

6 The Golden Era of Costeño Music— and After

The 1950s and much of the 1960s were the golden era of Costeño music. It competed on equal terms with the international Latin styles— mambo, guaracha, bolero, tango, rancheras—which continued to be important in the Colombian music scene. Artists such as Lucho Bermúdez were international stars, and Costeño music became *the* Colombian style, above all as dance music.

These years also saw the takeoff of the national recording industry. The early initiatives by Antonio Fuentes (fig. 6.1) in Cartagena and Emilio Fortou in Barranquilla were followed by the creation of other record companies. A few of these were in Barranquilla, but the majority were based in Medellín, with a couple in Bogotá. The capital of Antioquia, previously associated with tango and ranchera, became the capital of Costeño music. The underlying dynamic was commercial: Medellín was a powerful industrial and commercial center of the country. But, of course, issues of identity were involved. The *paisas* were proud of their business acumen, their industrial clout, and their efficiency. *Al ritmo paisa* (at the Antioqueño rhythm or pace) means at a rapid, efficient, businesslike pace. If there was good business to be done with music, then Antioqueños wanted to get their share of it: not only money but reputation was at stake.

In the late 1960s and into the 1970s, Costeño music began to change in various ways. Bands began to appear, made up of musicians from Antioquia and other regions of the interior—for example, Cali— which played cover versions of Costeño music or their own compositions along similar lines. The bands became smaller on average, often incorporating keyboards and electric guitars, and the music rhythmically simpler. Some Costeño bands followed this trend (although oth-

6.1 Antonio Fuentes (*on far right*) with colleagues. (By permission of Discos Fuentes.)

ers did not). Terminology changed to reflect this. *Música tropical* (or sometimes *música bailable,* dance music) became a generic term, used to refer to all varieties of Costeño music, and later to Dominican merengue as well (although salsa generally kept a separate label). Within this umbrella category, the newer, simpler style of Costeño music had various names. In the music industry, the term *cumbia* was generally used, displacing *porro* but maintaining some continuity with the past. Others coined pejorative terms to reflect what they saw as a loss of authenticity. In La Costa, it was often called *música gallega* (literally, music from Galicia in northern Spain) and was generally looked down upon. In the interior, it became known in some circles, especially among devotees of salsa, as *chucu-chucu* (an onomatopoeic word) or *raspa* (scraping, rasping), referring to a music seen as rhythmically mechanical and melodically simplistic. It might also be called *sonido paisa* (paisa sound), reflecting the influence of the Antioqueño bands and recording industry. These were never easily defined categories, since one person's cumbia was another's chucu-chucu.

By the 1970s, the newer style had practically become the sound of commercial Costeño music in Colombia. It sold very well in the interior from the late 1960s through the 1980s and also did well in Mexico. Thus, with the relocation of the recording industry to Medellín came certain transformations of "Costeño" music, changes that were seen as creative modernizations by many within the recording industry and among the buying public but as debasement and simplification by some others.

This was not a straightforward process of appropriation of a regional music by a national industrial elite. Costeño musicians were also centrally involved in producing music very close in style to that associated with the Antioqueño bands, whether one called it cumbia or chucu-chucu. The Costeño record company, Discos Fuentes, was a leading light in this respect (fig. 6.2). The shift of the record industry to Medellín was simply a pioneering step in an overall transformation of Costeño music powered by music capitalism. Costeño music retained a regional identity, partly because cumbia became a principal label used for it, but that identity became less clear cut and tended to merge into the broad category of música tropical that included Costeño music of various kinds, played by Costeños and non-Costeños (including many Venezuelans), and other styles such as merengue.

As ever in Colombia, national styles never dominated international ones in the domestic market. Although cumbia became the musical marker of Colombian nationality, it had to compete with transnational musical styles. Starting in the late 1950s and continuing through the 1960s, cumbia had to contend first with *la nueva ola* (the new wave) of rock and roll styles, first imported directly from the United States and later also from Europe and in Hispanic versions from Mexico and Argentina. This music tended to appeal to young, middle-class people, although it was by no means confined to these circles; it was embedded in overall 1960s youth radicalism and challenges to the values of the preceding generation. Also, Cuban-derived music was undergoing rapid changes in the United States, giving rise to short-lived crazes such as *charanga* music, pachanga, and *bugalú* in the early to mid-1960s. This is turn set the stage for the appearance of salsa as a powerful competitor in Colombia, beginning in bohemian and urban working-class circles and spreading quickly up the social scale during the 1970s and 1980s.[1] During this period too, rock music captured an increasing youth market, especially among the middle and upper classes, while international Spanish-language ballad singers began increasingly to satisfy the constant demand for romantic styles that boleros and Mexican songs had previously fulfilled.[2] Finally, Dominican merengue had, by the 1980s, become a transnational Latin music which was increasingly popular in Colombia (Austerlitz 1995: 127–129).

Class divisions—or rather, images of class—were important in

6.2 The Discos Fuentes studios in Medellín (with Fuentes at desk). (By permission of Discos Fuentes.)

these changes. Due to the association of Lucho Bermúdez and Pacho Galán with the fancy social clubs, porro could have something of an elitist image, although this could be contested by images of rustic Costeño origins. "Modernized" Costeño music also tended to have conservative middle-class associations in relation to salsa, which, precisely because it seemed to be rooted in the rebellious urban working class and marihuana-smoking bohemia, soon appealed to middle-class youth who identified with left-wing radicalism.

Costeño music marketing adapted to the new competition. Alongside the modernization—or, to some, the oversimplification—of the sound to appeal to wider audiences in the national market, there were also moves abroad. In the mid-1960s, Costeño music—under the label of cumbia—was already known in countries such as Mexico, Peru, Argentina, and Chile. In some countries, it spawned interpretations by local bands, and by the 1970s cumbia had become very popular, often in adapted forms or as part of the more general category of música tropical. Within Colombia, other Costeño styles also became more popular. In the early 70s, vallenato expanded from being a mostly regional music, or seen as basically "folkloric," to being a major player in the music market. In the process, it changed too, becoming more "romantic" and ballad-like in feel and being played by larger, more elaborate lineups. The orchestras of Lucho Bermúdez and Pacho Galán still played, but their time had passed and vallenato was taking over.

The social context for all these changes was very contradictory. On the one hand, capitalist development proceeded apace, and although a recession from the late 1950s into the 1960s slowed growth, the government protected national industrialization, aiding the emergence of chemical, metallurgical, and automotive assembly industries. Cities such as Bogotá and Medellín initiated ambitious plans of urban development, communications were improved by important infrastructural projects, the first supermarket chains appeared, and mass media—plus commercial advertising—became pervasive, with a national television industry starting in 1954.

On the other hand, political violence was rampant, beginning in 1946, when the Conservatives took power after a long period of Liberal rule, and there were violent reprisals and recriminations in rural areas. When the populist Liberal leader, Jorge Eliécer Gaitán, was assassinated in 1948 prior to a general election, partisan violence erupted, and it continued throughout the 1950s. Widespread killings, massacres, torture, and terrible atrocities were carried out by both Liberal and Conservative factions, but the Conservative Party retained control of the government. General Gustavo Rojas Pinilla was installed as a military leader between 1954 and 1958, but alongside his populist tendencies, official repression and partisan killing continued and people fled in large numbers from the countryside to the relative safety of the big cities. Urban centers expanded rapidly and often in uncontrolled ways as low-income settlements multiplied in their peripheries.

La Violencia more or less ended with the establishment of a power-sharing agreement between Liberals and Conservatives in 1958, but in the mid-1960s, based partly around the remnants of guerrilla Liberal fighters, left-wing guerrilla movements began to emerge. Some of these are still active today, despite widespread repression by state and paramilitary forces and despite attempts by different governments since the 1980s to demobilize them and integrate them into institutional politics. Finally, of course, the drug trade, starting in the 1970s with marihuana and shifting later toward cocaine, has generated its own forms of violence, which have interwoven in complex ways with guerrilla, paramilitary, and state forces.[3]

The transformations of Costeño music fitted very neatly into patterns of capitalist growth. Their relation to changing forms of violence is less clear, but in previous chapters I argued that one of the ideological fields within which Costeño identity is constituted and contested is that polarized by images of violence and peacefulness, with La Costa identified as less involved with violence in general and La Violencia in particular. That the golden era of Costeño music—remarked on by all as quintessentially *alegre*—was also one of grotesque violence is not, I think, coincidental.

"Al Ritmo Paisa": The Recording Industry

The growth of the domestic record industry in the 1950s was helped by a strongly protectionist regime which restricted the importation of certain consumables, including records. Medellín, already a manufacturing center, became the heart of the recording industry, and the first record company founded there was Sonolux (Industria Electrosonora), started in 1949 by Rafael Acosta, a businessman, and Antonio Botero, who had been the Discos Fuentes agent in Medellín and was also a technician. Acosta's brother, Lázaro, was also involved, and the initials of the brothers names, "Lázaro y Rafael Acosta," made up the name of their first label, Lyra, which recorded mainly Colombian artists; the company also distributed RCA Victor records. A large December 1950 advertisement for Lyra records in the national daily, *El Espectador,* shows that the company recorded and sold a wide variety of music by Colombian artists. Of the hundred or so records listed, Andean music, in the broadest sense, accounted for a half, with pasillos alone taking a third of the titles, followed by bambucos. Costeño music was about 20 percent, mostly porros and some paseos by Bovea y Sus Vallenatos. Cuban styles—mostly boleros—accounted for about 10 percent, as did tangos. The rest were canciones and other minor styles. The advertisement also made it clear that the company already had a national distribution network, listing sixty-five outlets in twenty-eight towns and cities across the country.

The outlook of this company was essentially commercial. An extract from a 1953 publicity leaflet distributed by Sonolux makes this abundantly clear, although alongside the commercialism there is the hint of a national project of happiness and thus, in my argument, of liberation:

> We look for new voices, we frame them in modern and agreeable arrangements with a repertoire that is chosen to suit the tastes of the masses, and naturally the public reacts favorably, buying with ever greater enthusiasm the records backed by our labels. And it is precisely

because we sell large quantities that our records are economical and rank among the least costly in the national market. The large volume of sales naturally reduces the costs of production, as in any industry of mass production, and we contribute to the happiness of the Colombian people by providing recorded music within the reach of everyone's budget. (*Los Discos,* no. 2, October 1953)[4]

Sonolux retained an important position in the national market, recording such stars as Lucho Bermúdez and Pacho Galán as well as many well-known Colombian artists specializing in other styles. Hernán Restrepo Duque, the great chronicler of Colombian popular music, was artistic director there for some twenty years, in addition to hosting his famous radio show, *Radiolente* (1952–1975), and Luis Uribe Bueno, Lucho Bermúdez's bass player, also worked as artistic director there in the early 1950s. Costeño composer and musician Antonio María Peñaloza worked as an arranger for the Orquesta Sonolux between 1959 and 1963.[5]

After Sonolux, other companies sprang up in quick succession. In Bogotá, Gregorio Vergara, a technician who owned a radio repair business, founded Discos Vergara in 1950, starting with "Los Camarones" by Julio Torres y Sus Alegres Vallenatos as the debut record (see chapter 5). He sold thirty thousand copies in the three months before Christmas.[6] Meanwhile, in Medellín, the Silver label was set up in about 1950 by Julio and José Ramírez Johns, Antioqueño merchants and industrialists who had also been distributing Columbia and Odeon records in the city. They recorded international and national artists, including a lot of material by Lucho Bermúdez, although the company did not specialize in any particular type of music. The firm lasted until the early 1960s, when it was taken over by Industria Nacional del Sonido.[7]

Also in 1950, Alfredo Diez Montoya, a record shop owner and son-in-law of the Ramírez Johns brothers, founded the Zeida label (A. Diez in reverse), after having imported a couple of presses from the United States in 1949, and collaborated briefly with Silver. In 1954, he changed Zeida into a limited company under the name Codiscos (Compañía Colombiana de Discos), which still exists today. Their Costeño label has been an important one for Costeño music, especially the vallenato artists, who are some of their biggest sellers. In 1952, one of the founders of Sonolux, Rafael Acosta, set up his own company, Ondina Fonográfica. This collapsed in about 1961, although it trailed on for a while under different management and some of its catalog—including porros of the period—is currently being produced by a new small company in Medellín, Disquera Antioqueña. Rather later, Otoniel Cardona, who had been working in Sonolux since 1952, decided in 1964 to form his own company, Discos Victoria, which still exists. He and his brothers also own a chain of record shops.

Discos Fuentes, feeling somewhat isolated in Cartagena, moved its factory to Medellín in 1954, a move facilitated by Antonio Fuentes's having an Antioqueño businessman as a father-in-law. Fuentes continues to be one of the principal national recording companies. The main Costeño recording company which stayed behind in La Costa was Discos Tropical, which in the 1950s moved into new premises where it came to have fourteen record presses and several foreign label licenses. However, after the mid-1970s, Tropical ceased to keep up with technological innovation and began to fade. In 1990, most of its catalog was sold to Discos Fuentes.

There were other small Costeño recording labels.[8] The most important was that of José María "Curro" Fuentes, the youngest brother of the Fuentes family, born twenty-two years after Antonio (fig. 6.3). In his early twenties, he worked a little with Antonio and ran a chain of record shops. In the early 1950s, he began to record artists on an ad hoc basis in the studios of Emisoras Nuevo Mundo in Bogotá, releasing the records under the Curro label. One of his first Bogotá recordings was in 1953, when he cut "Te Olvidé" (I Forgot You), composed and played by Antonio María Peñaloza, which later became the unofficial hymn of the Barranquilla carnival. In the mid-1950s, he set up his own studios in Cartagena in the original Discos Fuentes building and recorded many well-known Costeño artists. He often used the Sonora Curro, a session orchestra directed mostly by Pacho Galán and based on the musicians who played with him. In the 1960s, he moved back to Bogotá and began to work with Philips as an artistic director, recording mostly Costeño artists. Curro records declined from that time and eventually petered out (interview with Carlos Fuentes).

The early years of the 1950s thus saw the establishment of the Colombian recording industry by a small group of Antioqueño businessmen and industrialists.[9] The Costeño industry either fell by the wayside through lack of technological advance or moved into the Antioqueño circle. Bogotá entrepreneurs did not grasp the available opportunities in the same way, with only the Vergara label dating from this period. Latterly, the capital has caught up, largely through the activities of the multinationals, plus a couple of domestic companies.[10] The Antioqueño record industry men all knew each other, they often

6.3 José María "Curro" Fuentes. (Photo by P. Wade.)

worked together at different times, their factories were, initially at least, all located near each other, and together they dominated the national music recording industry for practically two decades, until bigger multinational companies began to take the lion's share of the market.[11]

The significance of this Antioqueño involvement is that it vitiates any simple idea of "the Costeños" commercializing "their" music as a project underwriting a cultural or political regional identity. The relation between the music and Costeño cultural identity was mediated through commercial interests, but to a large extent these were Antioqueño commercial interests. Nor can we think in terms of Costeño music simply being appropriated by Antioqueño capitalists. Discos Fuentes was a major player on the scene, and Antonio Fuentes a key figure in determining its output. In fact, the music that helped to constitute many people's images of La Costa and the Costeños, and that was inevitably part of many Costeños' self-image, was being managed by people whose overriding interest was in making money. Many of these had a greater interest in sustaining an image of dynamic Antioqueño entrepreneurialism than in promoting Costeño cultural identity. This did not mean, however, that the relation between music and Costeño cultural identity was not important, or that consumers of the music, Costeños or otherwise, could not invest it with their own meanings or rearticulate it according to their own perspectives. I will save an examination of this issue until the next chapter. In the next section I will look at some of the developments that took place in Costeño music from 1950 onward.

Changes in Costeño Music, 1950–1980

THE OLD GUARD

Figures such as Lucho Bermúdez and Pacho Galán occupied a central place in the continued spread of Costeño music in the early part of this period. Bermúdez was based in Medellín, working with the radio stations, hotels, and clubs there. He also played in the Club San Fernando in Cali, which inspired his famous song "San Fernando." In the early 1950s, Lucho and Matilde visited Cuba, where they met Ernesto Lecuona and played alongside La Sonora Matancera, the classic Cuban orchestra active since 1932. They went on to Mexico and recorded an LP with RCA Victor, backed by musicians from the orchestra of Rafael de Paz and that of Dámaso Pérez Prado, the Cuban artist who had moved to Mexico and popularized the mambo there with worldwide success. Returning to Colombia, Lucho's orchestra signed a contract with the Hotel Tequendama in Bogotá. At this time, inspired by contacts made in Cuba, in Mexico, and during a visit to the United States (where he met Machito, Tito Rodríguez, and Tito Puente, leaders of some of the best-known orchestras playing Afro-Cuban music, mambo, and cha-cha-cha), Lucho started to compose crossover rhythms such as tumbasón, porro-pachanga, and gaita-jazz; he also wrote "Porro Operático," which appropriated elements of Bizet's *Carmen* (Arteaga 1991). Also at this time, Lucho made his debut on television, appearing on one of the first programs in 1954, and the orchestra toured all over Central America and the United States.

   In Medellín, Cali, and Bogotá, the orchestra was basically an eleven-piece lineup, with two saxophones, two trumpets, piano, drum kit, maracas, and bass, plus Lucho on clarinet and two vocalists. The personnel underwent various changes over time: the bassist Luis Uribe Bueno left before the Bogotá contract. Matilde Díaz continued to be Bermúdez's main singer, accompanied by other "crooners" such as Bobby Ruiz (Arteaga 1991).[12] In about 1965, Matilde Díaz left the orchestra and married the son of Alberto Lleras Camargo (president, 1958–1962), causing a national scandal in elite circles; her singing career continued, but at a much reduced level. The boom period of Lucho Bermúdez and his orchestra was over by now, but the band continued to appear on television and radio and to play live gigs. In the

1980s, Lucho was honored by President Belisario Betancur (fig. 6.4), was awarded the Order of Rafael Núñez, and had his compositions played by many different symphonic orchestras. He died on Saturday, 23 April 1994, at the age of eighty-two.

Some of the news reports on the occasion of his death sum up nicely the role of Lucho Bermúdez's music. One says that he took his orchestra to Bogotá at a time when "the Caribbean for the Bogotanos was quite close to Japan." The writer goes on: "they came . . . to suffer the cold, in a Bogotá atmosphere filled with hats, overcoats, and umbrellas. When, among the pasillos and the waltzes, the most radical movement was produced by boleros, Lucho brought the waves and the sea. This was when Bogotá began to emerge from the cold. . . . Lucho presented to [high] society his gaitas, porros, and sones dressed up in tails" (Sierra 1994). This imagery presents La Costa as entirely foreign to the Bogotanos and uses the stereotypes of coldness and being covered up against the cold which were common in people's perceptions of the capital and which are still purveyed today. La Costa was, and is, seen as hot and tropical, and Lucho is presented as having introduced movement—the sensuous bodily movement of the waves—and heat, which together brought Bogotá out of its coldness and overdressed immobility and, in a word, liberated the city. Nevertheless, the music was dressed up in style: nothing too plebeian would do.

An unsigned report on Lucho's death reproduced the text of a statement made by President César Gaviria (which actually was the same as that read by him a year before, when Bermúdez was given the National Order of Merit). It said: "Lucho Bermúdez composed works which by virtue of their artistic quality and their profound popular roots today form part of the cultural heritage of the folkloric patrimony of our country" (El Espectador, 26 April 1994). The music is portrayed as highly artistic, but also rooted in the people ("popular," "folkloric"); above all, it is now claimed as a national patrimony. Gaviria's choice of words points up how Bermúdez's music bridged the difficult space between upper class (artistic quality) and lower class (popular roots) and between heterogeneity (folklore) and homogeneity (our country). Nevertheless, another report on the funeral stated that friends and colleagues complained that not enough had been done to officially honor the dead man (El Tiempo, 25 April 1994): he had been only a musician and a "popular" one at that, not to mention having been a Costeño.

Pacho Galán was mostly based in Barranquilla during the whole of this period. The basis of his orchestra, the Rodríguez brothers,

6.4 President Betancur (*left*) and Lucho Bermúdez, 4 January 1984. (By permission of El Espectador.)

had been in Bogotá in about 1951–1954 under the name of Lucho Rodríguez y su Orquesta (see chapter 4), and when they returned to Barranquilla, Pacho Galán joined them and began to direct the band, which was then called the Orquesta de Pacho Galán. At this time, Galán had been recording in Cartagena with the Orquesta Emisora Fuentes and with Sonora Curro, and the Rodríguez brothers also played with him there. In 1955, he was invited to go to Medellín by a colleague, pianist Ramón Ropaín, to play in the Club Medellín. Galán at first refused, but his son, Armando, who was by then playing trumpet in his band, went along and later persuaded his father to join him.

One song that Curro Fuentes had turned down in Cartagena, "Cosita Linda," was recorded in Medellín with the help of Luis Uribe Bueno, Lucho Bermúdez's ex–bass player who was by then artistic director at Sonolux, plus various musicians from the orchestras of Ramón Ropaín and Lucho Bermúdez. This record, an instrumental piece with a vocal refrain, went on the market in November 1955 as a *merecumbé*, supposedly a mixture of merengue and cumbia. The invention of "new" rhythms was not unusual and was part of the continuous search for commercial success, but this one proved to be very successful. Pacho returned to Barranquilla and to his own band. He gave the drummer, Pompilio Rodríguez, license to adorn the basic porro rhythm of "Cosita Linda," and Pompilio, according to his own account, created a beat which gave the merecumbé its distinctive quality (interviews with Armando Galán and Pompilio Rodríguez). "Cosita Linda" was rerecorded with Discos Tropical, this time with full lyrics sung by Emilia Valencia, and became a smash hit. Merecumbé became very popular, Pacho Galán recorded whole albums in this style, and many famous artists did covers of his numbers, including La Sonora Matancera. On the basis of this success, Pacho Galán's band toured Central America and Venezuela in the late 1950s. There were also gigs in Bogotá and Cali. In general, however, he stuck to Barranquilla.[13] The Rodríguez brothers left the orchestra in the early 1960s, new musicians were added, and the orchestra played New York and Chicago various times in the 1970s. But, as with Lucho Bermúdez, the apogee had passed, and by 1980, Pacho had more or less withdrawn from an active role in the band. He died on 21 July 1988.

The bands of Lucho Bermúdez and Pacho Galán best represent the large orchestras which played Costeño music between 1950 and 1970, according to models already established in the 1940s. It is worth mentioning, however, two other orchestras which were also prominent and followed a similar style. Edmundo Arias (fig. 6.5) was born in 1925 in Tuluá, Valle Province, to Joaquín Arias, an Antioqueño musician. Edmundo, nicknamed Cabeza-de-nido (Bird's-nest-hair), was a light-skinned black, and he played bass and guitar. He moved to Medellín in about 1952 and formed the Sonora Antillana, which later became the Orquesta de Edmundo Arias. As a composer, arranger, and band leader, he focused almost exclusively on Costeño music—porros, cumbias, gaitas—recording with Ondina, Sonolux, and Discos Fuentes, among others.[14] Some of his later recordings show the attempts to modernize Costeño styles which became characteristic of other artists in the 1960s and 1970s (see below). For example, his porro "Las Cosas de la Vida" (The Things of Life) has a salsa-style piano and bass line and two of his cumbias, "Ave'Pa'Ve" (Let's See Then) and "Cumbia del Caribe," have an electric keyboard part which is very typical of the post-1960s música tropical sound that some denigrated as "chucu-chucu." [15]

A second important band was La Billo's Caracas Boys. This Venezuelan band was actually formed by the Dominican band leader Luis

6.5 Edmundo Arias. (By permission of Discos Fuentes.)

María "Billo" Frómeta (b. 1915), who left the Dominican Republic, then under Trujillo's dictatorship, and arrived in Caracas in 1938 and founded the Billo's Caracas Boys in 1940. This was a typical large dance orchestra playing a variety of Caribbean, Latin American, and some North American styles. Billo specialized in playing Costeño music as well, however, and was a frequent visitor to Colombia, often playing the Barranquilla carnival. Sometimes his covers of Colombian numbers were more successful than the originals. The orchestra still survives today and in fact played the 1995 carnival in Barranquilla.

The Colombia-Venezuela connection was important for Costeño music, and there were other orchestras which specialized in these styles and played in Colombia, especially during the Venezuelan oil boom of the 1960s. Los Melódicos, founded by Renato Capriles (b. 1931), was similar to La Billo's and indeed was formed when Billo was temporarily out of action with legal problems (some say marital, others immigration) in 1958; Billo did a number of arrangements for them. There were several other Venezuelan bands that played Costeño music as an important part of their repertoire—often in a modernized form and increasingly alongside salsa in the 1970s—and some of them won the prized Congos de Oro for outstanding musical performances in the Barranquilla carnival; several still play today.[16]

Venezuela was not the only important connection for Costeño music at this time, although it probably had the most influence for Colombian audiences. Pérez Prado also recorded porros, as did La Sonora Matancera—just as Colombian musicians recorded Cuban styles and sang with Cuban orchestras (Betancur Alvarez 1993). Costeño music represented Colombia abroad, completely displacing bambuco and related Andean styles.

ROOTS

A slightly different current in Costeño music was formed during the 1950s by bands that tended to play a more "rootsy" style of porro and, to a lesser extent, cumbia. Central figures here were Pedro Laza, Rufo Garrido, and Climaco Sarmiento, all of them old-timers but not important commercial figures until the 1950s. Pedro Laza was born in about 1906 and worked for some time as a journalist. In his youth, he played in local bands in Cartagena and other towns in Bolívar Province.[17] His main fame came with the formation of Pedro Laza y Sus Pelayeros in about 1952. (As I discussed in chapter 3, San Pelayo is one of the towns reputed to be the "cradle of porro" in histories and myths about the origin of porro.) This band was formed on the initiative of Antonio Fuentes, who asked Laza to round up some of the best musicians in the area: Rufo Garrido on saxophone and Climaco Sarmiento on clarinet were prominent figures in the band.[18] Laza's band was popular throughout the 1950s and 1960s, making many LPs with Fuentes, including two with the Cuban singer Daniel Santos in 1958; Garrido also recorded with Curro Fuentes. The band broke up in about 1973.[19]

The main repertoire of Laza's band was porros, fandangos, and a few cumbias; after the mid-1950s they also recorded a number of merecumbés. The interesting aspect was their ability to combine numbers in a smooth orchestral style very similar to that of Bermúdez, Galán, or Arias with others—often composed by Garrido or Sarmiento—that had a rather rougher, more gutsy sound that evoked much more immediately the local wind bands of the savannah of Bolívar, where the musicians came from.[20] Numbers with the latter sound were generally instrumental—lyrics were a later addition to "traditional" porros—and the percussion was foregrounded, as were strident trumpets and clarinets. Records made with Discos Fuentes sometimes reinforced this

6.6 Wilson Choperena. (Photograph by Jorges Torres, 1976. By permission of Cromos.)

image: one was called *Fiesta y corraleja,* with a picture of a rural Costeño bullfighting festival (issued on vinyl as DF 200030, n.d.).

This "roots" current of music was also evident in smaller conjuntos which tended to focus on cumbia. A classic example is Wilson Choperena's big cumbia hit, "La Pollera Colora" (The Red Petticoat), recorded on Discos Tropical by Pedro Salcedo y Su Conjunto in 1962 and since covered many times. (See fig. 6.6.) This original starts with a simple conga drum beating duple time (as does the llamador drum in folkloric styles of cumbia). This is joined by a heavy drum kit tom-tom playing uneven rolling patterns (which recall the tambor alegre of the folkloric groups), a maraca playing the same rhythm as the conga drum, hand claps, and a scraper which takes the classic chi-qui-CHA-chi-qui-CHA rhythm that one finds in much Costeño music. Then comes a single clarinet weaving the melody over various saxophones honking out a two-chord riff. These are joined by a heavy acoustic bass which settles into a one-two-three pattern as the male lead vocalist, in a high, strained, nasalized voice, sings of dancing and women. His verses are followed by call-response sections with a male chorus, and these vocal parts alternate with the clarinet and saxophone parts. In the background, a piano simply marks the rhythm with single chords that fall between the beats of the conga drum (see appendix B, "Musical Examples").

A later version of the tune adds a larger horn section, which takes over some of the melody from the clarinet, reducing the feeling of interweaving patterns. Electric piano is added, which evokes elements of a salsa keyboard line, while the electric bass starts with the same one-two-three rhythm but often switches to a simpler one-two pattern during the verses. The heavy tom-tom is replaced by timbales, mostly hit on the frame to the chi-qui-CHA-chi-qui-CHA rhythm of the scraper. The maraca disappears (although occasionally imitated by the high hat), and a wooden block (plus what sounds like a synthesized hand clap) carries the simple duple beat. The overall feel is lighter, smoother, with a more regular beat.[21]

To a certain extent, then, the progressive stylization of Costeño music was braked in this type of music, which had a less elitist air—although Laza did also play some elite social clubs.[22] Costeño music was by then fairly well accepted in the cities of the interior, and it seems there was less need to "dress it in tails." Still, much of Laza's music did fit into the Bermúdez or Galán mold, and it is worth noting that Laza, Garrido, and Sarmiento were hardly "blacks" by Colombian standards. Laza was light skinned, Garrido's grandfather was a Spaniard, and Sarmiento was more often identified as of indigenous origin than black. Of course, in Bogotá, they might have been identified as blacks in the same way that any Costeño of obviously mixed heritage might be so labeled.

INNOVATORS

Discos Fuentes, under the firm leadership of Antonio Fuentes, was instrumental in bringing new combinations and crossovers into Costeño music in the 1960s, changes which distanced this music somewhat from the classic porros of the 1940s and 1950s. The most important band from the Fuentes stable in this respect was Los Corraleros de Majagual (fig. 6.7), from which basis various individuals made careers as solo artists, among them the accordionists Alfredo Gutiérrez and Lisandro Meza and the salsa band leader Julio "Fruko" Estrada.[23]

The founding members of Los Corraleros were mostly working in their own bands in the late 1950s. Eliseo Herrera (fig. 6.8), apart from his job as a stevedore in Cartagena, sang with La Sonora Cordobesa, an orchestra similar to Laza's Pelayeros, although less well known. Various others—Calixto Ochoa, Lisandro Meza, César Castro—had smaller accordion-based conjuntos. Tony Zúñiga was singing with Rufo Garrido, while Chico Cervantes and Nacho Paredes were also local singers. Many of these people were already working with Fuentes at the time, recording porros, cumbias, and paseos. Herrera was taken along one day in about 1958 to display his specialty of singing com-

6.7 Los Corraleros de Majagual in traditional Costeño dress. *Above, left to right:* Edilberto Benítez, Chico Cervantes, Neil Benítez, Lucho Pérez, Tomás Benítez, and Mario Londoño. *Below, left to right:* Gilberto Benítez, Carmelo Barraza, Calixto Ochoa, and Alfredo Gutiérrez. (By permission of Discos Fuentes.)

plex, tongue-twisting lyrics (*trabalenguas*): he sang "Chule Vende Chica," and this was recorded with the Sonora Cordobesa.[24]

Herrera then became a regular singer with various bands in the Fuentes stable and met up with the young accordionist Alfredo Gutiérrez (fig. 6.9) in Medellín in the early 1960s. Alfredo himself recounted that he began to record with Fuentes from about 1958, when he was a mere fourteen years old. In any event, it was not long after this that Antonio Fuentes had the idea of grouping together various different musicians in a lineup that started as a studio-based recording group. This was a fairly typical setup in Fuentes: bands were often created by Antonio Fuentes and staffed by changing combinations of artists who also played with other Fuentes bands or alone.

The crucial musical innovation of Los Corraleros—which most seem to agree was the inspiration of Fuentes himself, although these matters are not likely to have been straightforward at the time and are probably even less so in retrospect—was to put one or more accordions in combination with a brass section drawn from the Sonora Cordobesa and Laza's Pelayeros.[25] Whoever invented the idea, it created a crossover between what had until then been two rather different line-

6.8 Eliseo Herrera. (By permission of Discos Fuentes.)

ups: the orchestra, usually concentrating on porros, fandangos, and cumbias, and the accordion conjunto, which, although it would also interpret cumbias and porros, focused more on paseos, merengues, and sones—in other words, what by then was commonly known as vallenato. Fruko, who was working as a gofer in Discos Fuentes in the early 1960s and who, in his teens, joined the band as a percussionist, said this: "After Lucho Bermúdez, which was Colombian music dressed in tails, came Los Corraleros, which was a *conjunto típico* [a traditional conjunto]. . . . It was the first group to use an electric bass, and that gave the group a lot of body, and made it sound good.[26] There were some changes of rhythm too, a special rhythm was invented, the caja and the sound of the horns, since there were a saxophone, a bombardino, and a trombone, and often a trumpet." (Oddly, he does not mention the most distinctive feature, which was the combination of accordions and horns.) As usual, a new sound had to have a new name, and the label *paseaíto* (a little paseo) was chosen by

Fuentes, who, according to Herrera, coined it for the second song Herrera recorded.[27] This became a common label for songs by Los Corraleros and a well-established label in the Costeño music repertoire. It
was essentially similar to a paseo (see appendix B, "Musical Examples"), but the brass section and accordion gave it something of the feel
of porro or cumbia. It was generally faster than most paseos or porros
and had a simple, strongly marked beat carried by the bass, a wooden
block and/or cowbell (playing a one-two rhythm), and a scraper (playing the chi-qui-CHA-chi-qui-CHA pattern), and often with the occasional interjection of a cymbal syncopating with the main one-two
rhythm. These were accompanied by a small caja drum (typically used
in accordion conjuntos), which functioned much like bongos, adding
rapid flourishes, while a *tumbadora* (conga drum) played a very muted
role. The songs were typically sung verses alternating with parts by the
horns and the accordion, which sometimes interwove in the classic
porro or cumbia style, but more frequently played in unison or sepa-
rately. The trademark of Los Corraleros was a strong element of brash
humor, with tongue-twisting lyrics, occasional risqué double enten-
dres, whoops, and yells (e.g., "¡nos fuimos!": we're off!). The lyrics
typically dealt with partying, particular events and features of a mostly
rural nature (e.g., festivals, animals, and individuals with odd charac-

6.9 Alfredo Gutiérrez (*left*) with Rafael Escalona. (By permission of Cromos.)

teristics), and sometimes romance. For the first few albums, Los Corraleros was a studio band, only later venturing onto the road to tour
Colombia and then Venezuela and the United States. However, by the
late 1970s, the band had passed its golden era, and several of its members concentrated on their solo careers.[28]

Alfredo Gutiérrez, both in Los Corraleros and as a solo artist, has
been an important innovator in Costeño music, as his nickname, the
Rebel of the Accordion, implies. After leaving Fuentes, he recorded
with Sonolux and later with Codiscos. In Alfredo's own words,

> I began to do a vallenato that was different from what had been done be-
> fore. Instead of doing *costumbrista* lyrics [i.e., dealing with local cus-
> toms and events], I made it very romantic with songs like "Los Novios."
> Instead of saying, like a traditional song by Escalona called "Playonera,"
> which is very traditional, very costumbrista—"I left the beaches on the
> banks of the Cesar River / I am the one who knows how to lasso the wild
> bullocks"—I said that vallenato music was very pretty, a beautiful coun-
> try girl but who didn't have the clothes to be presented in society. So I
> chose songs like "Los Novios" which said, "We love each other, long
> live love, long live the newlyweds when they love each other with all
> their hearts."[29] (Interview)

Alvaro Arango, vice-president of Codiscos in 1995, joined the company in 1960 when it was taking an increasing interest in Costeño music. In the late sixties, it set up its "Costeño" label dedicated to Costeño
music, particularly accordion music, although one of the first bands
was a Corraleros look-alike called Los Caporales del Magdalena, led
by Alfredo Gutiérrez. Arango recalled the growing impact of the type
of Costeño music that Los Corraleros played:

> Now the themes were not so regional, not so folkloric as before. Instead,
> easier songs appeared, songs that the people from the interior could un-
> derstand easily, some of them were tongue twisters, with sayings, jokes,
> very happy songs. Also with the way these groups presented Costeño
> music, it was a lot easier to dance to. That is, us people from the interior
> are not very good dancers, we don't dance Costeño music very well. . . .
> But when new elements were introduced and perhaps some rhythmical
> adjustments were made to the music and when the themes became eas-
> ier to understand for the people of the interior, I think that all these
> things made us, the cachacos as they call us in La Costa, assimilate this
> music more easily.

It was precisely the paseaíto that Arango identified as having an easy, danceable beat. The same types of changes were taking place, he thought, with vallenato itself, although this term was only beginning at that time to acquire the definite meaning, on a national scale, that it now has.

> Alfredo Gutiérrez was the beginning of vallenato at Codiscos. . . . At that time, perhaps because of Alfredo, vallenato began to become distanced from vallenato as very regional, very narrative, from the vallenato of Escalona . . . and began to take on a very romantic feel. From that moment on, vallenato started becoming national. And also in a similar way, I think, to what happened with Los Corraleros, because they began to introduce new elements into vallenato: the electric bass, and perhaps someone might dare to use a guitar. And a polemic developed between those who defended pure vallenato and those who—like Alfredo—were saying that it was important to introduce new elements if vallenato was really to be promoted first into the interior of the country and, in the future, abroad.

I will say more about vallenato in a later section, since its emergence as a major commercial style needs more extensive treatment.

Another important innovator was Aníbal Velásquez. His impact was lessened in Colombia by his lengthy residence in Venezuela during the 1960s and 1970s, but his use of the accordion to interpret Cuban and Mexican styles represented a significant change, and his records sold quite well in Colombia. He was born in 1936 in Barranquilla and picked up the accordion from his older brother, Juan. On the radio he heard a lot of Buitrago's guitar-based vallenato songs and also occasionally accordionists such as Pacho Rada, Luis E. Martínez, Abel Antonio Villa, and Alejo Durán. He started playing in a group called Los Vallenatos del Magdalena[30] in the early 1950s, and with its demise Aníbal formed another group called Los Dardos with brothers Juan and José "Cheíto," who organized a horn section of trumpet, sax, and trombone. This combination of accordion and horns did not prove as successful as Los Corraleros, and Aníbal tended to stick more to the accordion, but his later records still had some brass accompaniment. His main claim to fame, however, was the "guarachas" he played on the accordion:

> I called it guaracha because I thought that it was a rapid rhythm and I could call it guaracha, but you know that guaracha isn't only what I

play. There are two sorts of guaracha: the Cuban one and mine. My guaracha is a bit faster, a bit hotter. [Question: Did it have any Cuban influence?] Yes, a bit, because in the arrangements I did on my first records I put in a little bit of Cuba, but that gradually disappeared and I did my own style. Instead of the bongo that's in the [Cuban] guaracha and rumba, I used the caja, and it wasn't a caja with wedges, because I had a ring made for it, like for a bongo, and my brother, José, instead of putting a leather skin on it, put a *radiografía* [X-ray film] on it and it sounded like a bongo. Then the tumbadora and the cowbell and the drum kit—in fact I put in almost the same instrumentation [as in the Cuban guaracha].

This type of caja—with a plastic membrane held in place by a metal ring instead of a leather skin held in place by ropes tightened with wooden chocks—is now standard in vallenato lineups, although I have no confirmation that it was introduced by the Velásquez brothers. Velásquez's repertoire was characterized by the great mixture of styles that he dealt in: rumbas and danzones by the Puerto Rican Rafael Hernández, Dominican merengues, paseaítos, paseos, porros, cumbias, the occasional boogaloo, and the so-called *pasebol,* a mixture of paseo and bolero, which both he and Alfredo Gutiérrez claim to have invented. All these styles were given a similar feel by his instrumental lineup, the sound of the accordion and the almost constant presence of the high hat or cymbal in the percussion section, syncopating with the bass and wooden block, which together drive a strong and simple rhythm.[31]

In sum, through groups such as Los Corraleros and artists such as Aníbal Velásquez and Alfredo Gutiérrez—and others from Los Corraleros, such as Lisandro Meza and Calixto Ochoa—Costeño music that used the accordion began to move into the interior of the country alongside the orchestrated arrangements of porros and cumbias. Prior to this, although accordion music was available on record from Discos Fuentes and Discos Tropical, the accordion had remained rather restricted to La Costa. These groups also marked certain "modernizations," which consisted not only of novel instrumental combinations, but also of rhythmic simplifications. This was a trend that was being pursued in other ways at the same time.

"MODERNIZING" COSTEÑO MUSIC

In the 1960s and the 1970s, several groups emerged which, although made up almost exclusively of musicians from the interior of the country, played mostly Costeño music, sometimes mixed in with some versions of the twist, rock and roll, and other nueva ola North American music. These groups included Los Teen Agers, Los Hispanos, Los Graduados, Los Golden Boys, and Los Black Stars, and most of them came out of Antioquia or nearby provinces. In Cali, Los Bobby Soxers were also important (Ulloa Sanmiguel 1992: 403). However, the changes that these bands represented were not just confined to the interior: Costeño music as a whole was undergoing changes in which what I have called the "old guard" and the "roots" currents, while still present, were being dominated by forms that were seen as either more "modern" or more "degenerate," depending on one's point of view.

A central figure of this movement in Medellín was Gustavo Quintero, who sang in several of these groups. He was born in the mid-1940s in Rionegro, Antioquia. His family had a farm in La Costa, so he grew up visiting the region on a regular basis.

His first band was Los Teen Agers (formed in 1957), which he joined as a percussionist in 1961, soon becoming their lead singer. This was a band, like many in Latin America at the time, that played some rock and roll and related styles. An early LP of theirs (*Exitos por docenas* [Zeida LDZ 20179, n.d.]), for example, includes "Celia" (a "rock-calipso," which actually sounds like a bolero and was written by the Argentinean ballad singer Leo Dan), "El Payaso" (The Clown, a "twist"), and "Canta El Corazón" (The Heart Sings, a "fox[-trot]"). But they also included a good deal of Costeño music—porros, cumbias, and gaitas. The Teen Agers made eighteen LPs before changing their name to Los Ocho de Colombia, a group which has released another score of albums of the same type of music, all with Discos Fuentes.

Quintero went on to become part of Los Hispanos, and he was by then known as "El Loco" Quintero by virtue of his antics on stage, leaping about, laughing, shouting, and generally lending a comic air to the gigs; he became known for putting on wigs and false teeth and leaving the stage to dance around with the audience. The band had as musical director Jaime Uribe, the son of Lucho Bermúdez's saxophonist, Gabriel Uribe. In 1969, they changed their name to Los Graduados (fig. 6.10), although Los Hispanos did continue thereafter with a different membership and its lead singer was later the Costeño Rodolfo Aicardi, who had been a popular ballad and bolero singer until he moved into música tropical. He later formed his own group, Rodolfo y Su Típica RA7, which had great success with the cumbia "La Colegiala" (The Schoolgirl), a hit in France in the early 1980s and to be found on most collections of cumbia available internationally. Los Graduados continued to play into the 1990s, and Quintero, who has recorded over one hundred albums, was in 1995 as active as ever, singing and occasionally playing the accordion. Live, the band has played a wide variety—from Benny Goodman numbers, through porros, to paso dobles—but their recordings have been almost entirely música tropical, based on Costeño music, although with salsa and other such genres added in (interview with Gustavo Quintero and his wife, Consuelo Ruiz).

The instrumental lineup of these groups varied but was smaller than the lineups of the big dance orchestras. Instruments included electric bass, drum kit, guacharaca, cowbell, saxes, and trumpet; sometimes a clarinet would be added. But the distinctive touch was given by an electric guitar and some kind of electronic keyboard, usually a Hammond organ, a Hammond Solovox, or in later years, an electric piano.[32] As time went on, these bands would include some salsa and merengue in their repertoires, and the presence of the keyboards in particular facilitated this move. The music that they produced was often seen by Costeños and by salsa and rock fans as "simplified" and inauthentic— "chucu-chucu"—and was also sometimes seen as a specifically Antioqueño product, but it proved to be commercially very successful among audiences in the interior of the country. Many albums by Los Graduados and Los Hispanos are still available from Codiscos and Discos Fuentes. Songs by Los Graduados were collected by a French label on the first LP of a series called "La Colombie y sa musique" (Barclay 0920274), so their music has even come to be seen as representative of the country, at least by some outsiders.

The idea of the debasement of Costeño music by these Antioqueño bands comes from a supposedly simplistic rhythm. In her account of Hernán Restrepo Duque's life, Ana María Cano writes about the power of Medellín in defining, or at least purveying, popular music between 1950 and 1975 and says: "The strongest criticism of the *paisa* [Antioqueño] influence on popular music comes from the movement which changes the country's rhythm; bands of 'boys' such as Los Graduados, Los Hispanos, and Los Black Stars emerged, all Antioqueños who took the music of the Caribbean coast and, with a very elemental local rhythm, 'degenerated' it, in the opinion of many" (Cano 1986: 26). Felix Chacuto, a radio disc jockey who started his career in Santa Marta in 1940, recalled that the music of these groups, "música gallega" for the Costeños, was not very popular in La Costa in the 1960s and 1970s: "Because their way of playing the music is too regular: a

6.10 Los Graduados, with Gustavo Quintero (*front center*). (By permission of Discos Fuentes.)

beat which is repeated and repeated; and that's what they call música gallega here. So when the musicians from here are going to play something that the musicians from the interior play, they do a different arrangement and they take out that regularity. It was what happened at the beginning with the music that the Venezuelans played: they also played Costeño music but with a very regular beat, so regular that it became monotonous, too repetitive." Some of the most caustic criticisms of "chucu-chucu" came from young urban salsa fans, who felt that salsa was musically more sophisticated, but also grittier and more hard edged and rebellious by virtue of its lyrics and its association with the urban working class—this was important in the context of the 1960s left-wing radicalism which was popular with some of the urban middle-class youth. For example, in Andrés Caicedo's classic novel, *Que viva la música* (1977), which tells the story of a girl from Cali—reputed to be the salsa capital of Colombia—and her love affairs with Anglo-American rock and salsa, there is a scene in which Ricardo "Richie" Ray and Bobby Cruz play a salsa gig in Cali, a story based on a real concert during the 1969 Cali Festival. Puerto Rican New Yorker

Richie Ray was already a hero among Colombian fans of what was being called salsa, but the support band was Los Graduados and the narrative relates how Ray made fun of "the foolishness" of Quintero on
stage: "There's talk of the public shaming of the paisas, they weren't
given a chance, they couldn't take even a little pressure, go back to
school I'm telling you that you just can't compete with me, they were
obliged to leave the stage because of their sugary style, poor devils with
a busted butt, and there was nothing but celebration, making a racket
and behaving badly with tremendous salsa" (Caicedo [1977] 1985:
129). In Caicedo's story, the organizers were scandalized by Richie
Ray: "'If we'd known that we were bringing an orchestra of homosex-
uals and drug addicts, we'd have put on records.' The daughters of the
organizers complained: 'Mummy, what is the Bugalú, you can't dance
to that, what vulgarity . . . why don't Los Graduados come on again,
little Gustavo was so lovely?'" (130).[33] Richie Ray's return was eagerly
awaited by his fans, one of whom, in the novel, printed posters every
year which said: "The people of Cali reject Los Graduados, Los Hispanos, and the other exponents of the 'paisa sound' made to suit the
bourgeoisie and their vulgarity" (136). España, in his anecdotal account of chucu-chucu music, refers to it also as that "vulgar *paisa*
sound" (1995: 174). It should be noted, however, that Quintero pos-
sesses a prized Carreta de Plata (Silver Cart) award for that performance at the Cali Festival.[34]

Ulloa Sanmiguel, in his history of salsa in Cali, also criticizes this
music, which he calls *raspa* (literally, scrape, referring to the regular
rhythm supplied by the scraper). "If raspa has done anything in Colombia it is to make banal the tropical Colombo-Caribbean music,
which in the 1950s had reached the heights and the quality of the most
important popular dance styles of the continent. Raspa simplified its
melodic and rhythmic structure and, in a search for easy tastes and
profitable markets, reduced its musical expression to a minimum. But
this approach would be the most successful from a commercial point
of view" (Ulloa Sanmiguel 1992: 403; see also Waxer 1998: 112–113).

There are two social divisions implied in these comments, one of
class, the other of region. As Caicedo's narrative made clear, Los Graduados were seen as playing to a middle-class audience—although
paradoxically one with "vulgar" tastes which preferred the inauthentic to the authentic—and this is something that Quintero himself recognized. While he claimed that "We have everyone, from the lottery
ticket seller and the security guard to the well-off gentleman," he also
recognized that his main audience was middle class. He added that an

arrangement was arrived at in Codiscos according to which, for ex-ample, "Alfredo Gutiérrez would record [sings] 'La negra dice que no me quiere . . .': he would record it on the accordion and I would record it in the same factory, I'd record the same song but with that slightly higher [class] arrangement." In this sense, Costeño music was, as be-fore, straddling class divisions. Previously, Lucho Bermúdez and his like catered mainly to elite and middle-class tastes—although work-ing-class people listened to him as well—while the accordion had ple-beian connotations. Then the "sonido paisa" and other modernized versions of Costeño music retained a middle-class connotation, while the accordion kept its basically "popular" orientation.

Some caution is needed with simple class divisions. For example, Ulloa Sanmiguel proposes that, in Cali at least, Afro-Cuban music, ex-pressed forcefully through dance and erotic gestures, became the mu-sic of the "popular strata" and the "workers," while the "scandalized bourgeoisie" took refuge in European music and the porros and cum-bias of Lucho Bermúdez and La Billo's Caracas Boys (Ulloa Sanmiguel 1992: 266–267). However, it is clear that things were not quite so simple: Afro-Cuban music was widely accepted by the middle classes, particularly the bolero; the music of Lucho Bermúdez was not just for the bourgeoisie, while some of Pedro Laza's or Rufo Garrido's music was even less so; Daniel Santos, who according to Ulloa (1992: 266) became the emblem of Afro-Cuban music for Cali's blacks and mu-lattoes, also made two albums of porros with Pedro Laza;[35] and, of course, Costeño music was not only vital dance music, but was also seen as erotic by many people. If Ulloa's attempt to, as it were, prole-tarianize Afro-Cuban music in general—prior to its later appropria-tion by the "dominant classes" (Ulloa Sanmiguel 1992: 267)—is over-stated, it is true that *connotations* of class were important. Modernized Costeño music, played by Antioqueños or Costeños, was popular across a wide range of classes—that was, after all, the basis of its commercial success—but there was always the possibility of associating it with a bourgeois quality, especially where "bourgeois" was thought to mean distanced from the hard realities of life. This was particularly so in a context in which salsa—apparently hard edged, rebellious, and new—was making increasing inroads.

The second division implied in the comments by Cano, Chacuto, and España is one between the interior (or at least Antioquia) and La Costa. Ulloa is less explicit here, since he does not overtly label raspa a product of the interior; nevertheless, the bands he cites as its precur-sors are mostly from the interior (1992: 403). But this division is also not as straightforward as it seems. The singer for Los Hispanos, Rodolfo Aicardi, was born in the Costeño town of Magangué, for example, and Costeños were active in the production of this sort of music. A singer with Los Black Stars, Gabriel Romero, was also a Costeño. Indeed, as I said earlier, Discos Fuentes was a prime mover of music in this style, recording Los Teenagers, Los Ocho de Colombia, Rodolfo Aicardi, and many others. By the 1970s it had effectively become the "modern" sound of Costeño music.

An example is La Sonora Dinamita, a band originally put together in 1960 by Antonio Fuentes for studio recording purposes, using a changing set of artists that originally included Pedro Laza on bass. A 1962 recording of a cumbia by them reveals what would have been heard by most as a fairly traditional sound, with a heavy drum beat produced by a tumbadora or tom-toms, a brass section, maracas, and a male lead vocal alternating with a female chorus. Already, however, the electric bass is playing a one-two rhythm, an accordion carries most of the melody after an initial introduction by the horns, and there is a guitar floating in the background ("Ritmo de Tambó" [Drum Rhythm; a cumbia by Bernardo Saldarriaga], on *Cumbia, cumbia 2* [World Circuit WCD 033, 1993]).

This group was disbanded in 1963 and reformed in 1977 as another flexible outfit that played music much closer to what would be called "chucu-chucu" by some people: the electric piano is prominent (sometimes bringing in elements of salsa), the bass plays a simple one-two rhythm, the percussion is generally more muted, and there is an electric treble guitar on many tracks. This is the typical sound of Costeño music in the 1970s and 1980s. Seven of the eleven singers who have recorded with La Sonora have been Costeños, including Rodolfo Aicardi and Lucho Argaín (real name Lucho Pérez Cedrón), a sometime member of Los Corraleros de Majagual, who had been in the original Sonora Dinamita lineup. La Sonora Dinamita became particularly popular in Mexico, where they won several platinum disks and other awards and were instrumental in the international popularization of "cumbia" (which by that time included numbers very distant from that 1962 recording).[36]

By the 1980s, the type of music played by La Sonora Dinamita fell for many people into a general category of música tropical, within which distinctions between cumbia, porro, and gaita or between the music of Lucho Bermúdez and that of Los Graduados were not very important. Categorizations are, of course, highly flexible and subjective, depending in this case mainly on region of origin, class, and age.

Some people like to maintain a distinction between "real" or "good" música tropical—by which they mean the music of what I have called the old guard and the roots orchestras—and "bad" raspa or chucu-chucu, with salsa as a separate category. Ulloa Sanmiguel elaborates such a classification in his book on salsa (1992: 557). But, as he himself admits, some bands cross his category boundaries, and, in any case, many people, especially among those whose youth came after the golden age of the old guard, do not draw much of a distinction between the first two categories: it is all música bailable (dance music).[37]

There are, of course, real differences between particular recordings. For example, "La Subienda" (The Shoal) by Gabriel Romero y su Orquesta has many elements that might make it a reasonably "authentic" cumbia for some: clarinets alternate with a wind section given a full sound by trombones (and perhaps tubas), the scraper plays a slow chi-qui-CHA-chi-qui-CHA rhythm, and the bass plays a one-two-three beat. There is a piano but it carries a simple syncopated beat. The lyrics refer to a fisherman in a rural environment. In contrast, in "Capullo y Sorullo," by La Sonora Dinamita, the piano and electric guitar are prominent and carry most of the melody, while the brass section plays a lesser role and is undifferentiated, with no interplay of different instruments. The lyrics, sung by a smooth polished female voice, are humorous and refer to the eponymous couple of the song, who are both blond and have eight blond and one black child: the mother, when challenged, insists that black child is the only legitimate offspring of the father.[38] All this would make it easily classifiable as chucu-chucu or raspa. But both songs were recorded by Discos Fuentes and both are labeled cumbia.

In summary, then, in the hands of the Antioqueño-dominated recording industry, but with Discos Fuentes also in the vanguard, much of Costeño music became either "simplified" or "modernized," depending on one's point of view, often including some salsa arrangements and, in the 1980s, some Dominican merengue. The old guard and roots music did continue, but by 1980 it was in decline. It was, however, played in cover versions—"debased" or "modernized"—by the newer bands.

THE INTERNATIONALIZATION OF CUMBIA

Costeño music had been an international success since the 1940s: Lucho Bermúdez toured and recorded in Argentina, Cuba, Mexico, and the United States; Pacho Galán had toured Central America and Venezuela. In addition, Cuban, Venezuelan, and Mexican orchestras recorded versions of Costeño music. By 1960, Colombia was already better known for a "tropical" sound than for string ensembles playing bambuco.

In the 1960s, with the consolidation of the national record industry, Costeño music had an even greater impact abroad.[39] Stigberg (1985) states that in the mid-1960s, Mexican ensembles led by Mike Laure and Carmen Rivero had best-selling hits with adaptations of Colombian cumbia. This made a national success from what had previously been popular only in certain regions. In Mexico, cumbia was assimilated into the general category of música tropical, which included Cuban and other Caribbean styles: "The cumbia is different from the established formats of música tropical, but it also has much in common with them: earthy, often ribald lyrics, solo and choral singing in call and response patterns, and an emphasis on percussion and on rhythm, with rhythmic complexity achieved through the combination of layers of contrasting repeated patterns played by several instruments" (Stigberg 1985). In the late 1960s and 1970s, however, the same changes that occurred in Colombia took place in Mexico. Larger orchestras were replaced by smaller conjuntos with electric bass, organ, and a reduced brass section. A mid-1970s band, Costa Azul, led by Rigo Tovar, took still further this "tendency towards the simplification of the style of música tropical itself," a tendency "viewed with disapproval by many of those dedicated to the established Afro-Cuban forms." This and other similar groups dispensed with brass and reed instruments and reduced the "distinctive rhythm of cumbia . . . to its bare essentials" (Stigberg 1985). The identification of cumbia with Colombia was, however, maintained by textual references to Colombian, or rather Costeño, places and by band names such as Los Nueve de Colombia. The connection was reinforced by Colombian bands such as La Sonora Dinamita, which had great success playing cumbia and other styles of música tropical in Mexico. In the 1990s, cumbia remains a very important popular style in Mexico, with groups such as Los Bukis specializing in cumbia and the *bandas* that have become popular in the 1990s including cumbias in their repertoire, alongside rancheras and norteño music.

Colombian cumbia and other tropical rhythms made a similar sort of impact in Peru in the 1960s, mostly among urban middle-class youth. In the 1970s, however, these circles started to listen more to rock or salsa, and cumbia became linked to poorer urban migrants. *Cumbia andina* or *chicha* emerged as hybrid form that combined the melodic structure and cadence of the highland *wayno* (or *huayno*) style with a cumbia rhythm carried by the bass and percussion. It was the children of Andean migrants to the cities, "involved in the construction of a new identity," who really identified with this musical innovation (Turino 1993: 178; see also Bullen 1993; Cloudsley 1993: 20–26; and Turino 1990). However, the dividing line between salsa and cumbia or música tropical is not always sharply drawn in Peru, and I have heard styles that would be labeled música tropical by most Colombians—or even "chucu-chucu" by some—called salsa by some young middle-class Peruvians.

This process of internationalization—which also reached into Argentina, Chile, and particularly Central America—raises a number of questions which need further investigation. It is not very clear why the cumbia boom took place at this time, although it is probably related to the consolidation of the Colombian record industry and the production of the new sounds and instrumental lineups, discussed above, which clearly appealed to tastes in other Latin American countries in the same way they did to audiences in the interior of Colombia: a modern-sounding but still identifiably Latin American music. This would need comparative research in Mexico and other countries.

The question of why Costeño music became internationally most popular under the label *cumbia,* rather than *porro,* also needs more research. It doubtless has to do with the fact that porro was associated with the 1940s and 1950s and that record companies, keen to emphasize the (apparently) new rather than the old, began to leave porro behind. This was, after all, happening within Colombia too, as new names were created for "new" styles, including Pacho Galán's mere-cumbé, the paseaíto of Los Corraleros de Majagual, and others which never really took off such as *patacumbia* and *tumbasón.*

Finally, one of the things that might strike the reader who is familiar with the Latin American music scene is the relative lack of prominence of cumbia compared to other styles, such as salsa and merengue. Cumbia became very popular in certain areas, but it seems to have been less successful than salsa or merengue in capturing the international market. This would need comparative research to substantiate—it may be more a question of cumbia's lesser impact on the U.S. record industry—but there may be some features of cumbia that explain such a pattern. First, Colombians have always been avid consumers of foreign styles of music, whether in the 1950s or the 1990s. Cuban, Mexican, and North American styles have always been major and even dominant players. This may relate to the regionalization of the country, with markedly different tastes apparent in La Costa, the

Pacific coastal region, and different areas of the interior. Also, there was never in Colombia, as there was in the Dominican Republic, a concerted effort by the state to make a single musical style *the* national style (cf. Austerlitz 1995; Pacini Hernández 1995). The state has generally taken a hands-off approach to popular music. Finally, and related to this, Colombian emigrants to the United States have been less numerous than Dominicans, Cubans, and Puerto Ricans, and they have not been able capture a market niche there with a single Colombian style—this is in contrast to both salsa and merengue.[40]

These questions aside, the interesting thing about the international popularity of cumbia is that Colombia's image abroad was principally that of a "tropical" country, whatever the representations being made of it by a literate or political elite based in the highlands. Gabriel García Márquez and other writers and artists were clearly influential here, but music was much more so, at least outside literate and intellectual circles. The impact of music was simply much more pervasive. Also, vitally, this music commonly involved dancing and socializing as well as solitary listening. Without arguing that reading a book or viewing a painting is an asocial or unembodied activity, the point can still stand that this music entered into and mediated contexts of social relations which were highly charged with emotional and embodied meanings—often involving sexual relations as well. It thus helped to constitute Colombian identity abroad, not only pervasively, but in a particularly potent way. It is no surprise that when Gabriel García Márquez went to collect his Nobel Prize for literature in 1982, he was accompanied by Los Hermanos Zuleta, a vallenato group, and by Totó la Momposina y Sus Tambores, a group specializing in "traditional" Costeño music.

VALLENATO

In chapter 3, I looked at the origin myths surrounding vallenato. On the one hand, there is a rather regionally particularist view which holds that accordion music based on paseo, merengue, and son was native to the region of "La Provincia"—that is, Valledupar and its environs—and was interpreted from the late nineteenth century by a long sequence of locally born exponents, becoming gradually commercialized, acquiring the generic label of vallenato in the process, and, in the later stages of this process, often becoming degenerate. Accordion music from elsewhere in La Costa is seen as derivative or of secondary importance. This narrative is contested by those who maintain that vallenato as a coherent style of music emerged only in the 1940s, with the advent of modern communications and through the direct mediation of local elites seeking exactly the regional particularity which the traditionalist narrative helps to sustain (Gilard 1987a, 1987b). I would support Gilard's view with the argument that, although accordions were present in La Costa in small numbers and were used to accompany various styles—anything from sung verses to mazurkas—there was no "tradition" or established repertoire which then simply became commercialized into "vallenato." The latter itself emerged with the recording industry and became consolidated in the 1960s. It is significant, for example, that Gabriel García Márquez, writing for a Barranquilla audience in 1950, saw fit to explain that "música Vallenata" was so called because it came from the Valledupar region: the term was apparently not well known (García Márquez 1981: 167).

As I showed in chapter 4, accordion music was recorded early by Discos Fuentes and Discos Tropical, but it remained a mainly regional market, with the guitar-based "vallenatos" of Guillermo Buitrago and Julio Bovea having more success in the interior and accordion music being seen as either very plebeian or "folkloric" in the interior, and indeed to some extent in La Costa too. However, vallenato music and the region around Valledupar were already gaining some powerful political allies in Bogotá. Ex-president Alfonso López Pumarejo's mother came from Valledupar, the family had a farm in the area, and his son, Alfonso López Michelsen, visited the region in the late 1940s with companions from Bogotá: their parties were, of course, always held to the accompaniment of música de acordeón. Meanwhile, several individuals from Valledupar who had good political connections were living in Bogotá at the time. These people, in an informal grouping called Los Magdalenos, arranged a visit of vallenato composer Rafael Escalona to Bogotá in 1953, which was noticed in several prominent papers and magazines. The dictator Rojas Pinilla was in power at the time, and Escalona wrote a tune for him, "El General Rojas," which was later arranged by Antonio María Peñaloza for the Orquesta Sinfónica Nacional and broadcast on the Radio Nacional.

The emergence of vallenato as a genre was thus also mediated by the particular set of Liberal political links between Valledupar and Bogotá which gave prominence to the accordion music of this particular region just at the time when such music was also being recorded and given radio airtime and when the area of La Provincia was being integrated into the wider region by infrastructural projects backed by López Pumarejo. These political links continued in the 1960s with President Guillermo León Valencia (1962–1966), who also held parties in Bogotá at which Rafael Escalona and vallenato music were guests (Arau-jonoguera 1988).

Then, under Lleras Restrepo (1966–1970), there was a campaign for the creation of the administrative province of El Cesar—basically the territories of La Provincia. At the time, several new such depar-tamentos were under consideration and there was debate about the pros and cons of creating more administrative divisions. As part of the campaign for El Cesar, Escalona and vallenato musicians—among them the famous accordionist Colacho Mendoza—toured the country, participating in "Encuentros Vallenatos" (Vallenato Meetings).[41] One doubter asked if the separatists thought that the division would be achieved "by the magic of their rhythms condensed with the alcoholic inspiration of whisky" (*El Heraldo,* 10 December 1966, p. 3). Another journalist noted: "Even though Cesar Province may have at times given the frivolous impression of having been won with paseos vallenatos and notes from an accordion, it is true that its folklore is one of the richest in the country" (*El Heraldo,* 18 November 1966, p. 3). Whether through frivolity, magic, or hard-nosed politics, El Cesar was duly created. Alfonso López Michelsen was its first governor, and he named Rafael Escalona as his public relations chief.

The consolidation of vallenato as a "tradition" born in La Provin-cia occurred in 1968 with the initiation of the Festival de la Leyenda Vallenata (Festival of the Vallenato Legend). This was purportedly based on an informal get-together organized in 1963 for Gabriel Gar-cía Márquez by Rafael Escalona when the former returned to Colom-bia after seven years' absence abroad and wanted to hear all the best in vallenato music (García Márquez 1991: 426). The festival as such was organized by Alfonso López Michelsen with the help of Consuelo Araujonoguera—a well-known writer on vallenato music—and the event first took place in the large colonial house of her family. García Márquez has frequently sat on the festival's panel of judges. There were long-standing traditions in La Costa of duels between accordion-ists, and the festival took the form of a competition. The idea was to maintain the authenticity of vallenato, and conjuntos were initially restricted to the "traditional" lineup of accordion, caja, and gua-characa, with the accordionist as vocalist, although later a separate singer was permitted. Each year a king is chosen, the first being Alejo Durán (fig. 6.11). Despite the aura of authenticity, the record compa-nies maintain a keen interest and may promote the winner into a new star (see Gutiérrez Hinojosa 1992: chap. 15; and Quiroz Otero 1982: chap. 10).

6.11 Alejandro Durán receives his trophy and a check from Cecilia Caballero de López Michelsen (wife of the governor of Cesar Province). (By permission of El Espectador.)

Meanwhile, vallenato as a commercial music was taking different directions. With Los Corraleros de Majagual and the individual artists associated with them, especially Alfredo Gutiérrez, accordion music became more widespread in the interior of the country, often played with horn and reed instrument parts, and including new styles such as paseaíto and pasebol.

In the early 1970s, vallenato in its more characteristic form, based simply on the accordion, bass, and percussion, without a brass section, remained a basically lower-class music and popular mainly in La Costa. From that time, however, building on the successes of Alfredo Gutiérrez and others, its popularity began to expand exponentially. At the same time, it began to change musically as well. There are many artists and companies involved here, but certain names stand out. CBS (now Sony) had begun recording operations in Colombia in 1965 and, in the early 1970s, started recordings with the Costeño singer Jorge Oñate fronting Los Hermanos López and also with Los Hermanos Zuleta, Emiliano on accordion and Poncho on vocals. Later they added Diomedes Díaz to their list, and he, with several different accordionists, has proven to be one of the best-selling vallenato singers.[42] These artists were still playing and recording in the late 1990s.

The involvement of CBS with vallenato was not automatic: it started recording with Lucho Bermúdez, and, in the early 1970s, when it began to develop its catalog of national artists, ballad singers were a principal focus. Gabriel Muñoz, who, after working for a year with Discos Tropical in Barranquilla, started in artists and repertoire with CBS, was a vallenato enthusiast, despite having been born in Manizales, Caldas Province: "They say I'm more Costeño than Caldense, because I really like música tropical." He was a mover behind the investment in vallenato artists, although he saw himself as swimming against the company tide. "I always believed that vallenato was a rich vein of music, because it was a music that, despite being very regional, could be turned into something more generic. And the only people who could play it were them [the Costeños]. Música tropical can be covered and it can sound the same; salsa's the same. Any type of music but that. That music you can't imitate."

This suggests a concern with authenticity, and Muñoz reiterated this: "The principal quality [I'm looking for] is the authenticity of the artist: that's absolutely vital to me . . . . If it's the composer, then he should have his own writing style; if it's the accordionist, then he needs his own particular playing style which can be identified when you hear it on the radio. That's vital for us." Authenticity here is individuality or nonimitation, rather than traditionality. It is being true to one's muse, rather than to one's roots. But the two overlap when "only the Costeños" can produce the authentic sound. Nevertheless, too much traditionality was to be avoided. Muñoz was from the start looking for something that he saw as not entirely traditional: the split between singer and accordionist was important, in his view, giving each the opportunity to concentrate on his part. Hence, Jorge Oñate and Poncho Zuleta were just vocalists. Also, lyrics had to be more than just regional: "Because there are some songs that are very regional, but that say a lot—such as 'Alicia Adorada' . . . —and that are so great, so well done, that everyone can assimilate them perfectly.[43] But there are songs that are too folkloric, very much their own [the Costeños'], and they're not liked in the interior. So I always had that criterion: to make songs a little more generic, looking precisely to widen the national market."

Codiscos already had Alfredo Gutiérrez in its stable, and he was selling a lot of records. Its next major success came in 1978 with El Binomio de Oro (The Golden Pair) who have recorded some twenty-five albums with the company. Israel Romero plays accordion and Rafael Orozco was on vocals until his death in 1993 (at the hands of drug traffickers according to some rumors, the fruits of philandering according to others). According to Fernando López, head of artists and repertoire at Codiscos, El Binomio broke the barrier which still limited vallenato as a product in the interior of the country. "Today, vallenato has left authenticity 100 percent behind. Today, people dance a more pop vallenato. That's what we did, with the idea of getting into other countries. For us, the clearest case is El Binomio de Oro. El Binomio de Oro gave a very refined character to vallenato; they dressed it up in a dinner jacket. And that allowed vallenato to sell strongly in the interior of the country, to leave La Costa and include the whole country." Authenticity here is simply provincialism and limited traditionality, something to be left behind in seeking out a more cosmopolitan audience.

A less easily assessed element in the popularization of vallenato was the influence of drug trafficking. In the 1970s, during the marijuana boom which was centered for a while on the Sierra Nevada mountains, between Santa Marta and Valledupar, the newly ascendant Costeño drug traffickers sponsored vallenato artists, who in return would name them in their songs. In later years, when the drug traffic moved to cocaine and centered on Medellín, some of the big traffickers would again fly vallenato groups, among other musicians, into their private estates for weekend parties. It is not clear to what extent this did anything other than speed up a process that was already under way, but it may have helped vallenato to gain an image that went beyond the rural and the folkloric. Some people also hold the drug traffic influence responsible for what they see as the loss of authenticity in vallenato, but again it is likely that this process of commercialization and musical change was happening anyway.[44]

Musically, the newer styles of vallenato used some of the same innovations that the "modernized" tropical Costeño music employed: by this time, the electric bass was standard, and in the 1980s electric keyboards and electric guitars began to be added on occasion. There was also an expansion in the rhythm section: the caja had already been supplemented by a conga drum, and this was followed by timbales. Vocalists began to use backing singers, usually two male voices, one often being a high contralto. Later, electronic drum kits appeared, drum and accordion parts might be double or triple tracked, and backing vocals might be done by three voices, perhaps without the high, constrained sound of the contralto. The lineup of one of these vallenato bands became almost like an old orchestra in size, often comprising a dozen musicians and singers, not counting at least one accordion technician. It is worth noting, however, that these changes were partly in relation to the nominally "traditional" lineup of accordion/vocals, guacharaca, and caja. Buitrago's music of the 1940s, although not labeled "valle-nato" as such (e.g., in the Discos Fuentes catalog of 1954), included a variety of instruments (guitars, bass, clarinets). Backing singers were also used long before the 1970s, for example, by Bovea y Sus Valle-natos. On the other hand, the accordion was used alongside various different instruments in the late nineteenth and early twentieth centuries (see chapter 3).

Vallenato had always included many romantic themes—or more accurately themes about male-female relations (Wade 1994a). It also had a certain picaresque quality, relating events and mentioning people, often with a somewhat satirical tone. Some of the songs could be fully understood only by those to whom these places and personalities were known (Posada 1986). The literature on vallenato frequently mentions that it was an oral musical form of newspaper (see the texts on val-lenato cited in chapter 3).[45] In the newer styles of vallenato, local themes lost importance, although they did not disappear and places were still often named, without much effect on listeners who did not know their exact location, since the songs often simply reiterated the origins of vallenato in La Provincia. The main move in lyrical terms was to greatly increase the emphasis on romantic themes, usually treated in a more abstract way. Rafael Escalona's songs included typi-cal themes of love affairs, lovesickness, unrequited love, and the jeal-ous woman, but these were always about an identifiable, named per-son. He also included tales about local people and events which had narrative elements in them. In contrast to Escalona's literate style, Alejo Durán's songs are lyrically simple, often consisting of a few two-line verses which, like Escalona's songs, tend to refer to particular places, people, and events, with his relations with women forming a major theme. If one compares El Binomio de Oro, the same romantic themes prevail, but now to the virtual exclusion of other subjects. The woman is usually an abstract person, and the overriding feelings de-scribed are pain and lovesickness due to the heartlessness of women or their intransigent families. The poignant simplicity of Alejo Durán is left behind for a more literate lyrical style.[46]

Exactly as with música tropical, the record companies have tended to see these changes as progress and modernization, while many oth-ers, often middle-class people, but others as well—for example, the

6.12 Leandro Díaz.
(By permission of
Cromos.)

older generation of Costeños—have bewailed the "degeneration" of
vallenato. Despite its acceptance in the interior of the country, vallenato was still widely seen as "the music of maids and taxi drivers" and
represented vulgar, common tastes; only very recently has this mold
been partially altered (see chapter 8). If middle-class people or fans of
rock and salsa admitted a liking for vallenato, this was, and usually
still is, qualified by deprecating comments about El Binomio de Oro
and a preference for the "real" thing, represented by Alejo Durán,
Emiliano Zuleta the elder, Juancho Polo Valencia, and Leandro Díaz
(fig. 6.12)—the older generation of vallenato artists.

Conclusion

The story of Costeño music during the decades after 1950 is one of
increasing commercialization, as porro's position at center stage was
taken over by cumbia and then finally by vallenato. In one sense, this
is a story of the appropriation and transformation of a regional music
by national music capitalism operating in a transnational market. There

was a transformist hegemony at work here creating a national music from local roots. This story runs the risk, however, of oversimplification: while one could suggest that the central role of Costeños was just as musicians being exploited by the music industry, this argument does not hold for Antonio Fuentes, a Costeño, who was one of the prime movers behind the commercialization and innovation of Costeño music. Discos Tropical in Barranquilla also continued to be important into the 1970s, and Discos Curro was significant, if transient: both took part in the overall transformation of Costeño music.

Just as important as the risk of oversimplification are the underlying implications of such a story: the idea that Costeño music, in its early commercial form, was a cultural product tied to La Costa in some authentic way and that its commercialization by the national recording industry was a simple process of alienation. This may be the way that some people understand the process—a good example is Ulloa Sanmiguel (1992), with his deprecatory comments on raspa and his praise for Colombo-Caribbean tropical music—but it is clearly inadequate to see the music of Lucho Bermúdez or Pacho Galán as simply "authentically" Costeño: it was national and international music from the start, although its *image* was Costeño.

A broader perspective needs to avoid opposing the authentic region to the alienating nation and instead see Costeño music in the context of a growing music industry that took the nation as its object of attention (and aspired to the international market). The fact that the industry was centered outside La Costa or that it was run mainly by Antioqueños is significant but not determinant—the overriding point is that it was an industry. The mission of Sonolux was to earn profits by making the Colombian people happy, and Costeño music was just one way of achieving this end. Costeño record producers, musicians, and composers were just as keen to have their products be successful and "nationalized." This is perhaps truly the sense of a transformist *hegemony:* all these people were pursuing the same goal in their different ways. But the image of the music as Costeño, or at least tropical, was not erased in this transformation. Here we need to focus on what Costeño music was thought, or could be made, to represent for "the public" in general. As I argued in the previous chapter, Costeño music was located in an ambivalent space between modernity and tradition, regionality and nationality, homogeneity and heterogeneity, and its potential for making this space productive was what made it powerful.

If we look at the overlapping progression from porro through cumbia to vallenato, the common feature is precisely the presence of this ambivalent space. Porro lost some of its appeal because it could increasingly be seen as too old and too folkloric: Lucho Bermúdez was aging; Pedro Laza seemed too tied to rural Costeño themes. Cumbia seemed more modern, yet still located in a specific place that could be regional and/or national, depending on emphasis. Yet for some people, cumbia went too far in the opposite direction. It came to represent falsity: the glossy, superficial, overcommercialized detritus of modernity, vulgar in a way that was sham and bourgeois rather than authentic and plebeian. It also became appropriated by Mexican bands to such an extent that some controversy started over whether cumbia was Colombian or Mexican in origin. It was increasingly difficult to read the música tropical of the 1980s as authentic, with roots either in a particular region or even country (as porro could be read) or in the lower class (as salsa could be read, at least in that period).

This is at the heart of many Costeños' distaste for the chucu-chucu that is often associated with the Antioqueño bands: much of Costeño music in the "cumbia" mold was going in a direction symbolized by these bands, and many Costeños found it hard to identify such music as their own, even if only in image. In this sense, the hegemonic transformations of the music were contested by Costeños (and indeed others) for whom it no longer articulated an authentic sense of the regional differences and identities of the nation. For the Costeños, the contestation could take the form of seeing this degeneration as Antioqueño-led; for others, the decline could be seen as bourgeois commercialization. These two discourses of regional ethnicity and class were not necessarily opposed; rather, they could easily be combined—to construe, for example, "good" Costeño music as rooted in an authentic regional working class.

It was at this time that vallenato was being established as a truly authentic but also incipiently national sound. It had the legitimation of the Festival of the Vallenato Legend, with big names such as García Márquez to vouch for its authenticity, but it was also becoming highly successful commercially. As usual, the debate among aficionados, musicians, and record producers came to focus on the relative merits of sounds held to be more or less traditional or modern (and more or less distanced from its rural working-class roots). From this perspective, the search was constantly on for music that would work effectively in the ambivalent, tense space between tradition and modernity—both of which, of course, were themselves ambivalent and constantly subject to reelaboration. For the musicians and record producers this seems to have been an enduring feature: Fuentes constantly experimented with

changing lineups and new arrangements; Bermúdez and others contin-
ually invented "new" rhythms—some disappeared without a trace,
while others were smash hits; Fernando López of Codiscos revels in the
fact that El Binomio de Oro has left "authenticity 100 percent behind"; Gabriel Muñoz seeks the exact balance between modernity and
authenticity—the latter, for him, being the unique quality of a (Costeño) artist. What is interesting, of course, is that so much of this took
place, and is still taking place, within the ambit of Costeño music,
broadly defined. This music allowed the search to continue fruitfully.
Such potential, as I have already argued, lay largely in the music's connotations of happiness and—not unrelatedly—in its association with
blackness and potent sexuality (whether seen as voluptuous frisson or
as social liberation). In the next chapter, I will explore further the aspect of sexuality.

7 Costeños and Costeño Music in the Interior
REJECTION AND ADAPTATION, 1950S–1980S

From the 1950s through the 1980s, in the interior of the country, Costeños and Costeño music were a cultural presence that was subject to different readings and at times actively contested. This was not just in arenas defined by authenticity and degeneration versus commercial success, but as a representation of regional identity, racial heritage, sexual morality, and values of civilization and primitiveness, modernity and tradition, and peace and violence. From the 1950s, Costeño music was fairly well established in the interior of the country. In Medellín, especially, Costeño and other Caribbean music became an integral part of the city's culture (alongside the tangos and rancheras which the "paisas" are still reputed to love). But musics putatively belonging to particular regions and the way of listening, dancing, and partying to music were still seen by all concerned as different for Costeños and people from the interior. Music and dancing were important aspects of people's identities and modes of identification of themselves and others. In all this, there was a relationship of mutual mediation between music, gender relations, and sexuality in which Costeño music and Costeños themselves represented a sexual power which was both libertarian and liberating.

Costeños were an increasing presence in both Bogotá and Medellín, although they never constituted more than 1.5 percent of the urban totals. In the accounts of Costeños and people from Bogotá and Medellín, migrants from La Costa are presented as mainly male and mainly students. Data are available only to confirm 1980s educational patterns—showing that Costeños in these cities were indeed well educated—but it is clear that men predominated only until the 1960s;

even before then about 40 percent of Costeños in Bogotá and Medellín were women.[1]

The lines of debate about Costeños and Costeño music were similar to those traced in previous chapters, but for this later period I present the testimonies of Bogotá and Medellín residents compared with those of Costeño migrants to these cities. I include people's memories of music and dance in general, because it is important to see that these were often important and active parts of people's lives, as they were in previous decades. The increased presence of radio and recorded music, including Costeño music, simply increased this tendency—especially, it seems, in Medellín. The image frequently purveyed by Costeños and people from the interior alike—that cachacos did not know how to dance and rarely did so—is not accurate. Like many stereotypes, it is usually deployed for contrastive effect: compared to the Costeños, it was *as if* people from the interior did not dance.

Bogotá: Resistance

Stella de Briceño, a teacher who lived in Bogotá from about 1946, remembered that, as a girl, she and her cousins would go dancing almost every weekend at one of the elite social clubs where orchestras played, or at the Gril Colombia, a venue for the well heeled, with orchestra and dance floor, or to records in friends' houses during empanadas bailabes (Saturday afternoon dances) or evening parties.[2] Such house parties were controlled by parents who prepared the drinks and kept an eye on how close the partners were dancing, especially during the slow, romantic boleros. They danced mainly porro, bolero, and some tango, but also the cha-cha-chá and merecumbé. Meanwhile, Stella also went to ballet school and took part in musical *tertulias* (get-togethers) in her house where people would sing, play the piano and recite. Her image of the Costeños was that they were "very *alegres,* noisy, magnificent singers, impressive dancers, because everybody used to say, as they say now, that the Costeño carries music in his blood and it's true, they listen to music and it's like they begin to move, even their eyes begin to dance; and they're very extrovert and very frank—sometimes they go a bit too far and become rude." Her first impression of La Costa was when she went to Cartagena as the Boyacá Province candidate for the national beauty contest there, so she had a particular and privileged experience of La Costa.

Despite the popularity of the porros of Lucho Bermúdez and the merecumbés of Pacho Galán, Costeños themselves were often not well

regarded. Ema Valderrama, the middle-class teacher in Bogotá introduced in chapter 5, remembered that "Costeños were rather rejected
because it seemed to us who lived in the center of the country that we
were cultured, refined, respectful, decent, intelligent and that they were
bullangueros [noisy] and vulgar—opinions which arose without much
basis." As a result, when Costeño music first arrived, people danced to
it "with timidity because the older people were against it, rejected it,
and considered it ordinary, vulgar; [they would say] how could a girl
to move to the rhythm of a cumbia or a porro?—what a scandal! But
it gradually entered [into Bogotá society] because the rhythm is so
sabroso [delicious, nice], so exciting that there are no hips that don't
move to the rhythm of that music—it's impossible."

She herself went to La Costa in about 1960. Before this, her main
impression of the region was from the music itself, with associated
ideas of revelry and noise, plus rather vague notions about the sea;
there was also an underlying notion of the relative blackness of the region. Her experience impressed on her the friendliness and openness of
the Costeños, and she commented that negative ideas about blacks
were transformed by this and the sight of "those black women, so wil-
lowy and graceful, carrying fruits and *cocadas* [coconut sweets] on
their heads . . . with that rhythm, with that waist swaying and those
hips moving so rhythmically." The sea also fascinated her: "I couldn't
believe that there was so much beauty in life. The sea absorbed me
completely and stayed forever in my soul and my eyes."

Music, rhythm, graceful bodies, and the sea: all these were exciting
and fascinating, but noisiness and explicit sexuality were also threatening to some people's ideas of propriety. This was certainly the experience of Ligia de Márquez, the Bogotá-born teacher, whose father
disapproved strongly of the Costeño man interested in his daughter.
She met this man at the university: he was "very *alegre,* very intelligent, [but] my father couldn't [bear to] see him even in a picture.
There was a terrible rejection and my father never let him enter the
house"—despite the fact that he was the brother of the rector of the
university where they both studied and so hardly likely to be of lower-
class origins.

Often, Costeño migrants to Bogotá and Medellín came to study and
tended to come from middle-class backgrounds, so class as such was
not necessarily the issue. If, however, as Stella de Briceño said, people
thought that Costeños carried music "in the blood," then a monied
background was not necessarily enough: for many middle-class people,
simply singing and dancing to popular music—especially outside the

domestic sphere—evoked images of impropriety and lower-class activity. If music was seen as being "in the blood," then this was difficult to offset with money. And if, every now and then, the Costeños "went too far," it only proved the point.

Another parent, María Helena Ramírez, opposed her daughter's relation with a Costeño man, although in retrospect she regretted her attitude. In the 1950s, her husband was killed and she moved with her three daughters to Bogotá to work as a teacher. For her, around that period, dancing was a common enough activity. There were parties with friends at which they danced to bambucos, pasillos, and fox-trots, but also to mambos and the music of the Cuban orchestra La Sonora Matancera; they might go out to a night club. She remembers rather little Costeño music, even though her sisters had Costeño friends who were teachers or students. The general image people had, according to her, was that Costeños were "not very trustworthy, a bit outrageous in terms of delicacy. Perhaps because of the hypocrisy of Andean people . . . the Costeño character was too aggressive." [3] Presumably she shared this view, because she fought with her daughter about the latter's Costeño boyfriend, who happened to be "moreno"—dark skinned. Costeños seem to have been ambivalent figures for her at that time: friends on the one hand, a threat on the other.

People's images varied, of course. Alfredo Arroyo, who declared himself to be of "upper-middle-class origins," went to a boarding school in Bogotá in the mid-1940s when many of the live-in students were Costeños. "There was an idea that they didn't have much urbanity because they were more open, uncomplicated—and everyone here wore a tie, very formal." There were also jokes referring to the supposed vulgarity of the Costeños. But Alfredo Arroyo made many friends among them and later, at the university, enjoyed the Costeños' parties, which were different because "there was more drink, the women were more open." In contrast, three Bogotá residents interviewed together—María Angélica Burgos, María Eugenia Goubert, and Luis Alfredo Rueda—remembered the reputation of the Costeños as being negative. People thought "that they were the noisiest, they were *pesados* [literally, heavy, boorish], sort of loud and bad mannered, that any party where there were Costeños would end badly. What else can I tell you? That was their reputation." In their comments, there was a general association of Costeños with blackness and laziness. Recounting more personal experiences—visits to Cartagena, university companions—there was agreement that individual Costeños were "very pleasant, *alegre.*" There was also constant reference to color: "She was very nice; she was from a Costeño family but she wasn't *de color* [colored]"; "we have a friend, a very famous colored doctor, and when you're talking to him you forget what color he is"; "some of my brothers are married to Costeños. Yes, but they're not colored." As far as the music was concerned, for these three it was a generational issue: their elders did not like it, but they did.

These comments were all from middle-class people, but the same general themes emerged from working-class people. As in the 1930s and 1940s, dance continued to be a normal feature of urban life for working-class people in Bogotá, as it was for middle-class people. However, parties and dancing seem to have been occasional activities for most people. Samuel Urbina, for example, a government employee in Bogotá, danced to the radio during occasional parties in private houses—mostly guitar music, Mexican rancheras, and boleros—and sometimes in the cinema on Sunday mornings, where he remembers dancing to boleros and to Bovea y Sus Vallenatos.

Since many Costeños migrated for secondary and university schooling, fewer working-class than middle-class people had met Costeños in Bogotá and so there was greater reliance on general stereotypes. One shopkeeper had visited La Costa a lot and liked Costeños because they were "*alegre,* boozers"—somewhat after his own tastes—although he also saw them "as a bit lazy." A security guard who first visited La Costa in 1953 thought that the Costeños "lacked culture and were very arrogant." A domestic servant commented that Costeños seemed "alegres" to her, while a government employee said: "There are Costeños of all kinds. Some are good workers, others are very idle. They like to party, to drink, to have fun, to go out—not so much to work." One woman shopkeeper who had visited Cartagena in the late 1960s observed: "Well, you see those blacks dancing mapalé and all that: they're easy to get on with. . . . They've always been more *alegre* than oneself." A female bank cashier, whose chief experience of Costeños came from a year spent in Santa Marta with some compadres, said she generally liked Costeños, although they were "a little licentious: they speak openly and it seems sort of licentious to me, but that's their temperament." She added that they were lazy workers but good dancers. Almost all these people remembered that Costeño music was well accepted in Bogotá and it seems that the sexual morality of dancing and ideas about excessive noise were a more middle- and upper-class preoccupation (from interviews with, respectively, Pedro Guarnizo, Jaime Clavijo, Hilda María Sánchez, Samuel Urbina, Lucía Ramírez, and María del Carmen Villalobos).[4] Nevertheless, ambivalence and ambiguity mark many reactions, regardless of class: people in Bogotá found Costeños both gay and vulgar or even threatening; they enjoyed the music but also thought that it could be improper.

Medellín: "More Costeño than La Costa"?

Judging from interview material, by the 1950s Medellín was already more lively than Bogotá: music and dance were a more central aspect of people's memories. For some, dance and "rumba" (partying) were practically a way of life. Jairo Colorado, a leather worker in Medellín, prided himself on his ability to dance rock and roll, porro, bolero, fox-trot, paso doble, mambo, guaracha, and so on:

> Everyone had his own original steps which we'd practice in front of the mirror. We'd go and see a film and then we'd go home or to the bar. In the bar there were mirrors and we'd practice the steps. And sometimes we'd change things around. We'd add something to the steps. . . . We had moves in rock and roll which we'd never seen in the American films. . . . On Sundays, we'd get up at six in the morning and get the train to Botero. There we'd swim and dance all day long. And dancers from Salvador, Gerona, and La Toma [barrios of Medellín] would turn up. We'd all meet there and learn from each other.

No interviews in Bogotá turned up individuals such as Colorado, while those in Medellín revealed several. Antonio Tapias, a contemporary of Colorado's, recalled that dancing and music were vital parts of his youth. Guayaquil was bursting with music and particular styles predominated in different streets: tangos, rancheras, the music of La Sonora Matancera, Costeño music, and so on. House parties were a frequent occurrence in his working-class neighborhood and were informal in style: the doors were open and neighbors came and went without an invitation. Porros and Cuban music were the staple diet. By the age of fourteen, he was a good dancer and would escape with his *barra* (gang, group of friends) to El Bosque de la Independencia (a public park), the bars of Guayaquil, or other dance halls to dance with women there. Barras from different barrios would compete on the dance floor, and older men might give tips to good dancers. A neighborhood could often be identified by the particularities of its dancers' style: a man from Enciso, for example, tended to keep his hand open and horizontal against his partner's back. The boys usually had a specific dance partner from their barrio, but since a girl's freedom was more controlled, they would also pick up temporary dance partners if they went to dance halls. As with Colorado, people would practice in their houses, with and without their partners. Porro was an integral part of working-class Medellín culture.

Interestingly, these dancers also began to adapt the dance styles. In the 1950s, according to Antonio, who is now a dance teacher, the *porro paseado* (strolled or walked porro) was the main style; this was "quite gentle, with moves from the fox-trot." Then dancers started to add "moves from the paso doble and from the bolero-mambo." In the mid-1980s, people in Enciso (Antonio's barrio) began to dance the *porro marcado* (marked porro), "putting more emphasis on the beat of the music." More recently, they began to add moves taken from tango and salsa and make up their own moves. In the mid-1990s, a visit to one of the several dance halls catering to amateur dance enthusiasts revealed young and old people performing very complex turns to old Lucho Bermúdez numbers and including obvious tango moves in their routines. Porro danced in this way is a specifically Antioqueño fashion through which the "paisas" have appropriated a Costeño dance, transforming it with elements drawn from dance styles associated with the tango, which has been such a strong influence in Medellín.

This experience of dance was not simply a working-class matter. Dario Ruiz, a university teacher of middle-class origins, recounted: "As a student, I used to go to a trade union [center] and there were nothing but [female] workers there and—go for it! It was great there, dancing with those workers." He added:

> The Antioqueño is very serious and there has been and still is a very conservative class here, very serious, distanced from *alegría:* work for work's sake, no? And there was some subversion in dancing, because dancing was a way of living, of showing off. That is, when one was a kid in the barrio, the way of defending yourself was to dance the best; that's why I was a good dancer. . . . You'd go to a popular place, to a union center or El Bosque de la Independencia—on Sundays, you'd go there to watch the black women and everyone dancing, and you'd ask someone to dance and people saw that you danced well and they respected you, there was no problem. . . . We used to go everywhere. . . . [We'd say] Let's go to Manrique [a working-class barrio]. So we'd set off and—exactly [as expected]—about four in the afternoon, you'd hear music in a house: so we'd stand in the doorway, until the lady of the house said "Do you want to come in, boys?" Of course! And right away—let's dance!

William Ramírez, born in Medellín in 1933, had close links with the music world through his father, who owned the Hotel Europa, where many artists stayed and performed; he later worked in the hotel himself. He recalled famous cafés and "grills," such as the Covadonga (which he knew as a youngster) or the Gril Piedamonte, owned by Adolfo Podestar, the saxophonist of the Italian Jazz Band. For middle-class men, the red-light districts were also important sites of music and dance. Lovaina was a relatively upmarket zone: there men would congregate in the early hours of the morning, drinking and listening to music on the *pianos* (jukeboxes) of Café Milancito or Café Ventiadero. Guayaquil was a cheaper red-light district: "[In Guayaquil] there was a street called la Calle de los Tambores [the Street of the Drums] because in one café they set up the jukebox and beside it they put a drum kit with a guy playing along to the rhythm of the jukebox, and there was another man, a maraca player. And so they called it the Street of the Drums because it was the most fantastic noise in the world. And apart from that, the area filled up with women, women of the good life [i.e., prostitutes]. And even *gente de bien* [well-off people] would go around Guayaquil, down Carabobo [Street] and back again." Arturo Zuluaga, a singer with various orchestras in Medellín in the 1950s, remembered that there was a plethora of work for musicians: there were many clubs (such as Club Medellín, Club de Profesionales, Club Unión, Club Campestre, Club Miraflores), and scores of hotel, nightclub, and bar venues, not to mention the radio theaters. There were many orchestras made up of musicians from the interior which played Costeño music, Cuban music, mambo, cha-cha-chá, bolero, and so on.

Music and dance, including Costeño styles, were thus an integral part of Medellín life by the 1950s. And this is despite the fact that La Violencia led to the repression of urban nightlife, especially street life. Today, Medellín people often say that porro has found a better home in their city than it has in La Costa, where salsa and merengue have largely displaced it.

This acceptance of Costeño music was not, of course, the same as the acceptance of Costeños, but it is interesting that interview material from residents of Medellín was much less explicitly derogatory with respect to Costeños than that of their Bogotá counterparts. There was the odd comment about the supposed noisiness or laziness of Costeños, but usually there was emphasis on *alegría*, rather than lack of culture and vulgarity. This is despite the fact that, in recent decades in the toilets of the University of Antioquia, graffiti could be seen that included the slogan "Hacer patria es matar costeños, entonces haga patria" (to be patriotic is to kill Costeños, so be patriotic). There is no doubt that the exclusivism and racism of some Antioqueños extends toward some Costeños—as I shall show below—but it seems that the general image of the Costeño as vulgar, common, uncultured, and licentious was and is less powerful in Medellín than in Bogotá (cf. Wade 1993a).

Summing up reactions to Costeños in both in Bogotá and Medellín, there was very general agreement that Costeños were *alegre*. This held also for their music, since Costeños were widely identified as good dancers and sometimes spoken of as having music in their blood: the association with music was often construed as physical, imbuing body and blood. *Alegría* could, however, be both good and bad, implying fun, openness, and sincerity (as opposed to Andean "hypocrisy") but also laziness in work, indelicacy, loudness, vulgarity, and licentiousness. The latter traits were also strongly identified with blackness. This link was more ambiguous, because although people might imagine that Costeños were generally black, experience soon taught them that many were not, especially the middle-class Costeños who went to Bogotá to study. However, color and racial identity often prompted pondering, and the nonblackness of certain Costeños was often a cause for thought and comment, indicating a typical association of La Costa with blackness.

Ambivalence, then, was a central feature in imaginings about Costeños and Costeño music. The "good" side of the Costeños was, for many people, precisely their music and the feeling or idea of freedom which it seemed to imply. Jairo Vasco, a trumpet player with El Combo Di Lido, observed: "The music is the best thing the Costeños have, the music and the sea. We Antioqueños have a different sort of music: bambuco, pasillo, and the music of the interior. So what we have to dance to is their music . . . because although our music is very nice, it's not dance music. So if you've got *un corazón de negro* [the heart of a black person]—at least that's how I feel it—you feel the music, you feel it so strongly you have to play it, you have to dance to it."[5] Even though música tropical was an integral part of his life and that of the city where he lived, he still identified "his" music as being bambuco and pasillo—which was not danceable, as far as he was concerned. "Their" music was danceable and was able to reach to his heart; "in his heart," he already felt "black," so he could not resist the urge to play and dance to their music. Striking here is his use of embodied metaphors: blackness is a physical presence within him, located in the heart, the seat of emotion. It is outwardly invisible in itself, but inwardly it resonates with the music and cannot help but express itself physically through music and dance. Mestizaje here does not erase blackness, nor is blackness blended into some indeterminate amalgam: it persists as an identifiable element within the person.

The Costeños in Bogotá and Medellín

RACE, DIFFERENCE, AND SOLIDARITY

Antonio María Peñaloza arrived in Bogotá in about 1940 and got a job with the orchestra of the Emisora Nueva Granada, directed at the time by Francisco Cristancho (see chapter 4). The first piece he was required to play was a bambuco with which, like many Costeño composers, he was already very familiar. Peñaloza had his own ideas about bambuco and ventured the opinion that the piece was wrongly written.[6] "We [he and Cristancho] had been presented very politely, in Bogotá style, but when I said that, the guy *me negreó* [called me, treated me like, a black] straight away: 'Listen, *negrito*, you should know that in order to play bambuco you have to eat *chunchullo, sobrebarriga,* and chicha.'"[7] Peñaloza might have been a good trumpeter and musician, but he was also a Costeño and a black man, albeit light skinned—and this "cachaco" band leader would not tolerate being taught his "own" business.

Matilde Díaz, Lucho Bermúdez's singer, recounted problems of racism when the band played at the opening of a new building in about 1947 in Bogotá:

> We had a great drummer, called El Negrito Virolí, who was a tall man, very good looking, who didn't have black [facial] features—beautiful eyes, aquiline nose, nice teeth—and he was black, black [i.e., very dark skinned]. And I remember when we did the opening of that building, we were in the elevator and people were going up to the dance. And one of those men said, "I don't know why they let blacks into the lifts." So he [Virolí] said, "Hold on, I'll get out"—because he was very decent. But the orchestra said, "No sir, let the other man get out: all the musicians are going together." And we made him get out.

These incidents show that some Costeños suffered racism, but the ambiguity of the racial identity of many Costeños meant that blackness was by no means always a factor. It was always there as a possibility, as I showed above, but it was not an automatic identification. The main image was rather of the Costeño as common, loud, and vulgar— traits that were, however, often linked stereotypically to the idea of blackness in the Colombian, and indeed Latin American and Caribbean, set of values (cf. Cooper 1993).

For the Costeños who moved to the interior, apart from the feeling that they were looked down on by some people, there was a strong perception of undergoing a radical change, even as late as the 1970s. The teacher Wilson Fuentes recalled: "When I came to Bogotá [in the early 1970s], it was a brutal change, a change from heaven to earth. Not because there were no other people like myself, but because of the customs. One thing that amazed me was that one doesn't know one's neighbor, one's neighbor doesn't know one's name and vice versa, people go past and don't say hello." Jackie, who went to Bogotá in the 1970s to study *bachillerato* (that is, to get a secondary education) in a convent school, said: "For me Bogotá was horrible; I cried tears of blood." To her, the school, its teachers, and its pupils were cold, stiff, and formal. She, like many other Costeños, recalled the cold, the rain, the grey and black colors of people's clothes, and the overcoats, umbrellas, and hats, all of which added up to a feeling of repression and suffocation.

Parties were different too. José Portaccio recalled that, "You go to a party in Bogotá and you're looking around to see where it is, because you can't hear anything [from outside the house]. But in Barranquilla, the neighbors protest if you don't turn the *picó* [sound system] up to full volume." The picó (literally, pickup) became an institution in La Costa from the 1960s, following Caribbean fashions: it is a large, mobile sound system, used for private parties, street dances, and other such events (Pacini Hernández 1993).

Feelings of difference led to solidarity among Costeños, despite the recognition of subregional identities and loyalties. José's brother, Rosni, said: "You try to find the people from your land: they might not be from Barranquilla, but we're all Costeños. So, being here, you make a separate camp. I'd meet Costeños and wanted to make friends: 'Hey, how are you? Give me your phone number. Listen, have you got a party for Saturday night?'" This type of comment was repeated by many Costeños in Bogotá and Medellín.

NOTHING BUT BAMBUCO

Rosni and José Portaccio arrived in Bogotá in about 1958, to study bachillerato. Rosni went to Chiquinquirá, a small town near the city: "I found that people only danced to the rhythms of the interior of the country—bambuco, pasillo—and that Costeño music was still considered sort of rough, sort of coarse. . . . So, without realizing it, you'd gradually introduce your own music, your own dance. Then the cachacos and the cachacas said to me, 'Why don't we get together in such-and-such a school and you can teach us to dance cumbia.' So I taught them cumbia, merecumbé, and porro. I'd sing music from the interior—bambuco and pasillo—and every now and then I'd sing porro, vallenato, and it began to stick." There was a generational difference: the parents of Rosni's peers considered Costeño music vulgar and crude; for their children, it was an exciting new fashion. He talked as if Costeño music hardly existed at the time (although he admits that the radio played boleros and so on), which is not true: even in Chiquinquirá, listeners would have been able to tune into La Hora Costeña and buy records. But according to him, the impact of Costeño music was mainly among the middle and upper classes and it was thus *as if* this music had no real impact at all. Rosni, who is now a semiprofessional singer, considered himself the catalyst of change: when he left Chiquinquirá in 1964, "people no longer wanted bambuco."

In Medellín, Eduardo Villalba, a Costeño disc jockey who started La Hora Costeña on Radio Claridad in 1949, said that his show was the first inkling people had of Costeño music (although, in fact, Lucho Bermúdez played Medellín social clubs and radio stations from 1948). The social milieu was "hostile," because the Antioqueños' regionalism made it hard for outsiders to find work, but Costeño music, although initially seen as a bit strange, was soon happily accepted: "As [the music] became known, it began to give free rein to *alegría,* and people mixed in with it and danced to the music." However, Costeños were not so easily integrated: "We were not well regarded here. Because at a party, people from Barranquilla, Cartagena, and Santa Marta would get together and create the biggest racket of all time. And they [the Antioqueños] didn't accept that: 'We Antioqueños are refined people, we're well mannered'and I don't know what else. Then there'd be fights."

By the sixties and seventies, despite the importance of Costeño music in the city, Costeño migrants often recall "nothing but tangos." Moisés Martínez and Salvador Gómez were two students from Cartagena who arrived in the early sixties, stayed on, and both became teachers. Moisés told me that "at that time the problem was that there was nothing but jukeboxes, and we'd come and put on a porro or a vallenato, but the jukebox was monopolized by tangos. There was friction with respect to the music; the Antioqueños didn't accept [Costeño music]." There were certain bars in the city center where Costeño music was played, such as the Salón Suizo or the Atlántico, "so great numbers of Costeños would congregate there and the Antioqueños would go to other places where they could listen more easily to tango."

Pedro Morán, now a university teacher, arrived in Medellín in 1969, and he now tells a similar story. "Costeño music was very limited here; there were very few places where you could listen to anything but tango. All of the city center and Guayaquil was bars, but with tango music; 'old music' were the words [the bars would use] to attract custom. It was music which one couldn't locate or understand, [just] as they didn't understand our music. But there were two or three meeting places for Costeños. One was nothing but vallenato. Salsa was scarce." As a result, the students arranged their own parties: "The parties we had were memorable. Two or three days of continuous *escándalo* [racket] which was what scandalized the neighbors and everyone. Because people were accustomed to drinking alone, listening to their tangos and crying, but not to shouting and making a racket." (Crying is often semihumorously associated with tangos and rancheras—*música para llorar,* music for crying to—the image being of a solitary man, drunk and maudlin, weeping at the tragedy of his own life, reflected in the lyrics of the music.)

Miguel Granados Arjona went to Bogotá in 1952 to work as a disc jockey on the La Hora Costeña radio show, which had been running for some ten years. Like Rosni, he recalled that the musical scene was dominated by bambucos. This was hardly the case, but in his account, he was concerned to make the enduring contrast between La Costa and the interior:

> They are two completely different spirits: the open spirit of the coasts, especially the Caribbean, and that of here, of the altiplano, completely Andean. But that was displaced by Costeño music, which was extraordinarily strong in the fifties and especially the sixties. . . . When I started here in Bogotá, the programming was very stiff necked; everyone had a very serious radio [presentation style]; there wasn't the spontaneity that the announcers have today. And the announcers from La Costa contributed to that [spontaneity]. Because I was—if you'll pardon the expression—a *mamagallista* [joker] . . . and people liked that.[8]

On the other hand, "on the phone people would say, 'No, take that [music] off: how could you think of playing Alejo Durán; the music from here is better.'" Protests notwithstanding, "in the end they accepted." The Bogotanos, according to Granados, thought of themselves as the "most cultured, the most intelligent, the best," so they looked down on the Costeños. But in the long run, because it was danceable and *alegre,* they had to accept Costeño music and the Costeño spirit—"our Caribbean spirit, which of course has something of Africa." Many Costeños—and Bogotanos—add that it was not only the musical tastes that changed: people also began to wear more colorful clothes, to leave behind the grey suits and black hats. The fact that Bogotá's climate also physically became warmer only served to reinforce this feeling that the influence of the Costeños "heated up" the interior of the country.

Manuel Zapata Olivella, who went to Bogotá to study medicine in 1939–1943, returning in 1947 to finish his studies, recounted that the music of Lucho Bermúdez was initially received "very badly." Doubtless he was referring to the bad press it got in some papers. People in Bogotá "considered that it was blacks' music, vulgar music. . . . But with time, the Costeño colony grew here and that was decisive." Costeño students' dance parties were often held on Saturdays, along the lines of the empanadas bailables that were common in all cities, and they would play the records they had taken to Bogotá from La Costa.

Relations between Costeños and Bogotanos were varied. On the one hand, according to Zapata Olivella,

> the view people had of Costeños at that time was of *patanes* [louts], that they weren't well behaved. Popular sayings refer to that. When someone [Costeño] did something loutish, the popular adage—which is still often used—was "Costeño tenía que ser" [just had to be a Costeño]. . . . And a phenomenon that I haven't been able to explain, but which I can confirm, is that the Costeño there in his own environment [in La Costa] was quite controlled, in the sense that behaving well was the parental norm. Here, without the parents, we behaved as outrageously as we could. On the buses we'd talk [loudly], we'd laugh loudly and it was frowned upon by people here. . . . So all that reflected on Costeño music . . . it was a young people's thing, it was frowned upon, it was this, it was that.

On the other hand, when people returned to Bogotá from holidays on the coast, "they didn't want to dance bambuco any more, but rather the music from La Costa—it was a kind of liberation." Zapata Olivella's sister, Delia, who also studied in Bogotá in the late forties and early fifties, remembered that Costeño student parties were popular among the other students from the interior, although their parents often thought the events were morally suspect and accompanied their daughters, if not their sons.

Totó la Momposina—her stage name—had a different theory

about the success of Costeño music.[9] "Colombia is a mixture of the Indian, the black, and the Spaniard, so the force of history imposes itself . . . and creates an identity which is that of the Indian, the black, and the Spaniard. For this reason, at this time people from the interior are accepting [Costeño culture] because they are becoming a minority. So the outcome which is happening musically, in that the Atlantic coast is taking over a feeling, is because that feeling is not only of Colombia but of all America." Her argument was that Costeño culture in general and music in particular represented the true identity of Colombia, and Latin America in general, and hence, "by the force of history," was imposing itself as a continued process of mestizaje, cultural and physical, between whites, indigenous people, and blacks. A mixed identity, in which blackness and indigenousness loom large, while whiteness becomes a minority element, is an authentic identity. In this account, there is a strong sense of liberation, of the discovery—or rather recuperation—of truth. Blacks' role in this process had traditionally not been recognized, she said, but it was there and its true presence was coming into the open and being reflected musically. Here, then, Costeño music was represented as being the reflection of a true and authentic identity.

Reviewing the comments of Costeño migrants to Bogotá and Medellín, it is clear that they saw themselves as different in ways rather similar to locals' perceptions—although the values attached to that difference were generally positive rather than negative. They also tended to see themselves as a transformative influence, even though local people in both cities danced and listened to music before the advent of the Costeños. The transformation they claim to have effected—one which is also admitted to some extent by local people as well—was perceived as a liberating one, banishing sadness. Here I think the role of ideas about sexuality were also very influential.

SEXUALITY

As I have shown, sexuality was a recurrent theme in ideas about Costeño music: the music and dance were seen not just as common, but as immoral too. Responding to a question about whether the music had connotations of immorality, Manuel Zapata Olivella said: "Yes, more than immorality, sexuality. The way of dancing, of moving the hips, of squeezing one's partner."

Salvador Gómez, talking of a later period in Medellín, encountered the same image of immorality: "I found that a lot. When I was in a sort of ecstasy [dancing] to a cumbia or a mapalé, there were confronta-

tions which were based on the way that one moves the waist, right?—
the pelvic movement as it's called. So that drew their [the Antioqueños'] attention because it seemed—and their teachers told them
this as well—a very vulgar thing. It's [just] a form of expression in that
type of music, but they held it to be something immoral." Moisés
added: "You have to bear in mind that Antioquia is one of the most
religious regions in Colombia and that the [bodily] contact, the closeness, and those movements caused a scandal." However, the Antioqueños were not simply shocked. "In that sense," said Moisés, "Antioqueño women wanted to learn how to dance more than the men;
they sought out the Costeños who knew how to dance, so that they
could learn. So there was a kind of displacement of the Antioqueño
man, who got jealous because the Costeños were taking away his partner to dance with her." In a neat phrase, Moisés said that Costeño men
were "a dream for the daughters, but a nightmare for the parents." For
Salvador, people liked to dance Costeño music because "it's a normal
expression of the person." This is a version of the view that Costeño
music and culture generally are "natural" and that the norms of the interior of the country "cover up" people's natural tendencies and, in this
case, physical desires.

    This imagery was not confined to Costeño men. Jackie, in her con-
vent school in Bogotá, decided to celebrate the birthday of the rector
in Costeño style: "Since one Costeño seeks out another, there were two
girls from Cartagena in the fifth year and all the others [in the school]
had a grudge against us. So I said to them [the Cartagena girls] that we
were going to have some fun with the school. [I said] 'You be the man,
I'll be the woman and we'll dance a bullerengue.' I took along [the
record] 'Josefa Matía' and a dress and I began to dance as I'd been
taught and of course that was worse. They said look how the Costeño
girl moves, how suggestive, she's going to go off with all the boys from
the schools." [10] Dominga Castaño remembered the differences in dance
styles that she noticed when she went to Bogotá in 1968 to study at
the university, after what she described as a very pious Catholic up-
bringing in Mompox: "Here the girls didn't know how to dance, so it
was the Costeños who danced and who created the atmosphere. One
laughed to see the others dancing: it was a horrible *brincado* [jumping,
hopping]. I taught my niece how to dance and people watched her and
were scandalized." Cecilia Delgado also remembered that Costeño
women were considered more liberated because of their dancing and
the way they "moved their shoulders," even though, in her opinion,

Costeño women were actually more closely guarded by their families than the women in Bogotá.

Sexuality has always been a vital part of the presentation and reception of commercial Costeño music, and the lyrics of Costeño music play upon sexual themes at times. Numbers by Lucho Bermúdez or Pacho Galán avoided this, since they were directed at a mainly middle-class and elite audience, but José María Peñaranda has been famous for the double meanings and sexual allusions of his lyrics, and indeed some of his LPs are marked "For adults only." More recent numbers are clearly suggestive: "El Africano," with the refrain "Mamá, ¿qué será lo que quiere el negro?" (Mama, what could the black man want?); or "Mi Cucú" (My Butt); or "Las Tapas" (literally, The Lids, but also the buttocks).[11] This is not to say that sexual allusions can be found only in Costeño music or that most Costeño music has risqué lyrics—vallenato, for example, refers constantly to male-female relations in terms of love rather than sex—but these allusions are a salient feature.

A more striking aspect of female sexuality, and one consciously exploited by the record industry, is the images on album covers.[12] On albums by single artists or bands, the female body may be used as a motif, but it is not very common. On compilation albums of Costeño music—and those of salsa and merengue—photographs of seminaked or bikini-clad young women have been normal on the covers of albums since the 1960s, and by the 1980s and 1990s a cover could be little more than a close-up shot of women's tanga-clad buttocks. If models are not actually photographed on the beach or in the sea, the swimming costumes and oiled bodies suggest a beach environment, interweaving ideas of sand, sea, and sex with "música bailable."

It is notable that black women are rarely used as models on these album covers compared to women who, if not blond, are certainly not black in Colombian terms. Female sexuality is not explicitly racialized as black sexuality, even though the association of the music with a stereotypically tropical environment continuously hints at such a link. The element of blackness available to images of Costeño identity is not erased, but rather submerged in such a way that a "whiter" female sexuality is lent some of the meanings of sensuality and "hotness" that are typical in Colombia in ideas about young black women. In one sense this is simply offering to nonblack men, for mere transient consumption, a sexual quality associated with black women. In a deeper sense, the supposed hotness of black female sexuality is presented as something that can become an embodied part of nonblack women and thus nonblack men. Black sexuality is transformed into a white female sexuality which can, in turn, transform the male consumer. Appropriation of this sexuality is not just consumption, understood as ephemeral, but a change in ownership, a process of consumption understood as transformative of personhood. Costeño music and sexuality is presented as a potential national identity: tropicality, sensuousness, and sexual openness can become part of everyone, not just the property of a region and much less a "race." As Taussig (1993: 21) suggests, mimesis involves not only copying, but also contact: the copy incorporates within itself something of the sensory concreteness of the original; copying the other hints at becoming the other (1993: 21).

Only occasionally is black male sexuality suggested on album covers. One Pedro Laza album used a racialized sexual image by showing a group of very black musicians with their instruments, playing to a fully dressed young white woman who is looking at them wistfully and yet turning away (*Fandango* [Discos Fuentes LP 200011]; fig. 7.1). This is very explicitly an image of black sexuality open for consumption by whites—perhaps here with a hint of forced consumption—but it is the only such image I have seen in this corpus of material.

Ideas about Costeño sexuality have thus been a crucial aspect of the processes of conflict and change of identity which I am examining through the medium of music. These ideas are a version of old, durable, and often heavily racialized images of "primitive" versus "civilized" people which have very deep roots in Western thought (see Hall 1992 for a summary; see also Nederveen Pieterse 1992; Rousseau and Porter 1990; Said 1985; Stocking 1968; and Taussig 1987, 1993; see also the literature cited in chapter 1 on race and sexuality). It is not my intention to examine whether Costeño culture does have a more "open" sexuality than the interior—if it were indeed possible to begin to separate "truth" from "ideology" in this complex area. It is the case that family patterns in Costeño society show significant differences from those in the interior, whatever the subregional and class variations within each complex. In very general terms, formal marriage is less common in La Costa, and a man may often have a wife or principal woman (even if they are not formally married) and one or more other "lovers" with whom he has socially recognized children. While this may also occur in regions of the interior, it is generally less overt and socially accepted. There is also a tendency for matrifocal households to form as men and women change partners over time. To explain these Costeño patterns, different authors have referred to the

7.1 Cover of *Fandango* (Discos Fuentes LP 200011). (By permission of Discos Fuentes.)

weakness of the church in La Costa, especially in colonial times, to the geographical mobility of the population, especially men, in the face of unstable economic opportunities, and to possible African influences (see Gutiérrez de Pineda 1975; Dussán de Reichel 1958; and Friedemann 1978; see also Wade 1993a, 1994a for a brief summary). All this, of course, by no means adds up to a society in which sexuality is relatively "free" or even overt, although it may suggest such an image to others. Such patterns may even have a repressive effect, at least for women in middle-class families intent on preserving honor. As I mentioned above, several Costeño women—of middle-class status—said they found control over women to be stricter in La Costa than in Bogotá.

Costeño dance styles, which are often taken to be highly erotic, are not necessarily this at all. A cumbia dance, as practiced in a rural context, is a highly ritualized courtship dance in which there is no physical contact at all between men and women. Such contexts are now relatively rare, but even the Costeño dance troupes which present "traditional" dances to audiences all over the country tend to maintain this "respect" between men and women in their renditions of cumbia. However, they also often emphasize aspects of other dances—typically, the fast and energetic mapalé dance—which appear erotic to their audiences: certain movements are exaggerated, more revealing clothes are worn, and so on (Simon 1994). To a great extent, I would argue, the "open" sexuality of the Costeños is a construction—in which Costeño intellectuals have participated as much as others—which draws on various aspects of actual family arrangements in La Costa, on a generalized notion of Caribbean "relaxation," and above all on long-established racialized imagery about black sexuality.[13] The ideas about Costeño frankness and sincerity are all linked to ideas about an unrepressed sexuality.

It is important to grasp that the migration of Costeños to Bogotá and Medellín was taking place in a context of rapid social change in which conservative religious values were coming increasingly into question. Elvira Ceballos and Gloria Ramírez told me their memories of dance in middle-class Medellín and small-town Antioquia in the 1940s and 1950s, when they were teenagers. Gloria said that her mother liked to dance: "But that was a condition that my father imposed. [He said], 'We'll get married if you stop dancing.'" Later her father also learned to dance, but he would not permit his daughter to do so. For men there was little control in this respect. Elvira said: "The first thing which the older men of the family did when a boy got long trousers at that time was to take him to a brothel so he could be a real man." Dance was associated with prostitution to some extent. Elvira recounted that in Manizales, men danced tangos but never in a "decent" dance salon. "They would go to the brothels in the red-light districts, which were strictly established with borders and so on." Gloria, who grew up in provincial town, said: "In the towns there was nowhere to dance except the red-light districts, or on the outskirts of town, where the men would go, after their wives had gone to bed, and dance with the town's *avionas* [flighty women]. Elvira added: "And what's more, [people said that] if you died after going dancing you'd go straight to hell in mortal sin."

In this context, Costeño music and dance could obviously be seen as breaking with parental traditions which restricted women's movements with repressive ideas about modesty and decency. The image of Costeño sexuality was thus a more "modern" sexuality (despite also being supposedly base, coarse, and "primitive"): it fitted into new and often "foreign" ideas about a woman's place and relations between men and women in which there was more freedom of movement for women and new definitions of what counted as modest behavior. Colombia remained—and remains—a country in which there is great gender inequality in economic, political, and symbolic spheres, and ideas about propriety still control women's freedom of movement in every sense. But ideas about decency and modesty have changed greatly since the 1940s, and Costeño music and dance (as well as styles such as bolero, guaracha, and rock and roll) were an important symbol and constituent part of this change.

At the same time, women's economic and social position was changing. Londoño and Londoño note that in the 1940s, "in a city as traditional as Bogotá, women were no longer confined in their cosy homes" (1989: 338). In 1945, women gained voting rights. All over the country, a majority of the migrants to the big cities were women, many of whom became domestic servants. In Medellín, industry employed a large number of young females.[14] Research is scarce on the social life of these women, but I reproduced above some comments from Dario Ruíz, who recounted how he used to go to a trade union center in Medellín to dance with young female workers. It seems likely that there was some degree of freedom of movement for these women, who would also have had access to a cash income. Scattered comments from working-class women in Medellín in the 1940s and 1950s indicate that young women could go out dancing in groups, despite restrictive ideas about decency (see chapter 4).

The image of liberated sexuality that attached to Costeños and Costeño music was thus a major aspect of the growing popularity of the music in the interior of the country. Sexuality was not made explicit in the music of Lucho Bermúdez or Pacho Galán, yet it was imagined to be there by observers, Costeño or not, as I showed in chapter 4. The sexual mores the music evoked seemed to fit into new ways of thinking about relationships between men and women, new ideas about what constituted modest behavior—even if these new ways continued to be patriarchal. Dancing to the music held out the possibility of expressing something that was inside and eager to get out, and also of appropriating new elements and thereby transforming oneself, acting on oneself, and especially one's body—as an "unfinished project," to use Chris Shilling's phrase (1993: 114)—to create something new. The sensuality and *alegría* attributed to La Costa could become part of all people in their identities as a Colombians.

This possibility has to be seen in the context of the increasing violence of the country—which, even if the cities were mainly spared, could not be entirely ignored by urbanites—and the image of La Costa as a relatively peaceable region where noise and conflict lead less often to overt violence and death. Sommer (1991) argues that the concern with erotic love in nineteenth-century Latin American romantic novels represented a smoothing over of the internal divisions of the new nations. I would argue that dancing to Costeño music was to some extent an identification with tropical love rather than Andean violence. Or, more than an identification, it was an attempt to turn oneself into a body for love, rather than a body for death.

Such a transformation was itself potentially dangerous, however, since the Costeños were also generally agreed to be vulgar, loud, uncouth, and sometimes black—even if one's own Costeño friends were usually nice people. So appropriating the "good" aspects of Costeño culture, via the embodied, transforming activity of listening and dancing to Costeño music, did not necessarily mean accepting blackness or "vulgarity," or rather becoming black and vulgar. Basic hierarchies of class, race, and region could be maintained. The classic paralleling of unification and differentiation that mestizaje has always involved was reiterated. In this process, it helped that Costeño music was only ambiguously black and that it was played by people who could be racially identified in varied ways. In the 1970s and 1980s, the connotations of *alegría* and sensuality were increasingly taken over for Colombian listeners by salsa and merengue, which unlinked these qualities from a specifically Costeño origin and reinforced their attachment to the more generalized Caribbean identity that bolero, rumba, guaracha, and mambo had already created.

Vallenato played a specific role here, because it was increasingly a romantic style that focused rather abstractly on the beauties of being in love, the pain of lovesickness and unrequited love, the problems of disapproving families, and jealousy—ideas about love more akin to those portrayed in ballads and soap operas than to the supposedly open sexuality and carefree joyfulness of cumbia and porro. Lyrics were rarely spicy, and half-naked women were less often used as album cover motifs. Nevertheless, vallenato added to images of Costeño sexuality through the way it was danced.

Dancing close—sometimes called *covar* in La Costa and *amacizarse* in the interior—was not a Costeño import: a bolero was the typical opportunity for a close, slow dance in many a party in the interior of the country, and parents often watched to make sure the dance was not too close.[15] The slow dancing style of the Costeños was, however, often seen as more intimate and sexually suggestive than the style in the interior, since it involved closer bodily contact. As Rosni Portaccio said: "With the Costeño, contact with the [other] person is a bit more direct. The Costeño there [in La Costa] places his face against the face of his partner and his partner doesn't get upset. Not here [in Bogotá]— well, I think perhaps today people do." His niece, brought up in Bogotá, but with a good deal of experience of La Costa, interjected: "The thing is that the Costeños always want to dance *amacizados* [close], here it's not like that . . . [or] only after a long time. If you don't know someone and you have a dance and he wants to dance close straightaway—forget it. In La Costa, they [even] dance rock *amacizados*." Whereas some forms of Costeño music and dance might be seen to suggest sexuality through open, expressive gestures, perhaps including pelvic movements, the slow vallenato dance suggested it through the small intimate movements of two bodies in an embrace.[16] Again, the active embodiment of dance as a consciously learned skill carried a potentially transformative charge, allowing people to refashion themselves through Costeño music and dance.

Ownership, Embodiment, and Identity

Powerful notions of ownership and embodiment were at work in all this. People felt that the inhabitants of the interior owned bambuco and pasillo: they owned them by virtue of having incorporated them into their bodies, just as they ingested the typical foods of the interior. The music had nourished them and become part of their bodily construction and their identity. Likewise for the Costeños and indeed even more so, since dance could be "in their blood," that is, heritable.

Hence the stark opposition that people tended to draw in their memories of music and dance: the people from the interior "could not dance," and there was "nothing but" tangos or bambucos; in contrast the Costeños were the sole owners of *alegría*—they possessed it, just as it possessed them. Different regions owned different bits of the nation, some with a higher status than others in dominant hierarchies of value. The Costeños' patrimony, however dubious some of its features, had aspects that seemed, at the time, to fit into ideas about modernity, especially when this was seen as progressive and liberating. To share ownership of this, it was necessary to mimic it, but also thereby to embody it, to live it, so that it could effect a personal transformation. Music and especially dance were the perfect vehicles for doing this, and I think this helps us to understand the role of music and dance in social life: dance in particular lends itself to processes of embodied appropriation and the transformation of identity. Although all human activity is by definition embodied, dance can involve a particularly potent dynamic of the interplay between creating and releasing physical and emotional tension. In this case, elements of Costeño identity could be appropriated, even while the Costeños themselves—or perhaps more precisely, the *image* of them as a category—might be kept at arm's length. Music and dance were easily detached from the aspects of Costeño identity seen as threatening (blackness, uncouthness), although, rather than being erased, these elements were kept in the background, to be reapplied to the Costeños themselves when hierarchical distinctions were sought. Music and dance were apparently trivial—one was not, after all, marrying a Costeño or moving to La Costa—but they were also pervasive and often vital aspects of relating socially, especially between men and women, and of identifying oneself and others.

These ideas about ownership are a long way from once standard anthropological notions about the correspondence of culture, identity, and even territory. We cannot talk here of the Costeños as a "group" with a particular cultural baggage which simply belongs to them. Even more sophisticated approaches to music and ethnic identity, which see both as in a dynamic and changeable relationship, are not necessarily adequate (see, e.g., Seeger 1994), because Costeños were a vague network of people, spread over the country, and because the music that was "theirs" was a mass-produced commodity, sold nationally and internationally. The reason it was "theirs" was that as individuals they claimed it by living it, by embodying it: this opened the possibility for them to talk about it *as if* culture, identity, and territory linked neatly together—that is, in a discourse of ownership; but by the same token it opened the way for other people to lay claim to the music as a personal possession.

These ideas about embodiment and transformation of the person relate to the reconceptualization of mestizaje that I have been suggesting at various points in this book. In chapter 1, I argued that a symbolics of origin persists alongside a symbolics of mestizaje which seems to erase origins. I cited the case of the María Lionza religious complex in Venezuela, where ideas about original "racial" ingredients are still vital symbols alongside an idea that all Venezuelans are somehow an amalgam of black, white, and indigenous. In this chapter, two parallels to this have emerged: first, the idea that a person can have a *corazón de negro* (a black person's heart) inside him; second, the idea that, through mimesis, elements of blackness can be appropriated into a body and person which are in the process of transformation as unfinished projects.

The first idea is ethnographically most obvious: tropes such as having *alma de blanco* (a white person's soul) or a *corazón de negro* are very common throughout the Americas. Perhaps the best known contexts are those in which a black person is said to be "white inside"— although this can be reckoned as either a good thing or a betrayal, depending on who is talking. Equally common in Latin America are tropes along the lines of "se le salió lo del negro" (the black in her/him came out), used when someone not normally classified as black does something thought to be characteristic of black people. Again, this can be seen as good or bad, depending on context: someone might dance well on a particular occasion or do something thought to be vulgar. These tropes can be seen as indicating purely metaphorical thought, but I am suggesting that they may point toward a more corporeal line of thought. They evoke an image of mestizaje in which different cultural elements—usually linked in some way to one of the "original" cultures—mix together but retain some separable identity rather than blending into indistinction.[17] These elements may then reside "inside" persons—in their blood, in their bodies—and express themselves in given contexts. As Colombian salsa combo Grupo Niche say in their song "Etnia": "Tiene cada quien del otro su poquitico" (everyone has a bit of the other in him/her; on the album *Etnia* [CBS 0081719, 1996]).

The second idea is less easy to support ethnographically: people did not volunteer in interviews very specific remarks about the way they did or did not transform their bodies and themselves. Rather, they talked about collective processes of transformation, focusing on how Costeños and their culture changed the cities of the interior, making them more colorful, "warming them up." I have also argued that Costeño music both reflected and promoted gradual changes in the moral evaluation of sexuality. Clearly, these collective processes had to occur through individual people who learned to enjoy and dance this music, who felt the color and the warmth—and who responded negatively with racist stereotypes or who reacted positively and changed themselves. Thus, Ema Valderrama's first experience of the beauty of La Costa "stayed forever" in her soul and her eyes, and she found that the rhythm of Costeño music was "so *sabroso,*" so delicious, that even in

Bogotá there were "no hips" that were not excited by it. This second notion of transformation is, of course, linked to the first idea of elements coexisting "inside." As well as appropriating new elements into one's person, one can cultivate and express (or leave hidden and repressed) different elements already inside, in a process of personal transformation spurred by a changing social context.

In short, then, these ideas suggest a different perspective on mestizaje as an ideology which recreates difference even as it suggests its erasure. This does not add up to an apology for mestizaje in general, because, as the history of Latin American nationalism clearly attests, such an ideology can have and has had very racist dimensions when it is construed either as a process of whitening—the erasure of blackness and indigenousness in favor of whiteness—or as a process of blending—the erasure of diversity in general. The point is that both these possibilities actually involve the recreation of diversity as the negative pole, the starting point, the primitive origin from which future mixture takes off. I have tried to show how that diversity remains in people's very concepts of themselves and others. It is a diversity that is clearly subject to different readings and always subject to being read anew.

8 Multiculturalism and Nostalgia:
THE 1990S

The 1990s have been characterized in Colombia by a sudden interest in the Costeño music of the 1950s and 1960s. There have been revivals of this music in cover versions—some of which have broken all previous record sales and gone international in an unprecedented fashion—soap operas based on famous Costeño composers of popular music, a proliferation of dance schools teaching porro, mambo, and similar dance styles, increased programming of older Costeño music on the radio, and, in La Costa itself, an informal movement under the slogan *el rescate de lo nuestro* (the rescue of what is ours). The research I undertook was not directed at a fine-grained analysis of these recent changes—which are clearly related to more general patterns of "postmodern" consumption in capitalist economies—but I will outline the nature of these developments before concluding with some thoughts about their causes and, more importantly, their significance for understanding the rather different image of Colombian national identity that has emerged recently—a postmodern, multicultural nationalism.

Patterns of Consumption in the 1990s

Data on the consumption of music in Colombia were very scarce: the market popularity of different styles of music could be gauged only in an impressionistic way and even then only for the CDs, LPs, and cassettes sold in formal retail outlets; the musical tastes of the significant population buying illegally reproduced cassettes from street stalls could only be guessed at. For 1995, approximate estimates of the formal sector indicated that tastes varied regionally. Vallenato led the market in Barranquilla and perhaps in Medellín but was much less significant in

Bogotá. Anglo-American and Latin rock and pop led in Bogotá, vied with vallenato in Medellín, and was relatively minor in Barranquilla. Música tropical was important everywhere, coming second in Bogotá and taking third place in Medellín and Barranquilla; the market share of this category expanded significantly in the few months leading up to Christmas. Salsa was second in Barranquilla, came in third in Medellín, and ranked alongside vallenato in Bogotá. These four main categories were followed by ballads, música de carrilera (including tangos, rancheras, and música guasca), merengue, reggae, and others.[1]

In the mid-1990s, radio programming had become much more diverse than in previous decades, with some stations specializing in particular styles. FM stations tended to be associated more with the middle-class listener, while AM radio catered to more popular tastes. Again, regional variation was apparent. Bogotá and Medellín each had about twenty FM stations, of which ten specialized in rock music, with three or four playing a mixture of salsa, vallenato, and música tropical. Barranquilla had six of its eleven FM stations playing this tropical mix, but only one rock station. Each city had at least one FM station that played mostly ballads, romantic music, and music associated with the interior of the country (including rancheras and tango), but Medellín had four of these. Each city also had at least one *emisora cultural* (cultural radio station), usually broadcasting from a university, which was strong on classical music, but also had specialist salsa programs, generally of older salsa and Cuban music, considered more authentic and less commercialized than recent trends in *salsa romántica* (softer, romantic styles of salsa).

AM radio stations were more numerous. None specialized in rock, but each city had at least one that played virtually nothing but vallenato; five of Bogotá's thirty-some stations did this, compared to two of Barranquilla's twenty-some stations and only one of Medellín's total of twenty-six. Again, some stations played mostly a mix of salsa, vallenato, and música tropical: six in Barranquilla, five in Bogotá, and two in Medellín.[2]

Vallenato was thus available nationwide on FM and AM—even in Bogotá there were vallenato-only stations—and other styles of Costeño music were also well represented, often including old hits of Lucho Bermúdez, Pacho Galán, Pedro Laza, and others. Interestingly, by 1994 about half of the specialist rock stations were beginning to include "crossover" programming which meant sprinkling a few salsa, merengue and vallenato hits—and perhaps some other Costeño numbers—into the rock, rap, and funk. This was confined to evenings and weekends and aimed at dancers and party-goers.

An important development has been the popularity in La Costa of *champeta* (or *terapia*)—a mixture of Zairean *soukous,* Nigerian high-life, Haitian *konpa, soca,* and reggae. This trend started in the 1970s in Cartagena and later spread to many areas of La Costa. Recently, Colombian champeta groups have formed playing their own versions of African music. Some champeta musicians come from Palenque de San Basilio, the old maroon settlement near Cartagena, and the symbolic association of champeta with palenques and black rebelliousness is overt. I have not been able to give champeta the attention it deserves, since I did not do extensive research in Cartagena, where it is most popular, and rather little has been written on it (although see Pacini Hernández 1992b, 1993; Streicker 1995; and Waxer 1997).[3] Champeta is clearly a subject of future research and is a development of great interest in tracing the interconnections of music, race, and nation. The music became popular mainly among working-class people in the cities and towns of the region, almost displacing salsa in some areas, although not vallenato (see Wade 1993a: 79–80). Champeta and its adherents, the *champetudos,* were from the start generally seen as loud and vulgar by others: the music was classed as repetitive and boring; the champetudos were seen as obstreperous, excessively flamboyant and tasteless in their choice of clothing, and outrageously explicit in the overt sexiness of their dance styles. Especially in Cartagena, these people were mainly black.

What is interesting here is the popularity of explicitly "black" and indeed "African" music among working class Costeños, even as cumbia and vallenato became nationalized and salsa and merengue, already internationally popular, also became as fashionable among middle-class people in Bogotá as it once had been among working-class people in La Costa (and in Buenaventura and Cali). This seems to indicate a desire for musical distinctiveness that has no qualms in opting for openly black and African associations. Some working-class Costeños are keeping one step ahead of the musical game, as it were: as Costeño music is nationalized and becomes mainstream, new forms are appropriated, setting up new distinctions which nevertheless recall previous ones in their moral connotations. There are familiar oppositions between blacks and nonblacks, vulgarity and civilization, sexual explicitness and sexual propriety, working classes and middle classes, and the regional and the national. At the same time, processes of nationalization are, perhaps, already under way. The label *terapia* (therapy) has emerged to rival *champeta* as a marketing term, evoking the supposedly therapeutic value of this "happy, sexy" music and avoiding the lower-class connotations of *champeta*. In 1982, Cartagena became the venue for the annual Festival de Música del Caribe, bringing artists from all over the Caribbean to perform in the city and giving their music a better reputation among the middle classes. It remains to be seen whether champeta will follow porro, cumbia, and vallenato and be adapted to become a mainstream national style.

Reviving Old Costeño Music

Within these, and other, patterns of consumption, there was a clear move toward a revival of older Costeño styles. Costeño music (other, that is, than modern vallenato) was still widely available in record stores and included material ranging from La Sonora Dinamita to Pedro Laza. At the same time, "folkloric" or "traditional" Costeño music could be heard live, usually performed by Costeño music and dance troupes, or on records made by groups such as La Cumbia Soledeña or Totó la Momposina y Sus Tambores, which saw their role as keeping alive the roots and traditions of Costeño music (interviews with Efraín Mejía, leader of La Cumbia Soledeña, and with Totó la Momposina; see also albums by Totó la Momposina y Sus Tambores: *La candela viva* [Talento/MTM/Realworld 7260-008019, 1993] and *Carmelina* [MTM 7262-008026, 1996]). What was new in the mid-1990s was the impact of new versions of Costeño music from the 1950s and 1960s on a broader range of the Colombian public and indeed abroad.

A major precipitant of this was the 1991 dramatization of the life of vallenato composer Rafael Escalona, shown on a television channel owned by Caracol, one of the two Colombian communications giants. Escalona was still a well-known public figure; his connections with García Márquez had helped, and he had also been appointed Colombian consul to Panama by López Michelsen in 1974. The lead role in the series was played by Carlos Vives, a Costeño actor from a wealthy Santa Marta family, who had previously released some albums of ballads with Sony that had made little impact. Escalona's music was prominent throughout the television series and was released by Sony on two albums that sold very well. The arrangements sounded quite traditional and were intended to keep to the spirit of the 1950s when the songs were composed: thus, the prominent instrumentation consisted of the accordion, caja, guacharaca, and bass. On closer examination, the presence of some wind instruments (trumpet, flute, trombone) was evident, as were a piano and a synthesizer (see, e.g., *Un canto a la vida*—*Escalona* [Sony CDC 464696, 1991]).

Carlos Vives, keen to exploit this potential—and, some said, brushing up a Costeño accent that had fallen into disuse—was not satisfied with his role simply as a voice. He proposed to Sony and Caracol a project based on reviving old vallenato classics, but in which he would have more artistic input. Sony turned him down, but he then proposed the idea to the Colombian record company Sonolux, owned by the Ardila Lulle group, one of the big Colombian conglomerates which also owns RCN, the other major communications company. With backing from Ardila Lulle, the project, rumored to be very costly, was taken on board. The best artists and arrangers were used, and the record, *Clásicos de la provincia,* was released in August 1993 with the full promotional power of Ardila Lulle and RCN behind it.

The album proved a major coup, breaking all sales records in the country. It also sold well in Mexico, Spain, and even the United States, where Vives won a gold disk and was nominated for a Grammy. It broke national and also class barriers: middle-class people (including intellectuals who generally disparaged vallenato) were among the buyers. Part of its success lay in the combination of elements it was seen to represent. Vives by then had long hair and wore jeans and leather on stage, as did most of the band (fig. 8.1). His accordionist, Egidio Cuadrado, however, retained the garb of a Costeño musician—plain trousers and shirt, but with the typical straw hat (*sombrero voltiao*) of La Costa;[4] Cuadrado had also been elected king of the Vallenato Festival in 1985, so his credentials were impeccable. A well-known jazz bassist and rock guitarist were featured on the album, and in the song arrangements, guitars, bass, and percussion were used to give a rhythmic basis influenced by rock and reggae. Flutes, saxophones, and a piano were used, but also a traditional Costeño gaita flute and a Dominican tambora drum.[5] The end result was widely seen as combining "the old and the new" and "dressing vallenato up in tails"—the comparison with Lucho Bermúdez's earlier "dressing up" of porro was made by several interviewees in the record industry. As such, some traditionalists deplored what they saw as the degradation caused by commercialization. A wide range of people, however, thought the innovations creative and admirable.

Most importantly, Vives broke into the middle-class youth market, which had previously consumed mainly Anglo-American music and salsa: his rock image was vital here. This change was different from the

8.1 Carlos Vives. (By permission of Sonolux S.A.)

kind of upward class mobility of musical styles which can be traced for porro and salsa—or indeed for other styles such as tango or rumba. It was not rearrangements of the contemporary vallenato of, say, Binomio de Oro or Diomedes Díaz that penetrated the edges of the middle-class market, but vallenato of thirty or forty years before. In short, Vives became a national phenomenon and his music was seen as Colombian as well as—indeed even more than—specifically Costeño. The incoming president, Ernesto Samper, had Vives's band play during his inauguration in 1994, while record industry interviewees recounted appreciatively how vallenato had, finally, "gone international"—but as a specifically Colombian product.[6]

Alongside Vives came other artists with similar projects of the revival of Costeño music, forming a trend generally known in the record industry as *tropical pop,* which included mostly non-Costeño artists such as Tulio Zuluaga, Café Moreno, Karamelo, Barranco (actually a

Venezuelan band), Luna Verde, and Aura Cristina. Tulio Zuluaga (with Discos Fuentes) was commonly labeled a Vives copy, but other artists did versions of Costeño music that were generally seen as more pop than Vives. Café Moreno, for example, was a recent group made up of three Colombian teenage girls—actresses and models from the interior—and a young South African man. They released an album in 1994 which included a cover of Costeño composer José Barros's old hit "La Momposina," used as title music for a television drama serial based loosely on the life of Barros; other tracks were covers and potpourris of well-known Costeño numbers, including ones by Lucho Bermúdez and Luis E. Martínez.

Such groups were seen by some as little more than record company inventions, made to cash in on a new trend, using actors and models for whom music was a sideline. Taken more seriously were the efforts of artists such as Costeño musician Moisés Angulo, who made an album of rock and funk versions of porros and a couple of vallenatos from the 1950s and 1960s (*Fusión* [BMG 74321238952, 1994]), an idea conceived by Rafael Mejía of Sonolux, who had also been involved with the Vives project.

Another established artist was Juan Carlos Coronel, who in 1994 released an album with versions of Lucho Bermúdez hits arranged by Carlos Piña, an experienced Costeño musician and arranger (*Un maestro, una voz* [Codiscos C9800177, 1994]). Coronel was born in Cartagena to a mother who had done some singing in the 1950s with local orchestras and a father who had done some work as a announcer with local radio stations. Coronel started singing in public as a boy, and ballads were his forte, but his first recording opportunity came when he was spotted and taken to Medellín to record with Fruko in Discos Fuentes. Moving to Codiscos, he recorded a few albums of música tropical with the band Nene y sus Traviesos, including the big 1983 hit "Patacón Pisao." Later he began a solo career as a salsa singer, releasing several LPs before his sudden shift toward older Costeño music; another album of Pacho Galán's merecumbés was in the pipeline in early 1995. Neither Coronel nor Angulo has had the success of Vives, but both participated in the wave of revival of Costeño music.

This revival was evident in other realms. At the end of 1993, an old porro number by singer Noel Petro was rereleased by a small Medellín record company and scored a major hit. Meanwhile, in Medellín, dance schools teaching porro, as well as mambo, tango, and paso doble, suddenly multiplied from a handful five years previously to several dozen in 1995, and they attracted young and middle-aged people from working- and middle-class backgrounds. The Colombian salsa star Joe Arroyo released an album (*Un toque de clase* [Sony CDC 464717, 1992]) with a track paying homage to Estefanía Caicedo, a well-known singer of Costeño music in the "traditional" mold, who had died shortly before; a 1994 release by Arroyo (*Sus razones tendrá* [Sony 52473269, 1994]) did the same for Irene Martínez, a similar Costeño figure. These homage tracks contained parts of songs written or made famous by these women singers, arranged with a salsa flavor, but with, in the first case, a flute part which clearly evoked the traditional Costeño gaita. This followed a style already established by Arroyo of occasionally taking Costeño rhythms and setting them to salsa arrangements.[7] A few years later, Grupo Niche, the well-known Colombian salsa band, released an album (*Etnia* [CBS 0081719, 1996]) which contained a cumbia track.

Finally, it is worth mentioning the rerelease of Colombian tropical music of various styles on international labels, even though this had little impact within the country. Although much of this was the music of Arroyo and other salsa bands such as Fruko y Sus Tesos or Los Latin Brothers, cumbia was also an important component, and while most of the numbers were of 1980s vintage, some date from the 1970s or even earlier.[8]

Costeño Music and Costeño Identity

Not surprisingly, although the trend toward reviving Costeño music has been national in scope, it has had particular resonance in La Costa. During my research in Barranquilla, there were several bars that specialized in playing old music (*música vieja, música de ayer*). This was often Cuban music, but Costeño music was also a major feature. Such bars were generally watering holes for record collectors and enthusiasts, but there was evidence that interest in older Costeño music was more widespread. In the period before the 1995 carnival, La Troja, a well-known salsa bar, mounted a series of Sunday afternoon sessions, under the slogan *el rescate de lo nuestro*, dedicated to Costeño music of earlier decades; local collectors brought in their record collections and acted as informal disc jockeys for a mixed audience of middle- and working-class people which included local media people and intellectuals. The same slogan could be heard on local radio and on Telecaribe, the regional television channel based in Barranquilla, which programmed a good deal of Caribbean and Costeño music. Meanwhile, a Barranquilla promotion company, Globo Musical, arranged a series of shows under the title "The Carnivals of the 1960s and 1970s: Carnivals of Yesterday, Today, and Always," which featured among others the reunited Corraleros de Majagual and Juan Carlos Coronel with his homage to Lucho Bermúdez.

This concern with "rescue" was given a boost at the local level by the organizers of the Barranquilla carnival, Carnaval S.A., who in July 1994 organized a meeting, El Primer Encuentro por el Rescate de Nuestra Música (First Meeting for the Rescue of our Music), with record companies, radio programmers, radio disc jockeys, musicians, collectors, musicologists, the music press, composers, and music business entrepreneurs. The theme was the assumed crisis of nonvallenato Costeño music. This crisis was held to consist of the weak commercial and public presence of Costeño music and its overpowering by salsa, merengue, and other musical styles generally seen as foreign. The Colombian record companies blamed the artists and composers for not producing a commercial sound and chastised radio programmers for their willingness to take bribes from foreign record companies. Artists and composers blamed the Colombian companies for not giving them a chance. Everyone agreed, however, that La Costa had musical talent and that the quality of the music made it competitive. All concurred that creative innovations were necessary: only on this basis could effective promotion take place. But "vulgarization" had to be avoided at all costs, and changes would have to respect the "roots" of the music— an issue of greater importance to the artists and composers than to the record companies. The meeting was, in effect, a call for a modernized but nevertheless distinctively Costeño musical identity to compete in a national arena dominated, as usual, by non-Costeño interests (in this case, the record companies and the radio stations controlled by the big communications companies, Caracol and RCN), which themselves had to deal with the global forces of music capitalism.[9]

At the regional level, the revival of Costeño music was thus closely linked to a concern with regional identity. The interest of local radio, television, and intellectual circles in promoting Costeño music was by no means single minded: salsa and merengue got more airtime than Costeño music (even including vallenato), and local intellectuals generally preferred salsa and Cuban music to Costeño material. But the increased popularity of Costeño music fitted well with an ongoing concern on the part of such people to promote Costeño regional identity in the national frame.

Thus, Adolfo González, university professor and investigator of Costeño music, wrote in 1985 that "the most important cultural manifestation of the Colombian Atlantic coast is its popular music." He saw this as more important than literature or plastic arts and continued: "it functions admirably as an effective corrosive of religious asceticism and even, in certain circumstances, of some social differences" (González Henríquez 1985: 49). For Jesús Ferro, rector of the Universidad del Norte in 1995, speaking at the Forum on the Costeño Way of Life in 1980, this way of life consisted of "a set of vital attitudes, a frank view of life, naturalness in behavior, even in those aspects seen as abominable in other cultures, with this system being impregnated with music, fandango, the carnivalesque, and the playful" (Ferro Bayona 1981: 45). Jaime Abello Banfi, then director of Telecaribe, said in an interview that an explicit objective of the regional television channel was to "be an instrument in a process of integration, consolidation, and creation of the concept of the region," a region looking for "autonomy, development, and integration." A principle tool here was Costeño culture: "the culture is what unites La Costa, and it has really been the main motor of the channel." Not surprisingly, music was a central element in Telecaribe programming, probably to a greater extent than other regional television channels.[10] In general, then, within an intellectual project of promoting regional identity, centered around notions of relaxedness, naturalness, sincerity, the absence of religious fanaticism, and even the amelioration of class difference, music played a central role, and the revival of Costeño music in the 1990s could be seen only positively from this perspective—as long, of course, as it was not "vulgarized."

At a formal political level, the role of music is less clear. Gustavo Bell Lemus, historian and governor of Atlántico Province (1991–1994) and vice-president of Colombia (1998–), thought that the political elite had never used music as a strategic weapon; rather, they had looked down on it or participated in it as a mere diversion. Only in the case of vallenato could a definite link be made between music and political strategies of a regional nature (see chapter 6). But, he said, the recent successes of Costeño music had been positive for Costeño identity and by extension for the political elite. Thus, he recounted that the deputy of a local senator gave big annual parties with local artists at which high-ranking central government ministers were now regular guests. Such officials were also being invited to the Barranquilla carnival (fig. 8.2) with political tactics in mind: even President Gaviria had attended in 1994. Nevertheless, music was a double-edged sword: "it has served from the point of view of the cachacos—who are more reserved, of course—to bring the Costeño [politicians] down a peg.

8.2 The carnival of Barranquilla. (Photo by P. Wade.)

Every time *El Tiempo* [newspaper] wants to bring a Costeño down a peg or two, they try to get a picture of him dancing vallenato, dressed up in a costume. Because they don't understand it, but they use it, they trivialize it. . . . If you want to be accepted at the central government level—be careful, because if you are *auténtico* [i.e., folkloric, typical], they'll disqualify you." In this sense, music has played a background role, more important to an intellectual elite in the promotion of regional identity than to a political elite in negotiations with central government. Nevertheless, there are some indications that, as with vallenato in the 1960s campaign for El Cesar Province, it is taking on a more overtly political role.

Like the Costeño music of previous decades, the recent revivals, re-releases, and rearrangements are caught up in ideas about tradition and modernity, mixture and purity, and regional and national identity. Juan Carlos Coronel, for example, recounted his involvement with Bermúdez's music as a career move, but also as a rediscovery of his own roots. When he went to see Lucho perform in 1992, he says, "I realized that this music was alive, that I was singing in a different current [salsa] which didn't belong to me, that I could perhaps join in, embrace my culture, embrace what was mine, and say I'm Colombian and I can do this. . . . I am interested in being known for my work, but for what is mine—Colombian. Right now I feel more Colombian than ever, especially when I travel [abroad]." While he recognized that the music he was performing was Costeño, he constantly referred to it as Colombian; his horizons were international, rather than regional.

The cover notes for the Café Moreno album, *Momposina* (Rodven 63-1337, 1994) are explicitly nationalist. They state that the aim behind the group was to internationalize Colombian music, specifically in the form of tropical pop, which is "as Colombian as coffee, that coffee which grows in our mountains and which takes the name of our fatherland throughout the world." The music, they say, has been known for three decades, and now it has a "young sound, a young style, without losing the essence, the rhythm and *sabor* [flavor, spiciness] which has always characterized us." Of course, locating música tropical in the coffee-producing regions of the highland interior rides roughshod over the history I have related in this book, but this is not unusual in promotional sleeve notes.

The public relations material for the album *Calor* by Aura Cristina (who was born in Mexico and moved to Colombia only in 1988) takes a different line, emphasizing universality and mixture: "In this record production we can see at once the mixture of many factors such as rhythms, cultures, instruments, and ethnic groups which fuse to give life to what man, combining his best features, can achieve: universality." The music fits into the new tropical pop category and, according to the public relations material, combines elements of cumbia, son, reggae, bossa nova, salsa, and Dominican bachata, each of which is given a potted history. The image is of Caribbean, or even Latin American, rather than Colombian identity; the phrase "meltin' pot" is mentioned (in English), and the product fits into the multiplex hybridizations that Wallis and Malm (1984: 300) have called transculturation. In some ways, it is similar to the French Caribbean celebration of *créolité* (Guilbault 1994), but the diversity of mixture is harnessed to universality in this public relations material, rather than to Antillean specificity.

Nevertheless, by explicitly associating each rhythm with its country of origin—salsa is located more complexly in the Cuban and Puerto Rican immigrant communities of the United States—the public relations notes reinscribe national boundaries at the same time as they promote an image of universality based on mixture. Cumbia is labeled Colombian, while the album's music as a whole is an international hybrid: as usual in discourses of mixture or hybridity, there is an evocation of the supposedly original essences which form the mixture.[11] Cumbia is portrayed as a national essence, while at a higher level the overarching figure of international hybridity resonates with the notion of mixture that is central in representations of Colombian national identity. Tellingly, in the public relations notes, the roots of cumbia are traced back to Africa, suggesting the mixed nature of this national icon. Each national essence is itself the result of mixture.

These examples indicate that, while Barranquilla intellectuals, musicians, and composers might see Costeño music as "theirs," the same music is seen by record industry marketers—but also by a Costeño artist such as Juan Carlos Coronel—as fundamentally Colombian. There is a contest over the cultural ownership of the music in which it may be construed as Costeño and/or Colombian. In any event, this is now a Colombia associated with heat, tropicality, *sabor,* and the Caribbean—in a word, with La Costa. Coffee itself, usually read nationally as the classic product of the Andean interior, is reread as a transnational symbol of tropicality. As a national icon, this music, like the Janus face of nationalism, is seen as having a traditional, pure essence while also being young, fresh, modern, and forward looking. And, as with the (hopefully felicitous) combination of old and new, the music also evinces regional and class (and by implication, racial) mixture: Carlos Vives singing "vulgar" vallenato to an incoming president in Bogotá; young white models from the interior singing the songs of an old Costeño composer. The image of mixture or a melting pot has long been involved in representations of Colombian national identity, as previous chapters have shown. In the 1990s, the tensions between tradition and modernity, region and nation, and blackness and whiteness are similar in some ways to those I analyzed for preceding decades. But the notion of mixture now has a new context of multiculturality within which these tensions are worked out in different ways.

A "Multicultural" Nation

There has recently been an attempt by the state to redefine Colombia as a multicultural nation. This can be understood as a response to some decades of native American and, more recently, black mobilization and to Colombia's reputation abroad as a violent country in which abuses of human rights are commonplace. Official recognition of multiculturality is a useful symbol to legitimate democracy. I think that the recent revival of older Costeño music has to be seen in this context, without arguing that the political situation has directly caused this revival. Rather, both grow out of the condition of postmodernity as it exists in Latin America and elsewhere today, a condition that includes, among other elements, two things.

First, there is a shift toward multiculturalism, spurred by the transnational mobilization of indigenous and black peoples and by the fore-grounding and radical development of long-standing challenges to the unifying metanarratives of Western science, progress, and modernity, which seemed to foretell the erasure of ethnic and racial identities or at the least the dominance of "white" Euro-American versions of moder-nity (see Alvarez, Dagnino, and Escobar 1998; Beverley, Oviedo, and Aronna 1995; Escobar and Alvarez 1992; Harvey 1989; Turner 1990; Wade 1997; and Whitten and Torres 1998). Second, there is a move toward the commoditization of places and their traditions (including "ethnic" traditions), prompted by processes of globalizing capitalism that, although centuries old, are increasingly accelerated and increas-ingly dependent on the production and circulation of information and images—including images of nostalgia, an essentially modern sensi-bility that is now, according to Robertson (1990), less driven by na-tionalist politics than by consumer capitalism. While some have seen globalization as erasing local difference, most see globalization and localization as two sides of the same coin. Within a rapidly shifting economy of signs and spaces (Lash and Urry 1993), the search by cap-italists for new sources of profit and the search by consumers and ide-ologues for new, or rather renewed, sources of personal and collective identification both contribute to the construction of localities, regions, and nations as special, saleable, and consumable. Cultural diversity is a commodity, and capitalists work through exploiting differences (of locality, gender, "race," and style) at the same time as homogeneity gives them profitable economies of scale. The drive toward sameness in production and consumption is always undercut by competition, which works on finding cheaper (female, migrant, black) labor, better loca-tions, and new products (see Harvey 1989; Massey and Jess 1995; Miller 1995b; Shields 1991; and Urry 1995).

The rise of multiculturalism thus responds to influences which are so varied as to include indigenous rights activism, the self-legitimation of national states, and consumer capitalism's continued search for profit. Bearing this broad context in mind, I will look briefly at the official redefinition of the Colombian nation, which, although it follows simi-lar redefinitions that have taken place elsewhere (e.g., Brazil), has its own dynamic as well.

The new constitution of 1991 stated that Colombia was a "pluri-ethnic and multicultural" nation. It enshrined certain rights for indig-enous minorities and allowed for the creation of a law—Law 70 of 1993—protecting the cultural identity of black communities and the titling of land for some such communities in the Pacific coastal region.

The constitution also made provision for greater regional autonomy, a measure which will doubtless strengthen cultural diversity. In chapter 2, I mentioned some of the representations of diversity which were allied to this process—the Regional Days of Popular Culture program and the Millenia of Cultural Diversity exhibition—showing how diversity was constructed and controlled. It is worth looking briefly at the background to the creation of the new constitution in order to show why such diversity has been officialized in the way that it has and what its limits are.

In simple terms, from the government of Belisario Betancur in the early 1980s, successive Colombian administrations have been engaged with a "peace process" in order to persuade the various guerrilla groups, which have been active since the 1960s, to demobilize. One of the counters in the bargaining process was that of constitutional reform, and the process of reform began in 1990, despite the fact that not all guerrilla groups had demobilized. Native Americans and blacks were not the primary targets of reform, but given the long history of indigenous protest and political mobilization, indigenous organizations could hardly be excluded from the discussions over the shape of the new constitution; black organizations also made their voice heard, despite a cool or even hostile reception in some quarters. In the end, both sets of organizations won some significant concessions, although there are important limits on their real impact.[12]

In addition to the peace process, there has been a long-standing concern in Colombia with regionalism and centralism, going back to the early days of independence and only partially resolved with the imposition of a strongly centralist constitution in 1886. As indicated in chapter 2, La Costa has always been a strong voice in favor of greater regional autonomy, allied with greater integration. In recent years, its politicians were instrumental in pushing through Law 076 of 1985, which created the Planning Region of the Atlantic Coast and opened the way to various such entities for other regions (Espinosa 1991: 27). In debates about the new constitution, the issue of territorial reordering was important, and provision was made for the creation of regional entities with unprecedented financial and planning control.[13] Since the cultural geography of Colombia is so regionalized (Wade 1993a), support for regional autonomy also translates into the official underwriting of cultural diversity—although it remains to be seen whether this is the eventual outcome.

Finally, during the peace process, there has been a "dirty war" of informal repression by paramilitaries and, reportedly, the armed forces of anything deemed by them to be subversive. This has given Colombia a very bad human rights record on the international scene (see Pearce 1990; Amnesty International 1988; CIIR 1992). The adoption of an image of multiculturality has also been, I would argue, part of an attempt to create for the outside world the image of a democratic, responsive, and sensitive government. In sum, the redefinition of the Colombian nation has been connected to the state's political strategies of control and legitimation in the face of challenges by guerrillas, indigenous and black minorities, and regional protest. Multiculturality may be connected to the postmodern condition, but it has to be seen as the locus of an intersection between strategies of political control and the emergence of multiple identities.

Where does the revived interest in older Costeño music fit in here? It would be false to argue that these state initiatives have actually caused the increased popularity of Costeño music. This stems in great measure from the commoditization of nostalgia that has gained ground as capitalists cater to consumers seeking renewed touchstones of identity in a world where deterritorialization has increased rapidly, especially since the 1980s, when the Colombian state began to open wide the doors of the national economy to global capitalism. This commoditization has indeed been most evident in the media industries, where the revival of Costeño music has been promoted and consumers over a wide range of classes and ages have accepted styles that emphasize different hybridizations of traditional and modern elements, recreating these as they are mixed.

My point is that the revival of Costeño music has to be seen in the context of the official redefinition of national identity; the first phenomenon exhibits what Weber might have called an elective affinity with the second. Costeño music fits the bill because it is regionally specific and has traditional roots, publicly nurtured by regional specialists in music and history, expressed at one extreme by popular presentations of "folklore"—often by people easily classed as "black"—and at the other in commercial arrangements of old examples of this music. As well as being local and traditional (and black), however, it can also be national, modern, and nonblack. Within the internationally located nation, Costeño music—as before in its history—mediates tensions between homogeneity and heterogeneity, between tradition and modernity. Now, the heterogeneity has a new legitimacy, but it cannot completely supersede some version of the nation as a unity. Tradition also has a new power, as the roots of a newly official cultural difference, but it cannot triumph alone in people's identifications of themselves and their localities.

Moreover, Costeño music is, as ever, *alegre:* it makes a heartening contrast—or, some might say, a macabre backdrop—to death by contract killers and massacres of peasants and rural workers by paramilitaries. This is difficult methodological terrain. It would be facile to argue that Costeño music was a veil drawn by instrumentalist hegemonic powers over the brutal conflicts of class and capital. It is less superficial to assert that citizens harrowed by years of violence sought refuge in "happy" music, especially music from a region with the reputation of being less violent than the interior of the country and that also made nostalgic reference to the past. Such an argument is lent weight by the constant association people make of La Costa with happiness and peacefulness, and of the interior with reserve and cold-blooded violence. It is also reinforced by the ideas I looked at in the previous chapter about the material as well as symbolic effects of dancing to "joyful" and "sexy" music—the embodied transformation from potential corpse to empowered lover.

It may be that some of the shift of representations of Colombian national identity toward images of the Caribbean and tropicality—and this includes the frequent personal self-representations of Colombians as *rumberos* (party loving)—stems from a desire to distance the nation and the person from overpowering images of violence, ruthlessness, and mistrust. The association of Caribbean tropicality with peacefulness is not a necessary one, of course, nor even always a convincing one, but the two images resonate powerfully for Colombians.

Conclusion

The foregoing raises the question of what is new about Colombian national identity in the mid-1990s. The emergence of minority voices, the embracing of multiculturalism, greater regional autonomy, the nostalgic revival of older, more "authentic" music, the seemingly final gasp of a Europhile elitist identity centered on the highlands, the triumph of a tropical popular culture—all these seem to be important innovations that reconstitute Colombia's nationhood in a postmodern world.

But, of course, there is as much continuity as novelty. First, heterogeneity has always been present in representations of Colombian identity, as I have tried to show throughout this book. The present multiculturalism, official and otherwise, is a different balance between the sameness and diversity that have always constituted the nation. Things are different now in important respects: real material and political gains have been won by ethnic minorities (albeit with severe pragmatic limits on them), and blacks and indigenous peoples have a rather different position in the nation from the one they previously occupied. Second, the recent trends in Costeño music indicate the continued play of modernity and tradition as powerful images in commerce, politics, and identity. In line with postmodern aesthetics, the play is now more ironic, self-reflexive, and purposive: the considered juxtaposition of old and new in Vives's material mockingly dares the consumer to denigrate it as a self-serving fabrication. But there is an important continuity involved.

Third, and relatedly, the commercialization of culture as commodity, although now more pervasive, is evidently not at all new to the music business. Urry (1990) has argued that tourism prefigured certain trends that have become more prominent with postmodernity: the role of spectacle and image, a preoccupation with nostalgia, authenticity, and the past, and the consumption of places. The same seems to be true of music capitalism with its mass production and mass consumption of music as a transnational commodity, based on highly flexible systems of global production and on the daring construction of transnational hybrids alongside notionally national repertoires—all dating back to the first decades of this century.

It is not my purpose here to argue that nothing is new under the sun or simply that *plus ça change.* . . . Clearly, real and important changes have taken place—not least, the one described at length in this book. But there are powerful strands of continuity which make today's cultural and political configurations new expressions of existing tensions and ambivalences, just as postmodernity, rather than being a radical rupture with the past, is an expression of the contradictions and dynamics existing within modernity. Thus, the gradual triumph of tropicalism in Colombian popular culture since the 1940s represents something different, but not something unheralded: it is located in the same tense, ambivalent space between modernity and tradition, between blackness and whiteness, and between region, nation, and globe that has always been at the heart of the Colombian nation.

9 Conclusion
WRITING ABOUT
COLOMBIAN MUSIC

One of the frustrating things I found in doing research was the difficulty of tying things down. Different people gave different and often conflicting accounts of what went on, not just as matters of opinion but as matters of fact. This is, of course, a trivial observation in some ways—even eyewitnesses differ over the simple facts of an event they all observed at the same time in the same place. Nevertheless, it often becomes an obsession when doing research. One tries to get some handle on "what actually happened," and this is especially so when constructing a history. In this research on Costeño music, for example, I frequently found myself focusing on dates. When did Discos Fuentes first press its own records? Which was the first record it ever produced? When exactly did Lucho Bermúdez arrive in Bogotá? I would pursue such questions with different sources of information (Discos Fuentes employees, record collectors, biographies, newspaper reports, etc.), lending each source more or less credence according to somewhat intuitive criteria of my own. In the final product—this book—these twists and turns of the chase are smoothed over and even concealed to some extent with phrases such as "it seems likely that" or "at about this time."

These very concrete details, which must theoretically have definite answers even if they are no longer discoverable, merge almost seamlessly into more difficult areas where a definite answer is perhaps not even theoretically possible. Where did porro come from? When did it emerge? Where was it "born"? These questions then disperse into larger even more contentious issues about the ownership and significance of porro or other styles of Colombian music. These problems are ones that are foregrounded in my writing, rather than smoothed over, but they are not disconnected from the more precise "matters of fact."

Ultimately, I, like everyone else, am caught up in the tangled webs of the production of knowledge, and I think it is interesting to reflect on the conditions for the production of different accounts, of different sorts of knowledge about Colombian music. Within academia, it has become fashionable in some circles to see all accounts as discursive productions produced by socially located actors and thus as not only ontologically but epistemologically equal.[1] One must concede that all accounts are, by their very nature, discourses and that they can be produced only by people who have a particular standpoint and perspective. But this does not, I think, make all accounts epistemologically equally valid. If it did, the whole enterprise of academia would have to be abandoned. I do not want to reinstate the authorial objectivizing authority that has been so effectively challenged in anthropology and other social sciences (see, e.g., Clifford and Marcus 1986; and Fabian 1983). But I think it can be said of some accounts that (*a*) they try to be systematic and comparative in their collection of data (e.g., by cross-checking sources and comparing historical trajectories), and, more importantly, (*b*) they try to take seriously that knowledge is a discursive production, but that as a human agent one is not locked forever into *particular* discourses (however much one is locked into discourse per se). Thus, some accounts do not question their own conditions of production, they are not self-reflexive, and they take certain categories for granted. In the case of the Colombian music which I was investigating, such categories would include modernity, tradition, authenticity, degeneration, working class, bourgeois, Costeño, and Colombian. The academic's task—not always achieved of course, given its difficulty—is to question the categories used by the people whose lives and histories are being studied and also the categories being used in the analysis. This leads inevitably to an endless regression, the critique without finality of poststructuralist deconstruction which always discovers the hidden agenda in any analysis only to have that discovery subjected to further deconstruction. A relapse into relativism seems to threaten, but in practice we have a recipe for a constructive critique (which is actually that at the heart of anthropology): to challenge categories which are taken for granted *in a given social context*. The critique is not final or universal, but is always made in relation to that context, which is, of course, in flux—partly as a result of the critique itself (cf. Giddens 1990).

Within Colombia, there are various accounts of Colombian and, for my purposes, Costeño music. These are produced by enthusiasts, record collectors, media industry workers (disc jockeys, record producers, etc.), and musicians—not to mention nonspecialist members of the listening, dancing, and record-buying public. There are also musicologists, sociologists, and historians who produce more academic accounts. These accounts have supplied some of the factual basis for my account, but also much of the subject matter of that account. Part of my purpose has been to analyze the representations different people make of the music, and, here, academic productions are not always that different from nonacademic ones, depending on the extent to which the academic accounts remain locked into certain perspectives. Thus, in my view, the accounts by Fortich Díaz (1994) of the history of porro and by Araújo de Molina (1973) of the history of vallenato, while they present a great deal of valuable data, do not question notions of tradition and authenticity and indeed actively reproduce them in much the same way as the journalistic writings on this music by García Márquez (see chapter 3).

Most of these varied accounts of Colombian music accept particular versions of regional, class, or national identities. They tell particular stories: Costeño music belongs to the Costeños or, on the other hand, to the nation; porro was a working-class music that was appropriated by the bourgeoisie; bambuco is the real heart of Colombian nationhood; cumbia represents the mestizaje that is the basis of Colombian identity; vallenato was born in La Provincia; and so on. The social conditions for the production of this knowledge about music are precisely the class, regional, and racial conjunctures that I have described in this book, all set in an international context, particularly that of the transnational recording industry. The effect of these accounts is generally to sustain the versions of identity which they accept.

My purpose is not to claim to produce a true account of Costeño music in the Colombian nation (and beyond). This purist, objectivist, and ultimately authoritarian goal is subverted not only by the difficulty of establishing certain concrete facts, but much more fundamentally by the impossibility of producing a definitive account of what Costeño music signifies in Colombia—not to mention what the Colombian nation itself signifies. Instead, I have striven to tell a story in which, at a basic level, certain facts have been cross-checked as far as possible, given the practical and methodological constraints that conditioned my research, and a story which tries to be critical of categories and ideas that are often taken for granted. Of course, I have inevitably done this from a particular perspective—that of an anthropologist in the context of late-twentieth-century theories about society and culture. From this perspective, categories such as tradition, modernity, authenticity, and commercial corruption all became open to question. As a lover of salsa myself, it was easy for me to identify with views that labeled chucu-chucu or raspa plastic, artificial music that had been corrupted and degenerated by commercialization. But the category of chucu-chucu had to be questioned. What did it include? According to whom? Who produced it? Who listened to it?

At a more general level, I found that some ideas that underlay accounts of music and its history in Colombia had resonances in more academic, theoretical approaches to conceptual issues. Again, there is no clear break between "lay" and "expert" accounts, just a constant attempt to be self-critical. For example, one of my central arguments has been that the nationalization of Costeño music has not involved a simple homogenization of difference, accompanied by the erasure of blackness. Academic approaches to nationalism often focus on homogenization, as I showed in chapter 1. The same tendency is evident in more lay accounts of Colombian music, which bewail the degenerative effect of commercialization or which see Costeño music as an authentic, regional product which has been appropriated by the national record industry in the hands of capitalists from the interior of the country. Now, there are powerful elements of truth in these ideas, in relation to both nationalism and Costeño music, because both capitalism and nationalism contain drives toward sameness, whether to create economies of scale or national solidarity and distinctiveness. But these ideas miss the vital point that heterogeneity and difference must remain and indeed are constantly referred to in nationalist discourse and in capitalism. They must remain because to obliterate them would deny hierarchical distinctions which are carefully maintained by those who are or want to be on the higher rungs of the social ladder and which open opportunities for the competition so central to capitalism. A tension is thus established between difference and sameness which is characteristic of nations in general and capitalism in general, a tension which is played out in different ways at different historical conjunctures.

Thus, in Colombia, Costeño music was marginalized as a national symbol in the late nineteenth century. Then, in the midcentury context of rapid modernization and the growth of mass media, it was accepted in adapted form as a national symbol. Then, in the 1990s, its older forms were revived for nostalgic consumerism. Cultural and racial difference were never completely denied in any of these periods, but were located differently (although blackness has generally been placed as inferior). At first, Costeño music and blackness were basically seen as primitive and savage; they were often linked to Africa and alienness. In the midcentury, these meanings remained as a crucial possibility, but were overlaid with ideas of the music as modern, exciting, and liberating, especially in a sexual sense. In the 1990s, all these meanings are still present, but now the notion of authentic nostalgia has become foregrounded.

Closely connected with this argument about difference and sameness is a second one about class, identity, and music that has been present throughout the book. My point here has been to contest that Costeño music is linked in a simple homological fashion to a particular class or social group and that simple continuities underlie its history. Again, this is a linkage implied in some academic theories about class and culture and is also an implication of some accounts of Colombian music that stress the traditional continuities of Costeño styles, their rootedness in locality, and their plebeian origins and that see all these as having been appropriated by the middle classes, the record industry, and national elites. Clearly, there are real and important continuities in Costeño music: to see the music as constructed completely anew at every historical conjuncture would be to fall into the trap of denying the input of Africans, black Colombians, and indigenous peoples into the music. Yet these continuities are not continuous, so to speak. They are examples of what Amiri Baraka (a.k.a. Leroi Jones) called "the changing same" (Jones 1970; see also Keil and Feld 1994: 23; and Gilroy 1993: 101). As Sahlins has so aptly put it: "syncretism is not a contradiction of . . . culturalism—of the indigenous claims of authenticity and autonomy—but its systematic condition" (1993: 19). That is, a *sense* of continuity and tradition is maintained through processes of syncretic change.

I have tried to argue that the processes of syncretism and hybridization involved in the history of Costeño music defy simple links between class, identity, and musical style and defy straightforward continuities. Costeño music in the twentieth century was produced in complex exchanges between Europe and the Caribbean, between New York, the Caribbean, and Colombia, between La Costa and the interior, between town and country, and between working and middle classes. The exact interactions between directors and players of provincial wind bands and between them and other local untutored musicians in the late nineteenth century, or the exchanges that occurred when Camacho y Cano went to New York to record "porros" with Rafael Hernández's band in 1929, or when Lucho Bermúdez drew around him a group of musicians from the interior in the 1940s—all these remain more or less hidden in their complexity. But I think it is misleading to see it all as a case of "traditional" plebeian music being "modernized" by capitalists and the middle classes. The traditional is as much a discursive construct as the modern; each is defined in relation to the other, and both are constantly on the move. As Taussig puts it, "modernity stimulate[s] primitivism" (1993: 231); that is, ideas about the new actively recreate ideas about the old. This is evident enough in the creation of the Festival of the Vallenato Legend in 1968 (not to mention the Festival of Porro and many other similar events), which was consciously set up as the guardian of authenticity for a "tradition" that may well have emerged as such only in the 1940s.

In addition, the modernization of Costeño music (its corruption, for some) that took place from the 1960s to the 1980s, led by the record industry in Medellín, cannot easily be seen as a simple process of class and regional appropriation. The music of Lucho Bermúdez made its initial impact as an elite music, played live in the prestigious social clubs; Bermúdez was also an international figure early on, inspiring band leaders in Buenos Aires to play Costeño music. The modernized cumbia of the later period was popular across a wide range of classes, although it might have been defined as "bourgeois" (meaning glossy and inauthentic) by lovers of the gritty salsa associated with the streets and youth rebelliousness. Also, in regional terms, many Costeños—most notably Antonio Fuentes himself—were pioneers in the process of changing Costeño music in this direction. Although some people—often Costeños—labeled the music an "Antioqueño sound" (sonido paisa), it was not only Antioqueños who played or created it. In short, Costeño music was not simply a local traditional product which was then appropriated and nationalized; it was a transnational construct of appropriations to start with.

All this does not mean that we have to abandon differences of class and region (and of course race) in analyzing this music. These were crucially important, as I hope to have shown. People's ideas about different musical styles as vulgar, plebeian, bourgeois, or elite, as more or less black, white, and indigenous, or as Costeño, "paisa," or "cachaco" were all central to the social identity of those styles and how they changed. Musical tastes and choices were made in contexts shaped by hierarchies of class, race, and region. Gender and sexuality were also important, since music was also judged in terms of its moral propriety and this differed for men and women. A *sense* of continuity was established in part by forceful ideas about the supposed inferiority of blackness or the perceived sexual power of music associated with blackness. In these contexts, hegemonic ideas held sway, but they were not driven forward as an explicit and integrated project by a coherent set of people. Particular people or networks of people pursued their endeavors (to make music, to produce records, to run a radio station, etc.) in ways that they preferred, often driven by hopes of success in the market. But their choices of what to produce and what to consume were made in contexts molded by hegemonic values. The outcome of such choices is to some extent unpredictable. Hegemonic values do not just continue in an automatic, self-propelling way. People make choices that do not conform to them, although they are informed by them. The musicians in La Costa who chose to focus on the accordion in the 1940s and 1950s were making a choice that militated against commercial success at the time, given the overwhelmingly plebeian connotations of accordion music. Perhaps they were not bothered about success, or perhaps they were establishing themselves within a smaller social circle where a different set of values reigned, ones which vindicated plebeian and/or Costeño origins. In either case, such choices went against the grain of hegemonic values, whether this was conscious resistance or not. Whichever it was, these decisions laid the basis for the subsequent success of vallenato in the 1960s and 1970s; even then, however, vallenato changed in ways that reflected certain hegemonic values of nationalism (in lessening purely local references) and modernity (in terms of changes to instrumentation and presentation). Overall, in looking at Costeño music over a period of some seventy years, it is clear that basic values of modernity, whiteness, and nationalism have prevailed—always in tension with their counterparts of tradition, blackness (coupled to some extent with indigenousness), and regionalism (coupled with internationalism).

The central question I began with in 1994 was why Costeño music, with its connotations of tropicality and blackness, came to play such an important role in Colombian popular music during the twentieth century, when the dominant representations of Colombian national identity emphasized the country's highland regions of the interior and its people's supposed nonblackness, and when bambuco and other styles from the interior were glorified as the essence of national traditions. The answer has turned out to lie, in a structural sense, in the place of La Costa as a region whose major cities, especially Barranquilla, were lapped first by the ripples of economic and cultural modernity that were breaking over the country; La Costa was first in line here. Crucially, the region was also historically part of the bubbling musical cauldron of the Caribbean, and this gave it a lead in musical innovation. Thereafter, the success of Costeño music lay in great part in its multivocality, which meant it could be talked about productively by different people in many different ways, according to their points of view, their class positions, their regional allegiances, their moral attitudes, and their racial and gender identities. When I say productively, I mean that the music could be harnessed effectively to the constitution of identity, to the definition of selves and others, whether individually or collectively. At an analytical level, homological theories might not work very well, but people certainly talked about and related to music in a homological way, as if they owned it and it owned them. At the same time, as I argued in chapter 7, in harnessing music to their personal and collective projects, people did not only talk: they could listen to the music, imagine others listening to it, and imagine themselves in different places and conditions by listening to it; and they could dance to it, usually with someone else, usually of the opposite sex. By tapping these realms of imagination, embodiment, and romance, Costeño music and dance—and it is of course vital that most of this music was made for dancing—were especially productive in the realm of constituting identities.

APPENDIX A

List of Interviewees

The following list records the name of the interviewee, the date and place of the interview, the name of the interviewer, and, where appropriate, some brief notes about the interviewee. Interviews with people who were born in Bogotá or were born in the Andean region and had lived in Bogotá most of their lives were carried out by Javier Pinzón and Rosana Portaccio. Interviews of native Medellín residents were done by Manuel Bernardo Rojas. Interviews of Costeños resident in Bogotá were done by Lorena Aja. These assistants found their own interviewees, selected according to prespecified criteria of class, age, and gender, and carried out taped interviews, using interview guides prepared by me. They supplied me with the original tapes, plus transcriptions. I also carried out interviews with various individuals in all locations.

Abello Banfi, Jaime, 7 February 1995, Barranquilla (Peter Wade). Notes: Director of Telecaribe, La Costa's regional television station.
Arango, Alvaro, 17 November 1994, Medellín (Peter Wade). Notes: Vice-president of Codiscos.
Barros, Marco T., 30 November 1995, Barranquilla (Peter Wade). Notes: Radio announcer and newspaper columnist in Barranquilla.
Bell Lemus, Gustavo, 31 January 1995, Barranquilla (Peter Wade). Notes: Historian and governor of Atlántico Province (1991–1994).
Betancur Alvarez, Fabio, 28 September 1994, Medellín (Peter Wade). Notes: Sociologist at the University of Antioquia and writer on Cuban and Colombian music (Betancur Alvarez 1993).
Betancur, Teresa de, 19 September 1994, Medellín (Peter Wade). Notes: Medellín resident; b. 1937; working-class background.

Botero, Tomás, 20 September 1994, Medellín (Peter Wade). Notes: Medellín resident; social club member; b. c. 1920, Aranzazu, Caldas.

Briceño, Stella de, November 1994, Bogotá (Rosana Portaccio). Notes: Bogotá resident from the age of nine; teacher; b. 1937, Tunja, Boyacá.

Burgos, María Angélica, María Eugenia Goubert, and Luis Alfredo Rueda, November 1994, Bogotá (Rosana Portaccio). Notes: All Bogotá residents; a teacher and two dentists; all between fifty-five and sixty-five years old.

Campo Miranda, Rafael, 29 November 1995, Barranquilla (Peter Wade). Notes: Costeño composer who also was a white-collar worker all his life.

Castaño, Dominga, 21 December 1994, Bogotá (Lorena Aja). Notes: Teacher; moved to Bogotá in 1968 to study; b. 1931, Mompox.

Chacuto, Félix, 28 November 1994, Barranquilla (Peter Wade). Notes: Radio disc jockey; b. c. 1915, Santa Marta.

Clavijo, Jaime, November 1994, Bogotá (Rosana Portaccio). Notes: Bogotá resident; security guard; b. 1935, Bogotá.

Colorado, Jairo, 18 December 1994, Medellín (Manuel Bernardo Rojas). Notes: Medellín resident; leather worker; b. c. 1940.

Coronel, Juan Carlos, 4 February 1995, Cartagena (Peter Wade and Egberto Bermúdez). Notes: Singer who began as a balladeer, before moving to Costeño music, salsa, and most recently a homage album to Lucho Bermúdez; b. 1967, Cartagena.

Coronel, Mercedes de, 4 February 1995, Cartagena (Peter Wade and Egberto Bermúdez). Notes: Occasional singer for Orquesta de Roberto Lambraño and Orquesta Emisora Fuentes.

De la Espriella, Alfredo, 24 November 1994, Barranquilla (Peter Wade). Notes: Curator of Museo Romántico, writer, columnist, and radio announcer in Barranquilla.

Delgado, Cecilia, 5 February 1995, Bogotá (Lorena Aja). Notes: Housewife; moved to Bogotá in 1957 when she married a man from Bogotá who worked as a hotel manager; b. 1937, Cartagena.

Díaz, Matilde, 8 November 1994, Bogotá (Peter Wade). Notes: Singer in Orquesta de Lucho Bermúdez and Bermúdez's wife.

Estrada, Julio (a.k.a. Fruko), 28 September 1994, Medellín (Peter Wade). Notes: Colombian salsa artist; also played with the Corraleros de Majagual in his youth; b. 1951, Medellín.

Fortou, Tony, 5 December 1994, Barranquilla (Peter Wade). Notes: Son of Emilio Fortou, founder of Discos Tropical.

Fuentes, José María "Curro," 4 February 1995, Cartagena (Peter Wade and Egberto Bermúdez). Notes: Brother of Antonio Fuentes of Discos Fuentes; owned Curro record label.

Fuentes, Wilson, 1 December 1994, Bogotá (Lorena Aja). Notes: Teacher; moved to Bogotá in early 1970s to study at university; b. Fonseca, La Guajira.

Galán, Armando, 1 December 1994, Barranquilla (Peter Wade). Notes: Son of Pacho Galán and musician in his orchestra.

González, Alberto, 30 September 1994, Medellín (Peter Wade). Notes: Barranquilla-born member of Trío Los Romanceros, a bolero trio, which started in Barranquilla and moved to Medellín in 1945.

Granados Arjona, Miguel, 10 November 1994, Bogotá (Peter Wade). Notes: Radio announcer on La Hora Costeña from 1952; b. Barraquilla.

Guarnizo, Pedro, November 1994, Bogotá (Rosana Portaccio). Notes: Bogotá resident from 1944; shopkeeper; b. 1924, Giradot, Cundinamarca.

Guerra, José del Carmen "Cheíto," 20 December 1994, Bogotá (Lorena Aja). Notes: Former musician with the Orquesta Radio Cartagena and Orquesta Emisora Fuentes in Cartagena; b. 1925, Arjona, Bolívar.

Gutiérrez, Alfredo, 5 December 1994, Barranquilla (Peter Wade). Notes: Accordionist, original member of Los Corraleros de Majagual, and important figure in Costeño music since the 1960s; b. 1944 in Sucre Province.

Herrera, Eliseo, 4 February 1995, Barranquilla (Peter Wade and Egberto Bermúdez). Notes: Founding member of Los Corraleros de Majagual; well-known for his tongue-twisting lyrics; b. c. 1925, Cartagena.

Jackie (no surname given), 5 December 1994, Bogotá (Lorena Aja). Notes: Runs dance school; moved to Bogotá for schooling in 1970s and remained there with her family; b. Barranquilla.

López, Fernando, 21 September 1994, Medellín (Peter Wade). Notes: artists and repertoire director, Codiscos.

Márquez, Ligia de, November 1994, Bogotá (Rosana Portaccio). Notes: Bogotá resident; teacher; b. 1929.

Martínez, Moisés, and Salvador Gómez, 23 September 1994, Medellín (Peter Wade). Notes: School teachers; moved to Medellín to study in the early 1960s; both b. Cartagena.

Mejía Donado, Efraín, 3 December 1994, Barranquilla (Peter Wade). Notes: Leader of band La Cumbia Soledeña, based in Barranquilla, which performs traditional Costeño folk music and dance; since 1960, they have recorded about twenty LPs, many with Philips; b. 1934, Soledad.

Morán, Pedro, 21 September 1994, Medellín (Peter Wade). Notes: University teacher; moved to Medellín to study in 1969; b. Cartagena.

Muñoz, Gabriel, 19 December 1994, Bogotá (Peter Wade). Notes: artists and repertoire director, Sony Music Entertainment Colombia; worked for a year in Discos Tropical before joining CBS in 1965.

Oñate, Julio, 13 December 1994, Barranquilla (Peter Wade). Notes: Record collector; specialist in the life of Guillermo Buitrago.

Parra, Orlando, 3 November 1994, Bogotá (Peter Wade). Notes: Director of ASINCOL, the record industry trade association.

Peñaloza, Antonio María, Barranquilla, 5 February 1995 (Peter Wade and Egberto Bermúdez). Notes: Costeño composer, arranger, and musician.

Peñaranda, José María, 25 November 1994, Barranquilla (Peter Wade). Notes: Costeño musician and early popularizer of Costeño music on the guitar; b. 1907, Barranquilla.

Pinzón, Adalberto, December 1994, Bogotá (Javier Pinzón). Notes: Bogotá resident; railway employee; b. 1910.

Portaccio, José and Rosni, 4 September 1994, Bogotá (Peter Wade). Notes: José was a radio announcer; Rosni is still a singer in different groups; both b. late 1930s, Barranquilla; moved to Bogotá in c. 1958.

Quintero, Gustavo, and Consuelo Ruiz, 22 November 1994, Medellín (Peter Wade). Notes: Gustavo Quintero has been lead singer of Los Teen Agers, Los Hispanos, and Los Graduados; b. mid-1940s, Rionegro, Antioquia; Consuelo Ruiz is his wife and manager.

Ramírez, Lucía, January 1995, Bogotá (Javier Pinzón). Notes: Bogotá resident from 1948; shopkeeper; b. 1927.

Ramírez, María Helena, December 1995, Bogotá (Javier Pinzón). Notes: Bogotá resident from 1950; teacher and housewife; b. 1920.

Ramírez, Oscar, 9 November 1994, Bogotá (Peter Wade). Notes: Publicity manager of Sonolux record company.

Ramírez, William, 20 September 1994, Medellín (Peter Wade). Notes: Medellín resident; hotel owner; b. 1933, Medellín.

Rodríguez, Pompilio, 3 February 1995, Barranquilla (Peter Wade and Egberto Bermúdez). Notes: Drummer in Orquesta de Lucho Rodríguez and Orquesta de Pacho Galán.

Ruíz Hernández, Alvaro, 9 December 1994, Barranquilla (Peter Wade). Notes: Radio announcer, amateur historian, and writer.

Sánchez, Hilda María, November 1994, Bogotá (Rosana Portaccio). Notes: Bogotá resident from 1970; domestic servant; b. 1945, Pacho, Cundinamarca.

Tapias, Antonio, 19 February 1995, Medellín (Peter Wade). Notes: Medellín resident; dance teacher; b. 1943, Medellín.

Totó la Momposina (real name Sonia Bazanta), 10 November 1995, Bogotá (Peter Wade). Notes: Singer of traditional Costeño music; played at Nobel Prize ceremony of Gabriel García Márquez in 1982; recorded with Peter Gabriel's Realworld label in 1991; b. 1944, Mompox.

Urbina, Samuel, January 1995, Bogotá (Javier Pinzón). Notes: Bogotá resident from 1942; driver and carpenter; b. 1935, Simijaca, Cundinamarca.

Valderrama, Ema, November 1994, Bogotá (Rosana Portaccio). Notes: Bogotá resident from early 1940s, when her family moved there from Fómeque, Cundinamarca; now a teacher; b. 1929.

Vasco, Jairo, 30 October 1994, Medellín (Manuel Bernardo Rojas). Notes: Trumpet player in El Combo Di Lido in the 1960s; also worked in a textile factory in Medellín; b. c. 1940; studied music in the conservatory of the University of Antioquia.

Velásquez, Aníbal, 12 December 1994, Barranquilla (Peter Wade). Notes: Accordion player who spent many years in Venezuela; played guarachas and boleros on the accordion; b. 1936, Barranquilla.

Villalobos, María del Carmen, January 1995, Bogotá (Javier Pinzón). Notes: Bogotá resident; bank cashier and housewife; b. 1934.

Zapata, Oliva, 24 October 1994, Medellín (Manuel Bernardo Rojas). Notes: Medellín resident; factory worker and domestic servant; b. c. 1924, Anorí, Antioquia.

Zapata Olivella, Manuel, 26 August 1994, Bogotá (Peter Wade). Notes: b. 1920, Cartagena; doctor, celebrated novelist and folklorist.

Zuluaga, Arturo, 14 February 1995, Medellín (Peter Wade). Notes: Singer with Los Swing Stars (1947) and Orquesta Medellín (1948) and director of Los Ases del Ritmo in the 1950s—all Medellín-based bands.

APPENDIX B

Musical Examples

This section and the accompanying musical transcriptions were prepared by Alex Miles, to whom I am most grateful. The brief characterizations of the three styles are based on her listening to the following material: various artists, *Escalona y su gran obra musical,* vol. 1 (Discos Fuentes E30005, 1994); Hermanos Zuleta, *Grandes intérpretes vallenatos: Hermanos Zuleta* (Columbia CDC464662, n.d.); Lucho Bermúdez, *Gaita caliente* (Polydor 5122222, 1995); various artists, *Rico, caliente y sabroso* (Codiscos C3250079, 1993); various artists, *Porros, sólo porros* (Discos Fuentes D10190, 1992); various artists, *Cumbia, cumbia* (World Circuit WCD 016, 1989); various artists, *Cumbia, cumbia 2* (World Circuit WCD 033, 1993); Totó la Momposina, *La candela viva* (Talento/MTM/Realworld 7260-008019, 1993).

PORRO

All porros are based upon tonic-dominant chords, usually lasting for a couple of bars each. The bass line, however (which determines this tonality), utilizes the second inversion of the dominant in every case. This does not alter the harmonic content; it creates a solid background as the main feature common to all porros. This tonality appears in the bass line as broken triads, and the entire porro never strays from these two chords.

Brass instruments in porros also occupy a prominent generic position. A short brass motif is repeated throughout each piece, played by a small ensemble consisting usually of trumpets and/or clarinets and saxophones. This repetitive brass motif is an important aspect of the porro, as it may provide the tonal base for any instrumental solo or vocal melody included. If a solo vocal or instrumental line is included, it will invariably be subservient to the brass motif; any pauses in the solo will be filled by the ensemble.

Percussion is another important aspect of the porro, consisting of at least maracas or shakers, a bongo drum, and a bass drum. The maracas may sustain a steady rhythmic pattern (usually ♪♫ ♪♫), while the bongo or other percussive instruments improvise on offbeats over this fixed base.

Porros are almost always performed in the minor mode and tend to be of similar tempi (around 180 bpm) in simple (4/4) time.

PASEO VALLENATO

The use of either an acoustic guitar or an accordion constitutes the most noticeable and common feature of the paseo vallenato. Occasionally, both instruments are used together, although the music never sounds "overcrowded." This is because the music always accommodates the vocal line, which may be solo with backing or all harmonized. The guitar and/or accordion is used to back up any voices (and not to replace them), although it may also fill any gaps between vocal lines. Instrumentation only really takes precedence during the introduction, where the guitar and/or accordion may take the lead (occasionally in conjunction with either woodwinds or brass).

Harmonically, the paseo vallenato will usually remain close to the tonic and dominant, although in some instances the subdominant is introduced and in others there is a fast rate of harmonic change. This does not, however, stray into the unexpected, and the music remains within predictable harmonic boundaries, invariably in the major mode.

The use of percussion is kept to a minimum. The motif is almost always included either on the maracas or cowbell, which may be reinforced by a bass drum and bongo or timbale. Simple time is always used, at a tempo of around 180 bpm.

CUMBIA

The cumbia is based largely upon the tonic and dominant of the scale, although it adopts other harmonic changes that differentiate it from, say, the porro. If it is in the minor mode, it may touch upon the relative major from time to time, or it may base itself upon the tonic and flatted seventh degree of the scale. The latter imparts an Aeolian modality to many, though not all, examples of the genre. The major key is sometimes used; there is no single rule governing the modality of a cumbia.

A strikingly common feature, however, is the use of a small brass and/or woodwind ensemble to introduce and punctuate the piece. The trumpet is especially prominent when such an ensemble is featured. Short, harmonized motifs appear throughout, at regular and predictable places, and it is these that characterize the melodic content of the cumbia.

The vocal lines of a cumbia are usually sung by soloists, with a group of backing vocalists "answering" at certain points of the piece. The lines are fast and often quite complex relative to the regularity of the brass motifs, which is probably why it is the brass lines, and not the vocals, which are the more memorable and "catchy."

Rhythmically, shakers or maracas provide the solidarity of the percussion section, while a heavier and deeper drum will reinforce these lighter sounds at random intervals. The beat may be further underlined by the use of piano chords on beats two and four of each bar.

Example B1. Cumbia: "La Pollera Colora," by Wilson Choperena. Source: Pedro Salcedo y su Orquesta, on *Música tropical*, vol. 7 (Discos Fuentes D10172, 1992); original recording 1962. (By permission of Sonointer [Promotora Sonolux Internacional S.A.].)

amañ - a _____ y al son - ar de la cañ - a _____

_____ va brin-dan-do sus amor-es _____ es la ne-gra Sol-e -

- dad _____ la que go - za mi cum - bia.

etc.

Example B2. Porro: "Fiesta de Negritos," by Lucho Bermúdez. Source: Lucho Bermúdez, *Gaita caliente* (Polygram Colombia 512222-2, 1995). (By permission of Fondo Musical Ltda.)

El Testamento
by Rafael Escalona

Example B3. Paseo vallenato: "El Testamento," by Rafael Escalona. Source: Guillermo
Buitrago y sus Muchachos, on *Escalona y su obra musical*, vol. 1 (Discos Fuentes E30005,
1994); original recording 1945–49. By permission of Discos Fuentes and Edimusica.

-ni - ta me voy por la ma - dru - ga - da que a - no - che di - jo

el ra - dio que ab - rie - ron el Lic - eo

y co - mo est -

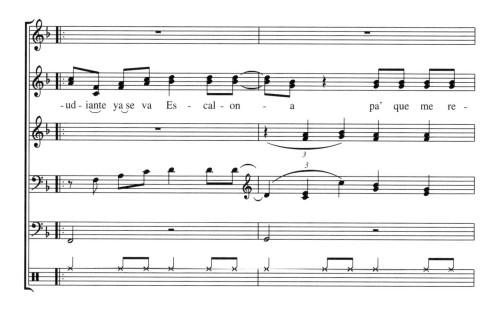

-ud - iante ya se va Es - cal - on - a pa' que me re-

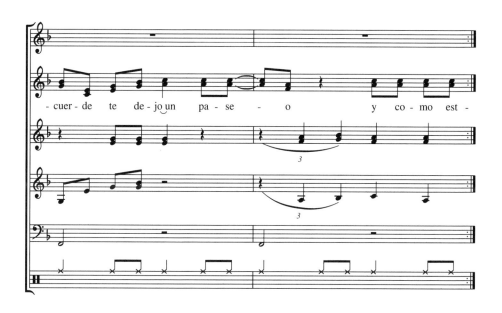

-cuer - de te de - jo un pa - se - o y co - mo est-

NOTES

CHAPTER ONE

1. The available sources, mostly published in Colombia, will become clear in the ensuing chapters. English-language sources include Bermúdez (1994), Burton (1994), List (1980, 1983), Manuel (1988: 50–53), Pacini Hernández (1992b, 1993), and Waxer (1997, 1998). Of these, Bermúdez and List are more concerned with what might be termed "folk" music.

2. For Latin America, Rowe and Schelling (1991: 38–42, 99–101, 151–172) give various cases of such nationalist projects, especially in the context of populist attempts to construct "the people" as a national body. For most of these, there is an emphasis on the imposition of homogeneity by the state or populist intellectuals. See also García Canclini's account of the National Anthropology Museum in Mexico City, where diversity is on display but subordinated to "the unification established by political nationalism in contemporary Mexico." The museum's collection "certifies the triumph of the centralist project, [and] announces that here an intercultural synthesis is produced" (García Canclini 1989: 167–168; my translation).

3. This process has been widely described for different styles. See, for example, Manuel (1995) for the Caribbean in general, Ulloa Sanmiguel (1991) for a general argument about modernity and Latin American popular music, Pacini Hernández (1995) and Austerlitz (1995) on merengue, Collier et al. (1995) and Savigliano (1995: chap. 4) on tango, Díaz Ayala (1981) and Moore (1997) on Cuban styles and Daniel (1995: chap. 6) on rumba in particular, and Manuel (1994) on Puerto Rican *danza*. Monsiváis (1997: 187) makes similar observations in relation to bolero. See also Washabaugh (1998b) for accounts of flamenco, tango, and *rebetika*. Pacini Hernández (1995: 232) notes that the emergence of working-class popular musics is a common phenomenon following processes of urbanization and that styles as varied as U.S. blues and polka, Nigerian *juju,* Greek *laika,* and Trinidadian calypso "have eventually percolated up into the mainstream." See also Keil (1985) for a general argument about mainstreaming.

4. Wilk (1995) makes a similar point in relation to Belizean culture in general. Averill (1997: 210) also notes this for lower-class Haitian musical styles. Washabaugh (1998b: 9) remarks that "every instance of popular music operates from both the center and the margin at the same time."

5. Gramsci himself referred to "transformism" (Gramsci 1971: 58) in his account of the Risorgimento in Italy. He thought that the formation of an "ever more extensive ruling class" since 1848 in Italy "involved the gradual but continuous absorption . . . of the active elements produced by allied groups—and even of those which came from antagonistic groups and seemed irreconcilably hostile" (Gramsci 1971: 58–59; see also Mouffe 1979: 182). Williams develops the notion of selective tradition: a tradition "always passed off [by the dominant culture] as *the* tradition,' *the* significant past,'" but which selects from a whole variety of meanings and practices, emphasizing some rather than others and perhaps reinterpreting and diluting them (1980: 39).

6. See also Middleton (1985), who develops a similar approach for the study of popular music but is more flexible in his view of articulating principles and attempts to analyze more fully what these might be in understanding popular music. See Manuel for a good discussion of appropriation in relation to Puerto Rican national identity: "appropriation is a socio-musical process, involving the resignification of the borrowed idiom to serve as a symbol of a new social identity" (1994: 274).

7. Frith (1987: 280) makes a similar point about the emergence of the British record industry, which began "as part of the electrical goods industry," not under the control of music publishers, promoters, and performers.

8. See García Canclini (1989), who argues that Latin American nations have not simply copied European models of modernity. Martín-Barbero (1987a: 165) argues that Latin America is characterized by a specific "noncontemporary modernity" which combines a historically produced backwardness (i.e., dependency) with a cultural heterogeneity that exists in spite of this backwardness, not because of it, as some culturalist explanations of backwardness would have us believe. Rowe and Schelling also examine debates about "imitation" in the context of nationalism and populism (1991: 165–168). See also Schwarz (1992: 1–18) and Prado Bellei (1995) on Brazil. More generally, Robertson (1990) argues that the process of globalization which began in the late nineteenth century involved both the universalization of particularism (i.e., the global spread of Euro-American models of, for example, the nation-state) and the particularization of the universal (i.e., the idea that every nation should be unique).

9. But see, for example, Martín-Barbero (1987a: 178), Rowe and Schelling (1991), and Stokes (1994a). See also Waterman (1990) on Nigeria. On the relation between music and identity in general, including national identity, see the literature cited in note 21.

10. It is important to note that, as elsewhere in the book, the "we" of this sentence probably refers to "blacks" or at least "black writers."

11. Useful texts on the concepts of "race" and "ethnicity" include Banton (1987), Eriksen (1993), Goldberg (1993), and Omi and Winant (1986).

12. In my view, racial identifications are analytically distinct from "ethnic" ones (see Wade 1997: chap. 1). The latter are used to classify people according to perceived cultural differences, and while they may include aspects of phenotype as cues for categorization, these do not have the same weight as the racial signifiers which form part of the global system of racial categories deriving from a particular colonial history, nor is a discourse of naturalization of difference as prominent. Of course, in a given historical context, ethnic and racial identifications may overlap and intertwine.

13. General accounts include Anthias and Yuval-Davis (1992), Segal and Handler (1992, 1993), and Williams (1989). For Latin America, central texts include Graham (1990), Helg (1995), Moore (1997), Skidmore (1974), Stepan (1991), Stutzman (1981), Urban and Sherzer (1991), Wade (1993a, 1997), Whitten ([1974] 1986, 1981), Whitten and Torres (1998), and Wright (1990). For the Caribbean, texts include Nettleford (1970), Nicholls (1979, 1985), Williams (1991), and Yelvington (1993).

14. Literature on Colombia which examines this theme includes Wade (1993a), Friedemann (1984), Bagley and Silva (1989), and Helg (1989). Friedemann (1984) argues that blacks, at least until the political changes of the 1990s, had been made "invisible" in Colombia. I argue that they had not been a main object of academic, state, or media attention mainly because for historical reasons they had not been institutionalized as a legitimate anthropological or political other. This minimized their presence in the nation, but it remained true that they were included in considerations of national identity in the sense that thinkers and writers commented on their presence and conceived of Colombia as a mestizo nation that was composed of black, white, and indigenous heritages. I elaborate on this in the next chapter.

15. "Racial origins" were also important in discussions about tango and national identity in Argentina (Savigliano 1995: chaps. 2, 4).

16. The imaging of women as "natural," or Nature as a woman, and thus subject to men's control is well documented: see, for example, MacCormack and Strathern (1980) and Merchant (1983).

17. Cf. Taussig's notion of the "moral topography" of Colombia (Taussig 1987: 253); see also Cowan (1990) on "moral geography" in a Greek village.

18. See, for example, Monsiváis (1997: 185) on the relation between romantic song and changing moral codes in Mexico of the 1920s and 1930s, spurred by the Revolution, the rise of single motherhood, the explosion in size of the urban female workforce, the growth of prostitution, and so on.

19. Some studies have examined the eroticism of musical forms as such, often using Roland Barthes's seminal essay "The Grain of the Voice" as a starting point, but this is not my main concern here. See Middleton (1990: 258–267) for an analysis of pleasure in popular music, a treatment which oddly barely mentions dance. For links between dance, the body, and sexuality, see Cooper (1993: 7–9), Foster (1996), Leppert (1993), Savigliano (1995), Vigarello (1989: 179), and Washabaugh (1998c).

20. Middleton admits that the authors he cites as taking the instinctualist

position often modify their arguments in a more sophisticated social constructionist direction (Middleton 1990: 259).

21. There is a huge literature on this topic. Among those studies which I have found useful—and with a bias toward Latin America—are the following: Austerlitz (1995), Averill (1989, 1994, 1997), Béhague (1994), Collins and Richards (1989), Duany (1984), Gilroy (1993), Hebdige (1979, 1987), Largey (1994), Larkey (1992), Manuel (1988, 1994, 1995), Pacini Hernández (1989, 1991, 1992a, 1995), Peña (1985), Reily (1992), Roberts (1979), Singer (1983), Slobin (1993), Stigberg (1978), Stokes (1994a), Turino (1993), Wallis and Malm (1984), Waterman (1990), and the special edition on Latin America of *Popular Music,* vol. 6, no. 2 (1987), edited by Jan Fairley and David Horn. Some of the earlier studies do not directly mention the question of identity, but their concerns are still relevant to the relation between social position and musical form.

22. Middleton's treatment is complex, and these are his broad criticisms of "culturalism" as an approach. Many of the actual studies he looks at—particularly that of the Birmingham Centre for Cultural Studies, exemplified in Hall and Jefferson (1976)—clearly address these problems at some level (see Stokes 1994b: 19), even if not entirely to Middleton's satisfaction.

23. See also Robertson (1990) on what he, following Tom Nairn, calls "wilful nostalgia," a politically driven quest for national traditions which also frame a search for the "authentic." In a very different context, Thornton (1995) examines how notions of authenticity are current in value judgments of music and club scenes made by young British clubbers. Many of the studies listed in note 21 make some reference to ideas about the authentic or inauthentic nature of particular musical styles.

24. See Averill (1989, 1997) for good examples of struggles over authenticity.

25. See, for example, similar fears expressed in the French Antilles (Guilbault 1993: 203).

26. Some accounts of globalization see it as beginning in the late nineteenth century (Robertson 1990) or even before (Smart 1990).

CHAPTER TWO

1. Parts of the Pacific coast may also be referred to as *la costa,* especially in southwestern Colombian provinces such as Valle del Cauca, Valle, and Nariño. In much of Colombia, however, the term *la costa* is understood to refer to the Caribbean coastal region, or *la costa atlántica,* as it is also popularly known.

2. I deal with this theme in much greater detail in Wade (1993a).

3. Perdomo Escobar (1963: 152–177) details the various attempts to compose a national anthem, which started soon after independence. The Núñez version was not adopted officially until 1920, although in practice it had been the national anthem since about 1887.

4. The important, centralist 1886 constitution—which finally fixed the political structures of the country (until the new constitution of 1991), after

decades of chopping and changing between centralist and federalist arrangements—ignored black and indigenous people in the sense that it ignored any reference to race at all, but this is not reflected in intellectuals' writing about the nation, which often mentioned blacks and indigenous people.

5. Helg (1989) stresses the divergent opinions of Colombian intellectuals of this period, some pessimistic about mestizaje and aligning themselves with Argentinean thinkers, others more optimistic and approaching the thinking of Mexican intellectuals. She locates López de Mesa in the first camp, not altogether correctly in my view.

6. An examination of the changing education system and a review of school textbooks was undertaken by a research assistant in Bogotá, Natalia Otero Correa. It is unfortunate that few textbooks dating to the 1930s were available. Textbooks were and still are produced by private publishers in accordance with government guidelines. The quotations cited here are my own translations. See also Rivera Reyes (1994) for an analysis of the representation of indigenous peoples in Colombian school texts.

7. The 1886 constitution stated that "The Roman Apostolic Catholic religion is that of the nation" and that education should be in accordance with Catholicism (see articles 38 and 41, cited in Noguero Laborde 1950, vol. 2). In 1887, a concordat was made with the Vatican which reinforced the role of the church, giving it the right to intervene in public education. Despite the removal of articles 38 and 41 in the liberalizing constitutional reform of 1936—which aroused vociferous protest from the clergy (Bushnell 1993: 189)—another concordat was signed in 1973 which stated that the Catholic religion was a "fundamental element in the common good and integral development of the community" (cited in Camargo 1987: 204).

8. In Latin American usage, *criollo* literally means native to the Americas and is generally used to refer to things (animals, plants, people) that were originally imported and became domesticated, rather than things that were autochthonous. In Latin American republican histories, "los criollos" usually refers to the American-born sons of Spanish parents, who would thus be socially classified as white. Given the frequency of sexual relations between white men and black and indigenous women, the word *criollo* often implied some kind of mixture.

9. The first edition was published in New York in 1854 by D. Appleton and Company. Later editions were also published in Paris, Lima, and Santiago. A recent edition was published in Mexico in 1983 by Editorial Patria. On Carreño's manual, see also Quintero Rivera (1996). See Peralta (1995: 80–98) for an analysis of other manuals of morality, current in nineteenth-century Bogotá, which emphasized moderation and restraint.

10. The examples given in the text, however, extend well into the 1960s. See also Wade (1993a) for other examples from the 1950s and for more recent representations of the Pacific coastal region (cf. Whitten 1985).

11. These decrees are, respectively, Law 198 of December 18, 1936 (*Diario Oficial,* no. 23838: 447–449); Decree 3418 of November 25, 1954 (*Diario Oficial,* no. 28647: 1013); Law 74 of 1966 (República de Colombia, *Leyes de*

1966, Bogotá: Imprenta Nacional, 1966); Decree 2085 of 1975; and Decree 284 of February 13, 1992. See also Decree 1480 of July 13, 1994. These last three were consulted as mimeographs in the library of the Ministry of Communications, Bogotá.

12. These titles are taken from a 1961 number of the monthly *Boletín de programas,* produced by the Department of Radio and Television, Ministry of Communications.

13. The quotations are, in order, from the Economic and Social Development Plan, 1969–1972, the Four Strategies Plan, 1970–1974, and the Change with Equity Plan, 1983–1986 (all cited in Mena Lozano and Herrera Campillo 1994: 126, 129, 134, 136).

14. Prior to this, the Ministry of Education had had, by 1950, a Department of Cultural Extension and Fine Arts which included a National Folklore Commission and a Department of Radio Broadcasting (which organized the state radio station). In 1960, a Section of Popular Culture was created. These moves reflected a concern with preserving or institutionalizing the culture of the "people" to form part of national cultural identity.

15. The quotations refer to, respectively, the National Integrated Program for Cultural Development, 1972–1976, and the Cultural Development Plan, 1976 (Mena Lozano and Herrera Campillo 1994: 144, 152).

16. These days were organized with community participation and empowerment high on the agenda, but state intervention and finance, and the subsequent national display of these days through state channels of publication and other media, meant of necessity—and perhaps independently of the aims of the organizers—that regional cultures were articulated to images of national identity.

17. For a sketch of the history of La Costa, see Wade (1993a: chap. 5). See also Bell Lemus (1988), Fals Borda (1976, 1979, 1981, 1984, 1986), Meisel Roca (1994), and Posada Carbó (1996).

18. Barranquilla is not actually on the sea, but near the mouth of the Magdalena River, which reaches right up into the Andean interior. Direct shipping access has always been a major problem, due to silting of the river mouth.

19. During the 1920s, a large amount of foreign capital entered Colombia, part of it the $25 million given by the U.S. government as an indemnification for the loss of Panama, the rest of it loans negotiated by government and private interests. In 1924, the Bogotá city council also took out a loan to modernize the city (Iriarte 1988: 213).

20. The history of the recording industry in Colombia is written up in only a very fragmentary way. The industry itself was very ad hoc in its early stages. It proved impossible to establish a definite date for the founding of Discos Tropical.

21. See Pacini Hernández (1993) on the impact of "Afrobeat" in Cartagena.

22. I say "apparently," because as Fals Borda shows, during the first decades of this century the capitalization of cattle farming made early inroads in

parts of La Costa, with new species of grasses, barbed wire, and unionization (Fals Borda 1976). Since about 1950, however, there has been a relative stagnation of this sector (Meisel Roca 1992).

23. From the late 1880s, carnival in Barranquilla—previously a mainly popular event—was increasingly organized and officialized by the city's elite, based in their social clubs (Friedemann 1985; Jiménez 1986; Orozco and Soto 1993; Rey Sinning 1992). The national beauty contest started in Cartagena in 1934.

24. Artel's poems included titles such as "Sensualidad negra" and "Romance mulato."

25. Obregón was born in Barcelona, but grew up in Barranquilla. Medina (1978) also mentions Enrique Grau, another influential Costeño painter, and Guillermo Wiedemann, a German-born painter who became a Colombian national in 1946: they also worked similar themes in their paintings.

26. See the discussion of sexuality in chapter 7 for more details on Costeño family structures and the relevant literature.

27. Pearce (1990) and Bushnell (1993) include general accounts of La Violencia. See Bergquist, Peñaranda, and Sánchez (1992) for more detail. These accounts show that La Costa was less affected by La Violencia than some areas of the interior. However, La Costa has not been immune from violence in general (see Fals Borda 1984, 1986), and the banana zone of Urabá region is now one of the most violent of the country (Steiner 1994).

28. Bell Lemus and Meisel Roca (1989: 17) show how ministerial jobs, especially key posts such as the minister of government and minister of hacienda, have favored politicians from highland provinces, in disproportion to the demographic weight of their electorates.

29. In 1934, the Inter-Provincial Assembly of the Coast was created with political aims, and in the 1950s the Costeño League was resuscitated by the editor of *El Heraldo*, the main Barranquilla newspaper. The Association of the Atlantic Coast Provinces was created in 1970 after the first meeting of all the provincial governors, and in the late 1980s the Association of Higher Education Institutions of the Atlantic Coast was formed. See Bell Lemus and Meisel Roca (1989) and Posada Carbó (1982, 1985, 1988, 1996: chap. 6). See also the report "Independencia federal," *Cromos*, July 27, 1992, pp. 16–24.

30. In 1967, the Electricity Corporation of the Atlantic Coast (CORELCA) was set up, and in 1974 planners invented the Regional Urban Planning System for La Costa (SIPUR). In 1985, the Planning Region of the Atlantic Coast was created, the first of various such entities, after efforts by Costeño politicians. Finally, the 1991 constitution has opened the way for the creation of autonomous regions, and some in La Costa think that their region should push for such status. See Acosta, Cabrera, and Mendoza (1991), Bell Lemus et al. (1993), Espinosa (1991), and Fals Borda (1988).

31. The current director of Telecaribe, Jaime Abello Banfi, said that the channel is more truly regional than the four others in the country, since an effort is made to cover events in all six coastal provinces and there are local news

programs in each province capital (interview). See appendix A for a list of interviewees.

32. See the works cited previously by these authors. During the Bell Lemus administration, the Gobernación del Atlántico published a series of books about aspects of Costeño history. The old customs house was also renovated as a splendid showpiece of Barranquilla's past glory, and it now houses the departmental library and archive, plus various commercial ventures.

33. For a general account and bibliography of Latin American popular music, including Colombian styles, see Béhague (1985).

34. This type of concern with triethnic origins is typical of Latin American ethnomusicology, according to Béhague (1991: 57). For literature on Colombian folk music—which varies in its use of documentary sources for history—see Abadía Morales (1973, 1983), Bermúdez (1985), Bermúdez et al. (1987), Davidson (1970), List (1980, 1983), Ocampo López (1988), Portaccio (1995), and Zapata Olivella (1960–1962). Major styles identified for the twentieth century include *bambuco* in the Andean region, played on small guitars and mandolins; *fandango, cumbia, bunde,* and *gaita* in La Costa, played with different combinations of drums, cane flutes, and rattles; *currulao* in the Pacific coastal region, played with drums, shakers, and the marimba, a type of xylophone; and *joropo* in Los Llanos region (the plains below the eastern cordillera), a style shared with Venezuela, played on guitars, harps, and maracas.

35. Miñana Blasco (1997) traces the bambuco to the Cauca region of southwestern Colombia and says it was formed as a national musical expression in the wars of independence.

36. For Colombia, there is little written on the history of popular music in the nineteenth century, but see Fals Borda (1981: 105A–111A), González Henríquez (1987, 1989a, 1989b), Pardo Tovar (1966), Perdomo Escobar (1963), and Ochoa (1997). The biographies in Restrepo Duque (1991) are also useful.

37. Bambuco is generally played with guitars, *tiples* (treble guitars), and *bandolas* (mandolins); a tambourine is sometimes used (Abadía Morales 1983: 157; List 1980: 577). It is a dance song in 3/4 or 6/8 meter in moderate quick tempo with a syncopated rhythm; the vocal part involves a duet of male voices singing in parallel thirds (Béhague 1985: 9; Durán 1950: 34; List 1980: 578; Ocampo López 1988: 106).

38. Caballero Calderón's use of "conceive" (Spanish *concebir*) implies the work of both imagination and physical procreation in creating the fatherland, even if it is probable that he was thinking primarily of mental conception. The suggestion is that the musical form permitted the nation to be imagined as an integrated whole sharing a common tradition and that, by enlivening romantic liaisons, it encouraged men and women to procreate and bring forth new citizens.

39. *Lira* means lyre. In addition to the usual strings, Morales's Lira had a violin and two cellos (Restrepo Duque 1991: 123).

40. All of these authors run through similar arguments about the origins of

bambuco, weighing African against European and Amerindian influences. Davidson, for example, spends nearly three hundred pages on these questions of origins, during which, although he discounts African and indigenous origins, he spends almost one hundred pages discussing African and indigenous music. Miñana Blasco (1997) and Ochoa (1997) both contend that bambuco's connection with black and indigenous people in the nineteenth century was whitewashed out of accounts of its origins in order that it could represent Colombian nationhood.

41. He is criticized by Ochoa (1997: 42) for denying the "corporeality" of the music, a feature she associates with blacks.

42. The precise numbers are as follows. In Rico Salazar (1984): bambucos, 165; pasillos, 61; boleros, 16; valses, 11; guabinas, 11; danzas, 9; porros, 6; cumbias, 4; paseos, 4; joropos, 4; pasajes, 4; others, 11. In Restrepo Duque (1991): bambucos, 36; pasillos, 14; porros, 13; cumbias, 7; vallenatos, 5; guabinas, 4; others, 23 (there are actually 102 songs listed).

43. Fagan and Moran (1986: 521) note that overseas recordings were done by Victor's traveling teams working out of hotels in Mexico and Cuba as from about 1905. In the 1920s and 1930s, Victor established its own factories in cities such as Santiago and Buenos Aires.

CHAPTER THREE

1. For example, the captain of a German vessel which docked near Barranquilla in the 1870s recounted that the local bands which he contracted to give a concert for the inhabitants of the city were composed of "blacks" who, although they "played by ear and without knowing a note of music," did so "with great precision" (Werner 1873: 324).

2. González Henríquez (1989a: 40) mentions the case of Montería in the 1880s, where the local band was directed by a Cuban musician. See also Fortich Díaz (1994: 49–52).

3. Cabildos were associations of slaves or free blacks permitted by the colonial and republican authorities which served as mutual aid societies and were also places of entertainment (and subversion). See Friedemann (1988) and Wade (1993a: 88). (Slavery was abolished in Colombia in 1851.)

4. Cartagena's festival of the Virgin of La Candelaria is described in the memoirs of General Joaquín Posada Gutiérrez, written in 1865 but referring to the 1830s. He mentions bailes de la tierra, without any details, except to say that they were "happy and vivacious" but entirely decent and courteous (Posada Gutiérrez 1920: 341).

5. In addition to the previous chapter and the sources cited therein, the reader can consult Añez ([1951] 1970), Davidson (1970), Fals Borda (1979: 48A, 1981: 105A–111A), González Henríquez (1987, 1989b), and Perdomo Escobar (1963). Hints about music in La Costa in the nineteenth century can also be gleaned from some memoirs and travelers' accounts: see, for example, Cordovez Moure ([1893] 1957: 484), Peñas Galindo (1988: 59), and Posada Gutiérrez (1920: 334–349). For a more general Caribbean perspective, see Bilby (1985) and Manuel (1995: 1–16).

6. Nowadays in rural areas and to some extent among the towns' lower strata, there are *conjuntos* (groups), often found today as a self-conscious recuperation of "traditions." These are made up of different combinations of native pipes, drums, and other percussion instruments. The pipes include the *caña de millo* (millet cane pipe), also known as the *pito atravesado* (transverse pipe), and the *gaita* or *pito cabece'cera* (a vertical cane pipe). The latter has a hollow feather quill sealed onto one end with beeswax and charcoal—hence the name *cabece'cera*, a shortening of *cabeza de cera*, head of wax—not as a reed but to channel air into the pipe itself. The instrument is of indigenous origin (Abadía Morales 1983: 244). Drums include (1) single-headed, open-ended varieties of various sizes, with different names according to region (the smaller size is called *llamador* [calling drum] or *tambor macho* [male drum]; the larger size is called *tambor alegre* [happy drum], *tambor hembra* [female drum], or *tambor mayor* [large drum]); and (2) the double-membraned *bombo*, or *tambora*, beaten with a stick. Other percussion instruments include the *guacharaca* (a gourd scraper), maracas, *guache* (a tube rattle, sometimes called *guacho*), *claves* (sticks beaten together), and *palmetas* or *tablitas* (small wooden paddles beaten together). Rare nowadays are the *marímbula* (thumb piano) and the *arco musical* (mouth bow). Groups composed of these instruments play a wide variety of styles, with locally varying names, which are said to derive mostly from African and indigenous sources, with less European influence: cumbia, porro, *mapalé, bullerengue,* gaita, and fandango are some of those frequently mentioned. In addition to these groups, there are work songs, funerary songs, and sung verses which are generally seen as remnants of more pervasive styles. See Abadía Morales (1983), Bermúdez (1985), Bermúdez et al. (1987), Davidson (1970), Escalante (1964), List (1980, 1983), and Zapata Olivella (1962).

7. Morales González (1989: 40) maintains that porro existed under that name at some notional time prior to the late nineteenth century, but she adduces no documentary evidence.

8. I use the masculine advisedly here, since it was men who are always depicted as playing the instruments, directing the orchestras, and writing the songs—even if their songs were about women, as in the case of the famous porro, "María Varilla."

9. See note 6 above.

10. On the indigenous origins of porro, Sandra Turbay, anthropologist at the University of Antioquia, Medellín, who did research among the Zenú (indigenous groups located in various areas of Sucre and Córdoba Provinces and speaking only Spanish), told me that they play what they call porro, which they say is of Hispanicized indigenous origins; they do not mention blacks as an influence.

11. Fortich uses Escalante (1980) as a source for the poro society.

12. Posada Gutiérrez (1920: 334–349), did not mention the word, talking instead of currulao, gaita, and mapalé. The nineteenth-century travelers cited by Peñas Galindo (1988) in his study of the *bogas* (boatmen) who worked the Magdalena river did not mention it either, again referring to currulao. Cor-

dovez Moure ([1893] 1957: 484), another traveler of the era, did likewise. Fals Borda (1979: 48A) interviewed a ninety-year-old ex-boga who referred to bunde, berroche, and mapalé. However, the black poet Candelario Obeso (1849–1884) talks of dancing a porro in his poem "Er Boga Charlatán," published in 1877 (Obeso [1877] 1977).

13. On this, see Bilby's incisive comments on the emergence of ska in Jamaica (Manuel 1995: 156–159).

14. There were Cuban musicians in the region at the turn of the century: see Betancur Alvarez (1993: 201–206, 220), Fortich Díaz (1994: 49–52), and González Henríquez (1989a: 40).

15. As with porro, there are some versions that privilege an indigenous origin; for example, the famous Costeño composer and artist José Barros argues this line (Restrepo Duque 1991: 7). The various authors in Discos Fuentes (1992) debate these different origins in a typically mythological manner.

16. The same sources that do not mention porro (see note 12 above) do not mention cumbia either, although continuities may be assumed. See, for example, how Escalante (1964: 149) cites Posada Gutiérrez as a reference for the history of cumbia. Perdomo Escobar's collection of comments on cumbia in his glossary is all from twentieth-century sources (Perdomo Escobar 1963: 336) and the same is true of those cited by Davidson (1970). The Costeño poet Candelario Obeso (1849–1884) does not use the term *cumbia* in his work (Lawrence Prescott, personal communication; see also Prescott 1985a). Going back to the late eighteenth century, colonial authorities in Cartagena outlawed fandangos but did not mention cumbias (Alzate 1980: 29; Bensusan 1984).

17. Simon (1994: 196) also cites Zapata Olivella (1962: 191), as well as interview testimony, to similar effect, although Londoño is the only one to mention a Spanish influence.

18. The work songs mentioned are often *cantos de vaquería* (cow-herding songs). Funerary songs are most famously exemplified in the *lumbalú* songs of the old maroon settlement, Palenque de San Basilio, which retain strong African characteristics. On these and other songs, see Abadía Morales (1983: 206–211), Friedemann and Patiño Rosselli (1983), Schwegler (1996), and Bermúdez et al. (1987). Atencio Babilonia and Castellanos Córdova (1982: 105–122) explore a black tradition of *romances* in the Cauca Valley. See Pacini Hernández (1995) on Latin American traditions of romantic song.

19. Pérez Arbelaez (1952), a botanist and amateur folklorist, classes the rural musics of La Costa's Magdalena Province as "porros," even though they are played on the accordion.

20. The names now used to describe the styles within vallenato are *paseo, son, merengue,* and *puya.* Merengue is said by Abadía Morales (1983: 210) to derive from the Dominican style of the same name; Quiroz Otero agrees (1982: 218). Others say that it is a Colombian, or rather Costeño, invention (Bermúdez et al. 1987: 91–92). The fact that Colombian merengue is in triple meter while the Dominican merengue is in duple meter might suggest distinct origins. On the other hand, merengue was a "pan-Caribbean genre" in the nineteenth century, with a number of regional variants all deriving from de-

velopments of the *contredanse* (Austerlitz 1995: 15). On vallenato generally, see also Araújo de Molina (1973), Carillo Hinojosa (1993), Gilard (1987a, 1987b), Gutiérrez Hinojosa (1992), Llerena Villalobos (1985), Posada (1986), Puello Mejía (1992), and Quiroz Otero (1982). Useful biographical material can be found in these and in Araujonoguera (1988), García Usta and Salcedo Ramos (1994), Hinestroza Llano (n.d.), Restrepo Duque (1991), Villegas and Grisales (1976), and Vergara (1981).

21. The term is disputed, but is often said to derive not from the name of the town, which comes from Valle de Upar (Upar is said to have been a native American chief), but from the *ballenato,* or baby whale, whose patchy colored skin is reminiscent of the skin discolorations of the local peasants, caused by a small insect ubiquitous in the area. See also Araújo de Molina (1973: 52).

22. Araújo de Molina (1973) and Gutiérrez Hinojosa (1992) clearly represent the continuist and localist approach to vallenato. The latter, for example, states that the puya variant (which is moribund in today's vallenato corpus) comes from the indigenous cultures of the nearby Sierra Nevada mountains. He recounts his search for the original sound, which he crowned by recording a version played by an ancient indigenous man on a gaita flute; this is supported by the testimony of a musicologist who says that the example has the same rhythmic and melodic structures as the current form played by accordionists (as if the old man's example were not also "current"). The possibility that the old man is playing a style of more recent origin is not considered. Gutiérrez then says that the merengue, another variant still played today, derives from the songs of the Africans of the Muserengue culture who were taken to the region (1992: 530–537).

23. On the hombre parrandero as a Costeño male identity, see Wade (1994a).

24. List (1980: 574) also observes that vallenato "originated" in the 1940s and 1950s.

25. Hinestroza Llano (n.d.: 63), in a biography of Pacho Rada, cites Armando Reclus, a late-nineteenth-century traveler, to the effect that accordions were also present in Panama. Also, in a biographical piece on Andrés Landeros, an accordionist born in San Jacinto in the 1930s, García and Salcedo report that the accordion was an "unknown instrument" in his home town as late as the early 1950s. Yet this town is not far from either the Magdalena River or El Plato, birthplace of Pacho Rada, one of "the four essential juglares of vallenato music," from whom, indeed, Landeros purchased his first accordion (García Usta and Salcedo Ramos 1994: 119–120). This suggests the patchy distribution of the accordion even in areas close to the "birthplace" of vallenato.

26. On the variety of styles played by accordionists, see the testimonies of old players in Gutiérrez Hinojosa's book. Most refer to themselves and their older compatriots as playing merengue, son, puya, and, at a later date, paseo— that is, the styles that still constitute the vallenato corpus. But, for example, one Samuel Martínez remembers his father (reportedly born in 1881) playing in cumbiambas, although the term refers to the events or parties rather than

the musical style as such (Gutiérrez Hinojosa 1992: 575). Antonio María Peñaloza, a well-known Costeño composer born in 1916, recounted that his grandfather played polkas and mazurkas on the accordion (interview). See also Bermúdez (1996: 116), who notes that accordions were used in a variety of contexts, including patron saint festivals and alongside wind bands.

27. The accounts of the origins of various styles of Costeño music contained in Discos Fuentes (1992) are good examples.

28. It is interesting to see how the same events are recycled in accounts of the Barranquilla carnival's history. Thus, Camargo Franco (1992), Jiménez (1986), Orozoco and Soto (1993), Rey Sinning (1992), and to a lesser extent Friedemann (1985) tend to reproduce events which seem to stem from Abadía Morales (1983: 365–378).

CHAPTER FOUR

1. The meaning of *echar colita* is not clear in a literal sense. *Colita* (literally, the diminutive form of *cola*, meaning tail, end, or line of people or cars) is said by Puello Mejía (1992: 181) to mean a spontaneous party; thus echar colita would mean to go to such a party. The Salón Carioca was one of a number of dancing places which opened in the 1930s which I discuss further on.

2. Uribe Celis (1992: 51–72) summarizes nationalist currents within Colombian arts and literature generally.

3. A sample of press advertisements and announcements was collected from *La Prensa,* a local newspaper, by looking at Friday and Saturday editions for December, January, and February (i.e., Christmas and carnival time) from 1925 to 1960. This work was done by Denirys Polo Calinda, assisted by Mónica Atequera.

4. *Zarzuela* is light opera.

5. These three had been contracted by the film agents Di Domenico Brothers, who owned the Teatro Colombia in Barranquilla. Squarcetta later founded a music conservatory in Ibagué (Mariano Candela, personal communication).

6. Of the seventy-four advertisements for artists in the sample for this period, fifty-four were for bands or orchestras and twenty-one of these were to play in clubs or the Hotel El Prado.

7. See Betancur Alvarez (1993) for a detailed account of musical links between Colombia and Cuba. In the 1950s, famous Cuban bands and artists such as the Sonora Matancera, Celia Cruz, Celina and Reutilio, Beny Moré, and Pérez Prado all toured in Colombia, often recording with Colombian artists.

8. Iriarte (1988: 189) notes that a gramophone was demonstrated in Bogotá in 1911 by Emilio Murillo, the musician mentioned in chapter 2 who had recorded with Victor in 1910.

9. Tango, with its roots in the late-nineteenth-century working- class and bohemian barrios of Buenos Aires and strongly associated with prostitution, became an international success in the 1910s in a sanitized form, first in Paris and then in the rest of Europe, the United States, and the rest of Latin America (Collier et al. 1995; Guy 1991: chap. 5; Roberts 1979; Savigliano 1995).

10. Béhague (1985: 6) says that the ranchera (or ranch song) is "distinctively Mexican in that it originated from folk-song tradition and retained specific performance characteristics of that tradition." It became urbanized and popularized in the 1920s and 1930s.

11. These record lists appeared in *La Prensa* between 1927 and 1934, with a total of 610 titles on the Victor, Columbia, and Brunswick labels. The lists carried record number, title, artist, and style (except for Brunswick, which omitted the artists' names). A more detailed breakdown, according to the terminology used to describe musical styles, showed the following patterns: Canciones accounted for 14 percent of the total. Some of the artists listed as performing this style were Mexican (e.g., Margarita Cueto, Carlos Mejía), but Cuban artists appeared (María Cervantes, Miguel de Grandy, Trío Matamoros), as did the Argentinean Agustín Magaldi. Fox-trot also took 14 percent of the total, and the various Cuban styles together constitute another 14 percent (principally danzón, bolero, son, with a few rumbas and guarachas). Tangos made up 11 percent and waltzes accounted for 9 percent on their own, with mazurkas, paso dobles, polkas, marchas, jotas, and schottis together making up another 6 percent. Pasillos were 3 percent and there were only three bambucos listed. The remaining third of the titles was made up of small amounts of many different styles.

12. Only three record lists appeared, two in 1941 and one in 1946, with a total of fifty titles. Of these thirty-three are "Cuban" music.

13. The coin-operated automatic piano was first marketed by Wurlitzer in 1898 (Tagg, Harker, and Kelly 1995). The jukebox could be found as an arcade amusement in the 1890s in the United States, but became widespread in the 1930s with advent of electric amplification (Paige 1969).

14. A Victor radio set, with a value said to be three hundred pesos, was raffled in 1930; General Electric radio sets cost thirty pesos in 1936 (*La Prensa*, 5 December 1930; 5 February 1936). The average worker's monthly family shopping basket in 1937 has been calculated as costing about twenty-four pesos (Archila Neira 1991: 160 n. 63).

15. In the Salón Carioca, entry was fifty cents for men and free for women, while the Rex Cinema cost between eight and thirty cents. Similarly, the Argentinean orchestra Sarrín y su Jazz played the Salón Arlequín with an entry charge of forty cents, having come from the Hotel Granada in Bogotá, an elite venue. The all-female Cuban band Orquesta Anacaona inaugurated the Casino Barranquilla with an entrance fee of forty cents. In comparison, a cocktail dance with the Costa Rican Orquesta Unión at the Hotel El Prado cost one peso, and a three-day ticket for the Club Barranquilla's carnival program cost twenty pesos (*La Prensa*, 17 January 1936; 20 January 1936; 22 January 1936; 22 January 1937; 18 January 1936; 22 February 1936).

16. Londoño and Londoño (1989: 364) mention the impact of North American music on all the urban elites of the 1920s. Restrepo Duque (1988: 533) mentions the "applauded Jazz Nicolás" which played fox-trots and one-steps in 1920s Medellín. Ulloa Sanmiguel (1992: 341) notes the existence of a jazz orchestra, La Voz del Valle, in Cali, although this appears to be in the

1930s. Iriarte (1988) and Puyo Vasco (1992) trace the rapid changes in urban form taking place in Bogotá which parallel those in Barranquilla.

17. The song "Paran Pan Pin" was recorded by Orquesta Casino de la Playa (Columbia 36270) in about 1941 and can be heard on *Memories of Cuba: Orquesta Casino de la Playa, 1937–1944* (Tumbao TCD-003, 1991). The lyrics De la Espriella sings translate roughly as "With your paran pan pin face . . . I have seen you with María at the door of the yard." The song "Tú Ya No Soplas" (literally, you don't blow any more) was a Mexican song from the motion picture *Oro Ponciano*, written by Lorenzo Barcelata as a corrido in 1937 (Columbia 5607-X) and recorded by many other people in the same year as a corrido, a polka, and a one-step (Spottswood [1990] lists six other versions). The final song says: "I saw it, I saw it, don't you hide it because I saw it." Julio Roque y su Orquesta recorded "Te Lo Ví" in 1934 as a son, written by R. Fábrega, with vocals by Antonio Machín (1904–1977), a famous Cuban artist with many Victor recordings to his credit between 1930 and 1935 (Victor 32186).

18. Díaz Ayala (1981: 158) notes of the jazz orchestras in 1930s Cuba that "in order to gain access to the private clubs, their main source of work, they had to be white orchestras, although occasionally some *entreverao* [mixed person] would sneak in, above all if he were a good artist, as happened with Miguelito Valdés."

19. Published biographical accounts of particular artists are often highly anecdotal, very selective, and tend to focus on the motives for writing particular songs. The details presented in this and subsequent chapters on bands and artists are generally composites, cross-referenced and cross-checked as far as possible, drawn from (i) interviews with artists, record collectors, radio announcers, and also knowledgeable individuals who combine qualities of journalist, writer, and amateur historian; (ii) secondary sources, which include newspaper articles, books, and journal articles; and (iii) primary sources such as contemporary newspapers. For La Costa, the following people were very helpful and knowledgeable: Mariano Candela, Nestor Gómez, Julio Oñate, and Alvaro Ruiz Hernández. Secondary sources that I found reliable include Betancur Alvarez (1993), Candela (n.d.), González Henríquez (1989c), Restrepo Duque (1991), Ruiz Hernández (1983), Salazar Giraldo (1990), and Zapata Cuencar (1962). Hernán Restrepo Duque, one of the kings of popular music history in Colombia—now unfortunately deceased—had produced a veritable mine of information: see Restrepo Duque (1971, 1986, 1988, 1991). On his life, see Cano (1986).

20. The Jazz Band Atlántico, directed by Simón Gómez, is mentioned in press announcements by La Voz de Barranquilla for its Saturday evening radio transmissions (e.g., *La Prensa*, 9 January 1932). The Jazz Band Colombia also crops up in advertisements in 1936 and 1938 (*La Prensa*, 8 February 1936; 28 January 1938).

21. González Henríquez (1989c: 87) calls this band the Orquesta de Pacho Lorduy, which had a violin, flute, saxophone, clarinet, bass, drums, piano, and lead vocals. See also Candela (n.d.). Betancur Alvarez (1993: 247), on the ba-

sis of an interview with the pianist Angel María Camacho y Cano, says that the band included porros, cumbias, and paseos in its repertoire.

22. Under the name Grupo Camacho y Cano, he cut forty-two tracks between 1929 and 1930 and also directed some recordings by the Orquesta Brunswick Antillana, a house orchestra (Spottswood 1990: 1721). Alcides Briceño contributed to some of these with vocals (e.g., "Por Lo Bajo," Brunswick 40873). Briceño was the Panamanian singer who teamed up with Jorge Añez on many recordings of bambucos (see chapter 2). On Rafael Hernández, see also Manuel (1995: 68).

23. The drum kit comprised a bass drum of Italian origin, a snare drum, three home-made *timbales* (actually similar to today's tom-toms), a single cymbal, and a *cajita,* or wooden block.

24. *Cachaco* (literally, dandy) is a term widely used in Colombia to refer to someone from the interior. As with any such term, its referent depends on the position of the speaker, so that in La Costa, it refers to anyone from the interior, but in Antioquia, where people identify themselves as *paisas,* it usually refers to people from Bogotá or surrounding areas.

25. See Arteaga (1991) for an account of Bermúdez's life. As always in these histories based mainly on oral sources, there are different accounts (e.g., Arango Z. 1985; Portaccio 1997).

26. The title means literally, "Sebastian, break your skin," that is, make a real effort. The song was recorded by Rafael Hernández's Grupo Victoria, as "Pobre Sebastían," a porro, arranged and sung by Mirta Silva, recorded in December 1940 in New York (Victor 83382; see Spottswood 1990: 2392).

27. Ernesto Lecuona was a major Cuban artist and internationally known pianist and composer (b. 1895) who also began to play popular Cuban music in the 1920s. He is known for such classics as "Siboney" and "María la O."

28. I am indebted to the record collector Julio Oñate for most of the following details, presented in a talk on Buitrago (11 December 1995, Barranquilla) and in an interview.

29. On radio in Colombia, see Múnera Gutiérrez (1992), Pareja (1984), Téllez (1974), Trujillo (1988), and Urueta Carpio (1994). I am indebted to Alvaro Ruíz Hernández for many details on the history of radio stations in Barranquilla (interview).

30. A large advertisement in *La Prensa* (30 December 1938) listed the New Year's Eve programming for stations in various cities. In Bogotá, listeners could hear the Metropolitan Jazz Band, a *conjunto de cuerdas* (guitars, tiples, etc.), Orquesta Ritmo, and Orquesta Nueva Granada. In Medellín, there were Orquesta Los Zíngaros and Orquesta Los Negritos, plus various duets and singers, including Obdulio Sánchez (a famous singer of "música colombiana"). In Cartagena, one could listen to the Estudiantina Bolívar, Pedro Laza y su Trío (Laza became famous in the 1950s for playing porros), Sexteto Nacional, and the Cuarteto Hawaiano (Antonio Fuentes played the Hawaiian guitar). In Cali, the Orquesta La Voz del Valle was playing with a couple of duos. In Barranquilla, the Orquesta Sosa and the Orquesta Blanco y Negro were playing. In 1942, Emisoras Unidas of Barranquilla advertised a program, sponsored by

Coltabaco, called "Discos de Estreno" (new releases) and listed various pieces of "carnival music," classed as porros, cumbias, fandangos, and mapalés (several of these are numbers by the Orquesta A Número Uno, recorded on the Victor label). Another program later in the week featured "new music" and listed rumbas, boleros, and guarachas (*La Prensa*, 14 February 1942; 21 February 1942).

31. The records advertised are a rumba, a fox-trot, a cumbia, and a fandango (Brunswick 41209 and 41191). The labels "parranda" and "aire colombiano" appear on Brunswick 40873 and 41126 (personal collection of Julio Oñate). See also Spottswood (1990: 1721).

32. Unlike radio, there is virtually nothing substantial and coherent written on the history of music recording in Colombia. The origins of Discos Fuentes are rather vaguely known even by the present-day company itself. There are scraps of information in the writings on radio and music already cited, but much of my material comes from oral sources, and I am especially indebted to the collectors Julio Oñate in Barranquilla and Manlio Bedoya in Medellín. Luis Felipe Jaramillo and Isaac Villanueva of Discos Fuentes were also very helpful. The occasional magazine, *Escuche*, of ASINCOL (Colombian Phonographic Producers' Association) has been useful, especially the twenty-fifth-anniversary edition, September 1988.

33. Restrepo Duque (1991: 35) says that Lucho Bermúdez's hit "Marbella" was recorded and pressed in this way. Other recordings that have found their way into the hands of collector Julio Oñate include "El Pollo Pelongo" (Fuentes 2000), a "fandango bolivarense" (a fandango from Bolívar Province) written by Joaquín Marrugo and recorded by the Orquesta A Número Uno. Oñate and others date this at about 1942. The number 2000 does not indicate that two thousand recordings had already been made; more likely, this was the first of a series. Number 2001 has "La Vaca Vieja," a porro by Joaquín Marrugo (later often attributed to the clarinetist Climaco Sarmiento), also recorded by the Orquesta A Número Uno, directed by Lucho Bermúdez, and on the other side, "El Doble Cero," a "danzón cartagenero" (a danzón from Cartagena) by Lucho Bermúdez, recorded by the same lineup. In an interview in 1949, Bermúdez dated these recordings at about 1940, although he says they were sent to Buenos Aires for one thousand copies of each song to be pressed (article reproduced, shortly after Bermúdez's death, in *Semana*, 3 May 1994, p. 76).

34. Salcedo died in poverty in Medellín.

35. *Querer* means to want and to love. The use of the word *negra* is complex in Latin America, since although literally it means black woman, it is often used as a term of endearment by men for their sweethearts or partners (as, less often, *negro* is used by women for their men), whatever their racial identification might be in more general terms.

36. These recordings are now available on CD (Buitrago, *16 éxitos de navidad y año nuevo,* Fuentes D10018, 1993). This CD falsely attributes the song "Qué Criterio" to Buitrago; it in fact is the well-known "Gota Fria" by Emiliano Zuleta.

37. "Hambre del Liceo" was recorded by Trío Bovea y los Piratas de Bocachica (Fuentes 0161). "Honda Herida" was recorded by Angel Fontanilla [a
member of Bovea's trio] y los Piratas de Bocachica (Fuentes 0162). See Araujonoguera (1988) for a full list of Escalona's songs and their lyrics and music.
These are mostly available on CD both in early versions recorded by artists
such as Bovea and Buitrago (e.g., *Escalona y su gran obra musical,* Fuentes
E3005, 1994) and in a variety of cover versions (e.g., *Un canto a la vida:
Escalona,* Columbia CDC464696, 1991).

38. I heard this phrase used of Lucho Bermúdez by various people, including a record collector, a record producer, a musician, and Matilde Díaz, the
main singer in Bermúdez's orchestra. See also Sierra (1994), who says, "Lucho
presented to [high] society his gaitas, porros, and sones dressed up in tails."

39. See note 33.

CHAPTER FIVE

1. On the history of Bogotá, see also Zambrano (1988).

2. I am grateful to Luis Javier Ortiz Mesa (1996) for allowing me to read
his manuscript in advance of publication, including these references to Espagnat (1983: 227, 251) and Brisson (1899: 62-63).

3. Posada Carbó (1987a, 1996: 30) notes the relative weakness of the
church in La Costa in general and the scant participation of Costeños in the
clergy. Pérez Ramírez (1961: 115, 132) shows that, in the 1960s, the Colombian clergy was dominated by men from the Andean zone, particularly Medellín and Bogotá; very few came from La Costa. Archila Neira (1991: 65) comments that, in La Costa, "There was not the rigid control [by the church] of
daily life that could be observed in the Andean regions." Gutiérrez de Pineda
(1975: 277), writing of the "black family complex" within which she includes
La Costa, remarks that "the church did not imbue the social structure of this
complex and it has not influenced morality as in the Andean zone." Bell Lemus
(1991: 149-161) examines the bishop of Cartagena's late-eighteenth-century
report lamenting the neglected state of his rural flock. For travelers' accounts
of Barranquilla, see, for example, Espagnat (1983) and O Drasil ([1893]
1994). Bobadilla ([1901] 1994) gives a satirical account of Barranquilla in his
novel *A fuego lento.*

4. See Wade (1993a: chap. 4) for a summary view of Antioqueño identity,
the mythology surrounding it, and some of the relevant references, including
Twinam (1980). On the contentious question of the democratic nature of Antioqueño society, see also Zambrano (1991), who sees claims to democracy as
part of the mythology of Antioqueño identity. See also Payne (1986), who emphasizes the conservative, elitist nature of Medellín high society. See Williams
(1991) for a regional treatment of the Colombian novel which contrasts Bogotá and Medellín literary cultures.

5. There is little systematic information on prostitution during this period.
Payne (1986) has some details about Medellín, and Sepúlveda's study, using
post-Second World War figures, shows that prostitution was much more
prevalent in Bogotá and especially Antioquia (where every town has its recog-

nized red-light district) than in La Costa, where "there is a greater cultural flexibility with regard to sexual relations" (Sepúlveda 1979: 17).

6. An assistant, Rosana Portaccio, carried out a search of *El Tiempo*, 1940–1960. The first decade and a half was covered in detail, with every issue being scanned for articles on and notices for music and dance. The period 1955–1960 was covered only for the month of December (the main partying period) in each year. *El Tiempo* was disrupted with censorship and closure during the dictatorship of Rojas Pinilla (1953–1957). No search of the press was undertaken for Medellín.

7. *Pachanga* is actually the name for a fast dance which became popular in the 1960s New York Latin American music scene (Roberts 1979).

8. Aguardiente is grain or cane spirit, usually flavored with anise. Tejo is a game, particularly popular in the Andean region, in which metal missiles are thrown at small explosive packets placed on a small sand pit; a score is made when a packet is hit and detonates.

9. The word *orchestra* was introduced into the conversation by the interviewer; it is not a word normally used to refer to a guitar-based group.

10. Los Llanos are the flat plains which lie to the east of the mountain range in which Bogotá is situated. Joropo is the main style of music there, similar to the Venezuelan joropo, which is played with guitars, tiples, harps, and maracas.

11. The interviewees were either not old enough or, in the couple of cases in which they were, talked at length about everything except music!

12. *Música guasca* is a term which was originally used to designate various guitar-based styles from the Andean rural areas of Cundinamarca and Boyacá. It was used later for guitar-based music associated strongly with the rural areas and small towns of Antioquia and related provinces. Such music has some affinities with Mexican rancheras.

13. *Pagando una promesa*, paying for a promise, involves promising to undertake an act (usually of self-sacrifice) for God in exchange for asking a favor. The promise then has to be fulfilled.

14. *Popular* is a term that means "of the people" and is a common euphemism for working or lower class.

15. The corrido is a form of traditional narrative ballad which became urbanized in the 1940s (Béhague 1985: 7).

16. On these three musicians, see Arteaga (1991: 56), Betancur Alvarez (1993: 228, 248), Portaccio (1995, 2:162–175, 304–311), Restrepo Duque (1991: 24–25, 65–67, 77–79), Ruiz Hernández (1983: 109), Salazar Giraldo (1990), and Zapata Cuencar (1962).

17. This number was recorded in Bogotá by Jaime Glottman, the RCA Victor agent there, and pressed in the United States by Victor. Milciades Garavito played the same kind of style in Bogotá and recorded with Victor and Odeon.

18. *La Prensa* (9/2/46) carries a Victor record list which includes "Porro Kikiriki" by Efraín Orozco y Su Orquesta, with a bolero on the B side (Victor 60-0350).

19. On Alex Tovar, see Arteaga (1991: 66, 85), Restrepo Duque (1991:

116–118), and Salazar Giraldo (1990). Tovar did not stay long with Bermúdez and kept his own orchestra going, later joining the Sinfonía Nacional. His arrangements of Lucho Bermúdez's music for symphonic orchestras were played in Bogotá in the 1980s.

20. Bermúdez met Uribe at a radio station, Emisora Nueva Granada, in 1945. Uribe was playing with a guitar trio, Los Norteños, specializing in bambuco, and he accompanied Matilde Díaz on a couple of pasillos Bermúdez had written for her.

21. On Barros, see Navia (1993), Restrepo Duque (1991: 4–9), and Rodríguez Calderón (1982). A version of "La Piragua" by Gabriel Romero can be heard on *Cumbia, cumbia* (World Circuit, WCD 016, 1989).

22. Important stations included Radio Santa Fe and Emisora Nueva Granada in Bogotá and La Voz de Antioquia and Ecos de la Montaña in Medellín. The Bogotá-based daily *El Tiempo* carried a Fuentes record list in 1949; Tropical and Fuentes lists appear in 1950, with Fuentes presenting a long-playing format (e.g., *El Tiempo*, 20 March 1950; 27 December 1950).

23. *El Tiempo* (22 March 1943, p. 5) notices the first anniversary of La Hora Costeña, although without comment. Manuel Zapata Olivella stated that his brother, Juan, actually started the show in about 1940 and that Ariza took over soon after (interview).

24. In 1952, the program passed to a different radio station, Mil Veinte, where Miguel Granados, a Barranquilla-born radio announcer, took it over.

25. Discos Tropical advertised "Danza Negra," a cumbia, and "Déjame Gozar, Suegra" (Let Me Have Fun, Mother-in-Law), a porro, by Francisco Galán y Su Orquesta (*El Tiempo*, 20 March 1950).

26. *El Tiempo* (31 December 1959) has an advertisement for Bovea y Sus Vallenatos playing the Country Club in Bogotá, with the Trío Los Isleños.

27. Discos Fuentes record lists from 1949 and 1950, published in *El Tiempo*, contained records by Guillermo Buitrago, the Trovadores de Barú (one of the resident Fuentes groups, often with José Barros), and the Trío Los Románticos, none of which would have had an accordion. But there is also one by Abel Antonio Villa y Su Conjunto, "La Zorra Me Anda Buscando" (The Vixen Is Looking for Me; Fuentes 0105)—listed as a porro in *El Tiempo* but a paseo (vallenato) in the Fuentes 1954 catalog; and a merengue by José María Peñaranda y el Conjunto Típico Vallenato, "Cosas de Nicolás" (Things of Nicholas; Fuentes 0237). Both these would have had accordions.

28. Luis Carlos Meyer had been a singer on occasion for the Emisora Atlántico Jazz Band, and he was in Bogotá during this period—possibly slightly prior to Lucho Bermúdez—and in Medellín, working with the local orchestras and radio stations. In the midforties, he went to Mexico, where he had great success with the Orquesta de Rafael de Paz, singing Barros's "El Gallo Tuerto" and the big hit "Micaela." El Negrito Jack (real name Ricardo Romero) was, it seems, not Colombian: Betancur Alvarez (1993: photographs between pp. 299–300) identifies him as Peruvian. *El Tiempo* (12 July 1941) carries an advertisement for a performance by Orquesta Ritmo "with the attraction of Negrito Jack, the expert Cuban drummer." The Orquesta Ritmo

was a midforties Bogotá-based lineup that included players such as Alex To-var, Gabriel Uribe, and Lucho Bermúdez (Betancur Alvarez 1993: 241).

29. Estudiantinas are string ensembles, playing pasillos, bambucos, and so on. I was not able to identify the song "El Vacilón" for 1940, although a Cuban chachachá of this name was popular in the 1950s. Alejandro Wills was discussed in chapter 2 as an exponent of bambucos and pasillos.

30. *Epa* is a common interjection in Costeño music, roughly similar to "Oh, yeah" in Western pop and rock music. *Dale compadre* (do it, compadre) is another such exhortation.

31. Cf. Cooper (1993: 7–9) on similar images of Jamaican popular culture.

32. Gilard (1986: 46, n. 2) identifies Gers as José Gerardo Ramírez, a journalist from Caldas who belonged to the most reactionary group of writers of the time.

33. It seems unlikely that there were actually an unusual number of Costeño politicians in central government at the time; in any case, these individuals would hardly have been "black" by Colombian standards. Historical research on this matter remains to be done, but a provisional list of Costeño ministers holding office between 1900 and 1950, drawn up by Eduardo Posada Carbó (personal communication), shows that under López Pumarejo, 1934–1938, there were about six Costeño ministers and between 1942 and 1945 there were about four. Being from the Costeño elite, these people would have been "white" for most Colombians, although one, Adán Arriaga, actually from Chocó Province of the Pacific coastal region, is often identified today as a *mulato* (Wade 1993a: 119). Other administrations had two or three Costeño ministers, but six were appointed under Pedro Nel Ospina in 1922–1926 and four under Enrique Olaya Herrera in 1930–1934, so the situation under López Pumarejo was not unprecedented.

34. I am grateful to Eduardo Posada Carbó for bringing these letters to my attention.

35. Gabriel García Márquez also noted in the same year of 1952 that a group of respectable Venezuelans had mounted a campaign against mambo, alleging that Pérez Prado was the "very incarnation of the devil" (García Márquez 1981, 2:539).

36. On these literary currents in Colombia, see Friedemann (1984), Jackson (1976, 1979, 1988), Prescott (1985a), and Williams (1985, 1991). *Négritude* as such was not a term or concept current in Colombia at the time. Although both term and ideology were developed by poets such as Léopold Senghor and Aimé Césaire in 1930s Paris, it was not really until Sartre wrote a preface to Senghor's 1948 anthology of black poetry that *négritude* took off (Hale 1978: 226; Vaillant 1990: 120).

37. Zapata Olivella's publications are too numerous to list here. See Friedemann (1984) for bibliographical references. On his novels, see Jackson (1976, 1979, 1988), Lewis (1987), and Williams (1985). My reading of Zapata Olivella is different from that of Richard Jackson, who emphasizes Zapata's militant antiracist stance. This is certainly present in his work, but it is not the only aspect (see Gilard 1986).

38. The original dates of all these pieces is 1954, although the last four were also published as one item in 1952 in *Lámpara,* a cultural magazine run by Esso.

39. Sánchez (1992: 90) lists some of the novels of the period that chronicled aspects of La Violencia.

40. Over the centuries, there have been, of course, many positions taken by different Western thinkers on this issue. See Hall, Held, and McGrew (1992).

41. Cf. Middleton (1990: 266) who argues that early jazz in the United States could be seen by whites "as both 'primitive' (instinctually liberating) and 'modern' (nervous, mechanical)." I argue that the modernity could be construed from the liberation that instinct might be thought to entail, rather than from a perceived "mechanical" quality of the music, but this simply indicates the variety of ways in which concepts such as modernity and tradition can be constructed.

CHAPTER SIX

1. On salsa—and on music in general of this period—in Colombia, see Arteaga (1990), Caicedo ([1977] 1985), España (1995), Giraldo (1994), Ulloa Sanmiguel (1992), and Waxer (1998). See Roberts (1979) for Cuban music in the United States.

2. Ballad singers who became popular all over the Spanish-speaking world from the 1960s onward include Nelson Ned (b. 1943, Brazil), Roberto Carlos (b. 1940, Brazil)—both of whom also sang in Spanish—Leo Dan (b. 1945, Argentina), Sandro (b. 1945, Argentina), Rafael (b. 1944, Spain), Camilo Sesto (b. 1946, Spain), Julio Iglesias (b. 1944, Spain), José-José (b. 1948, Mexico), and Juan Gabriel (b. 1950, Mexico). For some details on the success of the *balada,* see Stigberg (1985).

3. See Pearce (1990), Bushnell (1993), and Bergquist, Peñaranda, and Sánchez (1992) for more detail.

4. I am grateful to Manlio Bedoya, the director of Discos Ondina and Preludio in Medellín, for bringing *Los Discos* to my attention.

5. In the 1960s, Sonolux was strengthened by the backing of Bedout, a Medellín publishing house, and in 1974, the company was taken over by one of Colombia's major economic conglomerates, Ardila Lulle, which still owns it today. In 1991, the company broke Antioqueño ranks and moved operations to Bogotá. A few details on the history of Sonolux and other record companies can be found in *Escuche* (no. 1, September 1988), the magazine of ASINCOL, the record companies' trade association. See also Cano (1986) and Restrepo Duque (1971: 244; 1991). I also interviewed Oscar Ramírez, the publicity manager of Sonolux.

6. Discos Vergara kept going until about 1979, when it was bought out by FM Discos y Cintas.

7. After some changes of ownership, the Silver catalog rights are now held by Americana de Discos, a Medellín firm run by Guillermo Galeano.

8. As I mentioned in chapter 4, the Atlantic label was started in Barran-

quilla by a group of partners in 1949 and lasted until 1956, when Emigdeo Velasco, the Venezuelan who owned La Voz de la Víctor, bought its machinery and formed the Eva label.

9. *Semana* (30 December 1950, p. 26) noted that there were eight record factories in existence in Colombia, producing 110,000 records a month. It listed Fuentes, Lyra, Zeida, Silver, Tropical, Atlantic, Vergara, and Marango. The last was located in Pereira, but I have no other information regarding it.

10. CBS (taken over in 1988 by Sony) established a branch in Bogotá in 1965, taking a major role in the ensuing vallenato boom. Philips, previously confined to selling electrical equipment, began to distribute records in 1960 and in 1976 bought out a local record company, Fonotón, founded originally by Hans Reinbold, a German Colombian. It began its own recording activities in the capital in the 1960s, starting up *La Hora Philips* (The Philips Hour), a radio talent show. In 1994, Philips was taken over by Polygram. The Venezuelan firm Rodven and the German multinational BMG (Bertelesman Music Group) also have branches in Bogotá. National record companies in Bogotá include FM Discos y Cintas, founded in 1978 by Franciso Montoya, who had worked previously in Ondina and who also owns a chain of record shops, Prodiscos; it was he that bought up the Vergara catalog.

11. In the 1990s, Sony dominates the Colombian market with about 38 percent of sales. Together with Philips (now Polygram), BMG, and Rodven, the multinationals take 60 percent of the market. The remainder is split between the national companies, with Sonolux (Bogotá) and Codiscos (Medellín) taking about 10 percent each and Discos Fuentes (Medellín) about 8 percent. FM Discos y Cintas (Bogotá) and another Bogotá firm, MTM (Música, Talento y Mercado), have about 5 percent each, with Discos Victoria (Medellín) trailing behind with a 1 percent market share. Other smaller companies include Disquera Antioqueña (Medellín), Producciones Felito (Barranquilla), Discos Orbe (Bogotá), and Fonocaribe (Bogotá). I am grateful to Orlando Parra, the director of ASINCOL, the record industry trade association, for some of these details. It is worth noting that the phonogram market in Colombia is small, with its 30 million inhabitants taking only 3.6 percent of the total Latin American market for LPs, CDs, and cassettes in 1993. Mexico's 85 million people take 37 percent, and Brazil's 150 million account for about 32 percent (Moreno 1994). Of course, the informal market in bootleg cassettes is large and more or less unquantified, although some estimates reckon that pirate phonograms are about 16 percent of the total market in Colombia *(IFPI Newsletter* 8, no. 5 [November/December 1990]). One survey in Bogotá in 1990 estimated that illegal cassette sales equaled about 20 percent of the formal market total in the city (Castillo Vega and Libos Achkar 1990). These figures are relatively low by the standards of some African countries (Manuel 1993: 30).

12. *El Tiempo* (18 September 1950, p. 21) records the appearance of Bobby Ruiz as a new singer in the band.

13. Pacho Galán's band appeared in Barranquilla's *La Prensa* advertisements fourteen times between 1954 and 1960.

14. He is still known for several hits, including "Guepa Je" (the title is a Costeño shout), "Ligia" (a woman's name), "Algo Se Me Va" (I Lose It), and "Diciembre Azul" (Blue December); see, for example, *Edmundo Arias y Su Orquesta* (Sonolux CD065, 1991).

15. These recordings are on *Las 100 mejores bailables de todas las épocas*, vol. 1 (Discos Fuentes E50001, 1992).

16. Such Venezuelan bands included Nelson Henríquez y Su Orquesta (Henríquez had played with La Billo's), Los Blanco, Nelson (González) y Sus Estrellas, Pastor López (who had played before with Nelson Henríquez and formed his own band in 1975), and Chucho Sanoja. See España (1995).

17. Laza founded the Estudiantina Bolívar in about 1932 with a lineup of piano, guitars, flutes, and violins playing porros, fandangos, and pasillos and in 1937 started an orchestra called Nueva Granada. In 1938, Pedro Laza appeared with a trio on the Voz de Laboratorios Fuentes (*La Prensa*, 30 December 1938).

18. Garrido, born in about 1900 in Cartagena, had learned some music in his Salesian school. He played in Cartagena and Sincelejo and in Montería, where he had his own orchestra, Danube Azul, but his main period of fame came in the 1950s and 1960s with Laza and with his own orchestra. Sarmiento, born in Soplaviento in 1916, was a clarinetist who during the 1940s had played with the Emisora Atlántico Jazz Band in Barranquilla and with the Discos Fuentes house bands, La Orquesta Emisora Fuentes and Los Trovadores de Barú.

19. For some details on these artists see García Usta and Salcedo Ramos (1994), Gómez (1988), Muñoz Vélez (1995), and Ruiz Hernández (1982, 1983).

20. For example, "El Cebú" (a mapalé by Rufo Garrido; the title is the name of a breed of cattle) is a much rougher sound than "Lamento Naufrago" (Shipwreck Lament, a porro by Rafael Campo Miranda). Both are on *Exitos bailables* by Pedro Laza y Sus Pelayeros (Discos Fuentes D10047, 1993).

21. See the version by Pedro Salcedo y Su Conjunto on *Música tropical*, vol. 7 (Discos Fuentes D10172, 1992) and that by Los Inmortales on *Cumbia, cumbia* (World Circuit WCD 016, 1989). The date of 1962 for the original is given by Restrepo Duque (1991: 40).

22. For example, *La Prensa* (27 January 1956) announced a gig by Pedro Laza at the Club Alhambra in Barranquilla.

23. Most of my information on this band came from interviews with Julio Estrada, Alfredo Gutiérrez, and Eliseo Herrera. In terms of chronology, they gave slightly conflicting accounts, but the main trends were clear enough.

24. The lyrics started thus: "Si Chule le parte los chochos a Chocha, Chocha le bota la chicha a Chule." This translates roughly as: "If Chule breaks Chocha's pots, Chocha will spill Chule's chicha." Chule is a term for a young woman, Chocha one for an old woman; chicha is a grain beer.

25. Alfredo Gutiérrez said that the first track to use the brass-accordion combination was "Majagual" (a porro, written by him in about 1960), which combines the accordion with a single baritone bombardino (euphonium or

small tuba). This can be heard on *Album de Los Corraleros de Majagual* (Discos Fuentes E30004, 1994).

26. Fender first developed the Precision electric bass in 1951, followed in 1960 by the Jazz bass (Sadie 1984, 1:732). The early 1960s seems a little late for the first use of the electric bass in Colombia, but I have no other information on the matter.

27. This was the B side of his first record, titled "La Mafafa" and recorded with an accordion conjunto.

28. A Barranquilla music promoter, Marco Barrazo, reunited some of Los Corraleros in 1989 for that year's carnival, and in 1995 they were touring under the same name, with a mixture of some of the old members and some younger players, including the three sons of Alfredo Gutiérrez, Dino, Walfredo and Kike.

29. *Costumbrismo* usually refers to a nineteenth-century literary trend which focused on local color and characters. *Novios* can mean boyfriend and girlfriend, fiancés, bride and groom, or newlyweds, depending on the context.

30. This band was formed with Velásquez's brother and Roberto and Carlos Román. The group did some gigs in small cities in the interior but did not last long. Roberto Román died in 1955.

31. See, for example, *Los éxitos de Aníbal Velásquez y Su Conjunto* (Discos Fuentes D16053, 1993).

32. The Hammond organ was manufactured from the mid-1930s in the United States in the form of a "tone-wheel" instrument; the Solovox was an early type of chord organ produced from about 1940. The first fully electronic organ was the Allen organ, dating from 1939; Hammond produced its first fully electronic chord organ in the early 1950s. The electric piano was first successfully marketed in the early 1970s (Sadie 1984, 1:675–678).

33. Bugalú "blended the mambo with early black rock-and-roll" and was first recorded in the mid-1960s by Richie Ray (Roberts 1979: 167).

34. See also Ulloa Sanmiguel (1992: 410) for comments on Ray's visit and the reactions it provoked, despite the fact that the previous year, Ray's orchestra had been well received and judged the best of the festival.

35. Daniel Santos was a Puerto Rican singer best known for his boleros, but he also sang Afro-Cuban styles (for example, as a front man for the Cuban orchestra La Sonora Matancera, which he joined in 1948).

36. Some of these songs can be heard on *Las 100 mejores bailables de todas las épocas,* vol. 1 (Discos Fuentes E50001, 1992). La Sonora Dinamita remains an important band in the Fuentes stable: the 1994 catalog lists six albums by them, all available on CD, and the band also recorded six of the series "30 pegaditas de oro" (30 Golden Hits).

37. For example, the collection *Música tropical,* vol. 7 (Discos Fuentes D10172, 1992), includes 1950s tracks by Pacho Galán and the 1962 "Pollera Colorá" by Pedro Salcedo alongside 1970s and 1980s numbers which would certainly be classified as raspa by Ulloa Sanmiguel, such as "La Colegiala," played by Rodolfo (Aicardi) y Su Típica RA7, or "Carmenza," played by Joe Rodríguez y Su Grupo Latino.

38. Both songs are reproduced on *Las 100 mejores bailables de todas las épocas,* vol. 1 (Discos Fuentes E50001, 1992). *Capullo* means cocoon or flower bud, but also foreskin. *Sorullo* has no literal meaning as far as I know.

39. It remains to be investigated whether the success of cumbia outside Colombia was related to the decline of Cuban-U.S. relations after the 1959 Cuban revolution. Roberts (1979: chap. 7) notes that during the 1960s there was a retrenchment of Latin music in the United States which was related partly to this decline. However, immigrant Latinos and their U.S.-born offspring were quickly filling the gap left by visiting Cuban bands. Also, it is not clear whether this affected the popularity of Cuban music in other Latin countries. In Mexico, for example, Cuban styles played by local orchestras were well established and continued throughout this period (Stigberg 1978).

40. United States Immigration and Naturalization Service statistics for 1996, for example, record that Colombians made up 1.7 percent of immigrants into the United States, compared to 17.9 percent for Mexicans, 4.3 percent for Dominicans, and 2.9 percent for Cubans (see http://www.ins.usdoj.gov/stats).

41. *El Heraldo* (10 October 1966, pp. 1, 10) reports one such event in Barranquilla.

42. His accordionists have been Elberto López, Juancho Rois, Colacho Mendoza, Cocha Molina, and again Juancho Rois until the latter's tragic death in 1994.

43. "Alicia Adorada" is a song by Juancho Polo Valencia (1922–1978), a Costeño accordionist of the old school. See Restrepo Duque (1991: 58) for details on his life and the lyrics to this song. His records are still available on Discos Fuentes (D10242, LP 206236).

44. See Marre and Charlton (1985: chap. 7) for a rather sensationalist account of the relation between the marijuana mafia and vallenato. They document reactions by Costeños who see the relationship as having been deleterious to the quality of vallenato music.

45. Gilard (1987b) contests that vallenato ever had a truly narrative function, but he argues this in relation to a rather narrow model of the narrative song, based on the Mexican corrido.

46. Compare, for example, *Escalona y su gran obra musical* (Discos Fuentes E30005, 1994), *Alejo Durán y su época de oro* (Victoria 515296, 1980), and El Binomio de Oro's *Mucha calidad* (Codiscos 228-20960, 1983). See Pacini Hernández (1995: chap. 5) on the changing ways bachata lyrics have referred to women and romantic relations as the songwriters contend with greater female autonomy in urban contexts.

CHAPTER SEVEN

1. Data on Costeño immigrants in Bogotá and Medellín are not abundant. In the following table, I show figures for the relevant province (Cundinamarca and Antioquia) where data for the city are not available (figures in brackets are percentages of the total population of the province or city). The difference between province and city is greatest for Antioquia and Medellín since Antioquia

has borders with Costeño provinces and many Costeños live in parts of Antioquia outside Medellín.

Number of Costeño Immigrants to Bogotá and Medellín

Date	Cundinamarca Province	Bogotá	Antioquia Province	Medellín
1951	9,920 (0.62)		21,771 (1.2)	
1964		23,820 (1.4)	54,893 (2.2)	
1973		38,493 (1.5)		12,101 (1.1)
1981		52,520 (1.4)		14,973 (1.2)
1985		57,329 (1.4)		

Sources: Censuses for 1951, 1964, 1973, 1985. Figures for Medellín in 1973 come from *Boletín Mensual de Estadística,* no. 314 (September 1977), table 6. Figures for 1981 come from the Estudio de Población done in that year, a sample survey of about 10 percent of the population of various cities: expanded figures are given in *Colombia Estadística* (Bogotá: Departamento Nacional de Estadísticas [DANE], 1985), table 3.4. The figure for Bogotá in 1985 comes from a special breakdown kindly supplied to me by DANE.
Note: Figures in parentheses are percentages of total population.

In general, Costeño immigrants to Bogotá came in greatest numbers from Atlántico Province, followed by Bolívar and Magdalena. Those to Medellín came from Córdoba and Bolívar. Men tended to predominate in the early years, forming between 55 and 60 percent of Costeño migrants in 1951. By 1973, the sex ratio was more or less balanced. Figures for Bogotá from the 1985 census show that the Costeño immigrants on average are a well-educated group: taking those from Atlántico Province, which supplied the largest single category of Costeños in Bogotá, over a third had university education, compared with only 12 percent for the city as a whole.

2. In the interview, this woman was keen to make clear that the Gril Colombia was a high-class venue: for some, a gril (literally, a grill, but in this case meaning a night club) might be a place of ill repute.

3. This woman is invoking the stereotypical idea that people from the interior of the country do not reveal their true feelings.

4. My research assistants in Bogotá tended to get shorter interviews from working-class respondents, so their views are less well represented here.

5. The Combo Di Lido was an Antioqueño-based orchestra playing Costeño music and other dance styles (salsa, Cuban styles, etc.) during the 1960s. It also had some Costeño members, including Francisco Zumaqué (a well-known composer and artist, born in Montería in 1945, who now works in a variety of styles, from classical to salsa).

6. There has been a long-standing and rather sterile debate about whether bambuco should be written in 3/4 or 6/8 time. Peñaloza insists that it should be 6/8.

7. *Negrito* (little black) is generally a condescending term. Chunchullo is

fried pig's intestine; sobrebarriga is a cut of beef; both are foods associated with the interior of the country.

8. *Mamar gallo* is a Colombian usage of some complexity which means to make fun of, to tease, to undermine the authority or pretensions of people by leading them "up the garden path," to fool around, to not take things seriously, to have a laugh (often at someone else's expense). The literal meaning is to suck the cock, apparently from the practice of owners of gamecocks who would suck the blood from their bird's head and eyes after a damaging blow by the opposing bird (Alario di Filippo 1983).

9. Totó la Momposina (real name Sonia Bazanta) was born in La Costa, but her family moved to Bogotá in the late 1940s, when she was about five years old. She has a group called Totó la Momposina y Sus Tambores which plays Costeño music presented in a modernized folkloric style.

10. "Josefa Matía" is the name of a popular bullerengue of the 1970s, written by Efraín Mejía Donado, director of the group Cumbia Soledeña.

11. "El Africano" (a cumbia by Wilfredo Martínez and Calixto Ochoa) and "El Cucú" (a cumbia by Sidney Simien) became platinum record hits for La Sonora Dinamita in Mexico in 1986 and 1989, respectively. They can be found on *Las 100 mejores bailables de todas las épocas*, vol. 1 (Discos Fuentes E50001, 1992) and *El show de la Sonora Dinamita* (Discos Fuentes D10156, 1992). "Las Tapas" (a cumbia by Ivo Otero), played by Lisandro Meza y Su Conjunto, won a Congo de Oro in the 1981 Barranquilla carnival (see *Congos de oro del Carnaval de Barranquilla*, Discos Fuentes D16076, 1993).

12. The corpus of album covers I refer to is contained in the catalogs of Discos Fuentes, Codiscos, Sonolux, Sony, and Discos Victoria. Although these are 1994 catalogs, they contain records going back to the 1960s. There are differences between the record companies in their use of female models. Each national company has an annual release of their best dance music of the year; these almost always feature a bikini-clad woman. They also have other compilations of salsa, Costeño music, or merengue, most of which have such photographs. Codiscos tends to feature women on their vallenato compilation album covers, but the other companies do so less.

13. For a discussion of Costeño sexuality and its relation to dance, see Simon (1994). Streicker (1995) points out that in Cartagena, the idea exists that in dance contexts sexuality is expressed in an uninhibited way by blacker, lower-class people. Thus, the imputation is not just one imposed from the interior.

14. Kuznesof (1989) notes that all over Latin America, female employment expanded rapidly from 1940 to 1970. Colombian censuses from 1951 to 1973 show a 55 percent female participation rate in rural-urban migration; in the Colombian industrial census of 1945, women formed between 40 and 83 percent of the blue-collar workforce of the food, garment, textile, and tobacco industries (Sandroni 1982). Data for 1916–1940 show that female workers in Medellín's industries were mainly single and under twenty-five years old (Gladden 1988; see also Bohman 1984). On domestic servants, see Chaney and Gar-

cía Castro (1989). Peiss (1984) shows that young white working-class women in New York in the early decades of this century had active social lives, centering around cinemas, dance halls, vaudeville theaters, and amusement parks; a central feature of going out was to associate with men.

15. *Covar* is a word used to mean dig or excavate. *Amacizarse* does not seem to have a literal meaning but connotes squeezing or pressing, partly by its closeness to *amasar*, "to knead."

16. See also Wade (1993a: 247), where I describe how the slow dance style of the Costeños and the Pacific coast blacks shocked some Antioqueños.

17. I am indebted to Placido's doctoral thesis (1999) on the María Lionza religious complex, which helped me think through these ideas.

CHAPTER EIGHT

1. Data on record sales were solicited from the record distributor Prodiscos in Bogotá, Barranquilla, Medellín, and Cali, and from the distributor Disfocol in Medellín. In Bogotá, thanks to Prodiscos employee Carlos Varela, actual figures for sales of CDs (obviously a middle-class market) were obtained, broken down into forty-four categories! Combining some of these gave the following picture for Bogotá: tropical (16 percent), rock and pop (15 percent), ballad (11 percent), salsa (8 percent), vallenato (8 percent), Latin rock and pop (6 percent), boleros and *vejez* (old-time music; 5 percent), and classical (4 percent); all other categories scored 2 percent or less, including música de carrilera, merengue, reggae, and música colombiana (i.e., bambucos, pasillos, etc.). The share for música tropical went up from 10 percent to 16 percent between October and December.

In the other cities, personnel in the head wholesale offices gave estimates of citywide sales. The Medellín office included sales to Chocó Province, where salsa and vallenato predominate. The Barranquilla respondent reckoned that in Cartagena, vallenato was less dominant than in Barranquilla (20 percent compared to 40 percent), but that reggae and *terapia* (mainly African and Haitian pop; also known as *champeta*) were strong. In Cali, salsa was predominant, followed by música tropical (including boleros and merengue) and rock and pop.

For Bogotá, Castillo Vega and Libos Achkar (1990) quizzed four hundred buyers of pirate cassettes on their "favorite music." This showed a preference for guasca and ranchera (24 percent), followed by balada (19 percent), salsa (15 percent), rock (14 percent), merengue (13 percent), and others; oddly, vallenato and Costeño music hardly figured.

ASINCOL, the phonographic companies' trade association, gave me the results of a 1992 survey (*n* = 600) done in five cities by a national opinion polling company for a local production company acting on behalf of a Mexican record company. The question asked was "What type of music do you prefer to listen to?" but categories used included "Traditional/Typical Colombian" and "Tropical," and it is unclear what people might have understood by these categories or if they were post hoc classifications. The place of vallenato, in particular, is very problematic. "Typical Colombian" music might have included cumbia, porro, and vallenato for some people, but only pasillos, bambucos, and perhaps guasca for others. If only the latter meaning prevailed, the weight of this preference in the survey is quite at odds with patterns of purchase, radio programming, and live music performance. The results were as follows, in percentages (Bucaramanga is the fifth city):

Types of Music Played in Various Cities (as Percentage of Total)

City	Typical Colombian	Tropical	Rock	Ballad	Bolero	Classical
Bogotá	20	21	11	15	19	8
Medellín	24	18	9	31	10	8
Cali	25	14	7	27	11	16
Barranquilla	3	36	1	36	16	8
Bucaramanga	25	18	5	28	12	12
Total	22	21	8	25	14	10

2. These patterns are, of course, broad generalizations, since some stations may have special programs of old Costeño music amid an overall nonmusical output or one in which other types of music predominate. Information on radio programming was collected by Manuel Bernardo Rojas in Medellín, Rosana Portaccio in Bogotá, and myself in Barranquilla, using a list of stations published in Múnera Gutiérrez (1992). A mixture of phone calls, personal visits, and listening was used, and the completeness of the information gathered obviously varied from one station to another.

3. See also the video *Les rois créoles de la champeta*, by Lucas Silva and Sergio Arria, La Huit Production, Paris, distributed by Stacey Benoit, Paris (fax. [33-1]-01-43-95-54). The soundtrack to this video has been published on CD: *El vacile efectivo de la champeta criolla: A new African music from Colombia* (Palenque Records PAL 1086, 1998). Palenque Records is located at 62, rue Doudeauville, 75018 Paris.

4. A sombrero voltiao is a wide-brimmed straw hat with black and natural straw colorings interwoven to form intricate patterns. *Voltiao* (properly, *volteado*) means turned over.

5. For example, Emiliano Zuleta's "La Gota Fria" is given a light rock ballad feel, with a gaita flute prominent alongside the accordion (the song was later covered again by Julio Iglesias, with the gaita replaced by pan pipes). Juancho Polo Valencia's classic, "Alicia Adorada," is given a reggae beat with a large chorus chanting the refrain and a saxophone solo in the middle. Other tracks—Chema Gómez's "Compae Chipuco" and Luis E. Martínez's "La Tijera," for example—sound much more like standard modern vallenato versions (Sonolux 01013901937, 1993). Vives's second album, *La tierra del olvido* (Sonolux 01013902038, 1995) has a similar mix of styles and motifs.

6. Vallenato had had some international trajectory prior to this. In its typical modern form (as exemplified by El Binomio de Oro) it had found some

markets in Venezuela, among Hispanics in the United States, and even in Japan. Vallenato had also been hybridized, most famously by Roberto Torres, a Miami-based Cuban, who in the early 1980s rearranged vallenato tunes from the 1950s and 1960s into a *charanga* music style (see, e.g., *Roberto Torres y Su Charanga Vallenata,* vol. 2, Guajiro Records 4013, 1981).

7. An example of Arroyo's earlier salsa arrangement of a Costeño style is "El Trato," labeled as having a *chandé* rhythm on the album *El super congo* (Discos Fuentes D10120, 1990). Chandé (possibly from the French *chanter*) is most associated with Barranquilla carnival music. Another example is "A Mi Dios Todo Le Debo," which has a cumbia beat (on the album *Grandes éxitos de Joe Arroyo y la Verdad* [Discos Fuentes D10150, 1991]). Of Arroyo, Arteaga (1990: 126) says, "Arroyo's has never been traditional salsa. . . . His way of playing salsa is different, very Costeño." On Arroyo, see also Calvo Ospina (1995: 123) and Steward (1994: 490).

8. Mango Records, a division of Island Records, released a series of albums under license from Discos Fuentes. Number 11 in the series, *Tropical Sounds of Colombia* (Mango CIDM 1058 846756-2, 1990), includes various items from La Sonora Dinamita of the 1980s to Los Latin Brothers. However, two older tracks are featured: "Cumbia Cienaguera," performed by Luis E. Martínez, and "Cumbia en Do Menor," performed by Lito Barrientos y Su Orquesta. World Circuit Records, also under license from Discos Fuentes, has released two albums of cumbia recordings, *Cumbia, cumbia* (WCD 016, 1989) and *Cumbia, cumbia 2* (WCD 033, 1993). The former has numbers mostly from the 1970s and 1980s, but the latter focuses on an earlier period of Costeño music, collecting tracks recorded between 1954 and 1972.

9. I am obliged to Luz Alejandra Aguilar of Carnaval S.A. for giving me access to the results of the questionnaire filled in by all participants in the meeting. The meeting was also reported at length in *El Heraldo,* 10 July 1994.

10. There are unfortunately no hard data on the relative presence of musical programming on the different regional channels, but an informal comparison of Teleantioquia and Telecaribe certainly showed the greater importance of music in the latter.

11. David Byrne's *Rei Momo* album (Luaka Bop/Sire 925990-2, 1989) can be seen as a precursor in this trend, naming rhythms from all over Latin America. It includes a track labeled a cumbia, although no mention is made in the sleeve notes of the origins of the various styles that are used. A more recent album in the same style is Gloria Estefan's *Abriendo puertas* (Epic 4809922, 1995), which, according to the sleeve notes, takes inspiration from Colombian vallenato, cumbia, chandé, and currulao, as well as salsa, merengue, bolero, son, and Venezuelan and Panamanian rhythms. In the notes, each rhythm is given its national origin, with cumbia and vallenato being identified as Colombian, although a passing mention is made of the "north coast" of the country.

12. See Wade (1995) for an account of these processes and references to the relevant literature; important among the latter are Arocha (1992), Gros (1991), and Sánchez, Roldán, and Fernández (1993).

13. This is stipulated in Article 306 of the Political Constitution of 1991.

CHAPTER NINE

1. I am referring here to critiques of the notion of "invention of tradition" which assert that all culture is invented and there is no real distinction between an invented tradition and a real one. See Linnekin and Handler (1984), Hanson (1989, 1991), and Ulin (1995).

REFERENCES CITED

Abadía Morales, Guillermo. 1973. *La música folklórica colombiana.* Bogotá: Dirección de Divulgación Cultural, Universidad Nacional.
———. 1983. *Compendio general del folklore colombiano.* Bogotá: Fondo de Promoción de la Cultura del Banco Popular.
Abello Banfi, Jaime. 1994. La televisión regional en Colombia: Filosofía, realizaciones y perspectivas. In *Cuarenta años de televisión en Colombia,* edited by Inravisión. Bogotá: Inravisión.
Acosta, Alvaro, Manuel Cabrera, and César Mendoza. 1991. La planificación del desarrollo en la costa atlántica, 1950–1980. Master's thesis, Universidad del Norte, Barranquilla.
Alario di Filippo, Mario. 1983. *Lexicón de colombianismos.* Bogotá: Banco de la República, Biblioteca Luis Angel Arango.
Alvarez, Sonia, Evelina Dagnino, and Arturo Escobar, eds. 1998. *Cultures of politics, politics of cultures: Re-visioning Latin American social movements.* Boulder: Westview.
Alzate, Alberto. 1980. *El músico de banda: Aproximación a su realidad social.* Montería: Editorial América Latina.
Amnesty International. 1988. *Colombia Briefing.* London: Amnesty International.
Anderson, Benedict. 1983. *Imagined communities: Reflections on the origin and spread of nationalism.* London: Verso.
Anthias, Floya, and Nira Yuval-Davis. 1992. *Racialized boundaries: Race, nation, gender, colour and class and the anti-racist struggle.* London: Routledge.
Añez, Jorge. [1951] 1970. *Canciones y recuerdos: Conceptos acerca del origen del bambuco.* 3d ed. Bogotá: Ediciones Mundial.
Arango Z., Carlos. 1985. *Lucho Bermúdez: Su vida y su obra.* Bogotá: Centro Editorial Bochica.
Araújo de Molina, Consuelo. 1973. *Vallenatología: Orígenes y fundamenatos de la música vallenata.* Bogotá: Tercer Mundo.

Araujonoguera, Consuelo. 1988. *Rafael Escalona: Hombre y mito.* Bogotá: Planeta.

Archila Neira, Mauricio. 1991. *Cultura e identidad obrera: Colombia, 1910–1945.* Bogotá: CINEP.

Aretz, Isabel. 1977. Música y danza en América Latina continental (excepto Brazil). In *Africa en América Latina,* edited by Manuel Moreno Fraginals, pp. 238–278. Mexico City: Siglo XXI; Paris: UNESCO.

Arnason, Johann P. 1990. Nationalism, globalization and modernity. *Theory, Culture and Society* 7 (2–3): 207–236.

Arocha, Jaime. 1992. Los negros y la nueva constitución colombiana de 1991. *América Negra* 3:39–54.

Arteaga, José. 1990. *La salsa.* Bogotá: Intermedio.

———. 1991. *Lucho Bermúdez: Maestro de maestros.* Bogotá: Intermedio.

Asad, Talal. 1993. *Genealogies of religion: Discipline and reasons of power in Christianity and Islam.* Baltimore: Johns Hopkins University Press.

Atencio Babilonia, Jaime, and Isabel Castellanos Córdova. 1982. *Fiestas del negro en el norte del Cauca: Las adoraciones del Niño Dios.* Cali: Universidad del Valle.

Austerlitz, Paul. 1995. *Merengue: Dominican music and Dominican identity.* Philadelphia: Temple University Press.

Averill, Gage. 1989. Haitian dance bands, 1916–1970: Class, race and authenticity. *Latin American Music Review* 10 (2): 203–235.

———. 1994. *"Se kreyol nou ye"/*"we're creole": Musical discourse on Haitian identities. In *Music and black ethnicity: The Caribbean and South America,* edited by Gerard Béhague, pp. 157–185. New Brunswick, N.J.: Transaction.

———. 1997. *A day for the hunter, a day for the prey: Popular music and power in Haiti.* Chicago: University of Chicago Press.

Bacca, Ramón Illán. 1990. La narrativa en el Atlántico, 1920–1940: El mundo de *Cosme,* I. *Huellas* 30:21–29.

———. 1991. La narrativa en el Atlántico, 1920–1940: El mundo de *Cosme,* II. *Huellas* 31:29–38.

Bagley, Bruce, and Gabriel Silva. 1989. De cómo se ha formado la nación colombiana: Una lectura política. *Estudios Sociales* (FAES) 4:7–36.

Banton, Michael. 1987. *Racial theories.* Cambridge: Cambridge University Press.

Barber, Karin, and Christopher Waterman. 1995. Traversing the global and the local: *Fújì* music and praise poetry in the production of contemporary Yorùbá popular culture. In *Worlds apart: Modernity through the prism of the local,* edited by Daniel Miller. London: Routledge.

Barkan, Elazar. 1995. Victorian promiscuity: Greek ethics and primitive exemplars. In *Prehistories of the future: The primitivist project and the culture of modernism,* edited by Elazar Barkan and Ronald Bush, pp. 56–92. Stanford: Stanford University Press.

Barkan, Elazar, and Ronald Bush. 1995. Introduction. In *Prehistories of the fu-*

ture: The primitivist project and the culture of modernism, edited by Elazar Barkan and Ronald Bush, pp. 1–22. Stanford: Stanford University Press.

Bastide, Roger. 1961. Dusky Venus, black Apollo. *Race* 3:10–19.

Béhague, Gerard. 1985. Popular music. In *Handbook of Latin American popular culture*, edited by Harold Hinds and Charles Tatum, pp. 3–38. Westport: Greenwood.

———. 1991. Reflections on the ideological history of Latin American ethnomusicology. In *Comparative musicology and anthropology of music*, edited by Bruno Nettl and Philip Bohlman, pp. 56–68. Chicago: University of Chicago Press.

———, ed. 1994. *Music and black ethnicity: The Caribbean and South America*. New Brunswick, N.J.: Transaction.

———. 1996. Latin American music, c. 1920–c. 1980. In *The Cambridge history of Latin America*, vol. 10, *Latin America since 1930: Ideas, culture and society*, edited by Leslie Bethell, pp. 307–363. Cambridge: Cambridge University Press.

Bell, Daniel. 1976. *The cultural contradictions of capitalism*. London: Heinemann.

Bell Lemus, Carlos, and Jorge Villalón Donoso. 1992. Historia de Barranquilla: El periódo del Frente Nacional y la crisis de los años sesenta. *Ensayos de Economía* 3 (1): 75–93.

Bell Lemus, Gustavo. 1981. *Cosme o uan introducción al siglo XX de Barranquilla. Huellas* 2 (4): 30–35.

———. 1984. Barranquilla 1920–1930. *Huellas* 11:13–24.

———, ed. 1988. *El Caribe colombiano: Selección de textos históricos*. Barranquilla: Ediciones Uninorte.

———. 1991. *Cartagena de Indias: De la colonia a la república*. Bogotá: Fundación Simón y Lola Guberek.

———. 1993. Nieto y los comienzos del regionalismo costeño. Preface to *Juan José Nieto: Selección de textos políticos-geográficos e históricos*, edited by Gustavo Bell Lemus, pp. 7–12. Barranquilla: Ediciones Gobernación del Atlántico.

Bell Lemus, Gustavo, and Adolfo Meisel Roca. 1989. *Política, políticos y desarrollo socio-económico de la costa atlántica: Una visión histórica*. Barranquilla: CERES, Universidad del Norte.

Bell Lemus, Gustavo, et al. 1993. *La región Caribe: Perspectivas y posibilidades*. Barranquilla: Centro de Estudios Regionales, Universidad del Norte.

Bensusan, Guy. 1984. Cartagena's fandango politics. *Studies in Latin American Popular Culture* 3:127–134.

Bergquist, Charles, Ricardo Peñaranda, and Gonzalo Sánchez, eds. 1992. *Violence in Colombia: The contemporary crisis in historical perspective*. Wilmington, Del.: Scholarly Resources.

Bermúdez, Egberto. 1985. *Los instrumentos musicales de Colombia*. Bogotá: Universidad Nacional de Colombia.

———. 1994. Syncretism, identity and creativity in Afro-Colombian musical traditions. In *Music and black ethnicity: The Caribbean and South America,* edited by Gerard Béhague, pp. 225–238. New Brunswick, N.J.: Transaction.

————. 1996. La música campesina y popular en Colombia: 1880–1930. *Gaceta* 32–33: 113–120.

Bermúdez, Egberto, David Puerta, María Eugenia Romero, and Gloria Triana. 1987. *Música tradicional y popular colombiana* (text accompanying 12 phonograph records). Bogotá: Procultura.

Bernal Pinzón, Carmen. 1941. *Historia de Colombia para niños.* Bogotá: Ediciones la Idea.

Betancur Alvarez, Fabio. 1993. *Sin clave y bongo, no hay son.* Medellín: Ediciones Universidad de Antioquia.

Beverley, John, José Oviedo, and Michael Aronna, eds. 1995. *The postmodernism debate in Latin America.* Durham: Duke University Press.

Bhabha, Homi. 1989. Down among the women. *New Statesman and Society,* 3 March.

————. 1994. *The location of culture.* London: Routledge.

Bilby, Kenneth. 1985. The Caribbean as a musical region. In *Caribbean contours,* edited by Sidney Mintz and Sally Price, pp. 181–218. Baltimore: Johns Hopkins University Press.

Bobadilla, Emilio. [1901] 1994. *A fuego lento.* Barranquilla: Ediciones Gobernación del Atlántico.

Bohman, Kristina. 1984. *Women of the barrio: Class and gender in a Colombian city.* Stockholm: University of Stockholm Press.

Bonilla, Liliana. 1990. *Colcultura: Un espacio para la cultura: Informe de gestión, 1989–1990.* Bogotá: Colcultura.

Bourdieu, Pierre. 1984. *Distinction: A social critique of the judgement of taste.* London: Routledge and Kegan Paul.

Brisson, Jorge. 1899. *Viajes por Colombia en los años 1891 a 1897.* Bogotá: Imprenta Nacional.

Brugés Carmona, Antonio. 1943. Noción del porro. *El Tiempo,* 28 February, sec. 2, p. 2.

————. 1945. Vida y pasión del porro. *Sábado* 99: 11–14.

————. 1946. Defensa del porro. *El Tiempo,* 23 January, p. 5.

————. 1949. De Francia a las selvas del Sinú. *Revista de América* 16 (52): 357–362.

Bullen, Margaret. 1993. Chicha in the shanty towns of Arequipa, Peru. *Popular Music* 12 (3): 229–245.

Burton, Kim. 1994. ¡Cumbia! ¡Cumbia! In *World music: The rough guide,* edited by Simon Broughton et al., pp. 549–556. London: The Rough Guides.

Bushnell, David. 1993. *The making of modern Colombia: A nation in spite of itself.* Berkeley: University of California Press.

Butler, Judith P. 1993. *Bodies that matter: On the discursive limits of "sex."* London: Routledge.

Caballero Calderón, Eduardo. 1960. *Historia privada de los colombianos.* Bogotá: Antares.

Caicedo, Andrés. [1977] 1985. *Que viva la música.* Bogotá: Plaza y Janes.

Calvo Ospina, Hernando. 1995. *¡Salsa!: Havana heat, Bronx beat.* London: Latin America Bureau.

Camargo, Pedro Pablo. 1987. *Crítica a la constitución colombiana de 1886.* Bogotá: Editorial Temis.

Camargo Franco, Jaime Eduardo. 1992. Chandé, ritmo de carnavales. In *Música tropical y salsa en Colombia,* edited by Discos Fuentes, pp. 147–172. Medellín: Ediciones Fuentes.

Candela, Mariano. 1992. Pedro Biava con la época dorada de la música de Barranquilla. *El Heraldo,* 12 July, pp. 4E–5E.

———. n.d. Orquesta Emisora Atlántico Jazz Band. Barranquilla. Mimeographed.

Cano, Ana María. 1986. Hernán Restrepo Duque: La voz de la música popular. *Boletín Cultural y Bibliográfico* 23 (6): 15–29.

Carranza, Eduardo. 1944. Jorge Artel: El poeta negro. *Sábado* 26 (8 January): 4.

Carrasquilla, Tomás. 1964. *Obras completas.* Medellín: Editorial Bedout.

Carreño, Manuel Antonio. n.d. *Manual de urbanidad y de buenas maneras.* Paris: n.p.

Carrillo Hinojosa, Félix. 1993. El vallenato. Essay presented to the Casa de las Américas essay competition, La Habana, Cuba. Bogotá. Mimeographed.

Castillo Vega, Leonardo, and William Libos Achkar. 1990. El mercado ilegal de cassettes en la ciudad de Bogotá y su influencia en la industria fonográfica. Graduate thesis, Pontificia Universidad Javeriana, Bogotá.

Chaney, Elsa, and Mary García Castro, eds. 1989. *Muchachas no more: Household workers in Latin America and the Caribbean.* Philadelphia: Temple University Press.

CIIR (Catholic Institute of International Relations). 1992. *Colombia: Image and reality.* London: CIIR.

Clifford, James, and George Marcus, eds. 1986. *Writing culture: The poetics and politics of ethnography.* Berkeley: University of California Press.

Cloudsley, Peter. 1993. *A survey of music in Peru.* London: Department of Ethnography, British Museum.

Collier, Simon, Artemis Cooper, María Susana Azzi, and Richard Martin. 1995. *¡Tango!* London: Thames and Hudson.

Collins, John, and Paul Richards. 1989. Popular music in West Africa. In *World music, politics and social change,* edited by Simon Frith, pp. 14–26. Manchester: Manchester University Press.

Cooper, Carolyn. 1993. *Noises in the blood: Orality, gender and the "vulgar" body of Jamaican popular culture.* London: Macmillan Caribbean.

Cordovez Moure, José María. [1893] 1957. *Reminiscencias de Santa Fe y Bogotá.* Madrid: Aguilar.

Cowan, Jane. 1990. *Dance and the body politic in northern Greece.* Princeton: Princeton University Press.

Csordas, Thomas, ed. 1994. *Embodiment and experience: The existential ground of culture and the self.* Cambridge: Cambridge University Press.

Daniel, Yvonne. 1995. *Rumba: Dance and social change in contemporary Cuba*. Bloomington: Indiana University Press.

Davidson, Harry C. 1970. *Diccionario folklórico de Colombia*. 3 vols. Bogotá: Banco de la República.

Davis, Marta Ellen. 1994. Music and black ethnicity in the Dominican Republic. In *Music and black ethnicity: The Caribbean and South America*, edited by Gerard Béhague, pp. 119–156. New Brunswick, N.J.: Transaction.

Delpar, Helen. 1981. *Red against blue: The Liberal Party in Colombian politics, 1863–1899*. Alabama: University of Alabama Press.

Díaz Ayala, Cristobal. 1981. *Música cubana: Del Areyto a la nueva trova*. San Juan, Puerto Rico: Ediciones Cubanacan.

Discos Fuentes, ed. 1992. *Música tropical y salsa en Colombia*. Medellín: Discos Fuentes.

DNP and Colcultura. 1990. *La política cultural: Nueva orientación de una política cultural para Colombia*. Bogotá: Departamento Nacional de Planeación and Instituto Colombiano de Cultura. Also published in *Gaceta* 8:55–58.

Duany, Jorge. 1984. Popular music in Puerto Rico: Toward an anthropology of *salsa*. *Latin American Music Review* 5 (2): 186–216.

———. 1994. Ethnicity, identity and music: An anthropological analysis of the Dominican *merengue*. In *Music and black ethnicity: The Caribbean and South America*, edited by Gerard Béhague, pp. 65–90. New Brunswick, N.J.: Transaction.

Durán, Gustavo. 1950. *Recordings of Latin American songs and dances: An annotated and selective list of popular and folk-popular music*. 2d ed., revised by Gilbert Chase. Washington: Pan-American Union.

Dussán de Reichel, Alicia. 1958. La estructura de la familia en la costa caribe de Colombia. In *Minutes of Thirty-Third International Congress of Americanists*, 2:692–703. Mexico City: Universidad Nacional Autónoma de México.

Eriksen, Thomas Hylland. 1993. *Ethnicity and nationalism: Anthropological perspectives*. London: Pluto.

Escalante, Aquiles. 1964. *El negro en Colombia*. Bogotá: Facultad de Sociología, Universidad Nacional.

———. 1980. Las máscaras de madera en el Africa y en el carnaval de Barranquilla. *Divulgaciones Etnológicas* 1:29–36.

Escobar, Arturo, and Sonia E. Alvarez, eds. 1992. *The making of social movements in Latin America: Identity, strategy, and democracy*. Boulder: Westview.

Espagnat, Pierre d'. 1983. *Recuerdos de la Nueva Granada*. Bogotá: Ediciones Incunables.

España, Rafael. 1995. *Que viva el chucu-chucu: Crónicas de la música tropical*. Bogotá: Editorial Linotipia Bolívar.

Espinosa, Luis Manuel. 1991. *Autonomía regional: Del hecho al derecho*. 2d ed. Medellín: Proditécnicas.

Espriella, Alfredo de la, and Hernando Quintero, eds. 1985. *75 años del De-*

partamento del Atlántico: 1910–1988 bodas de diamante. Barranquilla: Museo Romántico de Barranquilla.

Fabian, Johannes. 1983. *Time and the other: How anthropology makes its object.* New York: Columbia University Press.

Fagan, Ted, and William R. Moran. 1986. *The encyclopedic discography of Victor recordings, 1903–1908.* Westport: Greenwood.

Fals Borda, Orlando. 1976. *Capitalismo, hacienda y poblamiento en la costa atlántica.* Bogotá: Punta de Lanza.

———. 1979. *Historia doble de la costa.* Vol. 1, *Mompox y Loba.* Bogotá: Carlos Valencia Editores.

———. 1981. *Historia doble de la costa.* Vol. 2, *El presidente Nieto.* Bogotá: Carlos Valencia Editores.

———. 1984. *Historia doble de la costa.* Vol. 3, *Resistencia en el San Jorge.* Bogotá: Carlos Valencia Editores.

———. 1986. *Historia doble de la costa.* Vol. 4, *Retorno a la tierra.* Bogotá: Carlos Valencia Editores.

———, ed. 1988. *La insurgencia de las provincias: Hacia un nuevo ordenamiento territorial para Colombia.* Bogotá: Instituto de Estudios Políticos y Relaciones Internacionales, Universidad Nacional, and Siglo XXI.

Fanon, Frantz. 1986. *Black skin, white masks.* London: Pluto.

Ferro Bayona, Jesús. 1981. Esbozo de una etnología sobre el modo de ser costeño. *Huellas* 2 (2): 40–45.

Finnegan, Ruth. 1989. *The hidden musicians: Music making in an English town.* Cambridge: Cambridge University Press.

Fortich Díaz, William. 1994. *Con bombos y platillos: Origen del porro, aproximación al fandango y las bandas pelayeras.* Montería: Domus Libri.

Foster, Susan Leigh, ed. 1996. *Corporealities: Dancing knowledge, culture and power.* London: Routledge.

Foucault, Michel. 1979. *The history of sexuality.* Translated by Robert Hurley. London: Lane.

Franco, Jean. 1967. *The modern culture of Latin America: Society and the artist.* London: Pall Mall.

Friedemann, Nina de. 1978. The study of culture on the Caribbean coasts of Colombia. UNESCO, Paris. Mimeographed.

———. 1984. Estudios de negros en la antropología colombiana. In *Un siglo de investigación social: Antropología en Colombia,* edited by Jaime Arocha and Nina de Friedemann, pp. 507–572. Bogotá: Etno.

———. 1985. *Carnaval en Barranquilla.* Bogotá: Ed. La Rosa.

———. 1988. Cabildos negros: Refugios de Africanía en Colombia. *Montalban* 20: 121–134.

Friedemann, Nina de, and Carlos Patiño Rosselli. 1983. *Lengua y sociedad en el Palenque de San Basilio.* Bogotá: Instituto de Caro y Cuervo.

Friedman, Jonathon. 1990. Being in the world: Globalization and localization. *Theory, Culture and Society* 7 (2–3): 311–328.

Frith, Simon. 1987. The making of the British recording industry, 1920–64. In *Impacts and influences: Essays on media power in the twentieth century,* edited by James Curran, Anthony Smith, and Pauline Wingate. London: Methuen.

———. 1996. Music and identity. In *Questions of cultural identity,* edited by Stuart Hall and Paul du Gay, pp. 108–127. London: Sage.

García Canclini, Néstor. 1989. *Culturas híbridas: Estrategias para entrar y salir de la modernidad.* Mexico City: Grijalbo.

García Márquez, Gabriel. 1981. *Obra periodística.* Vol. 1, *Textos costeños,* edited by Jacques Gilard. Bogotá: Oveja Negra.

———. 1982. *Obra periodística.* Vols. 2 and 3, *Entre Cachacos,* edited by Jacques Gilard. Barcelona: Bruguera.

———. 1991. *Notas de prensa, 1980–1984.* Madrid: Mondadori.

García Usta, Jorge, and Alberto Salcedo Ramos. 1994. *Diez juglares en su patio.* Bogotá: Ecoe Ediciones.

Gellner, Ernest. 1983. *Nations and nationalism.* Oxford: Blackwell.

———. 1994. *Encounters with nationalism.* Oxford: Blackwell.

Giddens, Anthony. 1987. *Social theory and modern society.* Cambridge: Polity.

———. 1990. *The consequences of modernity.* Cambridge: Polity.

Gilard, Jacques. 1986. Surgimiento y recuperación de una contra-cultura en la Colombia contemporánea. *Huellas* 18:41–46.

———. 1987a. Crescencio ou don Toba? Fausses questions et vraies réponses sur le "vallenato." *Cahiers du Monde Hispanique et Luso-Brésilien, Caravelle* 48:69–80. Also published as ¿Crescencio o Don Toba? Falsos interrogantes y verdaderas respuestas sobre el vallenato, *Huellas* 37 (1993): 28–34.

———. 1987b. Vallenato: ¿Cuál tradición narrativa? *Huellas* 19:59–67.

———. 1991. Voces (1917–1920): Un proyecto para Colombia. *Huellas* 31:13–22.

———. 1994. Le débat identitaire dans la Colombie des années 1940 et 1950. *Cahiers du Monde Hispanique et Luso-Brésilien, Caravelle* 62:11–26.

Gilman, Sander. 1986. Black bodies, whites bodies: Toward an iconography of female sexuality in late nineteenth-century art, medicine, and literature. In *"Race," writing, and difference,* edited by Henry Louis Gates, Jr., pp. 223–261. Chicago: University of Chicago Press.

Gilroy, Paul. 1987. *"There ain't no black in the Union Jack": The cultural politics of race and nation.* London: Hutchinson.

———. 1993. *The black Atlantic: Modernity and double consciousness.* London: Verso.

Giraldo, Carlos Alberto. 1994. La salsa en Medellín: Sonidos del goce y el dolor urbanos. *El Colombiano, Dominical,* 11 September, pp. 13–16.

Giraldo, Juan Leonel. 1989. Antonio María Peñaloza: El hombre de "Te Olvidé." *Revista Diners* 228:84–85.

Gladden, Kathleen. 1988. Women in industrial development: The case of Medellín, Colombia. *Journal of Popular Culture* 22 (1): 51–62.

Goldberg, David. 1993. *Racist culture: Philosophy and the politics of meaning.* Oxford: Blackwell.

Gómez, Laureano. [1928] 1970. *Interrogantes sobre el progreso de Colombia.* Bogotá: Colección Populibro.

Gómez, Nestor. 1988. Pedro Laza: El emperador de la música caliente. *El Diario del Caribe,* 8 April, p. 8B.

González Henríquez, Adolfo. 1985. Sociología de la música costeña. *Huellas* 14:49–56.

———. 1987. La música costeña en la obra de Fals Borda. *Anuario Científico* 6:57–92.

———. 1989a. Influencia de la música cubana en el Caribe colombiano. *Huellas* 25:34–42.

———. 1989b. La música costeña en la tercera década del siglo XIX. *Boletín Cultural y Bibliográfico* 26 (19): 3–12. Also in *Latin American Music Review* 9, no. 2 (1988): 187–206.

———. 1989c. La rumba costeña en los años 20. *Revista Diners* 228:86–91.

Graburn, Norman. 1995. Tourism, modernity and nostalgia. In *The future of anthropology,* edited by A. Ahmed and C. Shore, pp. 158–178. London: Athlone.

Graham, Richard, ed. 1990. *The idea of race in Latin America, 1870–1940.* Austin: University of Texas Press.

Gramsci, Antonio. 1971. *Selections from the prison notebooks of Antonio Gramsci.* Edited and translated by Quintin Hoare and Geoffrey Nowell Smith. London: Lawrence and Wishart.

Granados, Rafael. 1949. *Historia de Colombia.* Medellín: Editorial Bedout.

Gros, Christian. 1991. *Colombia indígena: Identidad cultural y cambio social.* Bogotá: CEREC.

Guilbault, Jocelyne, with Gage Averill, Edouard Benoit, and Gregory Rabess. 1993. *Zouk: World music in the West Indies.* Chicago: University of Chicago Press.

Guilbault, Jocelyne. 1994. Créolité and the new cultural politics of difference in popular music of the French West Indies. *Black Music Research Journal* 14 (2): 161–178.

Gutiérrez de Pineda, Virginia. 1975. *Familia y cultura en Colombia.* Bogotá: Colcultura.

Gutiérrez Hinojosa, Tomás Darío. 1992. *Cultura vallenata: Origen, teoría y pruebas.* Bogotá: Plaza y Janes.

Guy, Donna. 1991. *Sex and danger in Buenos Aires: Prostitution, family, and nation in Argentina.* Lincoln: University of Nebraska Press.

Hale, Thomas A. 1978. Les écrits d'Aimé Césaire: Bibliographie commentée. *Études Françaises* 14, no. 3–4 (special issue).

Hall, Stuart. [1986] 1996a. Gramsci's relevance for the study of race and ethnicity. In *Stuart Hall: Critical dialogues in cultural studies,* edited by David Morley and Kuan-Hsing Chen, pp. 411–440. London: Routledge.

———. [1986] 1996b. The problem of ideology: Marxism without guarantees. In *Stuart Hall: Critical dialogues in cultural studies,* edited by David Morley and Kuan-Hsing Chen, pp. 25–46. London: Routledge.

———. 1992. The question of cultural identity. In *Modernity and its futures,* edited by S. Hall, D. Held, and T. McGrew, pp. 273–326. Cambridge: Polity.

Hall, Stuart, David Held, and Tony McGrew. 1992. *Modernity and its futures.* Cambridge: Polity.

Hall, Stuart, and T. Jefferson, eds. 1976. *Resistance through rituals: Youth subcultures in post-war Britain.* London: Hutchinson.

Hanson, Allan. 1989. The making of the Maori: Culture invention and its logic. *American Anthropologist* 91 (4): 890–902.

———. 1991. Reply to Langdon, Levine and Linnekin. *American Anthropologist* 93 (2): 449–450.

Harvey, David. 1989. *The condition of postmodernity.* Oxford: Blackwell.

Hebdige, Dick. 1979. *Subculture: The meaning of style.* London: Methuen.

———. 1987. *Cut 'n' mix: Culture, identity and Caribbean music.* London: Methuen.

Helg, Aline. 1987. *Educación en Colombia, 1918–1957: Una historia social, económica y política.* Bogotá: CEREC.

———. 1989. Los intelectuales frente a la cuestión racial en el decenio de 1920: Colombia entre México y Argentina. *Estudios Sociales* (FAES) 4 : 37–53.

———. 1995. *Our rightful share: The Afro-Cuban struggle for equality, 1886–1912.* Chapel Hill: University of North Carolina Press.

Henao, Jesús María, and Gerardo Arrubla. 1967. *Historia de Colombia.* Bogotá: Voluntad.

Hernton, Calvin. 1970. *Sex and racism.* London: Paladin.

Hinestroza Llano, Alberto. n.d. *Remembranzas de una historia: Pacho Rada, vida de Francisco el Hombre.* Barranquilla: Gráficas Lucas.

Hobsbawm, Eric, and Terence Ranger. 1983. *The invention of tradition.* Cambridge: Cambridge University Press.

Honour, Hugh. 1989. *The image of the black in Western art.* Vol. 4, *From the American Revolution to World War I.* Pt. 2, *Black models and white myths.* Houston: Menil Foundation.

hooks, bell. 1991. *Yearning: Race, gender and cultural politics.* London: Turnaround.

Hurtado, Teodora. 1996. Las migraciones "norteñas" y el impacto sociocultural sobre la población urbana de Buenaventura. Graduate thesis, Universidad del Valle, Cali.

Iriarte, Alfredo. 1988. *Breve historia de Bogotá.* Bogotá: Oveja Negra y Fundación Misión Colombia.

Jackson, Richard L. 1976. *The black image in Latin American literature.* Albuquerque: University of New Mexico Press.

———. 1979. *Black writers in Latin America.* Albuquerque: University of New Mexico Press.

———. 1988. *Black literature and humanism in Latin America.* Athens: University of Georgia Press.

Jiménez, Pat. 1986. "En aquel tiempo: Eso que llamamos Carnaval." *El Diario del Caribe,* 30 January–8 February.

Jones, Leroi [Amiri Baraka]. 1970. *Black music.* New York: William Morrow.

Jordan, Winthrop. 1977. *White over black: American attitudes toward the Negro, 1550–1812.* New York: Norton.

Kastos, Emiro. 1972. *Artículos escogidos.* Bogotá: Banco Popular.

Keil, Charles. 1985. People's music comparatively: Style and stereotypes, class and hegemony. *Dialectical Anthropology* 10:119–130.

Keil, Charles, and Steven Feld. 1994. *Music grooves.* Chicago: University of Chicago Press.

Keith, M., and S. Pile, eds. 1993. *Place and the politics of identity.* London: Routledge.

King, John. 1990. *Magical reels: A history of cinema in Latin America.* London: Verso.

Kuper, Adam. 1988. *The invention of primitive society: The transformation of an illusion.* London: Routledge.

Kuznesof, Elizabeth. 1989. A history of domestic service in Spanish America, 1492–1980. In *Muchachas no more: Household workers in Latin America and the Caribbean,* edited by Elsa Chaney and Mary García Castro, pp. 17–36. Philadelphia: Temple University Press.

Largey, Michael. 1994. Composing a Haitian cultural identity: Haitian elites, African ancestry, and musical discourse. *Black Music Research Journal* 14 (2): 99–117.

Larkey, Edward. 1992. Austropop: Popular music and national identity in Austria. *Popular Music* 11 (2): 151–185.

Lash, Scott, and John Urry. 1993. *Economies of signs and spaces.* London: Sage.

Leppert, Richard. 1993. *The sight of sound: Music, representation and the history of the body.* Berkeley: University of California Press.

Levine, Lawrence. 1977. *Black culture and black consciousness: Afro-American folk* thought from slavery to freedom. New York: Oxford University Press.

Lewis, Marvin A. 1987. *Treading the ebony path: Ideology and violence in contemporary Afro-Colombian prose fiction.* Columbia: University of Missouri Press.

Linnekin, Joyce, and Richard Handler. 1984. Tradition, genuine or spurious. *Journal of American Folklore* 97 (385): 273–290.

List, George. 1980. Colombia: Folk music. In *New Grove dictionary of music and musicians,* edited by Stanley Sadie, 4:570–581. London: Macmillan.

———. 1983. *Music and poetry in a Colombian village.* Bloomington: Indiana University Press.

Llerena Villalobos, Rito. 1985. *Memoria cultural en el vallenato.* Medellín: Centro de Investigaciones, Universidad de Antioquia.

Londoño, Alberto. 1989. *Danzas colombianas.* Medellín: Editorial Universidad de Antioquia.

Londoño, María Eugenia. 1985. Introducción al vallenato como fenómeno musical. In *Memoria cultural en el vallenato,* edited by Rito Llerena, pp. 125–134. Medellín: Centro de Investigaciones, Universidad de Antioquia.

Londoño, Patricia. 1988. La vida diaria: Usos y costumbres. In *Historia de Antioquia,* edited by Jorge Orlando Melo, pp. 307–342. Medellín: Suramericana de Seguros.

Londoño, Patricia, and Santiago Londoño. 1989. Vida diaria en las ciudades colombianas. In *Nueva Historia de Colombia,* vol. 4, *Educación, ciencias, luchas de la mujer, vida diaria,* edited by Alvaro Tirado Mejía, pp. 313–397. Bogotá: Planeta.

López de Mesa, Luis. [1934] 1970. *De cómo se ha formado la nación colombiana.* Medellín: Editorial Bedout.

López de Rodríguez, Cecilia. n.d. *La costa atlántica: Algunos aspectos socioeconómicos.* Bogotá: Fedesarrollo.

Lotero Botero, Amparo. 1989. El porro pelayero: De las gaitas y tambores a las bandas de viento. *Boletín Cultural y Bibliográfico* 26 (19): 39–53.

MacCormack, Carol, and Marilyn Strathern, eds. 1980. *Nature, culture and gender.* Cambridge: Cambridge University Press.

Manuel, Peter. 1988. *Popular musics of the non-Western world: An introductory survey.* Oxford: Oxford University Press.

———. 1993. *Cassette culture: Popular music and technology in North India.* Chicago: University of Chicago Press.

———. 1994. Puerto Rican music and cultural identity: Creative appropriation of Cuban sources from danza to salsa. *Ethnomusicology* 38 (2): 249–280.

Manuel, Peter, with Kenneth Bilby and Michael Largey. 1995. *Caribbean currents: Caribbean music from rumba to reggae.* Philadelphia: Temple University Press.

Marre, Jeremy, and Hannah Charlton. 1985. *Beats of the heart.* London: Pluto.

Martin, Wendy. 1995. "Remembering the jungle": Josephine Baker and modernist parody. In *Prehistories of the future: The primitivist project and the culture of modernism,* edited by Elazar Barkan and Ronald Bush, pp. 310–325. Stanford: Stanford University Press.

Martín-Barbero, Jesús. 1987a. *De los medios a las mediaciones: Comunicación, cultura y hegemonía.* Barcelona: Gustavo Gili.

———. 1987b. Tecnología y cultura: Una relación necesitada de historia. *Aportes* 23:73–80.

Martínez, Luis. 1924. *Geografía de Colombia.* Bogotá: n.p.

Martinez-Alier, Verena. 1974. *Marriage, colour and class in nineteenth-century Cuba.* Cambridge: Cambridge University Press.

Massey, Doreen, and Pat Jess, eds. 1995. *A place in the world? Places, cultures and globalization.* Milton Keynes: Open University Press.

McCaa, Robert. 1984. *Calidad, clase* and marriage in colonial Mexico: The case of Parral, 1788–90. *Hispanic American Historical Review* 64 (3): 477–501.

McClary, Susan, and Robert Walser. 1994. Theorizing the body in African-American music. *Black Music Research Journal* 14 (1): 75–84.

McClintock, Anne. 1993. Family feuds: Gender, nationalism and the family. *Feminist Review* 44:61–80.

———. 1995. *Imperial leather: Race, gender and sexuality in the colonial contest.* London: Routledge.

Medina, Alvaro. 1978. *Procesos de la historia del arte en Colombia.* Bogotá: Instituto Colombiano de Cultura.

Meisel Roca, Adolfo. 1992. *Economía regional y pobreza: El caso del Caribe colombiano, 1950–1990.* Barranquilla: CERES, Universidad del Norte.

———, ed. 1994. *Historia económica y social del Caribe colombiano.* Bogotá: Ediciones Uninorte and Ecoe Ediciones.

Meisel Roca, Adolfo, and Eduardo Posada Carbó. 1993. *Porque se disipó el dinamismo industrial de Barranquilla y otros ensayos de historia económica de la Costa Caribe.* Barranquilla: Ediciones de la Gobernación del Atlántico.

Mena Lozano, Ursula, and Ana Rosa Herrera Campillo. 1994. *Políticas culturales en Colombia: Discursos estatales y prácticas institucionales.* Bogotá: Mena y Herrera Editoras.

Merchant, Carolyn. 1983. *The death of nature: Women, ecology and the scientific revolution.* San Francisco: Harper and Row.

Middleton, Richard. 1985. Popular music, class conflict and the music-historical field. In *Popular music perspectives,* edited by David Horn and Philip Tagg, pp. 24–46. Göteborg and Exeter: International Association for the Study of Popular Music.

———. 1990. *Studying popular music.* Milton Keynes: Open University Press.

Miller, Daniel. 1995a. Consumption as the vanguard of history. In *Acknowledging consumption: A review of studies,* edited by Daniel Miller, pp. 1–57. London: Routledge.

———, ed. 1995b. *Worlds apart: Modernity through the prism of the local.* London: Routledge.

Miñana Blasco, Carlos. 1997. Los caminos del bambuco en el siglo XIX. *A Contratiempo* 9:7–11.

Monsiváis, Carlos. 1997. *Mexican postcards.* Translated by John Kraniauskas. London: Verso.

Moore, Robin. 1997. *Nationalizing blackness: Afrocubanismo and artistic revolution in Havana, 1920–1940.* Pittsburgh: University of Pittsburgh Press.

Morales Benítez, Otto. 1984. *Memorias del mestizaje.* Bogotá: Plaza y Janes.

Morales González, Verena. 1989. Descripción y análisis de la música popular y folclórica del Sinú como manifestación sociocultural. Graduate thesis, Universidad Autónoma Latinoamericana, Medellín.

Mora Patiño, Orlando. 1989. *La música que es como la vida.* Medellín: Ediciones Autores Antioqueños.

Moreno, Claudia Pilar. 1994. Mercado musical en Colombia: En marcha al ritmo del compact-disc. *Publicidad y Mercadeo* 15 (162): 42–51.

Mouffe, Chantal. 1979. Hegemony and ideology in Gramsci. In *Gramsci and*

Marxist theory, edited by Chantal Mouffe, pp. 168–204. London: Routledge and Kegan Paul.

Múnera Gutiérrez, Luis Fernando. 1992. *La radio y la televisión en Colombia: 63 años de historia.* Bogotá: Apra Editores.

Muñoz Vélez, Enrique Luis. 1995. Los nostálgicos años veinte. *El Universal,* 29 January, p. 4D.

Nairn, Tom. 1977. *The break-up of Britain.* London: New Left Books.

———. 1988. *The enchanted glass: Britain and its monarchy.* London: Hutchinson.

Navia, José. 1993. José Barros se las sabe todas. *El Tiempo,* 28 February, p. 9A.

Nederveen Pieterse, Jan. 1992. *White on black: Images of Africa and blacks in Western popular culture.* New Haven: Yale University Press.

Nettleford, Rex. 1970. *Mirror, mirror: Identity, race and protest in Jamaica.* Kingston: William Collins and Sangster (Jamaica).

Nicholls, David. 1979. *From Dessalines to Duvalier: Race, colour and national independence in Haiti.* Cambridge: Cambridge University Press.

———. 1985. *Haiti in Caribbean context: Ethnicity, economy and revolt.* London: Macmillan; Oxford: St. Antony's College.

Nichols, Theodore E. 1954. The rise of Barranquilla. *Hispanic American Historical Review* 34 (2): 158–174.

Noguero Laborde, Rodrigo. 1950. *Constitución de la República de Colombia y sus antecedentes desde 1885.* 2 vols. Bogotá: Pontificia Universidad Católica Javeriana.

Obeso, Candelario. [1877] 1977. *Cantos populares de mi tierra.* Bogotá: Fondo de Publicaciones de la Fundación Colombiana de Investigaciónes Folclóricas.

Ocampo López, Javier. 1988. *Las fiestas y el folclor en Colombia.* Bogotá: El Ancora Editores.

Ochoa, Ana María. 1997. Tradición, género y nación en el bambuco. *A Contratiempo* 9:34–44.

O Drasil. [1893] 1994. *Viaje de O Drasil de Bogotá a Barranquilla.* Barranquilla: Ediciones Gobernación del Atlántico.

Omi, Michael, and Howard Winant. 1986. *Racial formation in the USA from the 1960s to the 1980s.* New York: Routledge.

Orozco, Martín, and Rafael Soto. 1993. *Carnaval: Mito y tradición.* Barranquilla: Editorial Antillas and Publicaciones Cultura Caribe.

Ortega, Lorenzo. 1945. Sobre la música nacional. *La Prensa,* 3 February, p. 10.

Ortiz, Fernando. [1950] 1965. *La africanía de la música folklórica cubana.* La Habana: Editorial Universitaria.

Ortiz Mesa, Luis Javier. 1996. Viajeros y forasteros: Vida cotidiana en Medellín, siglos XIX–XX. In *Historia de Medellín.* Medellín: Suramericana de Seguros.

Pacini Hernández, Deborah. 1989. Social identity and class in *bachata,* an emerging Dominican popular music. *Latin American Music Review* 10 (1): 69–91.

———. 1991. *La lucha sonora:* Dominican popular music in the post- Trujillo era. *Latin American Music Review* 12 (2): 105–123.

———. 1992a. Bachata: From the margins to the mainstream. *Popular Music* 11 (3): 359–364.

———. 1992b. Review of *Cumbia, cumbia; Tropicalísmo,* by Peregoyo y su Combo Vacano; *Rebelión,* by Joe Arroyo; *Cantando!* by Diomedes Díaz and Colacho Mendoza; and *Vallenato Dynamos,* by the Merino Brothers. *Ethnomusicology* 36 (2): 288–296.

———. 1993. The picó phenomenon in Cartagena, Colombia. *América Negra* 6:69–115.

———. 1995. *Bachata: A social history of a Dominican popular music.* Philadelphia: Temple University Press.

Paige, E. 1969. The jukebox story. *Billboard,* 27 December, pp. 84–90.

Palacios, Marco. 1986. La fragmentación regional de las clases dominantes en Colombia: Una perspectiva histórica. In *Estado y clases sociales en Colombia.* Bogotá: Procultura.

Pardo Tovar, Andrés. 1966. *La cultura musical en Colombia.* Bogotá: Ediciones Lerner.

Pareja, Reynaldo. 1984. *La historia de la radio en Colombia, 1929–1980.* Bogotá: Servicio Colombiano de Comunicación Social.

Park, James William. 1985. *Rafael Núñez and the politics of Colombian regionalism, 1863–1886.* Baton Rouge: Louisiana State University Press.

Parker, Andrew, et al. 1992. *Nationalisms and sexualities.* London: Routledge.

Partridge, William. 1974. *Exchange relations in a North Colombian coastal community.* Ann Arbor: University Microfilms.

Payne, Alexander. 1986. Crecimiento y cambio social en Medellín. *Estudios Sociales,* vol. 1.

Pearce, Jenny. 1990. *Colombia: Inside the labyrinth.* London: Latin American Bureau.

Peiss, Kathy. 1984. "Charity girls" and city pleasures: Historical notes on working class sexuality, 1880–1920. In *Desire: The politics of sexuality,* edited by Ann Snitow, Christine Stansell, and Sharon Thompson, pp. 127–139. London: Virago.

Peña, Manuel. 1985. From ranchero to jaitón: Ethnicity and class in Texas-Mexican music (two styles in the form of a pair). *Ethnomusicology* 29 (1): 29–55.

Peñaloza, Antonio María. 1989. La música en el Carnaval de Barranquilla. In *Memorias de los foros del Carnaval,* edited by Adolfo González Henríquez and Deyana Acosta-Madiedo. Barranquilla: Cámara de Comercio.

Peñas Galindo, David. 1988. *Los bogas de Mompox: Historia del zambaje.* Bogotá: Tercer Mundo.

Peralta, Victoria. 1995. *El ritmo lúdico y los placeres en Bogotá.* Bogotá: Planeta.

Perdomo Escobar, José Ignacio. 1963. *La historia de la música en Colombia.* 3d ed. Bogotá: Editorial ABC.

Pérez Arbelaez, Enrique. 1945. Literatura popular del Magdalena. *Revista de América* 2 (6): 379–384; 4 (12): 360–367.

———. 1952. La cuna del porro. *Revista de Folclor* 1 (1): 18–98. Also published as *La cuna del porro* (Bogotá: Ed. Antares, 1953).

Pérez Ramírez, Gustavo. 1961. *La iglesia en Colombia: Estructuras eclesiásticas.* Fribourg: FERES.

Peristiany, Jean G. 1965. *Honour and shame: The values of Mediterranean society.* London: Weidenfeld and Nicolson.

Piñeres Royero, Fernando. 1991. Expansión económica e imagen de Barranquilla, 1935–45. *Ensayos de Economía* 2 (1): 37–55.

Placido, Barbara. 1999. Spirits of the nation: Identity and legitimacy in the cults of María Lionza and Simón Bolívar. Ph.D. diss., University of Cambridge.

Ponce Vega, Eugenio. 1994. Fue un conjunto "cachaco" el primero en ganar. *El Heraldo,* 6 November, p. 6E.

Portaccio, José. 1995. *Colombia y su música.* Vol. 1, *Canciones y fiestas de las llanuras Caribe y Pacífica y las islas de San Andrés y Providencia.* Vol. 2, *Canciones y fiestas de la región andina.* Vol. 3, *Canciones y fiestas llaneras.* Bogotá: José Portaccio.

———. 1997. *Carmen tierra mia: Lucho Bermúdez.* Bogotá: José Portaccio.

Posada, Consuelo. 1986. *Canción vallenata y tradición oral.* Medellín: Universidad de Antioquia.

Posada Carbó, Eduardo. 1982. Identidad y conflicto en la formación de la regionalidad, 1900–1930. *Huellas* 3 (7): 4–13.

———. 1985. La Liga Costeña de 1919: Una expresión de poder regional. *Boletín Cultural y Bibliográfico* 22 (3): 34–46.

———. 1986. Karl Parrish: Un empresario colombiano en los años veinte. *Boletín Cultural y Bibliográfico* 23 (8): 3–20.

———. 1987a. Iglesia y política en la costa atlántica. *Huellas* 19:5–8.

———. 1987b. *Invitación a la historia de Barranquilla.* Bogotá: CEREC and Cámara de Comercio de Barranquilla.

———. 1988. Estado, región y nación en la historia de la costa atlántica colombiana: Notas sobre la Alianza Regional de 1919. In *El Caribe colombiano,* edited by Gustavo Bell Lemus, pp. 49–67. Barranquilla: Ediciones Uninorte.

———. 1996. *The Colombian Caribbean: A regional history, 1870–1950.* Oxford: Oxford University Press.

Posada Gutiérrez, Joaquín. 1920. *Ultimos días de la Gran Colombia y del libertador.* Madrid: Editorial America.

Prado Bellei, Sérgio Luiz. 1995. Brazilian culture in the frontier. *Bulletin of Latin American Research* 14 (1): 47–61.

Prescott, Laurence E. 1985a. *Candelario Obeso y la iniciación de la poesia negra en Colombia.* Bogotá: Instituto Caro y Cuervo.

———. 1985b. Jorge Artel frente a Nicolás Guillén: Dos poetas mulatos ante la poesía negra hispanoamericana. In *Ensayos de literatura colombiana,* edited by Raymond L. Williams, pp. 129–136. Bogotá: Plaza y Janes.

Primer Foro de la Costa Atlántica. 1981. Autonomía y Desarrollo. Santa Marta. Mimeographed.

Puello Mejía, Carlos Daniel. 1992. Vallenato: Una historia menospreciada por la aristocracia. In *Música tropical y salsa en Colombia,* edited by Discos Fuentes, pp. 173–200. Medellín: Ediciones Fuentes.

Puyo Vasco, Fabio. 1992. *Bogotá.* Madrid: Editorial MAPFRE.

Quintero Rivera, Angel. 1996. The somatology of manners: Class, race and gender in the history of dance etiquette in the Hispanic Caribbean. In *Ethnicity in the Caribbean,* edited by Gert Oostindie, pp. 152–181. London: Macmillan.

Quiñones Pardo, Octavio. 1948. El alma popular: El porro. *Revista de América* 13 (37): 82–86.

Quiroz Otero, Ciro. 1982. *Vallenato: Hombre y canto.* Bogotá: Editorial Icaro.

Ramón, Justo. 1948. *Significado de la obra colonial, independencia y república.* Bogotá: Librería Stella.

———. 1967. *Geografía de Colombia.* Bogotá: Librería Stella.

Rasch Isla, Enrique, ed. 1928. *Directorio comercial pro-Barranquilla.* Barranquilla: Sociedad de Mejoras Públicas de Barranquilla.

Reily, Suzel Ana. 1992. *Música sertaneja* and migrant identity: the stylistic development of a Brazilian genre. *Popular Music* 11 (3): 337–357.

———. 1994. Macunaíma's music: National identity and ethnomusicological research in Brazil. In *Ethnicity, identity and music: The musical construction of place,* edited by Martin Stokes, pp. 71–96. Oxford: Berg.

Restrepo, Luis Antonio. 1988. El pensamiento social e histórico. In *La Historia de Antioquia,* edited by Jorge Orlando Melo, pp. 373–382. Medellín: Suramericana de Seguros.

Restrepo Duque, Hernán. 1971. *Lo que cuentan las canciones: Un cronicón musical.* Bogotá: Tercer Mundo.

———. 1986. *A mí cánteme un bambuco.* Medellín: Ediciones Autores Antioqueños.

———. 1988. Música popular. In *Historia de Antioquia,* edited by Jorge Orlando Melo, pp. 527–538. Medellín: Suramericana de Seguros.

———. 1991. *Las 100 mejores canciones colombianas y sus autores.* Bogotá: RCN and Sonolux.

Rey Sinning, Edgar. 1992. *Joselito Carnaval.* Barranquilla: Eds. Costa Caribe.

Rhodes, Colin. 1994. *Primitivism and modern art.* London: Thames and Hudson.

Rico Salazar, Jaime. 1984. *Las canciones mas bellas de Colombia.* Bogota: Centro Editorial de Estudios Musicales.

Riedel, Johannes. 1986. The Ecuadorean pasillo: *"Música popular," "música nacional"* or *"música folklórica"*? *Latin American Music Review* 7 (1): 1–25.

Rivera Reyes, Honorio. 1994. Ethnic representation in Colombian textbooks.

In *The presented past: Heritage, museums and education,* edited by Peter G. Stone and Brian L. Molyneaux, pp. 398–407. London: Routledge.

Roberts, John Storm. 1979. *The Latin tinge: The impact of Latin American music on the United States.* New York: Oxford University Press.

Robertson, Roland. 1990. After nostalgia: Wilful nostalgia and the phases of globalization. In *Theories of modernity and post- modernity,* edited by Bryan Turner, pp. 45–61. London: Sage.

Rodado Noriega, Carlos. n.d. *El alegato de la costa.* N.p.: Poligrupo Comunicación.

Rodríguez Calderón, Rodolfo. 1982. José Barros: Una vida con ritmo de cumbia. *El Espectador* 22 May, p. 7B.

Rousseau, G. S., and Roy Porter, eds. 1990. *Exoticism in the Enlightenment.* Manchester: Manchester University Press.

Rowe, William, and Vivian Schelling. 1991. *Memory and modernity: Popular culture in Latin America.* London: Verso.

Ruiz Hernández, Alvaro. 1982. Por muchas razones hay que llamarlo el "Gran Pedro Laza." *Intermedio* (supplement of *El Diario del Caribe*), 10 January, p. 20.

———. 1983. *Personajes y episodios de la canción popular.* Barranquilla: Luz Negra.

Sadie, Stanley, ed. 1984. *New Grove dictionary of musical instruments.* London: Macmillan.

Sahlins, Marshall. 1993. Goodbye to tristes tropes: Ethnography in the context of modern world history. *Journal of Modern History* 65:1–25.

Said, Edward. 1985. *Orientalism: Western concepts of the Orient.* Harmondsworth: Penguin.

Salazar Giraldo, Noel. 1990. *Ayer y hoy en mis canciones.* 4th ed. Manizales: Andina.

Sánchez, Enrique, Roque Roldán, and María Fernández. 1993. *Derechos e identidad: Los pueblos indígenas y negros en la constitución política de Colombia de 1991.* Bogotá: Coama and Disloque Editores.

Sánchez, Gonzalo. 1992. The Violence: An interpretive synthesis. In *Violence in Colombia: The contemporary crisis in historical perspective,* edited by Charles Bergquist, Ricardo Peñaranda, and Gonzalo Sánchez, pp. 75–124. Wilmington, Del.: Scholarly Resources.

Sánchez, Hernando. 1966. *Elementos de geografía general y de Colombia.* Medellín: Bedout.

Sandroni, Paula. 1982. La proletarización de la mujer en Colombia después de 1945. In *Debate sobre la mujer en América Latina y el Caribe,* vol. 1, *La realidad colombiana,* edited by Magdalena de León, pp. 72–83. Bogotá: ACEP.

Savigliano, Marta E. 1995. *Tango and the political economy of passion.* Boulder: Westview.

Schwarz, Roberto. 1992. *Misplaced ideas: Essays on Brazilian culture.* Edited by John Gledson. London: Verso.

Schwegler, Armin. 1996. *"Chi ma nkongo": Lengua y rito ancestrales en El*

Palenque de San Basilio (Colombia). 2 vols. Frankfurt: Vervuert Verlag; Madrid: Iberoamericana.

Seeger, Anthony. 1994. Whoever we are today, we can sing you a song about it. In *Music and black ethnicity: The Caribbean and South America*, edited by Gerard Béhague, pp. 1–16. New Brunswick, N.J.: Transaction.

Segal, Daniel. 1991. "The European": Allegories of racial purity. *Anthropology Today* 7 (5): 7–9.

Segal, Daniel, and Richard Handler. 1992. How European is nationalism? *Social Analysis* 32:1–15.

———. 1993. Introduction: Nations, colonies and metropoles. *Social Analysis* 33 (special issue, *Nations, colonies and metropoles*, edited by Daniel Segal and Richard Handler): 3–8.

Sepúlveda, Saturino. 1979. *La prostitución en Colombia: Una quiebra de estructuras sociales*. Bogotá: Tercer Mundo.

Sevcenko, Nicolau. 1995. Brazilian follies: The casting, broadcasting and consumption of images of Brazil on both sides of the continent, 1930–50. Paper read at conference, Ways of Working in Latin American Cultural Studies, King's College and The Institute of Latin American Studies, University of London, 5–7 April.

Shields, Rob. 1991. *Places on the margin: Alternative geographies of modernity*. London: Routledge.

Shilling, Chris. 1993. *The body and social theory*. London: Sage.

Sierra, Luz María. 1994. Un porro a la eternidad. *El Tiempo*, 24 April, p. 11A.

Simon, Alissa. 1994. The Costeño hip movement: A conceptual framework for understanding sexuality in Afro-Colombian folkloric music and dance. Ph.D. diss., Department of Ethnomusicology, University of California, Los Angeles.

Singer, Roberta. 1983. Tradition and innovation in contemporary Latin music in New York city. *Latin American Music Review* 4 (2): 183–202.

Skidmore, Thomas. 1974. *Black into white: Race and nationality in Brazilian thought*. New York: Oxford University Press.

Slobin, Mark. 1993. *Subcultural sounds: Micromusics of the West*. Hanover, N.H., and London: Wesleyan University Press and University Press of New England.

Smart, Barry. 1990. Modernity, postmodernity and the present. In *Theories of modernity and postmodernity*, edited by Bryan S. Turner, pp. 14–30. London: Sage.

Smith, Anthony D. 1986. *The ethnic origin of nations*. Oxford: Blackwell.

Sojo, José Francisco. 1942. *El Club Barranquilla: Carnavales*. Barranquilla: n.p.

Solano, Sergio Paolo, and Jorge Enrique Conde Calderón. 1993. *Elite empresarial y desarrollo industrial en Barranquilla, 1875–1930*. Barranquilla: Ediciones Uniatlántico.

Sommer, Doris. 1991. *Foundational fictions: The national romances of Latin America*. Berkeley: University of California Press.

Spottswood, Richard K. 1990. *Ethnic music on record: A discography of eth-*

nic recordings produced in the United States, 1893 to 1942. 7 vols. Vol. 4, *Spanish, Portuguese, Philippines and Basque.* Urbana and Chicago: University of Illinois Press.

Steiner, Claudia. 1994. Héroes y banano en el Golfo de Urabá: La construcción de una frontera conflictiva. In *Territorios, regines y sociedades,* edited by Renán Silva, pp. 137–149. Bogotá: CEREC and Departamento de Ciencias Sociales, Universidad del Valle.

Stepan, Nancy Leys. 1991. *"The hour of eugenics": Race, gender and nation in Latin America.* Ithaca: Cornell University Press.

Stigberg, David K. 1978. *Jarocho, tropical* and "pop": Aspects of musical life in Veracruz, 1971–72. In *Eight urban musical cultures,* edited by Bruno Nettl, pp. 260–295. Urbana: University of Illinois Press.

———. 1985. Foreign currents during the 60s and 70s in Mexican popular music: Rock and roll, the romantic ballad and the *cumbia. Studies in Latin American Popular Culture* 4:170–187.

Stocking, George. 1968. *Race, culture and evolution: Essays in the history of anthropology.* Chicago: University of Chicago Press.

Stokes, Martin, ed. 1994a. *Ethnicity, identity and music: The musical construction of place.* Oxford: Berg.

———. 1994b. Introduction: Ethnicity, identity and music. In *Ethnicity, identity and music: The musical construction of place,* edited by Martin Stokes, pp. 1–28. Oxford: Berg.

Stoler, Anne. 1995. *Race and the education of desire: Foucault's "History of Sexuality" and the colonial order of things.* Durham: Duke University Press.

Streicker, Joel. 1995. Policing boundaries: Race, class, and gender in Cartagena, Colombia. *American Ethnologist* 22 (1): 54–74.

Stutzman, Ronald. 1981. El mestizaje: An all-inclusive ideology of exclusion. In *Cultural transformations and ethnicity in modern Ecuador,* edited by Norman E. Whitten, pp. 45–94. Urbana: University of Illinois Press.

Tagg, Philip. 1989. "Black music," "Afro-American music" and "European music". *Popular Music* 8 (3): 285–298.

Tagg, Philip, Dave Harker, and Matthew Kelly. 1995. Music media chronology from Anglocentric perspective, version 4.2. University of Liverpool. Mimeographed.

Taussig, Michael. 1987. *Shamanism, colonialism and the wild man: A study in terror and healing.* Chicago: University of Chicago Press.

———. 1992. *The nervous system.* New York: Routledge.

———. 1993. *Mimesis and alterity: A particular history of the senses.* London: Routledge.

———. 1997. *The magic of the state.* London: Routledge.

Téllez, Hernando. 1974. *50 años de radiodifusión en Colombia.* Medellín: Ed. Bedout.

Thornton, Sarah. 1995. *Club cultures.* Cambridge: Polity.

Torgovnick, M. 1990. *Gone primitive: Savage intellects, modern lives.* Chicago: University of Chicago Press.

Triana, Gloria, ed. 1990. *Aluna: Imagen y memoria de la Jornadas Regionales de Cultura Popular.* Bogotá: Presidencia de la República, Plan Nacional de Rehabilitación, Colcultura.

Trujillo, Luis Fernando. 1988. *Estructura general de una cadena radial: Historia, legislación e información.* Bogotá: Ed. Epoca.

Turino, Thomas. 1990. "Somos el Peru": Cumbia andina and the children of Andean migrants in Lima. *Studies in Latin American Popular Culture* 9:15–37.

———. 1993. *Moving away from silence: Music of the Peruvian altiplano and the experience of urban migration.* Chicago: University of Chicago Press.

Turner, Byran S. 1990. Periodization and politics in the postmodern. In *Theories of modernity and postmodernity,* edited by Bryan S. Turner, pp. 1–13. London: Sage.

Turner, Terence. 1994. Bodies and anti-bodies: Flesh and fetish in contemporary social theory. In *Embodiment and experience: The existential ground of culture and the self,* edited by T. Csordas, pp. 27–47. Cambridge: Cambridge University Press.

Twinam, Ann. 1980. From Jew to Basque: Ethnic myths and Antioqueño entrepreneurship. *Journal of Inter-American Studies* 22:81–107.

Ulin, Robert. 1995. Invention and representation as cultural capital: southwest French winegrowing history. *American Anthropologist* 97 (3): 519–527.

Ulloa Sanmiguel, Alejandro. 1991. Modernidad y música popular en América Latina. *Iztapalapa: Revista de Ciencias Sociales y Humanidades* 11 (24): 51–69.

———. 1992. *La salsa en Cali.* Cali: Ediciones Universidad del Valle.

Universidad Nacional, ed. 1984. *El nacionalismo en el arte: Textos.* Bogotá: Universidad Nacional.

Urban, Greg, and Joel Sherzer, eds. 1991. *Nation-states and Indians in Latin America.* Austin: University of Texas Press.

Urueta Carpio, Mike. 1994. *Historia de la radiodifusión en Barranquilla.* Barranquilla: Ediciones Uniautónoma.

Uribe Celis, Carlos. 1992. *La mentalidad del colombiano: Cultura y sociedad en el siglo XX.* Bogotá: Ediciones Alborada and Editorial Nueva América.

Urry, John. 1990. *The tourist gaze: Leisure and travel in contemporary societies.* London: Sage.

———. 1995. *Consuming places.* London: Routledge.

Urueta, José, and Eduardo Gutiérrez de Piñeres. 1912. *Cartagena y sus cercanías.* Cartagena: Tipografía Mogollón.

Vaillant, Janet. 1990. *Black, French and African: A life of Léopold Sédar Senghor.* Cambridge, Mass.: Harvard University Press.

Valencia, Pedro Francisco. 1977. *Geografía general-física y de Colombia.* Bogotá: Ediciones Cultural.

Vergara, José Manuel. 1981. *Alejo Durán.* Bogotá: Tercer Mundo.

Vergara y Velasco, Francisco. [1901] 1974. *Nueva geografía de Colombia.* 3 vols. Bogotá: Banco de la República.

Vigarello, Georges. 1989. The upward training of the body from the age of chivalry to courtly civility. In *Fragments for a history of the human body*, pt. 2, edited by Michel Feder et al., pp. 148–199. New York: Zone.

Villegas, Jorge, and Hernando Grisales. 1976. *Crescencio Salcedo: Mi vida.* Medellín: Ediciones Hombre Nuevo.

Viviescas, Fernando. 1983. Medellín: El centro de la ciudad y el ciudadano. *Revista de Extensión Cultural de la Universidad Nacional de Colombia* 15:46–56.

Wade, Peter. 1993a. *Blackness and race mixture: The dynamics of racial identity in Colombia.* Baltimore: Johns Hopkins University Press.

———. 1993b. "Race," nature and culture. *Man* 28 (1): 1–18.

———. 1994a. Man the hunter: Gender and violence in music and drinking contexts in Colombia. In *Sex and violence: Issues in representation and experience*, edited by Peter Gow and Penelope Harvey, pp. 115–137. London: Routledge.

———. 1994b. Negros, indígenas e identidad nacional en Colombia. *Cuadernos de Historia Latinoamericana* 2 (special issue, *Imaginar la Nación*, edited by François-Xavier Guerra and Mónica Quijada), pp. 257–288.

———. 1995. The cultural politics of blackness in Colombia. *American Ethnologist* 22 (2): 342–358.

———. 1997. *Race and ethnicity in Latin America.* London: Pluto.

———. 1998. Blackness, music and national identity: Three moments in Colombian history. *Popular Music* 17 (1): 1–19.

———. 1999. Representations of blackness in Colombian popular music. In *Representations of blackness and the performance of identities*, edited by Jean M. Rahier, pp. 173–191. Westport: Greenwood.

Wagner, Roy. 1981. *The invention of culture.* 2d ed. Chicago: University of Chicago Press.

Wallis, Roger, and Krister Malm. 1984. *Big sounds from small people: The music industry in small countries.* London: Constable.

Washabaugh, William. 1998a. Fashioning masculinity in flamenco dance. In *The passion of music and dance: Body, gender and sexuality*, edited by William Washabaugh, pp. 39–50. Oxford: Berg.

———. 1998b. Introduction: Music, dance and the politics of passion. In *The passion of music and dance: Body, gender and sexuality*, edited by William Washabaugh, pp. 1–26. Oxford: Berg.

———. 1998c. *The passion of music and dance: Body, gender and sexuality.* Oxford: Berg.

Waterman, Christopher Alan. 1990. *Jùjú: A social history and ethnography of an African popular music.* Chicago: University of Chicago Press.

Waxer, Lise. 1997. Salsa, champeta, and rap: Black sounds and black identities in Afro-Colombia. Paper presented to the Annual Meeting of the Society for Ethnomusicology, Pittsburgh.

———. 1998. *Cali pachanguero: A social history of salsa in a Colombian city.* Ph.D. diss., University of Illinois at Urbana-Champaign.

Werner, R. 1873. La escuadra alemana en la Bahía de Sabanilla. *Revista de Colombia,* 28 November, pp. 323–324.

Whitten, Norman. [1974] 1986. *Black frontiersmen: A South American case.* 2d ed. Prospect Heights, Ill.: Waveland.

———. 1981. Introduction. In *Cultural transformations and ethnicity in modern Ecuador,* edited by Norman E. Whitten, pp. 1–44. Urbana: University of Illinois Press.

———. 1985. *Sicuanga Runa: The other side of development in Amazonian Ecuador.* Urbana: University of Illinois Press.

Whitten, Norman, and Arlene Torres. 1998. General introduction: To forge the future in the fires of the past: An interpretive esay on racism, domination, resistance, and liberation. In *Blackness in Latin America and the Caribbean: Social dynamics and cultural transformations,* edited by Norman Whitten and Arlene Torres, 1:3–33. Bloomington: Indiana University Press.

Wilk, Richard. 1995. Learning to be different in Belize: Global systems of common difference. In *Worlds apart: Modernity through the prism of the local,* edited by Daniel Miller, pp. 110–133. London: Routledge.

Williams, Brackette. 1989. A class act: Anthropology and the race to nation across ethnic terrain. *Annual Review of Anthropology* 18:401–444.

———. 1991. *Stains on my name, war in my veins: Guyana and the politics of cultural struggle.* Durham: Duke University Press.

Williams, Raymond. 1980. *Problems in materialism and culture.* London: Verso.

Williams, Raymond L. 1985. *Ensayos de literatura colombiana.* Bogotá: Plaza y Janes.

———. 1991. *The Colombian novel, 1844–1987.* Austin: University of Texas Press.

Wright, Winthrop. 1990. *Café con leche: Race, class and national image in Venezuela.* Austin: University of Texas Press.

Yelvington, Kevin, ed. 1993. *Trinidad ethnicity.* London: Macmillan.

Young, Robert. 1995. *Colonial desire: Hybridity in theory, culture and race.* London: Routledge.

Yuval-Davis, Nira, and Floya Anthias, eds. 1989. *Woman-nation-state.* New York: St. Martin's.

Zambrano, Fabio. 1988. *Historia de Bogotá: Siglo XX.* Bogotá: Fundación Misión Colombia, Villegas Editores.

———. 1991. Región, nación e identidad cultural. In *Imágenes y reflexiones de la cultura en Colombia: Regiones, ciudades y violencia,* edited by Foro Nacional Para, Con, Por, Sobre, De Cultura, pp. 145–157. Bogotá: Colcultura.

Zamudio, Daniel. [1936] 1961. El folklore musical en Colombia. *Boletín de Programas de la Radiodifusora Nacional* 20 (200–203): 3–13, 1–8, 1–8, 73–81.

———. 1978. El folklore musical en Colombia. *Textos sobre música y folk-*

lore. Vol. 1, *Colombia,* edited by Hjalmar De Grieff and David Feferbaum. Bogotá: Colcultura.

Zapata Cuencar, Heriberto. 1962. *Compositores colombianos.* Medellín: Carpel.

Zapata Olivella, Delia. 1962. La cumbia: Síntesis musical de la nación colombiana: Reseña histórica y coreográfica. *Revista Colombiana de Folclor* 3 (7): 189–204.

Zapata Olivella, Manuel. 1960–1962. Los pasos del folklore colombiano. *Boletín Cultural de la Biblioteca Luis Angel Arango* 3 (8), 4 (3,4,7,8), 5 (1,5,11).

INDEX

Abello Banfi, Jaime, 222
Academia Nacional de Música, Colombia, 31
Accordion music: Costeño vallenato, vii, 61–64, 176; growing popularity of, 179; minstrels playing, 81, 88; recordings of, 95, 177. *See also* Vallenato
Acosta, Rafael, 149, 150
Aicardi, Rodolfo, 167, 172
"Alicia Adorada," 180
Anderson, Benedict, 3, 25, 142
Añez, Jorge, 50, 51
Angulo, Moisés, 219
Antioqueños: elites, 107–8; in recording industry, 151–52; as regional types, 35
Arango, Alvaro, 164–65
Araújo, Consuelo, 23
Araujonoguera, Consuelo, 178
Archila Neira, Mauricio, 68, 108
Arcos, Pilar, 94
Ardila Lulle group, 217
Argaín, Lucho (Lucho Pérez Cedrón), 172
Argentina: cumbia in, 175; tango in, 17–18
Argentinean music: in Bogotá and Medellín (1920s, 1930s), 109; penetration in La Costa, 101–2
Arias, Edmundo, 156–57
Ariza, Enrique, 123
Armani, Eduardo, 96, 119

Arroyo, Alfredo, 190
Arroyo, Joe, 220
Artel, Jorge, 44, 131, 136
Atlantic record company, 95
Austerlitz, Paul, 141
"Ave'Pa'Ve," 156
Averill, Gage, 6

Bambuco: bambuco fiestero, 116; bambuco yucateco, 50; as Colombian national music, 51; criollo nature of, 51; as folkloric music, 52; lyrics of, 51; in national identity discourse, 48, 51; origins and creolization of, 51; popularization of, 48–50
Banda de la Policía, Barranquilla, 82, 84
Banda Española, 49
Bands: Jazz Band Atlántico, 78; Jazz Band Barranquilla, 78, 80; Jazz Band Colombia, 78; local bands in Barranquilla (1920s–1940), 78–88; playing Costeño music (1950s–1960s), 144–46; popularity of brass, 48. *See also* Wind bands (bandas de viento)
Barranquilla: AM and FM radio programming (1990s), 214; carnival, 44, 64–65, 102, 104; changes (1930s), 107; cinema theaters (1920s), 76; class differences, 67; class segregation by elite in, 67–68; class structure, 67; early radio stations, 91–92; elite social clubs, 68; Group of Barranquilla, 137; immigrant population, 43, 67; as

Glottman, Jaime, 121
Gómez, Laureano, 33
Gómez, Manuel, 124
Gómez, Salvador, 198, 201–2
Gómez, Simón, 78
González, Adolfo, 221–22
González, Alberto, 88, 122
Goubert, María Eugenia, 190–91
"Grab It/Him from Behind," 97
Gramophones: in cafés and bars, 75;
  Panatrope, 74; sales in Barranquilla
  (1920s–1940s), 74
Granados Arjona, Miguel, 199
"Grito Vagabundo," 98
Group of Barranquilla, 137
Groups, musical: bands playing Costeño
  music (1950s–1960s), 144–46; play-
  ing and singing early Costeño music,
  88–91; playing modernized Costeño
  music, 166–73
Grupo Niche, 220
Grupo Victoria, 79
Guabinas, 50
Guarachas: of Aníbal Velásquez, 165–66
Guarnizo, Pedro, 191
Guerra, José del Carmen "Cheíto," 86
Guerrero, Cipriano, 94
Guilbault, Jocelyne, 23
Gutiérrez, Alfredo, 160–61, 163–66,
  179, 180
Gutiérrez, Gustavo, 63
Gutiérrez Piñeres, Virginia, 54
Guzmán, Roberto, 59

Hall, Stuart, 11
"Hambre del Liceo," 99
Handler, Richard, 3
Hegemony: concept of transformist
  (Williams), 9–10; Gramsci's notion
  of, 9–10; hegemonic values, 103,
  237; transformist, 184
Hernández, Rafael, 79, 86, 93, 109, 110
Herrera, Eliseo, 160–63
Heterogeneity: in Caballero Calderón's
  writing, 34; expressed in school text-
  books, 34–36; in national identity,
  3–16; retention of, 234; tension be-
  tween homogeneity and, 141–43
Hollopeter, Samuel, 41
Homogeneity: expressed in school text-
  books, 34–36; lacking in Colombian

nationalism, 234; in national identity,
  3–16; tension between heterogeneity
  and, 141–43

Identity, class: in Barranquilla, 68, 138;
  in Bogotá, 107–9; in La Costa, 67–
  74, 87–88, 91, 102–4; in Medellín,
  107–9, 110
Identity, Costeño, 42–47
Identity, national: blackness in, 6–7, 10,
  14, 104, 127–28, 138, 196–97;
  bound to racial identity in Colombia,
  16; in cultural policy, 1, 36–39; heterogeneity and homogeneity in, 3–16,
  141–43; linked to racial identity and
  nationalism, 16; mestizaje in Latin
  America, 15; music in discourse related to, 48; related to national culture, 1–2, 34–52; representations of
  whiteness, 32; transformation in
  Colombia, 2–11
Identity, racial: ambiguity of Costeño,
  196; in Colombia, 16, 30–31; of
  Costeño musicians in Colombian interior, 124–25; as gendered process,
  17–18; of La Costa, 42–47; linked to
  nationalism and national identity, 16;
  in national identity, 14–15; relation
  between sexuality and, 18; spatial
  pattern in Colombia, 30–31; as
  transnational process, 16
Ideologies, hegemonic, 10–11
Immorality: perception of Costeño music,
  78
Indígenas, 39
Indios, 40
Instruments: for cumbia music and
  dance, 60–61, 245–46; in Orquesta
  Nuevo Horizante, 80; for paseo vallenato, 245; for porro, 57–59, 63,
  244–45; for rumba criolla, 117; used
  in modernized Costeño music, 166–
  73; for vallenato, 61–64
Integration, national: diversity of culture
  linked to, 38–39
Iriarte, Alfredo, 106

Jardín Aguila, 93
Jazz Band Atlántico, 78
Jazz Band Barranquilla, 78, 80
Jazz Band Colombia, 78

Moore, Robin, 8
Morales, Abadía, 48, 51
Morales Benítez, Otto, 34
Morales Pino, Pedro, 48–50
Morán, Pedro, 199
Moscote, Francisco "El Hombre," 62
Mouffe, Chantal, 10
Movie films: influence in Colombia
(1920s–1940s), 76
"Muchacha Cartagenera," 98
Multiculturalism, Colombia, 1–2, 225–
30
Muñoz, Gabriel, 180, 186
Murillo, Emilio, 49–50, 117, 119
Music: Afro-Cuban music, 93; of Alfredo
Gutiérrez, 164; for black Atlantic di-
aspora, 13; changes in Barranquilla
and La Costa (1920s–1940s), 72–
100; early radio, 92–94; of Edmundo
Arias, 156; effect of commercializa-
tion in Colombia, 27–28; emergence
of national popular music styles, 7–8;
influence in La Costa of foreign
(1920s–1940s), 72–100; origins of
Latin American, 15–16; role in Colombian nationalism, 31; styles in rural and urban Colombia in nineteeth
century, 47–48. *See also* Costeño music; Popular music; Rural music
Music, Colombian popular, 47–52; bambuco, 48–49; danza, 47–49; pasillo,
47–49
Música bailable, 145
Música de carrilera, 115
Música gallega, 168
Música guasca, 115
Musical styles: with commercialization,
27; with diversification, 27; standardization, 27
Música tropical: cumbia in Mexico, 174;
referring to Costeño music, 145
Music capitalism: of Caribbean coastal
region, 25–29

Nationalism: bound to racial identification in Colombia, 16; of Colombian
music, 224; emergence in Colombia,
31–32; ethnographic, 12; as gendered
discourse, 16–17; Janus-faced, 4–5,
7, 12; Latin American cultural, 7;
Latin American musical, 7–10, 51–

52; postmodern, multicultural Co-
lombian, 213; related to mestizaje
ideology, 212; in school textbooks,
34–35; women in nationalist dis-
courses, 16–17
Nederveen Pieterse, Jan, 18–19
Nene y Sus Traviesos, 219
New York: Afro-Cuban music, 93;
Colombian porro music, 93
Nieto, Juan José, 45, 70
Nieto Caballero, Agustín, 130
night clubs, Bogotá and Medellín, 109
Nóbile, Eugenio, 96, 119
"No Como Conejo," 98
North American music: in Bogotá and
Medellín (1920s, 1930s), 109; pene-
tration in La Costa, 101, 103
Nuñez, Rafael, 31, 129

Obligado, Rafael. *See* Camacho y Cano,
Angel María
Obregón, Alejandro, 44
Ochoa, Calixto, 160
Oñate, Jorge, 179, 180
Ondina Fonográfica (record comapny),
150–51
Orchestras: in Barranquilla (1920s–
1940s), 78–88
Orozco, Efraín, 116, 117, 119
Orozco, Rafael, 181
Orquesta A Número Uno, 79, 84, 98
Orquesta Casino de la Playa, 77, 78, 80,
85
Orquesta Cristancho, 110
Orquesta Cubana Topacio, 77
Orquesta de Edmundo Arias, 156
Orquesta de José Pianeta Pitalúa, 84
Orquesta del Caribe, 85–86, 118
Orquesta de los Hermanos Lorduy, 79
Orquesta de Lucho Bermúdez, 119–20
Orquesta de Pacho Galán, 80, 155
Orquesta de Roberto Lambraño, 104
Orquesta Emisora Fuentes, 93, 95, 98,
104, 155
Orquesta Garavito, 117, 122
Orquesta Melodía, 95
Orquesta Nueva Granada, 121
Orquesta Nuevo Horizonte, 78–80
Orquesta Pájaro Azul, 83
Orquesta Panamericana, 96
Orquesta Ritmo, 110, 119